# Statistix®

## Version 4.0

## User's Manual

Analytical Software P.O. Box 12185 Tallahassee FL 32317-2185
Telephone 904-893-9371

**License Statement**

*Statistix* software is protected by both United States copyright law and international treaty provisions. You must treat this software just like a book, except that you may copy it onto a computer to be used and make archival copies of the software for the sole purpose of backing up our software.

By saying "just like a book", Analytical Software means, for example, that this software may be used by any number of people, and may be freely moved from one computer location to another, as long as there is no possibility of it being used at one location while it is being used at another.

**Limited Warranty**

Analytical Software warrants the physical diskettes and physical documentation enclosed herein to be free of defects in materials and workmanship for a period of 90 days from the purchase date. The entire and exclusive liability and remedy for breach of this Limited Warranty shall be limited to replacement of defective diskettes or documentation and shall not include or extend to any claim for or right to recover any other damages, including but not limited to, loss of profit, data, or use of the software, or special, incidental, or consequential damages or other similar claims. In no event shall Analytical Software's liability for any damages to you or any other person ever exceed the lower of suggested list price or actual price paid for the license to use the software.

Analytical Software specifically disclaims all other warranties, express or implied, including, but not limited to, any implied warranty of merchantability or fitness for a particular purpose. The user assumes the entire risk as to the quality, performance, and accuracy of this product. Analytical Software shall not be held responsible for any damages that may result from the use of this product, whether through Analytical Software's negligence or not.

**Copyright Notice**



Publisher: Analytical Software
Editor: Joan Siegel
Cover design by Diann Parrott

ISBN 1-881789-00-4 (IBM 5 1/4" format)
1-881789-01-2 (IBM 3 1/2" format)
1-881789-02-0 (User's Manual)

# P R E F A C E

*Statistix* is a very fast, easy-to-use data analysis program designed to encourage you to "play" with your data. Manipulating data becomes simple and straightforward, allowing you to focus on your research and not your software.

## Capabilities of *Statistix*

- Descriptive statistics
- Nonparametric tests
- Linear regression
- Stepwise regression
- Logistic regression
- Analysis of variance/covariance
- T tests
- Residual analysis
- Association tests
- Probability distributions
- Time series analysis
- Statistical process control
- Powerful transformations
- Graphs

## Features of *Statistix*

- Compact—only 1.4M disk space
- Lotus 1-2-3 and ASCII support
- Menu driven
- Spreadsheet data editing
- Free technical support
- Fast and accurate

## New Features of Version 4.0

**High resolution graphs**

*Statistix* offers a long list of high resolution graphs, including histograms, scatter plots, time series plots, and more. Graphs are displayed in high resolution on the screen and can be printed using "printer resolution" on many dot matrix, laser, and PostScript printers and pen plotters. You can also print graphs using character mode for speed.

**Quality control charts**

*Statistix* now offers Statistical Process Control charts, including the p chart, c chart, X bar chart, R chart, and S chart.

**String, date, and integer data types**

Now *Statistix* can store alphanumeric string data and dates, adding flexibility. You can also take advantage of the space-saving integer type.

**Variable and value labels**

You can increase the readability of *Statistix* reports by using variable and value labels. With value labels, you can combine the simplicity of numeric codes with the readability of names.

## Hardware Requirements

*Statistix* runs on IBM PC, XT, AT, or PS/2 and 100% compatible computers. A minimum of 512K RAM and DOS version 2.1 or higher is required. You must install *Statistix* on either a fixed disk or diskettes with a minimum capacity of 720K.

Graphics procedures require a CGA, MCGA, Hercules, EGA, or VGA monitor. *Statistix* reports can be printed on any ASCII text printer. *Statistix* graphs can be printed on a variety of printers that support graphics including Epson- and IBM-compatible dot matrix printers, Postscript printers, HP LaserJet, HP DeskJet, HP PaintJet, and HP pen plotters.

Hardware and software that increase the performance of *Statistix* but are not required include math coprocessor, mouse, expanded memory, and disk cache.

## What's Included

*Statistix 4.0* includes this manual, program diskettes, and a registration card. **Please mail us your registration card to receive:** (1) free technical support, (2) special upgrade prices, and (3) product announcements.

## Technical Support

Should you need help using *Statistix*, call our office for free technical support at 904-893-9371 Monday-Friday, 8:00 a.m.-5:00 p.m. Eastern Time.

## Acknowledgements

We'd like to thank the people who gallantly waded through early versions of 4.0 and offered their help and advice:

Mark Berenson
Baruch College

Douglas Hawkins
University of Minnesota

David Hosmer
University of Massachusetts

Ben King
Florida Atlantic University

Stanley Lemeshow
University of Massachusetts

David Levine
Baruch College

Donald Richter
New York University

Harry Roberts
University of Chicago

Herbert Spirer
University of Connecticut

Janet Wagner
University of Massachusetts

# C O N T E N T S

C H A P T E R

# 1

# Introduction

Welcome to *Statistix 4.0*, the latest version of our award-winning data analysis software.

You're going to find this program useful whether you're a rocket scientist or a beginning stats student. Why? Because you can easily do sophisticated analyses, such as logistic regressions, as well as basic descriptive statistics.

Here are some reasons why you'll like *Statistix*: It's fast—due to the way data are stored—and compact, so it doesn't eat up megabytes of disk space. It's computationally accurate, assuring the correct answer every time. The user's manual is clear and concise; it has lots of examples and references, too, if you want to dig deeper.

The most frequent comment we hear from *Statistix* users is, "It's so easy to use". They like the program's unique "feel", describing it as "clean" and "intuitive". Also, *Statistix* encourages the kind of creativity that marks the difference between good and routine data analysis. By its very design, *Statistix* invites you to be adventurous—to explore, play around, and get to know your data.

So jump in and get started.

# Using This Manual

If you're like most people, you'll run the software before reading the manual. That's OK with us because *Statistix* is far easier to use than it is to read about. However, if you haven't tried *Statistix* yet, install the software now by following the directions in the Getting Started section on the next page. Explore the *Statistix* menus and play around with the *Statistix* panels used to run statistical procedures. You can retrieve the sample data file CHOLESTE.SX supplied with *Statistix* or enter a small data set of your own. Get a feel for the program; it'll make it easier to understand the manual.

Once you've experimented with the software, read the rest of Chapter 1. The section titled Moving About the *Statistix* Menus describes how to use the menus. Two sections—Data in *Statistix* and Getting Data In and Out of *Statistix*—give an overview of how data are handled. *Statistix* Panels is an important section that describes how to make efficient use of input or model specification panels.

Before you get down to serious computing, you'll have to use the Install System procedure discussed at the end of this chapter. Use it to install your printer so that you can print *Statistix* reports and graphs and make configuration choices.

As you develop your *Statistix* skills, make it a high priority to read Chapter 2 on Data Management and Chapter 3 on File Management. Chapters 4 through 11 describe the statistical analysis procedures available in *Statistix*—Summary and Descriptive Statistics; One, Two, & Multi-Sample Tests; Linear Models; Association Tests; Randomness/Normality Tests; Time Series; Quality Control; and Probability Distributions.

It's a good idea to at least skim these chapters so that you're aware of the range of *Statistix*' capabilities. If you come across statistical procedures with which you're unfamiliar, study the examples and references until you have a general understanding of when the analyses would be useful. The details of how the analyses are performed are unimportant; you can always look them up when needed. However, to fully utilize *Statistix*, you need to know which tools to apply to which tasks.

While concise, the *Statistix* manual provides useful background. Used in conjunction with appropriate references, it's a valuable learning tool.

# Getting Started

*Statistix* is delivered on either two $5^1/_4$"diskettes labeled Disk 1 and Disk 2 or on one $3^1/_2$" diskette labeled Disk 1/2. You can't run *Statistix* using the distribution diskettes; the files are compressed and must first be decompressed using the install program on Disk 1.

You can install *Statistix* on diskettes or a fixed disk (hard disk). *Statistix* performs better on a fixed disk, so install *Statistix* on your computer's fixed disk if it has one.

The installation program INSTALL decompresses the program files and copies them to your fixed disk or working program diskettes. It doesn't modify your autoexec.bat or config.sys files.

## Installing *Statistix* on a Fixed Disk

Insert the distribution diskette labeled Disk 1 or Disk 1/2 into your computer's diskette drive. Then enter A:INSTALL at the DOS prompt to start the installation program. An options panel appears on the screen.

```
                  STATISTIX 4.0 INSTALLATION

   Install on a fixed disk or on diskettes (F/D)? .... Fixed disk

   Source disk drive used for distribution diskette .. A:

   Destination disk drive to install Statistix ....... C:

   Fixed disk directory to install Statistix ......... \SX

 Esc Exit  F1 Start
```

First select "Fixed disk" installation from the first prompt. Enter the letters corresponding to the diskette drive containing the distribution diskette (usually A or B) and the fixed disk (usually C). Finally, enter a valid directory name for the *Statistix* program (usually \SX). You can enter the name of a new directory or the name of a directory that already exists. If you have an earlier version of *Statistix* on your computer, you can use the same directory as before.

Press F1 to begin installation. The names of the files will be listed on the screen as they are decompressed. If your distribution diskettes are 5 ", you'll be prompted to insert the second diskette once the first diskette is decompressed.

To run *Statistix*, use the DOS change directory (CD) command to select the *Statistix* directory (i.e., CD \SX). Then enter SX to run the program.

After browsing around the program, be sure you look at the **Install System** procedure discussed on page 18.

## Installing *Statistix* on Diskettes

*Statistix* can be installed on two 720KB 3 " diskettes or two 1.2MB 5 " diskettes. (The program files are too large to be installed on 360KB 5 " diskettes.) We'll call these the working program diskettes to distinguish them from the distribution diskettes. Format two diskettes using the DOS format command and label the diskettes SX1 and SX2.

Put the distribution diskette Disk 1 in drive A: and the new diskette SX1 in drive B: (If your computer only has one diskette drive, drive A: will play the roles of both drives A: and B:; start with Disk 1.) Enter A:INSTALL at the DOS prompt. The installation options panel will appear on the screen.

```
                  STATISTIX 4.0 INSTALLATION

   Install on a fixed disk or on diskettes (F/D)? .... Diskette

   Source disk drive used for distribution diskette .. A:

   Destination disk drive to install Statistix ...... B:

   Fixed disk directory to install Statistix ........

Esc Exit  F1 Start
```

Select "Diskette" installation and then enter A: for the source drive and B: for the destination drive. Press F1 to begin installation. You'll be prompted to exchange diskettes partway through installation.

To run *Statistix*, insert the SX1 diskette in drive A: and enter SX at the DOS prompt. When properly installed, *Statistix* can be run on a dual diskette drive computer using both drives to store program diskettes (see **Install System, Other Options** on page 22), which reduces program diskette swapping. When this is done, it's best to keep SX1 in drive A: at all times and to use drive B: to alternate between the SX2 diskette and your data diskette. The data diskette only needs to be in a drive when you use a **File Management** procedure, such as **Retrieve** or **Save**. When you select a procedure and the correct program diskette is not in one of the drives, you'll be prompted to insert it.

After browsing around the program, be sure to use the **Install System** procedure discussed on page 18 to configure the software for your equipment.

## Program Files

The *Statistix* software consists of five program files: SX.EXE, SX1.EXE, SX1.OVR, SX2.EXE, and SX2.EXE. All of these files are required to operate *Statistix*.

This program also uses graphics driver files. Four screen driver files and several printer driver files are included with the software and are required for displaying graphs on your screen and printing graphs on your printer. These files are listed below.

CGA.BGI  CGA and MCGA
HERC.BGI  Hercules monochrome
EGAVGA.BGI  EGA and VGA
PC3270.BGI  IBM PC 3270
$FX.BGI  Epson/IBM 9 pin
$LQ.BGI  Epson 24 pin
$PP24.BGI  IBM Proprinter X24
$IBMQ.BGI  IBM Quietwritter
$PS.BGI  PostScript
$LJ.BGI  HP LaserJet
$DJ.BGI  HP DeskJet
$PJET.BGI  HP PaintJet
$HP7475.BGI  HP pen plotters

The screen drivers are the property of Borland International, Inc. The printer drivers are the property of Fleming Software. These files are copyrighted by their respective owners and can only be used with the *Statistix* software.

The file named GDHEAD.PS is required when printing graphs using a PostScript printer. The file GCOPY.EXE is a graph file printing program described on page 16.

The distribution diskettes include two sample *Statistix* data files. The file CHOLESTE.SX contains the example data used in Chapter 4. The file HALD.SX contains the Hald data used for many of the procedures described in Chapter 6.

Any of these files can be decompressed individually from the two compressed files DISK1.EXE and DISK2.EXE (DISK1 contains the files SX.EXE, SX1.EXE, and SX1.OVR; DISK2 contains the rest). For example, to extract the file $LJ.BGI from DISK2, enter the following command at the DOS prompt.

```
A:DISK2 $LJ.BGI C:\SX
```

# Moving About the Statistix Menus

When you first run *Statistix*, the base menu appears on the screen. All of the selections listed on the base menu are themselves menus. These menus offer a variety of data management and statistical procedures.

```
STATISTIX BASE MENU

Data management
File management
Install system
Summary statistics
One, two, & multi-sample tests
Linear models
Association tests
Randomness/normality tests
Time series
Quality control charts
Probability distributions
```

To select one of the topic menus from the base menu, press the highlighted letter (usually the first letter) of the topic menu name. You can also make menu selections by moving the highlighted bar to your choice using the up and down arrow keys and then pressing Enter. When you select a topic menu, the menu appears on the screen overlapping the base menu. Press Esc to exit a topic menu and return to the base menu.

You can also select menu items with your mouse. Move the highlighted bar up and down using the mouse. Select a menu item by clicking the left button. Exit a menu by clicking the right button.

Exit *Statistix* by pressing Esc when the base menu is active.

Before attempting to use a statistical procedure, you must either create a data set using a Data Management procedure or retrieve a data set from disk using a File Management procedure.

Data in *Statistix* remain in *Statistix* as you move from procedure to procedure until you explicitly get rid of it. When you select a procedure, the data variables are listed at the top of the screen.

In addition to the topic menus listed above, the regression, analysis of variance, and several of the time series procedures display results menus after the initial analysis is specified and computed.

# Data In Statistix

In this section, we give an overview of how data are handled once entered into *Statistix*. The following section describes ways to get your data into *Statistix*. More details about data handling are given in Chapter 2.

## Variables and Variable Names

Data in *Statistix* can be viewed as a rectangular table of values. The columns of the data table are called variables, and the rows are called cases. All data in *Statistix* are referenced by variable names that you assign when data are entered. A variable name is one to nine characters in length, must begin with a letter, and can only consist of letters, digits, and the underscore character. You should assign meaningful variable names to help you remember what they represent. There are a few words reserved for other tasks, such as ALL, M, PI, and RANDOM, that you cannot use as variable names.

Variable names are used to manipulate the data. For example, a new variable VOLUME can be created from the variables HEIGHT and BASE using the **Transformations** procedure as follows:

```
VOLUME = PI * HEIGHT * SQR (BASE)
```

PI and SQR are examples of built-in functions available in Transformations, which we'll discuss in detail in Chapter 2.

Variable names are used to specify the source of data for statistical analyses. For example, to specify the regression of HEAT on CHEM1 and CHEM2 using the **Linear Regression** procedure, enter the name HEAT at the prompt for the dependent variable and then enter the names CHEM1 and CHEM2 at the prompt for the independent variables.

## Data Types

*Statistix* can handle four types of data: real, integer, date, and string. A variable can only contain values of one data type. The data type of a variable is established when you create the variable and can be changed to a different data type using the Transformations procedure.

The "real" data type is used to represent floating point numbers (e.g., 1.245). This format is the most flexible offered by *Statistix* and is used as the default data type when creating new variables.

Integer data in *Statistix* are whole numbers in the range -32767 to 32767. This data type uses only 25% as much space as the real data type. You can use the integer data type instead of the real data type, when appropriate, to increase the data set capacity of *Statistix*. This will also save disk space by reducing the size of *Statistix* data files.

The "date" data type is used to represent 20th century dates (e.g., 12/31/92). See the Install System, Other Options on page 22 for an option to select the order of month, day, and year.

The "string" data type is used to enter alphanumeric data, such as a subject's name. String variables can be used as grouping variables for statistical procedures that compute results by group.

## Cases and Data Subsets

The rows in the rectangular data table are called cases. The cases are numbered sequentially. The case numbers are listed when viewing the data using the **Edit Data** and **View Data** procedures. The Case function in **Transformations** and **Omit/Restore Cases** provides a method to refer to the case numbers.

Sometimes you'll want to temporarily work with a subset of all data cases. The **Omit/Restore Cases** procedure can be used to "hide" specified cases from the system. The subset selection is based on a condition that you specify.

```
OMIT IF (HEIGHT > 5) AND (WEIGHT < 100)
```

Until specified otherwise, *Statistix* only "sees" cases not omitted using the omit statement. The cases are not deleted, but hidden. You can easily restore the hidden cases at any time. More details on Omit/Restore Cases are given in Chapter 2.

## Data Set Size

Most *Statistix* procedures display the variables in your data set in a window at the top of the screen. The amount of available space is listed at the bottom of the variable name list, as shown on the next page.

```
AGE        HT         ID         LOW        LWD        LWT        PTD
PTL        RACE       SMOKE      UI

11 variable(s).  189 of 189 cases selected.  143K bytes free.
```

The amount of free space available for *Statistix* data is reported in kilobytes (1 KB = 1024 bytes). A real number requires eight bytes of storage. A real variable in a data set of 1000 cases requires 8000 bytes of storage. Integer data require two bytes, date data type requires four bytes, and string data requires one byte more than the maximum length.

The active *Statistix* data set must completely fit in the available random access memory (RAM) and the expanded memory (EM). A *Statistix* data set can have up to 200 variables, provided there is sufficient memory. Variables and cases compete for space in the data table. The more cases you have in a data set, the fewer variables you can add.

## Missing Values

When data are entered into *Statistix*, a value of "M" is used to indicate a missing value. When data are displayed, a missing value is displayed as an "M". The M function available in Transformations and Omit/Restore Cases is used to assign missing values and to make comparisons to missing values.

All *Statistix* procedures examine the data for missing values and treat them appropriately. If arithmetic is performed on a variable containing missing values using Transformations (e.g., A = B + C), the result of the equation will be missing for the cases that contain the missing values. When a statistic, such as the mean of a variable, is calculated, only the non-missing values for the column are used to compute the result. The Linear Regression procedure will drop cases that contain a missing value for either the dependent variable or any of the independent variables.

# Getting Data In and Out of Statistix

You can use three methods to enter data into *Statistix*:

1) Keyboard data entry
2) ASCII or Lotus 1-2-3 files
3) *Statistix* data files.

Keyboard data entry is performed using the **Data Entry** and **Edit Data** procedures. Both are found on the Data Management menu (Chapter 2). Keyboard data entry is often preferred when the amount of data being entered is fairly small.

*Statistix* can read ASCII files created using a word processor, a spreadsheet program, or some other PC program. *Statistix* can also read a Lotus 1-2-3 compatible spreadsheet file. ASCII text files provide a standard data exchange format between *Statistix* and other programs. Most popular programs offer the option of writing and reading data as ASCII text files. Many spreadsheet programs support the Lotus 1-2-3 format. Use the *Statistix* **Import** procedures to create or augment data sets using data stored in ASCII or 1-2-3 files. Likewise, *Statistix* data can be exported to a variety of programs using the **Export** procedures.

While running *Statistix*, your data set is temporarily stored in random access memory (RAM). Before you exit *Statistix*, you should save your data set using the **Save** procedure. A *Statistix* data file is a "snapshot" of *Statistix*' data memory, and it's an ideal method of storing data sets for future *Statistix* analyses. The advantages of *Statistix* data files are that they can be read and written very rapidly, are compact in terms of the diskette space occupied, and preserve such *Statistix* information as variable names, labels, and the case omit status. *Statistix* data files are described in more detail in Chapter 3. *Statistix* data sets are retrieved using the **Retrieve** procedure.

A *Statistix* data set is dynamic. You can increase or decrease its size in a variety of ways. For example, you can delete cases and variables when you no longer need them to conserve space. New cases and variables can be added from the keyboard, imported from ASCII and 1-2-3 files, or merged from *Statistix* data files. You'll often use **Transformations** to create new variables. Some of the statistical procedures can produce new variables, too. For example, **Linear Regression** can save residuals and predicted values as new variables. A *Statistix* data file can be saved at any time.

*Statistix* data files are version upward compatible, but not downward compatible, i.e., version 4.0 can be used to retrieve data files created using earlier versions of *Statistix*, but earlier versions cannot retrieve version 4.0 data files.

## Statistix Panels

Once you select a procedure using the menus, an options panel is displayed on your screen. A panel is a screen, divided into data display and data input areas, that you use to specify the details of a statistical analysis, data management, or file management procedure. To illustrate, we'll examine the panel for the Linear Regression procedure displayed below.

```
                           LINEAR REGRESSION                               HALD
 CHEM1      CHEM2      CHEM3      CHEM4      HEAT


 5 variable(s).  13 of 13 cases selected.  159K bytes free.

 Enter the name of the dependent variable.  Press F2 to select from list.
 HEAT

 List the independent variables.  You may specify ALL or use A .. Z syntax.
 Press F2 to select variables from the list.
 CHEM1 CHEM2 CHEM3


 Enter the name of the weighting variable (optional).

 Do you want the constant (intercept) fitted?
 Yes

Esc Exit  F1 Start  F2 Select variable
```

Because most *Statistix* procedures use data variables, the data set variables are listed at the top of the panel. File management procedures will often list file names as well. The remainder of a panel is divided up into prompts and spaces for your input. Your input can consist of a list of variable names, a file name, numerical values, or your selection from a list of options. The current "hot keys" (Esc, F1, and F2 in the example above) are listed on the bottom line of the panel.

First you enter a value for the prompt where the cursor is positioned and then you press Enter. The cursor moves on to the next prompt. To make any changes, you can move up and down the panel using the up and down arrow keys. When you're ready to begin an analysis or data/file management procedure, press F1, the start key. If you decide not to run the analysis, press Esc to return to the *Statistix* menus.

If you make a mistake while responding to the panel prompts, an error message appears at the bottom of the screen and your cursor will be positioned at the error. You correct the error by editing the input line (editing input lines is discussed on the next page).

### Variable Name Selection

Whenever you're prompted for a variable name or a list of variable names, press F2 and select the names from the list displayed at the top of the panel. When you press F2, a variable name in the list is highlighted (usually the first in the list). Move around the list using the arrow keys and the page up, page down, home, and end keys. Press Enter to select the variable at the cursor position. The variable name will appear underneath the prompt for the variable or variable list. If the prompt is for a variable list, the cursor remains in the variable list area so you can select additional variables. Press Esc when you're done, and the cursor will return to the variable list prompt.

To move about the list of variable names, press the first letter of the desired variable. Pressing the same letter a second time will advance the cursor to the next variable name that begins with that letter.

You can also select variables using a mouse. Click the left button when the cursor is at the variable name prompt. Use the mouse to move the highlighted bar around the list of variable names. Select a variable name by clicking the mouse's left button. Click the right button to exit from the variable list.

### A .. Z Syntax and the Key Word ALL

When prompted for a variable list, you can often abbreviate the list by using A .. Z syntax or the key word ALL. When using A .. Z syntax, all the variables that appear in the list between the variables A and Z are included in the list. The variable list CHEM1 CHEM2 CHEM3 in the example panel above can be abbreviated by entering CHEM1 .. CHEM3. You can use A .. Z syntax more than once in a list.

Variable lists are generally presented in alphabetical order. You can choose to have the variables listed in the order in which they were created (the spreadsheet editor order) by using the install system option discussed on page 22. In that case, the variable A need not precede the variable Z alphabetically; rather, it must appear before the variable Z in the list.

The key word ALL can be used to specify all variables in the data set. In the Linear Regression example above, the independent variable list CHEM1 .. CHEM4 could be specified by typing ALL. In this particular case, it's understood that the variable HEAT will be excluded because it was previously identified as the dependent variable.

## Editing Input Lines

When responding to prompts in a panel, you can edit what has been entered so far. Use the arrow keys to move the cursor to the desired position. Then use the various editing keys to delete, overwrite, and insert characters.

The insert key is used to switch back and forth between overwrite mode and insert mode. When in overwrite mode, the next character entered replaces the character at the cursor position. When in insert mode, the next character entered will be inserted before the character at cursor position. You can always tell which mode you're in by the size of the cursor; overwrite mode has a small cursor and insert mode has a large cursor.

You can use several keys to move the cursor while editing panels. They're described below.

| Movement Keys | |
|---|---|
| arrow keys | moves cursor one space in the direction of the arrow |
| ctl-right | moves cursor one word to the right |
| ctl-left | moves cursor one word to the left |
| home | moves cursor to the far left |
| end | moves cursor to the far right |

| Insert Key | |
|---|---|
| insert | switches between overwrite mode and insert mode |

| Deletion Keys | |
|---|---|
| del | deletes the character at the cursor |
| backspace | deletes the character to the left of the cursor |
| ctl-backspace | deletes the word at the cursor |
| ctl-end | deletes the line from the cursor to the end of the line |
| ctl-Y | deletes the entire line |

Function Keys

| | |
|---|---|
| F1 | the start key, used to begin an analysis or procedure |
| F2 | used to select variables and file names from lists |
| F3 | used to select transformation functions |

## File Name Selection

When prompted for a file name in a File Management procedure, you can select a file name from the list of file names that is displayed either by pressing F2 or by clicking the left button on your mouse. You can also change the file list displayed by entering a new drive, path, or file name mask.

```
                              RETRIEVE
EMPTY DATA SET


200 free variables.  160K bytes free.
Files:
AIRLINE.SX      ALFALFA.SX      BIRTHWT.SX      BL5ED.SX        CHEMCON1.SX
CHEMCON2.SX     CHOLESTE.SX     CIRCUIT.SX      COMPUTER.SX     DOUG1.SX
DOUGH1.SX       DOUGH2.SX       DREAMS.SX       E.SX            EXXON.SX
FUNGUS1.SX      HALD.SX         IBM.SX          JUICE.SX        LIZARDS.SX
LIZARDS2.SX     LIZARDS3.SX     NORTUP.SX       PAINT.SX        PISTONS.SX
ROSES.SX        ROSESTAT.SX     SHOCKS.SX       SMALL.SX        SMIRNOV.SX
SMOKER.SX       SOYBEANS.SX     T1.SX           T2.SX           TANKDEFT.SX
VASO.SX         VISIONC.SX      VISIONT.SX

Enter a drive designator, subdirectory, or file mask for directory listing.
C:\SX\40\*.SX

Enter the input file name.  Press F2 to select from the list.
ROSES.SX

Esc Exit   F1 Start   F2 Select file
```

To change the drive, path, or file mask, press the up arrow key to move the cursor to the mask prompt line. Edit the drive, path, and mask displayed, or type in a new name altogether. You can use the ? and * characters to build a mask in the same manner you use with DOS commands. Use *.SX for the mask to list all the *Statistix* data files. When you press Enter, the files in your new drive, path, and mask will be displayed.

You select a file from the list by pressing F2 when your cursor is at the file name prompt. Then you use the arrow keys and the page up and down keys to highlight the name of the file you want. Press Enter to select that file. The name then appears at the file name prompt. Press Esc if you decide not to select a file name.

You can also select a file name using a mouse. By clicking the left button when the cursor is at the file name prompt, you can use the mouse to move the highlighted bar around the list of file names. Select a file name by clicking the mouse's left button. Click the right button to exit from the file name list if you choose not to select a name.

## Saving Panels

The variable lists, file names, and other details that you enter on a panel are automatically saved. When you select a procedure for the second time, the data you entered on the previous visit automatically reappear. You can press F1 and rerun the same analysis, or you can use the input line editing features described above to make changes. When you save a data set using the Save procedure, the options are saved as well as the data. When you retrieve the data file later, the panel options used earlier are available.

## Printing and Saving Reports

When you run a statistical analysis, the report is automatically displayed on the screen once the computations are completed. You can scroll forward and backward through the report using the up and down arrow keys and the page up and page down keys.

The prompt at the bottom of the report screen offers additional options:

```
Esc Exit  Print  File  Options panel  |  PgUp PgDn
```

Press Esc to exit the report and return to the *Statistix* menus. Press P to print the entire report. Once the report has been printed, you return to the *Statistix* menus. Press F to save the entire report in an ASCII file. Press O to return to the options panel used to produce the report.

When you press F to save the report in a file, you'll be asked for the file name. If you don't specify a drive or path, the current drive and path will be used. If the report file already exists, you can choose to overwrite the file or append the report at the end of the file.

```
File already exists  |  Esc Exit  Append  Erase
```

Press Esc to enter a different file name. Press A to append the new report to the end of the file. This is useful when you want to record a series of analyses for a particular data set in a single file. Press E to erase the existing file. This will erase the old file from the disk and create a new file to save the report.

## Printing and Saving Graphs

Most of the statistical analysis procedures in *Statistix* produce reports. A report is composed of text, which can be printed using a text printer or saved in an ASCII file. Some procedures, such as the Histogram and Scatter Plot, produce graphs. Graphs are displayed on your graphics monitor. They can also be printed using a graphics printer or plotter, and they can be saved in a graph file.

When a graph is displayed on the screen, a menu of options is presented below the graph:

```
Esc Exit  Print  File  Export  Titles  Options panel
```

Press Esc to exit from the graph and return to the *Statistix* menus. Press O to return to the options panel used to create the graph. Press T to edit the titles that appear on the graph. After you edit the various titles, press F1 to redisplay the graph using the new titles.

Press P to print the graph. You must install your graphics printer before you can print your first graph; see Install System, Printers on page 19.

Press F to save the graph in a graphics file. The resulting graph file is formatted for the graphics printer you select using the Install System procedure. The graph file can be printed using the GCOPY program after you exit *Statistix*, but only using the graphics printer you selected.

Press E to save the graph in a file if you want to export a graph to a different program, such as a word processing program. The file format used to create the graph file is the graph export file type you selected using the Install System procedure (either PostScript or HPGL).

If a graph file already exists when using the File command or the Export command, you can choose to overwrite the file or append the graph at the end of the file.

```
File already exists  |  Esc Exit  Append  Erase
```

Press Esc to enter a different file name. Press A to append the new graph to the end of the file. Press E to erase the existing file from the disk and to create a new file to save the graph.

Because printing graphs can be a very slow process, it's useful to be able to save a number of graphs in a single file and then print all the graphs in the file after exiting *Statistix*. If you intend to import a *Statistix* graph into another program, it's safer to save one graph per file.

Use the GCOPY program supplied with *Statistix* at the DOS prompt to print graphs you've saved. The syntax is:

```
GCOPY filetype filelist port
```

Filetype . the file format:
  DM . dot matrix
  LJ . . LaserJet or PaintJet
  PS . . PostScript
  HP . HP plotters
Filelist . . the list of files to print. You may use wildcards (? and *).
Port . . . . the printer port: COM1, COM2, LPT1, or LPT2.

## Mixing Report and Graph Files

When you save a *Statistix* report in a file, the file is an ASCII file that can be printed on a text printer using the DOS commands Print or Copy. When you save a graph in a file, the file is a graphics file that can be printed using the GCOPY command.

Usually, you'll keep your *Statistix* report files separate from your graphics files. However, you can save both reports and graphs in the same file and print the file using the GCOPY command provided your text printer is also your graphics printer. If you try this, be sure to install your text printer to force page ejects after each report (see Install System, Printers on page 19).

## ASCII Graphs

One of the graphics printers offered by *Statistix* is ASCII text. When a graph is printed or saved using the ASCII text graphics driver, the output consists of text just like a *Statistix* report. It can be printed on any text printer. You can import an ASCII text graph file into a word processor like any other text. The output are low resolution, and lines and curves are omitted. The advantages of ASCII text graphs is that they print faster and you can mix them with text from reports.

# Install System

The **Install System** procedures are used to configure *Statistix* for your computer and printer, allowing you to indicate your preferences for such options as screen colors. Once you've made a selection in an installation procedure, your choice remains in effect until you change it again. Your choices are stored in a data file named SXDRIVE.DEF.

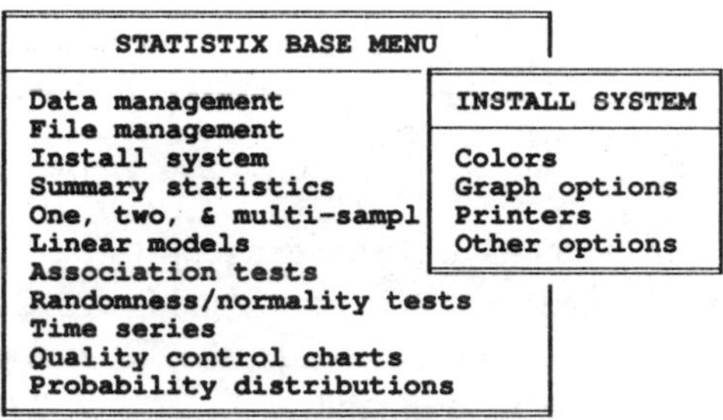


## Colors

The first item on the Install System menu is used to select colors. The standard colors panel is presented below.

```
                              COLOR INSTALLATION

Does your computer have a color monitor? ................. Yes

Panel colors:
   Background color (press F2 for list) ................... Blue
   Dim text color for instructions ........................ Light gray
   Bright text color for user input ....................... White
   Report text color ...................................... Green
   Select bar background color ............................ Black

Menu colors:
   Background color (press F2 for list) ................... Light gray
   Normal text color ...................................... Black
   Shortcut text color .................................... Red
   Select bar color ....................................... Green

Graph colors:
   Background color (press F2 for list) ................... Blue
   Titles, labels, and axis color ......................... White
   Primary plotted data color ............................. Light green
   Secondary plotted data color ........................... Light red
```

Some computers (usually laptops and notebooks) have a color graphics adapter installed, but with a monochrome screen. This situation, which *Statistix* cannot detect automatically, makes reading text on the screen difficult. Be sure to answer NO to the question regarding the color monitor if you have a monochrome monitor.

If you have a color monitor, you can change the colors used for *Statistix* panels, menus, and graphs. Press F2 to display the menu of color choices.

## Graph Options

There are a number of options regarding *Statistix* graphs. These can be changed by selecting Graph Options from the Install System menu. The graph options only affect high resolution graphs, not ASCII text graphs. These options are displayed below.

```
                         GRAPH OPTIONS

Display grid lines ................................. No
Single pair scatter plot symbol (press F2 for list)  Plus
Scatter plot symbol #1 ............................. Circle
Scatter plot symbol #2 ............................. Square
Sequence plot symbol #1 ............................ Circle
Sequence plot symbol #2 ............................ Square
Bar fill pattern ................................... Slash
```

Grid lines are dotted lines that are drawn vertically and horizontally to form a grid inside the rectangle of a graph.

You can use a number of symbols to mark points on X-Y plots (plus, start, circle, square, etc.). The "Single pair scatter plot symbol" is used to plot points on scatter plots when there is only one X-Y pair of variables. If there is more than one X-Y pair, we use different symbols to mark the different X-Y pairs. You can select the symbols you want to use for the first two X-Y pairs in multi-pair scatter plots. *Statistix* will select the remaining symbols for plots with more than two pairs.

Select the symbol you want *Statistix* to use for sequence plots (time series plots and control charts). You can plot up to five series on a single plot using the Time Series Plot procedure. You can select the symbols to mark the points for the first two time series variables plotted. *Statistix* will select the symbols for the others when more than two variables are used.

Select your preference for the bar fill pattern. It will be used to shade the inside of the bars in histograms and Pareto charts.

## Printers

The Printer installation panel (presented on the next page) is divided into three parts: text printer options for printing *Statistix* reports, graphics printer options for printing *Statistix* graphs, and export graphics options for exporting graphs to be used by other programs.

```
                    PRINTER INSTALLATION

Text Printer Details:
  Text printer port (press F2 for list) ............ LPT1
  Supports the IBM extended-character set? ......... No
  Use the "printer on line" test? .................. Yes
  Print a page eject after each report? ............ No

Graphics Printer/Plotter Details:
  Graphics printer ID (press F2 for list) .......... HP LaserJet
  Graphics printer port (press F2 for list) ........ LPT1
  Graph orientation (press F2 for list) ............ Half page portrait
  Print resolution (press F2 for list) ............. High
  Use resident Times Roman fonts? (HP LaserJet only) No
  Print in color? (PS, plotters, PaintJet only) .... No
  Titles, labels, and axis color ................... Black
  Primary plotted data color ....................... Green
  Secondary plotted data color ..................... Blue

Graphics Export File Details:
  Graphics export file type (press F2 for list) .... Postscript
  Export graph orientation ......................... Half page portrait
```

Select your text printer port (LPT1, COM1, etc). LPT1 is the most common.

If your printer supports the IBM extended-character set, enter YES to the second question. Printed output looks better using this option, especially graphs printed using the ASCII text graphics selection discussed on the next page. Many printers support this character set. The HP LaserJet offers support for what its manual calls the "PC-8 symbol set". However, you must specifically select the PC-8 symbol set using the LaserJet's control panel. Please see the LaserJet User's Manual for more details.

*Statistix* normally performs a "printer on line" test before trying to print a report. If you're using a shared printer or if you get erroneous "printer not on line" messages, enter NO at this prompt.

*Statistix* can print a page eject at the end of each report, or you can answer NO to the "page eject" question to let reports print one after another to save paper. If you have a laser printer, you should answer YES.

You must select a graphics printer before you can print *Statistix* graphs. Press F2 to display the list of graphics printers supported by *Statistix*. If your printer is not listed, it may be compatible with one that is (please see your printer manual). *Statistix* provides support for a number of 9-pin and 24-pin dot matrix printers, PostScript printers, HP LaserJet-compatible laser printers, and HP-compatible pen plotters.

One of the graphics printers listed is "ASCII text". High resolution graphs displayed on the screen are converted to low resolution text representations of the graphs and are printed using letters and symbols. Some graph features, such as the normal curve on a histogram and the line segments connecting points on a time series graph, are omitted from ASCII text graphs. ASCII text graphs aren't as pretty as real graphs, but they do have some advantages: (1) They can be printed using any text printer, (2) they take less time to print, and (3) ASCII text graphs can be mixed with *Statistix* reports in ASCII files. If you do use ASCII text to print graphs, be sure to answer YES to the IBM extended-character set question discussed on the preceding page.

Select the I/O port connecting your computer to the printer or plotter you want to use for printing graphs. Select the graph orientation—half page portrait, full page portrait, or landscape. Select the print resolution—low, medium, or high. Low resolution graphs print faster, and the graph files saved with the File command are smaller.

The HP LaserJet III has resident Times Roman fonts. *Statistix* can use the resident fonts to print the titles that appear on graphs. If you're using a LaserJet III or if you know your laser printer has a 12 point, 16 point, and 20 point resident Times Roman fonts, answer YES to the Times Roman font question to improve the quality of your graphs. *Statistix* can only use resident fonts (not downloaded fonts) and only when graphs are printed directly from *Statistix*.

The HP PaintJet, HP pen plotters, and some PostScript printers can print in color. If you're using a color printer, select whether or not you want *Statistix* to use color when printing graphs. Select the colors you want to use to draw the axes and titles and the first two colors to use when plotting "data" (points, lines, bars, etc.). You select colors using pen numbers for HP pen plotters. *Statistix* uses the PaintJet's eight-color mode for color graphs.

*Statistix* graphs can be exported to other programs that support graphics. For example, you may be interested in incorporating a *Statistix* graph in a document using a word processor. You can use either of two popular graphics languages to export graphs—PostScript or HPGL. Select the export file type supported by your software; if your software supports both languages, select PostScript for the best results. The Export command on the graph menu will use the graphics language you choose to create a graph file (see Printing and Saving Graphs above). You can also select the graph orientation for PostScript export files.

## Other Options

The Other Options selection on the Install System menu is a collection of miscellaneous options available in *Statistix* (see panel below).

```
                         OTHER OPTIONS
 Do you want variables to be listed in alphabetical order? ........ Yes
 Date format (MM/DD/YY, DD/MM/YY, or YY/MM/DD) .................. MM/DD/YY
 Maximum expanded memory usage by Statistix (megabytes) .......... 2.00
 If you are using a dual drive computer without a fixed disk,
 enter the letter for the second SX program drive (usually B:) ....
 Enter the starting default drive and path for data files.
```

*Statistix* displays the variable names of the active data set at the top of data management and statistical procedures panels. The variable name list can be kept in alphabetical order or in the order the variables were created. If you select the latter, you can reorder the variables using the Order command in **Edit Data** (see Chapter 2).

Select the date format you want to use for both data entry and reports—month/day/year, day/month/year, or year/month/day.

*Statistix* reserves all the available random access memory (RAM) for variable data storage. Computers with 640 KB of RAM provide for about 30,000 real numbers or 120,000 integers. *Statistix* will use up to 8 MB of expanded memory for additional variable storage, provided an expanded memory manager (EMM or LIM 3.2 or later) is installed. An expanded memory manager is a program that is often supplied with DOS (e.g., EMM386.EXE) or with an expanded memory board that must be installed in the CONFIG.SYS file (e.g., device=emm386.exe 2048). Using expanded memory, *Statistix* can handle much larger data sets (over one million real numbers). Enter the amount of expanded memory you want *Statistix* to use in megabytes.

If your computer doesn't have a fixed disk and you're running *Statistix* from diskettes, you can instruct *Statistix* to search a second diskette drive for *Statistix* program files. If you enter the letter for your second diskette drive (usually drive B:), *Statistix* will automatically search both drives for program files when it needs them. This allows you to keep SX1 in drive A: and the SX2 diskette in drive B:, reducing program diskette swapping. When you want to use a File Management procedure, insert your data diskette in drive B:

Enter the disk drive and disk directory where you want to store your *Statistix* data files at the last prompt in the Other Options panel presented on the preceding page. The drive and path you enter will be used when you save and retrieve data files. The file management procedures (Retrieve, Save, Import, etc.) list file names in their options panels. The disk drive and path you specify here dictates where *Statistix* will look for this list of files.

C H A P T E R

# 2

# Data Management

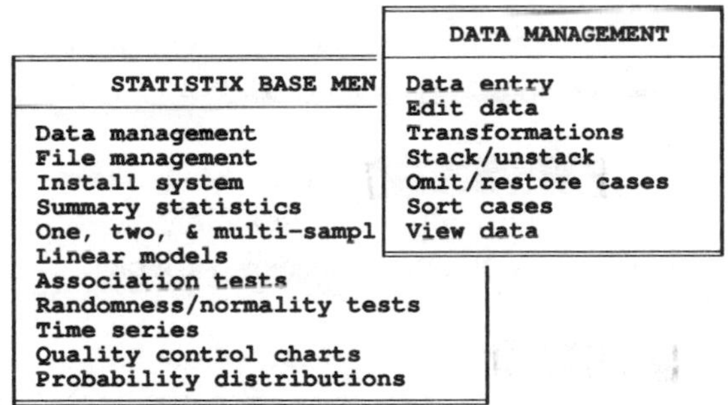


The **Data Management** procedures are used to enter data and manipulate data already entered into *Statistix.*

The **Data Entry** procedure is used to create a new data set by typing values into a spreadsheet-like format. You can also use it to add new variables to an existing data set.

The **Edit Data** procedure is used to edit the values of your active data set. It's also used to delete cases and variables, insert cases and variables, enter variable and value labels, and rename variables.

The **Transformations** procedure is used to modify the values of existing variables and to create new variables using algebraic expressions and built-in transformation functions.

The **Stack/Unstack** procedure stacks several variables end-to-end to create a single long variable and unstacks one variable into several shorter ones.

The **Omit/Restore Cases** procedure lets you "hide" or "omit" specified cases from the program. These rows are ignored by *Statistix*, although they can be restored at will. If a case is not omitted, we say that the case is selected. The omit status of a case refers to whether it is omitted or selected.

The **Sort** procedure is used to sort the cases of a data set based on the values of one or more variables.

The **View Data** procedure is used to print the contents of a *Statistix* data set.

A data set in *Statistix* can be thought of as a rectangular table. The columns are called variables and are identified by variable names. The rows are called cases and are numbered sequentially.

*Statistix* can handle four types of data: real, integer, date, and string. A variable can only contain values of one data type.

The "real" data type is used to represent floating point numbers in *Statistix*. This format is the most flexible offered by *Statistix* and is used as the default data type when creating new variables.

Integer data in *Statistix* are whole numbers in the range -32767 to 32767. This data type uses only 25% as much space as the real data type. You use the integer data type instead of the real data type, when appropriate, to increase the data set capacity of *Statistix*. This also saves disk space by reducing the size of *Statistix* data files.

The "date" data type is used to represent 20th century dates. The "string" data type is used to enter alphanumeric data, such as a subject's name. String variables can be used as grouping variables for statistical procedures that compute results by group.

When typing numbers using *Statistix*, you can enter a number in either decimal format (e.g., 2.45) or exponential format (e.g., 1.23E+05). Enter the letter M to indicate a missing value for integer, real, and date variables, but not for string variables. A blank string is the missing value equivalent for string variables.

# Data Entry

In *Statistix*, the **Data Entry** procedure is used to create a new data set by typing in values manually. It can also be used to add new variables to an existing data set. After selecting Data Entry from the menu, you enter a list of new variable names.

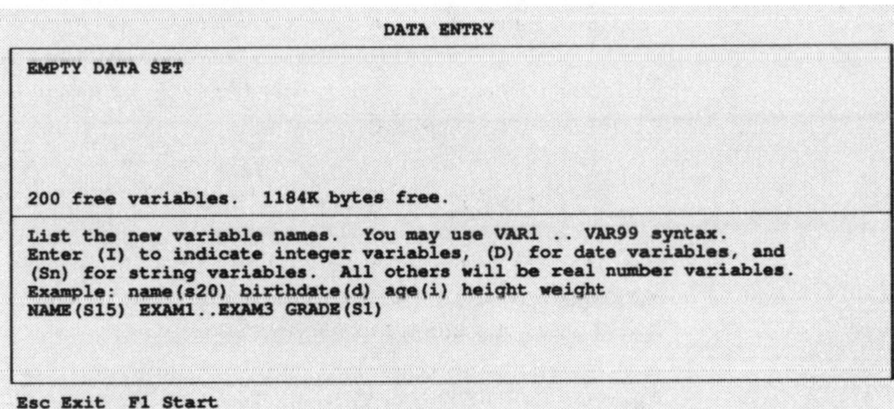


List a variable name for each column of data you intend to enter. Variable names must start with a letter and may contain letters and digits. They must be no more than nine characters in length.

In *Statistix*, data can be integer, real, date, or string. However, a particular column can only be used to store one type of data. You can specify the data type of variables when you list the variable names. Use the letters I, R, D, and S in parentheses after the variable names to identify integer, real, date, and string types. String types require a number after the letter S to indicate the maximum length. If you don't specify a data type, real is assumed.

In the example options panel above, the variable STUDENT is a string variable with a maximum length of 15 characters and the variable GRADE is a string variable with length 1. No data type is specified for the variables EXAM1, EXAM2, and EXAM3, so they are assigned the real data type.

The variable list EXAM1, EXAM2, and EXAM3 was abbreviated using what we call VAR1 .. VAR99 syntax. A data type entered at the end of the list is applied to all of the variables in the list (e.g., Q1 .. Q15(I)).

After listing the variable names, press F1 to begin data entry. An empty spreadsheet will appear, as in the following example.

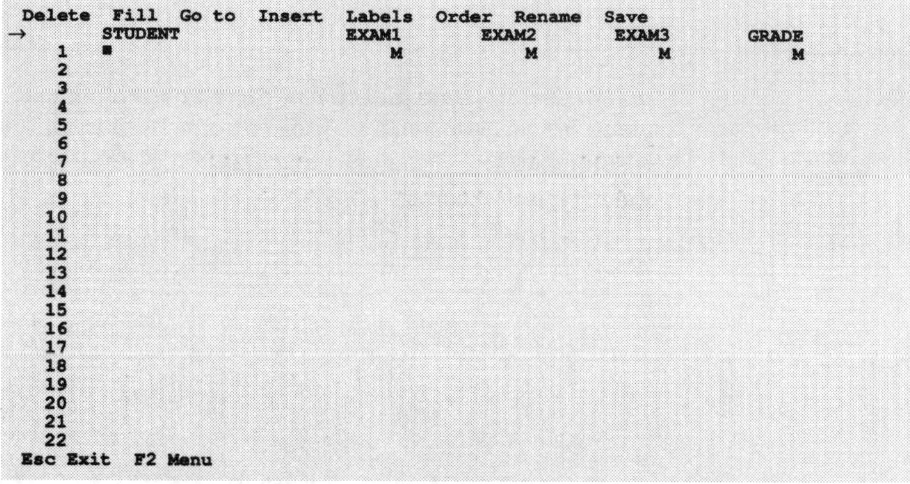


Variable names are listed along the top of the screen. Case numbers are listed along the left margin. Your cursor starts at the first variable and first case position. To enter data, simply begin to enter values for each cell, pressing either Enter or an arrow key after each entry. Enter the letter M for missing values in integer, real, and date variables, but not for string variables.

When you press Enter, the cursor moves in the direction of the "auto move arrow" displayed in the upper left corner of the screen. You can change the direction of the auto move arrow by pressing the right arrow key or the down arrow key.

You can use the arrow keys to go back and correct errors at any time. Simply type in a new value over the existing value in a cell.

A menu of edit commands appears on the top line of the screen. Press F2 or click the left button on the mouse at any time to activate the menu. The edit commands let you delete variables and cases, insert variables and cases, reorder variables, rename variables, enter variable and value labels, and save the data to disk. The edit commands are discussed in detail in the next section, **Edit Data.**

Press Esc to exit Data Entry and return to the menus.

# Edit Data

In *Statistix*, the **Edit Data** procedure is used to edit individual data items in your active data set. In addition, Edit Data lets you delete cases and variables, insert new cases and variables, reorder variables, rename variables, and enter variable and value labels.

While in the **Edit Data** procedure, the data are displayed in a spreadsheet format.

```
Delete  Fill  Go to  Insert  Labels  Order  Rename  Save
→          NAME               BIRTHDATE        STATE         AGE         CONC
   1    Dood, C                28/11/45         IA            46          181
   2    Fisher, E              02/11/39         IA            52          228
   3    Haley, J               10/01/53         IA            39          182
   4    Hickman, D             23/10/26         IA            65          249
   5    Johnson, M             01/01/38         IA            54          259
   6    Johnson, A             04/11/58         IA            33          201
   7    Lyttle, R              06/01/43         IA            49          121
   8    Payne, P               21/11/15         IA            76          339
   9    Sellman, G             20/10/20         IA            71          224
  10    Stadt, S               16/11/50         IA            41          112
  11    Thorn, J               16/11/33         IA            58          189
  12    Baur, J                24/12/73         NE            18          137
  13    Christianson, E        23/10/47         NE            44          173
  14    Farrow, C              14/10/58         NE            33          177
  15    Greer, R               28/11/13         NE            78          241
  16    Keller, G              13/12/40         NE            51          225
  17    Lauber, R              10/01/49         NE            43          223
  18    Neimann, P             07/10/47         NE            44          190
  19    Price, D               27/11/33         NE            58          257
  20    Stanley, J             15/12/28         NE            63          337
  21    Steele, A              09/12/72         NE            19          189
  22    Stock, W               17/10/49         NE            42          214
Esc Exit  F2 Menu
```

Variable names appear along the top margin of the screen. Case numbers appear along the left margin. Both selected and omitted cases appear on the edit screen. The case numbers of omitted cases are marked with a star (*) to remind you that the case is omitted. The values of omitted cases can be changed.

The value at the cursor is highlighted to show its position. The cursor can be moved around the spreadsheet using the arrow keys, page up, page down, home, and end keys. Press Ctl-left to page left and Ctl-right to page right. You can also move the cursor by moving the mouse.

The value at the cursor can be changed simply by entering a new value and pressing Enter. Enter the letter M for missing values for integer, real, and date variables, but not for string variables.

The "auto move arrow" displayed in the upper left corner of the screen points in the direction the cursor will move when Enter is pressed. Press either the left arrow or the down arrow key to change the direction of the auto move arrow.

The menu of edit commands—Delete, Fill, Go to, Insert, Labels, Order, Rename, and Save—appears on the top line of the screen. Press F2 or click the left button on the mouse at any time to activate the menu. The edit commands are discussed in detail below.

## Delete

Select **Delete** from the edit menu to delete cases or variables. You will be presented with a pull-down menu giving you three choices: Cases, Omitted cases, and Variables.

```
Delete  Fill  Go to  Insert  Labels  Order  Rename  Save
┌────────────────┐       BIRTHDATE      STATE        AGE        CONC
│ Cases          │        28/11/45        IA          46         181
│ Omitted cases  │        02/11/39        IA          52         228
│ Variables      │        10/01/53        IA          39         182
└────────────────┘D       23/10/26        IA          65         249
   5   Johnson, M         01/01/38        IA          54         259
   6   Johnson, A         04/11/58        IA          33         201
   7   Lyttle, R          06/01/43        IA          49         121
   8   Payne, P           21/11/15        IA          76         339
```

Use the delete cases command to delete one case or to delete a contiguous block of cases. You'll be asked to enter the first and last case numbers for the cases you want to delete.

You can also delete all omitted cases. This method of deleting cases gives you greater flexibility in selecting which cases to delete. The Omit/Restore Cases procedure discussed later in this chapter can be used to omit cases based on data values rather than case numbers.

To delete variables, select "variables" from the delete submenu. The delete variables panel is shown below.

```
┌──────────────────────── DELETE VARIABLES ─────────────────────────┐
│ AGE       AGECLASS  BIRTHDATE CONC      CONCLASS  NAME            │
│ STATE                                                             │
├───────────────────────────────────────────────────────────────────┤
│ List the variables you want to delete.  You may specify ALL or    │
│ use A .. Z syntax.  Press F2 to select variables from the list.   │
│ AGECLASS CONCLASS                                                 │
└───────────────────────────────────────────────────────────────────┘
Esc Exit  F1 Start  F2 Select variable
```

List the variables you want to delete. You can use A .. Z syntax in your variable list, or you can press F2 and select variables from the list displayed.

## Fill

The **Fill** command is used to fill a number of contiguous cells with a particular value.

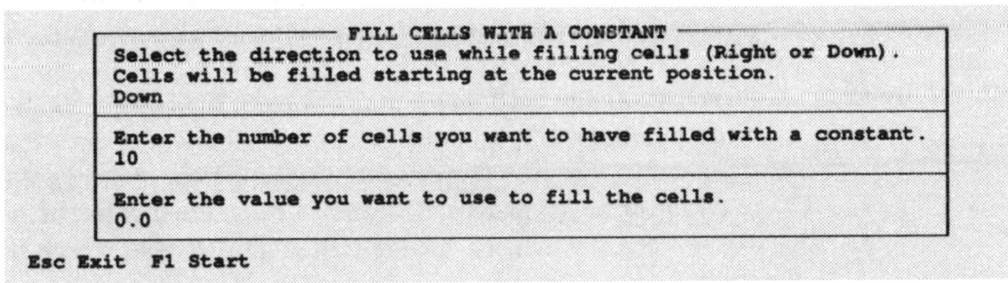


Cells will be filled starting with the current cursor position. First select the direction in which you want the filling to proceed, either down or to the right. Enter the number of cells you want to fill and the new value for these cells. If you select "right" for the fill direction, then filling will automatically wrap around when the end of a case is reached and will continue on the next row.

## Go To

Use the **Go to** command to jump to any position in the spreadsheet. This is particularly useful with large data sets.

```
GO TO CELL
AGE        AGECLASS   BIRTHDATE CONC       CONCLASS   NAME
STATE

Enter the target variable name ..................... STATE
Enter the target case number (1 - 30) .............. 17
Esc Exit  F1 Start  F2 Select variable
```

Enter the variable and case number of the cell you want to move to and press F1.

## Insert

The **Insert** command is used to insert new cases and new variables in the spreadsheet. You can select either cases or variables from the insert submenu.

The insert cases panel is shown below.

```
INSERT CASES
Enter number of the first new case (1 - 31).
31

Enter the number of cases to insert (1 - 2895).
20

Esc Exit  F1 Start
```

First enter the case number where you want to insert the case(s). Then enter the number of cases to insert.

To insert additional variables, you must enter a list of new variable names. The variables will be inserted after the variable where the cursor is currently positioned. The insert variable panel is shown below.

```
INSERT VARIABLES
List the new variable names.

Esc Exit  F1 Start
```

## Labels

The **Labels** command is used to enter or change the current values of three kinds of labels: the data set label, variable labels, and value labels. These labels are used to annotate *Statistix* reports and graphs.

The **data set label** is a one line comment used to describe the data set. It's printed at the beginning of each *Statistix* report.

**Variable labels** are comments for variables. When you return to a data set months after creating it, variable labels will remind you what data the variables contain and how they were created. Variable labels are incorporated into the heading of some reports, such as the stem and leaf plot. They are also used for axis labels for graphs (e.g., scatter plots and histograms).

The variables and variable labels are presented in a table as shown in the example below. Use the arrow keys and page up and page down keys to scroll up and down the list to enter labels in the table. Variable labels can be up to 40 characters long.

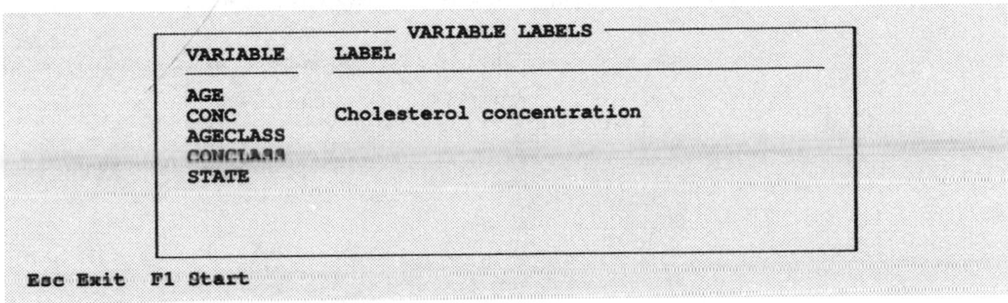


**Value labels** are strings attached to individual values for a variable. For example, it may be convenient for data entry purposes, to code states using numbers (1 for Iowa and 2 for Nebraska in the value labels example below.) A value label serves as a comment to remind you what the codes represent. These labels also appear in *Statistix* reports (e.g., cross tabulations) to improve readability.

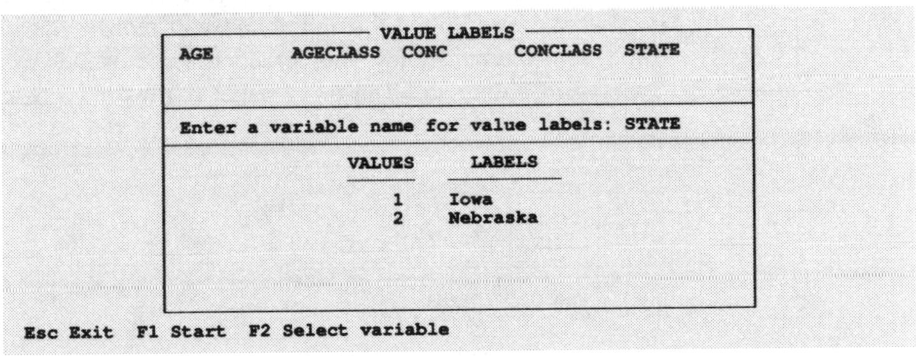


First select a data set variable. Then begin entering value and value label pairs in the table. Value labels can be up to ten characters in length.

The **Labels Report** lists the variable and value labels for the active data set. An example report is presented on the next page.

The Labels Report lists the data set label, variables and variable labels, and value labels. It also lists the data type (real, integer, date, and string) for each variable. After viewing the report on the screen, you press P to print the report.

```
STATISTIX 4.0                                          CHOLESTE, 23/05/92, 12:59
Age and blood cholesterol concentration of women from two states.

VARIABLE     DATA TYPE   VARIABLE LABEL
----------   ---------   ----------------------------------------
AGE          Real
CONC         Real        Cholesterol concentration
AGECLASS     Real
CONCLASS     Real
STATE        Integer

VALUE LABELS FOR STATE

VALUE  LABEL
-----  ------------
    1  Iowa
    2  Nebraska
```

## Order

The **Order** command is used to change the order in which the variables are displayed in the spreadsheet editor. If you have installed *Statistix* (see Install System, Other Options in Chapter 1) to keep your variable lists in the order they were created, then this command will reorder the variables in lists throughout the program. This affects the use of the A .. Z syntax (see A .. Z Syntax in Chapter 1). The order panel is illustrated below.

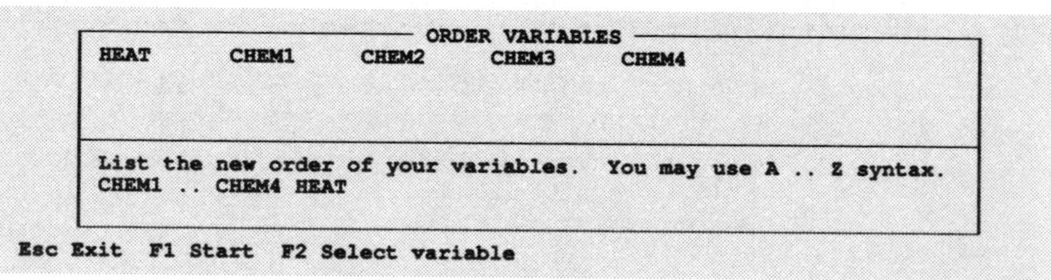


In the example above, the variable HEAT will be moved from the far left to the far right of the edit screen. If you omit variables from the new order list, they will be moved to the end (right side of the spreadsheet).

## Rename

After selecting **Rename** from the menu, the cursor highlights the name of the variable in the current column position, and you're prompted to enter a new variable name. Enter a new variable name and press Enter. The next variable to the right is then highlighted. You can continue renaming variables from left to right. Press Enter to skip a variable you don't want to rename. When you're finished, press Esc to return to editing.

## Save

You can use the editor's **Save** command to save the changes you've made in a *Statistix* data file without leaving the spreadsheet editor.

```
                          SAVE
  Enter the output file name.
  CHOLESTE.SX

Esc Exit  F1 Start
```

The existing file name, if any, appears in the space for the file name. Press Enter to save the data using the same file name, or enter a new file name.

## Exiting Edit Data

To exit the Edit Data procedure, press Esc. You'll be returned to the *Statistix* menus.

# Transformations

This powerful procedure is used to create new variables or to alter the values of the existing ones. It has two general forms: simple assignment and conditional assignment using the If-Then-Else construct.

```
                          TRANSFORMATIONS                              HALD
 CHEM1      CHEM2      CHEM3      CHEM4      HEAT



 5 variable(s).  13 of 13 cases selected.  159K bytes free.
 Functions:
 ABs (x)         ARCSin (x)      ARCTan (x)      ATkinson (x)    CAt (i, j)
 CASE            COS (x)         COUnt (x)       CUmsum (x [,y]  DAY (x)
 DAYOfweek(x)    DIff (x [,i])   Exp (x)         Geomean (x)     LAg (x [,i])
 LEngth (s)      LN (x)          LOG (x)         LOWcase (s)     M
 MAx (x)         MEAn (x)        MEDian (x)      MIn (x)         MODulo (i, j)
 MONth (x)       NOrmalize (x)   NRandom(m,sd)   PErcentile(x)   PI

 Enter a simple transformation (e.g., variable = expression) or a conditional
 transformation (e.g., IF condition THEN expression ELSE expression).
 Press F1 when finished to actually perform each transformation.
 LCHEM1 = LOG (CHEM1)

Esc Exit  F1 Start  F2 Select variable  F3 Select function
```

If you're not familiar with arithmetic and logical expressions, you should read the **Arithmetic and Logical Expressions** section at the end of this chapter.

## Specification

The **Transformations** panel illustrated on the preceding page is divided into three areas. The data set variables appear at the top of the screen. The *Statistix* built-in functions are listed in the middle area of the panel. (There are too many functions to display all at the same time. Press F3 and the various arrow and page keys to view the rest of the functions.)

The bottom area of the screen is the transformation expression work space. You have three lines available to enter a transformation expression. You can use the arrow keys to move about this area and edit your expression. Press Ctl-Y or Ctl-end to delete a line in the work space. Press F1 to compute the transformation. Press Esc to exit the transformations procedure.

## Simple Assignment

Suppose the variable NEWVAR is a new one you want to create or perhaps an existing one that you want to alter. Such a variable is called a **target variable**. In a simple assignment, a target variable is simply equated with an arithmetic expression:

```
{target variable} {data type} = {arithmetical expression}
```

To give a specific example, suppose you want NEWVAR to be the sum of the variables A, B, and C.

```
NEWVAR = A + B + C
```

A new variable called NEWVAR has now been created with the sum of the variables A, B, and C. If a variable called NEWVAR already exists, the variable's values will be replaced by the sum A + B + C.

A target variable's name may appear on both sides of an assignment statement provided the variable already exists.

```
TARGET = 2.75 + SQRT (TARGET)
```

Sqrt is an example of a built-in function that computes the square root of the argument. The built-in functions are described in the **Arithmetic and Logical Expressions** section on page 52.

*Statistix* can handle four types of data: real, integer, date, and string. Use the letters I, R, D, and S in parentheses after the name of the new variable to identify integer, real, date, and string types. String types require a number after the letter S to indicate the maximum length. If you don't specify a data type, real is assumed. The examples below illustrate how integer, date, and string variables can be created.

```
COUNT (I) = A + B + C
DUEDATE (D) = SALEDATE + 30
FULLNAME (S30) = FIRSTNAME + " " + LASTNAME
```

## Conditional Assignment

On occasion you may want to apply one assignment to the target variable when some condition is met and another assignment when the condition is not met. Conditional assignments employing the If-Then-Else construct are designed for this purpose. Its general form is:

```
IF {logical expression}
THEN {target variable} = {some arithmetic expression}
ELSE {target variable} = {some other arithmetic expression}
```

If a specified logical expression for a particular case is true, the THEN clause is performed; otherwise, the ELSE clause is performed. This construct is quite flexible, as the following examples illustrate.

Suppose you want to create a new variable—AGEGROUP—based on the values of a variable AGE. You want AGEGROUP to be the tens digit of age, but you want to group all ages of 60 or greater into one group.

```
IF AGE < 60
THEN AGEGROUP = TRUNC (AGE/10)
ELSE AGEGROUP = 6
```

The three key words—IF, THEN, and ELSE—need not be on separate lines. A short statement can be written on one line. The ELSE expression can be omitted from a conditional transformation, in which case the target variable is left unchanged when the logical expression is not true.

```
IF AGEGROUP > 6 THEN AGEGROUP = 6
```

The logical expression can include any valid arithmetic expressions, and the arithmetic expressions can include the target variable if it already exists. For example:

```
IF (A + B) <= (1.25 * SIN (C))
THEN A = 0.0
ELSE A = A + D + E
```

## Converting Variable Types

All of the values of a particular variable must be of the same data type, either integer, real, date, or string. The data type of an existing variable can be changed using a transformation. For example, suppose that the variable

CONC was originally created as a real variable and contains values for cholesterol concentration. You can convert the variable CONC to an integer variable using the transformation:

```
CONC (I) = ROUND (CONC)
```

An integer variable can just as easily be converted to a real variable:

```
HEIGHT (R) = HEIGHT
```

If a value for HEIGHT exceeded the limits for an integer variable (-32767 to 32767), the result would be missing.

The maximum length of a string variable can be changed using a transformation. Suppose you had created a variable NAME (S15) but later decided that 15 characters were insufficient. You could increase the maximum length using the transformation:

```
NAME (S20) = NAME
```

When a string variable is converted to an integer, real, or date variable, all values are assigned the missing value. When integer, real, and date variables are converted to string variables, all values are assigned blank strings. This kind of variable type conversion would only be useful to change a variable's data type before any data have been entered.

## Missing Values

If a number used in an arithmetic expression is missing, the result of the expression is also missing. After all, you can't perform arithmetic on numbers that don't exist. Consider the transformation:

```
A = B + C
```

If the value for the variable C is missing for a particular case, the expression B + C is missing and the case for the target variable A is assigned the missing value.

In the logical expression of a conditional transformation, it makes sense to make tests of equality using missing values. The expressions IF X = Y and X <> Y are evaluated normally if either X or Y is missing. However, a number can't be less than or greater than a missing value. So when X or Y is missing in an expression like IF X < Y, the logical expression can't be evaluated and the target variable is assigned a missing value.

The treatment of missing values is discussed at greater length in the **Arithmetic and Logical Expressions** section on page 50.

**Omitted Cases**

Cases that have been omitted using **Omit/Restore Cases** are basically ignored when a transformation is performed. If the target variable is a variable that already exists, omitted cases retain their old values, i.e., they are not transformed. If the target variable doesn't already exist, omitted cases are assigned the missing value when the transformation is performed.

**Dummy Variables**

There is a special transformation for creating dummy variables (indicator variables). A dummy variable contains the values 0 or 1 to indicate the absence or presence of some factor. The general format for the dummy variable transformation is:

```
DUMMY (variable level1 level2 ...) newvar1 newvar2 ...
```

For example, if you have a categorical variable named DOSE that contains the values 5, 10, and 15 and you want to create three dummy variables named LOW, MED, and HIGH:

```
DUMMY (DOSE 5 10 15) LOW MED HIGH
```

For cases where DOSE has the value 5, the new variable LOW will be given the value 1; otherwise, the value would be 0. For cases where DOSE has the value 10, the new variable MED will be given the value 1; otherwise, the value would be 0. For cases where DOSE has the value 15, the new variable HIGH will be given the value 1; otherwise, the value would be 0.

The source variable containing the existing levels can be an integer, real, date, or string variable. The levels listed for an integer or a real variable must be non-negative whole numbers. String values in the list of levels must be delimited using quotes.

```
DUMMY (STATE "Iowa" "Nebraska") IA NE
```

The list of levels can be omitted if the levels are consecutive numbers starting with 1. For example, if DOSE contains the levels 1, 2, and 3, the dummy function could be written as:

```
DUMMY (DOSE) LOW MED HIGH
```

# Stack / Unstack

The **Stack/Unstack** procedure is used to stack several variables end-to-end to create a single long variable, and to unstack one variable into several shorter ones based on the values of a grouping variable.

Data to be analyzed often can be broken down into groups of interest. For example, you may be interested in cholesterol concentration by age group or fat absorption of doughnuts by the type of fat used in cooking. There are two ways data of this type can be presented. Chapter 5 defines these methods of presentation as the "table" method and the "categorical" method. The table method puts the data for each group into a separate variable. The groups are identified by the variable names. The categorical method puts all the data into one column and uses a second grouping variable to identify the groups. You can stack variables to produce the categorical format and unstack variables to produce the table format.

## Stack

```
                            STACK/UNSTACK                              CHEMCON2
 QUICK     STANDARD



 2 variable(s).  8 of 8 cases selected.  159K bytes free.

 Select an operation (Stack or Unstack).
 Stack

 List the variables you want to stack one after another into one variable.
 You may enter ALL or use A .. Z syntax.  Press F2 to select from list.
 QUICK STANDARD

 Enter the name of the destination variable to accumulate the stacked data.
 CONC

 Enter the name of the destination class variable (optional).  This variable
 is used to capture class values representing each source variable.
 METHOD

 Esc Exit  F1 Start  F2 Select variable
```

First select "stack" or "unstack". We'll illustrate stack first. In the example panel above, we listed the variables QUICK and STANDARD as the variables to stack. The variable CONC has been entered as the destination variable. The grouping variable is optional. In the example above, the variable METHOD will capture the group numbers 1 and 2 for the source variables QUICK and STANDARD, respectively.

The resulting data set is presented below.

| QUICK | STANDARD | CONC | METHOD |
|---|---|---|---|
| 23 | 25 | 23 | 1 |
| 18 | 24 | 18 | 1 |
| 22 | 25 | 22 | 1 |
| 28 | 26 | 28 | 1 |
| 17 | M | 17 | 1 |
| 25 | M | 25 | 1 |
| 19 | M | 19 | 1 |
| 16 | M | 16 | 1 |
| M | M | 25 | 2 |
| M | M | 24 | 2 |
| M | M | 25 | 2 |
| M | M | 26 | 2 |

The eight values for the variable QUICK are copied to the new variable CONC followed by the four values for the variable STANDARD. The variable METHOD identifies the two groups.

### Unstack

Suppose you start with the variables CONC and METHOD, but you decide to make the two variables QUICK and STANDARD. You'd use the unstack operation to do this, as illustrated in the options panel below.

```
                         STACK/UNSTACK                          CHEMCON1
CONC     METHOD

2 variable(s).  12 of 12 cases selected.  159K bytes free.

Select an operation (Stack or Unstack).
Unstack

Enter the name of the source variable containing values to unstack.
CONC

Enter the name of the variable containing the class values to use to divide
the source values into the various destination variables.
METHOD

List the destination variables to capture the unstacked data.  You may use
VAR1 .. VAR99 syntax.  Press F2 to select variables from the list.
QUICK STANDARD

Esc Exit  F1 Start  F2 Select variable
```

Here both the source variable and the grouping variable are required. The grouping variable can be any data type (integer, real, date, or string). There can be no more than 200 groups. List the destination variables. You can use VAR1 .. VAR99 syntax to abbreviate the list. If there are n values for the grouping variable, you must enter exactly n variables in the list.

# Omit / Restore Cases

You may often want to analyze a select subset of the cases in *Statistix*. **Omit/Restore Cases** allows you to temporarily "hide" some of your data from the program. Once cases are omitted, they are ignored by the statistical procedures until they are "restored". Omitted cases can also be selectively restored using a "select" statement. The omit status of cases are saved when you use the **Save** procedure.

You specify the cases you want to omit using logical expressions. If you're not familiar with logical expressions, please refer to the **Arithmetic and Logical Expressions** section at the end of this chapter.

```
                              OMIT/RESTORE CASES                         CHOLESTE
 AGE        HEIGHT     SEX        WEIGHT




 4 variable(s).  85 of 100 cases selected.  158K bytes free.
 Functions:
 ABs (x)         ARCSin (x)       ARCTan (x)        ATkinson (x)     CAt (i, j)
 CASE            COS (x)          COUnt (x)         CUmsum (x [,y]   DAY (x)
 DAYOfweek(x)    DIff (x [,i])    Exp (x)           Geomean (x)      LAg (x [,i])
 LEngth (s)      LN (x)           LOG (x)           LOWcase (s)      M
 MAx (x)         MEAn (x)         MEDian (x)        MIn (x)          MODulo (i, j)
 MONth (x)       NOrmalize (x)    NRandom(m,sd)     PErcentile(x)    PI

 Enter an OMIT expression (eg. OMIT (TRT = 1) OR (TRT = 3)), a SELECT
 expression, or enter RESTORE to restore (select) all cases.
 Press F1 when finished to perform an omit/select/restore expression.
 OMIT AGE < 10 OR AGE > 65

 Esc Exit   F1 Start   F2 Select variable   F3 Select function
```

The **Omit/Restore Cases** panel shown above is divided into three areas. The data set variables and a description of the current number of cases selected appear at the top of the screen. The *Statistix* built-in functions are listed in the middle area of the panel. There are too many functions to be displayed at one time. Press F3 and the various arrow and page keys to view the rest of the functions. The bottom area of the screen is the logical expression work space. You have three lines available to enter a logical expression. You can use the arrow keys to move about this area and edit your expression. Press Ctl-Y or Ctl-end to delete a line in the work space. Press F1 when you want to begin omitting. Press Esc to exit the procedure.

You can enter three types of statements: "omit", "select", and "restore". The omit statement has the general form OMIT {logical expression}. Likewise, the select statement has the form SELECT {logical expression}. The restore statement is simply the word RESTORE, which instructs *Statistix* to restore the omit status of all cases to be selected.

The omit status of a case can be either selected or omitted. When a data set is created, all cases are selected. You can use the omit statement to selectively omit cases that currently have the status selected; the omit statement doesn't change the status of cases already omitted. Use the select statement to change the status of omitted cases back to selected; the select statement doesn't change the status of already selected cases.

Once you've entered and successfully executed an omit expression, a message appears at the bottom of the screen to indicate the result:

```
15 ADDITIONAL CASE(S) OMITTED
```

The successful omit or select expression remains in the work space and can be edited to create a new omit expression. To delete a previous expression from the work space, press Ctl-Y or Ctl-end to delete lines.

The effects of sequential omit expressions are cumulative; a second omit expression will only act upon the cases not omitted by the first expression. Thus, the two expressions "OMIT AGE < 10" and "SEX <> 1" entered one after the other have the same effect as the single expression "OMIT AGE < 10 OR SEX <> 1".

The omit expression can be as complex as you like and can span all three lines in the work space:

```
OMIT (CASE > 50) AND
(SEX = 1) OR
(SQRT (WEIGHT - 10) > HEIGHT)
```

A useful tip for using the omit command takes advantage of the fact that the arithmetic involving missing values always results in a missing value. Thus the omit expression

```
OMIT AGE + HEIGHT + SEX + WEIGHT = M
```

will omit a case if any of the variables have a missing value for the case and is easier to type than the alternative:

```
OMIT AGE = M OR HEIGHT = M OR SEX = M OR WEIGHT = M
```

Please see the **Arithmetic and Logical Expressions** section at the end of this chapter for more information about logical expressions and functions.

# Sort Cases

*Statistix* offers a **Sort Cases** procedure to sort the cases of a data set into ascending or descending order based on the values of selected key variables.

```
                              SORT CASES                              CHOLESTE
AGE        AGECLASS   CONC       CONCLASS   STATE




5 variable(s).  30 of 30 cases selected.  158K bytes free.

Select ascending or descending order.
ASCENDING

List any number of variables you want to use as sort keys.  Each case will
be ordered by the values that the sort key variables contain.  You may
specify ALL or use A .. Z syntax.
STATE AGE

List any number of variables that you want excluded from the sort.  Unless
you list a variable here, it will be sorted along with the key variables.
You may specify ALL or use A .. Z syntax.

Esc Exit  F1 Start  F2 Select variable
```

Select ascending or descending order by entering A or D.

List the variables you want to use as the key variables. The order in which you list the variables is important. The cases will be sorted by the first variable first, then by the second variable within the first, and so on.

Any type of variables (integer, real, date, or string) can be used as key variables. Sorting using string keys is not sensitive to upper and lower case letters (e.g., the keys "Iowa" and "IOWA" will be treated the same).

In most applications, you'll want the cases kept intact so that the values for the non-key variables are moved to their new positions along with the key variable values. Occasionally, you'll want to sort the values of a variable without disturbing the order of some or all of the remaining variables. In such cases, list the variables you want excluded from the sort in the bottom section of the options panel. You can specify ALL to indicate that all non-key variables are to be excluded from the sort.

Omitted cases are sorted along with selected cases. The omit status of a case moves with the key variables.

# View Data

The *Statistix* **View Data** procedure lets you to view a listing of your data on the screen. You can also print the listing or save it in an ASCII file. You select the variables you want to view. Omitted cases are not displayed, so **Omit/Restore Cases** provides a convenient method for viewing a subset of the data. You can control the listing format using a format statement.

```
                         VIEW DATA                                CHOLESTE
 AGE      AGECLASS  BIRTHDATE CONC     CONCLASS  NAME      STATE




 7 variable(s).  30 of 30 cases selected.  158K bytes free.

 List the variables you want to view.  You may specify ALL or use A .. Z
 syntax.  Press F2 to select variables from the list.
 NAME BIRTHDATE AGE STATE CONC

 Enter the output format (optional).  For example:  I3 5F10.3 1X A10
 1X A15 A11 I8 2X A5 F7.1

Esc Exit  F1 Start  F2 Select variable
```

List the names of the variables you want to view in the order you want them to appear. You can use A .. Z syntax (e.g., AGE .. CONC) or specify ALL, in which case all variables will be listed in alphabetical order. You can also press F2 and then select variables from the list displayed.

The output format statement allows you to control the widths of columns and the appearance of numbers displayed. The output format in the example View Data options panel above produces the following results:

```
CASE NAME               BIRTHDATE      AGE  STATE    CONC
   1 Dood, C             28/11/45       46  IA      181.0
   2 Fisher, E           02/11/39       52  IA      228.0
   3 Haley, J            10/01/53       39  IA      182.0
   4 Hickman, D          23/10/26       65  IA      249.0
   5 Johnson, M          01/01/38       54  IA      259.0
   6 Johnson, A          04/11/58       33  IA      201.0
```

The format statement is optional. If you don't specify a format statement, the data will be automatically formatted so that it can be printed on an 80-character-width printer. Real numbers will be formatted using the D10.5 specification, which provides for five significant digits. If the variable list contains more variables than can fit in 80 characters, all of the cases for the first few variables are listed first, with the cases for the remaining variables listed underneath.

If your output format specifies a line length of greater than 80 characters, the excess characters are truncated when displayed on the screen. However, the entire line will be printed, regardless of length, when sent to the printer. It's your responsibility to insure that the resulting line length can be accommodated by your printer.

The different format specifications are listed in the table below. In the table, "w" is the field width, "s" is the number of significant digits, "d" is the number of digits to the right of the decimal point, and "r" is the repeat factor.

| Name | General Format | Example Format | Example Appearance | Notes |
|---|---|---|---|---|
| Alphanumeric | Aw | A10 | John Smith<br>01/05/92 | |
| Decimal | Dw.s | D11.5 | 12.345<br>3.4523E-03 | s <= w - 4 |
| Exponential | Ew.s | E10.4 | 1.234E+01<br>3.452E-03 | s <= w - 4 |
| Floating point | Fw.d | F7.2 | 12.34<br>0.003 | d < w - 2 |
| Integer | Iw | I2 | 12<br>0 | |
| Space | rX | 10X | | inserts spaces |
| New line | / | / | | inserts line feed |

The A format is used for string and date variables. The D, E, F, and I formats are used for integer and real variables.

The X and / are not used as format specifications for variables. They're used to insert spaces and line feeds into the output record.

Any of the format specifications can have a number in front called the repeat factor. This is used to abbreviate the format statement when several variables are to be formatted in a similar manner. You can also use a repeat factor in front of a list of format specifications inside parentheses as follows:

```
3I5 2(I1 1X F4.2 F6.2) E10.4
```

Remember to make "w" large enough to account for the minus sign for negative numbers, and to allow for extra space between variables.

# Arithmetic and Logical Expressions

The data management procedures **Transformations** and **Omit/Restore** are powerful data manipulation tools. To appreciate the full potential of *Statistix*, you must understand the principles of arithmetic and logical expressions discussed in this section. This material will be familiar to people who are experienced in either database management software or programming languages.

## Arithmetic Expressions

The following arithmetic operators are available:

^ Exponentiation. For example, A ^ B is A raised to the B-th power.

* Multiplication. A * B is the product of A and B.

/ Division. A / B is A divided by B.

+ Addition. A + B is the sum of A and B.

- Subtraction or reversal of sign. A - B is B subtracted from A. The expression -A, unary negation, reverses the sign of A.

These operators are used to form arithmetic expressions with constants, variable names, and built-in functions. A constant is simply a number, such as 1.96 or 3.1416. Built-in functions are described in more detail below.

An example of an arithmetic expression is A + 2.75 * B, where A and B are variable names and 2.75 is a constant. *Statistix* evaluates this expression for each case by first taking the product of the constant 2.75 and the variable B. The values of variable A are then added to this to get the final result.

The order in which operators in an expression are evaluated is determined by some simple rules of precedence. The rules of precedence *Statistix* uses to evaluate arithmetic expressions are the same as those used in algebra. If all of the arithmetic operators in an expression are of equal precedence, they are evaluated in order from left to right. However, not all operators share equal precedence. The following table ranks the arithmetic operators according to precedence.

| | |
|---|---|
| Highest Precedence: | - (unary negation) |
| | ^ |
| | *, / |
| Lowest Precedence: | +, - |

Unary negation has the highest precedence and is always performed first if it occurs anywhere in an expression. Exponentiation (^) is performed next, followed by multiplication (*) and division (/). Multiplication and division are of equal precedence, so the order in which they appear in the expression determines which is done first. Addition (+) and subtraction (-) share the lowest precedence among arithmetic operators.

Any expression within parentheses is evaluated before expressions outside the parentheses. For example, in the expression (A + 2.75) * B, the sum A + 2.75 is evaluated first and the result is then multiplied by B. Parenthetical expressions can be nested, with the innermost ones being evaluated first. An example is (A + B * (C + D)) * E.

The simplest arithmetic expression is just a constant or variable by itself, in which case no arithmetic operators are involved.

### Date and String Arithmetic

Some arithmetic can be performed on dates and strings. A date can be subtracted from another date to compute the number of days between two events. For example, AGE = ("05/23/92" - BIRTH) / 365. You can also add a constant to a date. Multiplication and division of dates aren't allowed.

Addition can be performed using string variables and constants. For example, the expression FIRST + " " + LAST concatenates the strings in the variables FIRST and LAST with a space in between.

### Logical (Boolean) Expressions

When arithmetic expressions are evaluated, they return numerical values by case. On the other hand, logical expressions return the boolean values TRUE or FALSE by case. You, as a *Statistix* user, will never actually see the values TRUE and FALSE. What you will see are the consequences of some action that was based on whether the expression was TRUE or FALSE, for example, whether a case becomes omitted or not (see Omit/Restore Cases for details).

We now introduce two new classes of operators—relational operators and logical operators. These operators are used to construct logical expressions,

expressions that take the boolean values TRUE or FALSE when evaluated. The relational operators are:

| | | | |
|---|---|---|---|
| = | equal to | <> | not equal to |
| < | less than | <= | less than or equal to |
| > | greater than | >= | greater than or equal to |

The logical operators are NOT, AND, and OR.

Relational operators require arithmetic expressions for arguments—one to the left and one to the right of the operator (remember that the simplest arithmetic expression is just a constant or a variable name). Relational operators return the boolean values TRUE or FALSE when evaluated. Some typical examples of simple logical expressions using relational operators are A + B > C, A = 999, A ^ 3.45 >= B / C. The embedded arithmetic expressions are evaluated before the relational operators. All relational operators have the same precedence.

The logical operators NOT, AND, and OR are used to construct more complex logical expressions. Logical operators require boolean arguments, or to put it another way, the arguments for logical operators must be logical expressions. (Note: This is why they are called logical operators; they operate on logical expressions.) The NOT operator requires only one argument to the right; both AND and OR require two arguments, one on either side. The truth table below summarizes the action of these operators (T stands for TRUE, and F for FALSE):

| ARGUMENT VALUES | | VALUE RETURNED | | |
|---|---|---|---|---|
| X | Y | X AND Y | X OR Y | NOT X |
| T | T | T | T | F |
| T | F | F | T | F |
| F | T | F | T | T |
| F | F | F | F | T |

In their most general form, logical expressions are built with relational and, when needed, logical operators. Some further examples of logical expressions are:

```
A > B
(A + B) <> C
(A > B) AND (A = 1)
NOT ((A + B) > C)
((A = B) AND (B = C)) OR ((A <> D) AND (A < 1.96))
```

There are often many ways to express the same condition. Use the one that is clearest to you, not necessarily the most "elegant". In such expressions, embedded arithmetic operators are evaluated first, followed by relational operators. Logical operators have the lowest precedence of any operator. NOT takes precedence over AND and OR; AND is evaluated before OR. The order of evaluation is easy to control with the use of parentheses. Be careful to use enough parentheses to insure that things are evaluated in the intended order. The following table summarizes the precedence ordering of *Statistix* operators and built-in functions.

| | |
|---|---|
| Highest Precedence: | parenthesized expressions |
| | built-in functions |
| | - (unary negation) |
| | ^ |
| | *, / |
| | +, - |
| | =, >, <, >=, <=, <> |
| | NOT |
| | AND |
| Lowest Precedence: | OR |

## Machine Precision and Tests for Equality

Computers do not perform decimal arithmetic exactly. While the rounding error that occurs during arithmetical operations is usually negligibly small, there is one situation where it is extremely important: tests for exact equality. For example, suppose you want to perform the transformation Y = 9*X/9. You might expect Y to equal X, but it may not because of very small rounding errors. Therefore, it's not certain that the logical comparison IF Y = X will return the value TRUE. It's safer to perform the comparison using the expression IF Abs (X - Y) < d, where d is some small number and Abs is the absolute value function.

## Handling of Missing Values

Missing values require special consideration when arithmetical or logical expressions are evaluated. In arithmetical expressions, if any of the arguments have the value missing, the expression is automatically evaluated as missing. This is only reasonable—you can't perform arithmetic on numbers that don't exist.

Logical expressions are somewhat trickier. Different actions are taken depending on the context in which the relational expression is used. The following truth table shows the rules used with missing values for

Omit/Restore Cases.

| ARGUMENT VALUES | | VALUE RETURNED | | | | | |
|---|---|---|---|---|---|---|---|
| **X** | **Y** | **X=Y** | **X<>Y** | **X>Y** | **X<Y** | **X>=Y** | **X<=Y** |
| M | NOT M | F | T | F | F | F | F |
| M | M | T | F | F | F | F | F |

The If-Then-Else construct has the same truth table for X = Y and X <> Y. However, it avoids the issue for the other inequalities by assigning the target variable the value missing.

You may think it would make sense to always assign the target variable the value missing. After all, how do you decide if two unknown values are equal? The reason we use these rules is so you can manipulate the missing values. For example, perhaps you want to replace all of the missing values with 0.0:

```
IF X = M
THEN X = 0
ELSE X = X
```

You should be aware, however, that sometimes you may not be satisfied with these rules. Consider, for example:

```
IF X = Y
THEN NEWVAR = 1
ELSE NEWVAR = 2
```

If both X and Y are missing, *Statistix* will evaluate the ELSE expression and assign 2 to NEWVAR. You really want NEWVAR to be missing as well. This is easily done with a second transformation:

```
IF (X = M) OR (Y = M)
THEN NEWVAR = M
ELSE NEWVAR = NEWVAR
```

Remember that if the value for any variable in an arithmetic expression is missing, the expression is evaluated as missing. This can be exploited in a variety of ways. For example, suppose you have the variables A, B, C, D, and Y, and you want Y to be missing whenever A, B, C, or D is missing. One way of doing this is:

```
IF (A = M) OR (B = M) OR (C = M) OR (D = M)
THEN Y = M
ELSE Y = Y
```

But a more compact method is:

```
IF A + B + C + D = M  THEN Y = M  ELSE Y = Y
```

## Built-in Functions

There are 50 built-in functions that can be included in arithmetic expressions. Most of them require arguments. The arguments of most functions can be any valid arithmetic expression. This will be represented as "x" in the following descriptions. Note that x can include built-in functions, including the function it is an argument for, such as Sqrt (Sqrt (VAR)). If x has the value missing when it is evaluated, the function is also assigned as missing. In a few cases, an integer constant is required for an argument, such as CAT (5, 1). Integer constants are represented as "i" or "j" in the following descriptions. Functions Case, M, Pi, Random, and Selcase do not require input arguments. The available built-in functions are:

| | | | | |
|---|---|---|---|---|
| ABs (x) | ARCSin (x) | ARCTan (x) | ATkinson (x) | CAt (i, j) |
| CASE | COS (x) | COUnt (x) | CUmsum(x [,y]) | DAY (x) |
| DAYOfweek(x) | DIff (x [,i]) | Exp (x) | Geomean (x) | LAg (x [,i]) |
| LEngth (s) | LN (x) | LOG (x) | LOWcase (s) | M |
| MAx (x) | MEAn (x) | MEDian (x) | MIn (x) | MODulo (i, j) |
| MONth (x) | NOrmalize (x) | NRandom(m,sd) | PErcentile(x) | PI |
| POS (s, s) | POWer (x, y) | RANK (x) | RANDOM | ROund (x) |
| SD (x) | SELCASE | SIN (x) | SQR (x) | SQRT (x) |
| STudentize(x) | TAn (x) | TOtal (x) | TRunc (x) | UNitize (x) |
| UPcase (s) | VAriance (x) | Year (x) | ZInverse (x) | ZProb (x) |

The table above appears in the options panel when you are using the Transformations or Omit/Restore Cases procedures. When you include a built-in function in an arithmetic expression, you need only type the capitalized letters. Functions can also be selected by pressing F2 and moving the highlighted bar to the desired function.

Most of the functions operate using one case at a time. For example, Sqrt (x) computes the square root of the expression x, case by case. Some functions compute a single value for an entire column x. The Mean (x) is an example of this type; it computes the mean of the column x. Column functions are normally used as part of a larger expression (e.g., x - Mean (x)). The nine column functions are Count, Geomean, Max, Mean, Median, Min, SD, Total, and Variance.

Most of the functions expect numerical arguments and return numerical results. There are four string functions (Upcase, Lowcase, Length, and Pos) and four date functions (Day, Month, Year, and Dayofweek).

A description of each of the functions follows.

**Abs (x)** Absolute value of x.

Arcsin (x) Arcsine of x in radians.

Arctan (x) Arctangent of x in radians.

Atkinson (x) Computes the transformation for the Atkinson score method used to determine what power transformation, if any, is needed in a linear regression analysis (Weisberg, 1985). The argument of the transformation is the dependent variable in the regression analysis. The transformed variable is added as an independent variable in the regression analysis to test for a power transformation (see Weisberg for an example).

Cat (i, j) Categorical index generator. This function generates index values. The integer argument i gives the number of categories in the index, and the integer argument j is the repeat factor. This function generates the numbers 1 through i, repeating each value j times. First j 1's are generated, then j 2's, etc., up to j i's. After i x j values are generated, the process repeats.

Both i and j must be specified as positive integers.

Some examples are shown below. The example assumes that there are 12 cases in the data set, and all have been selected.

Y = CAT (3,2) Y : 1,1,2,2,3,3,1,1,2,2,3,3

Y = CAT (3,3) Y : 1,1,1,2,2,2,3,3,3,1,1,1

Y = CAT (4,3) Y : 1,1,1,2,2,2,3,3,3,4,4,4

Y = CAT (5,1) Y : 1,2,3,4,5,1,2,3,4,5,1,2

Y = CAT (2,4) Y : 1,1,1,1,2,2,2,2,1,1,1,1

Although this may initially appear to be a rather simple-minded function, it is extremely useful for creating categorical variables needed for numerous types of analyses. For example, suppose you have data from a randomized block design with 4 blocks and 3 treatments applied within each block. Then suppose your data is ordered such that the 3 observations for block 1 came first, followed by the 3 observations for block 2, etc. To create your block index, you would specify: BLOCK = CAT (4,3). The treatment index is created as: TREAT=CAT (3,1).

Note that if the data had been ordered such that the 4 values for treatment 1 came first, followed by the 4 values for treatment 2, etc., the indices would be generated as BLOCK = CAT (4, 1) and TREAT = CAT (3, 4).

Case — Case index. Case indicates the position of a value in the data set. If the data set is thought of as a rectangular table of numbers, the variable names identify the columns and the case indices identify the rows. Case is incremented for cases that are omitted. The Selcase function discussed below skips omitted cases.

Cos (x) — Cosine of x. Units of x are assumed to be radians. Angles can be converted from degrees to radians as: RADIANS = DEGREES / 180 * PI.

Count (x) — Number of usable cases of x. This function returns the total number of usable cases (i.e., selected and not missing). It is not a running counter; please see Case above for such a function.

Cumsum (x, k) — This function is two functions in one. When used with a single argument x, it computes the running sum of x. The value it returns for the i-th case is the sum of the first i cases of x.

When used with the two arguments x and k, it computes the decision interval cusum. The value returned for the i-th case $S_i$ is defined as $S_i = \max(0, S_{i-1} + x_i - k)$.

Day (x) — Day of month. The argument must be a date.

Dayofweek (x) — Day of week (1 = Sunday, 2 = Monday, etc.). The argument x must be a date.

Diff (x, i) — Difference of x and x lagged by i cases. The value of this function for the j-th case is x at case j minus x at case j-i. The argument i may be omitted, in which case i = 1 is assumed. See also Lag (x, i).

Exp (x) — Exponentiation; e raised to the power x.

Geomean (x) — Geometric mean of the column x.

Lag (x, i) — Lag x by i cases. The value of this function for the j-th case is the (j - i)-th case of x. Cases 1 up to i receive the value missing. Only selected cases are treated. If the (j - i)-th case of x is missing, Lag will return the value missing for the j-th case. The integer lag factor i is optional; it defaults to 1 if omitted.

| | |
|---|---|
| Length (x) | Computes the length (number of characters) in the string x. |
| Ln (x) | Natural (base e) log of x. |
| Log (x) | Base 10 log of x. Use the Power function discussed below to compute antilogs (e.g., Power (10, x)). |
| Lowcase (x) | Converts the string x to all lower case. |
| M | Missing value indicator. This can be used to assign a variable a missing value (e.g., VAR = M). It can also be used to test a variable for missing data (e.g., IF VAR = M). |
| Max (x) | Maximum value of x over all selected cases. |
| Mean (x) | This function returns the mean of x over the selected cases. |
| Median (x) | This function returns the value of the median for x over all selected cases. |
| Min (x) | This function returns the minimum value of x over all selected cases. |
| Modulo (x, y) | Computes the modulus of x by y (the remainder of x divided by y). x and y may be expressions but must have integer values less than 99,999. Example: Modulo (12, 5) = 2. |
| Month (x) | The month of the year. The argument x must be a date. |
| Normalize (x) | Normalize scales x such that the sum of all values of x equals 1. |
| NRandom (m, sd) | Normal random number generator. Generates a normal random number with mean m and standard deviation sd. See also Random. |
| Percentile (x) | Percentile of x. Suppose you have a variable SCORE that contains the test scores for all students in a class. The transformation PSCORE = Percentile (SCORE) creates a new variable PSCORE that contains the percentiles of each test score. |
| Pi | The constant pi, 3.1415926. |
| Pos (x, y) | Returns the starting position of the string x where it appears in the string y. |

If the string x does not appear in the string y, zero is returned. Example: Pos ("def", "abcdefg") = 4.

| | |
|---|---|
| Power (x, y) | Raises the value x to the power y. Produces the same result as x ^ y. This function is defined for nonnegative values for x and for negative values for x when y is a positive whole number. |
| Rank (x) | Ranks of x. The value of this function for the i-th case of x is the rank of that case. If some cases are tied, these cases receive the appropriate average rank. |
| Random | Generates a uniformly distributed random number on the interval 0.0 to 1.0. You change the scale of the random numbers produced by multiplying the function result by a constant. See also NRandom. |
| Round (x) | Rounds x to the nearest whole integer number. |
| SD (x) | Standard deviation of x. This function returns the sample standard deviation for the column x. This is the so-called unbiased estimate of the standard deviation; the divisor is the square root of n - 1, where n is the number of usable cases. |
| Selcase | Selected case index. Selcase indicates the position of a value in the data set with respect to the selected cases. If the data set is thought of as a rectangular table of numbers, the variable names identify the columns and the case indices identify the rows. Selcase is not incremented for cases that are omitted. Selcase ranges from one to the maximum number of selected cases. Case counts all cases regardless of their omit status. |
| Sin (x) | Sine of x. Units of x are assumed to be radians. |
| Sqr (x) | Squares the value of x. |
| Sqrt (x) | Square root of x. |
| Studentize (x) | Studentizes x. A variable is studentized by subtracting the sample mean from the original values and dividing the deviations from the sample mean by the sample standard deviation. Once x has been studentized, it'll have a mean of zero and a standard deviation of one. If x was originally normally distributed, x will be nearly standard normally distributed after studentizing. |
| Tan (x) | Tangent of x. Units of x are assumed to be radians. |

**Total (x)** This function returns the sum of all selected cases for x.

**Trunc (x)** Truncates the decimal portion of a number. For example, 1.98 when truncated becomes 1.0.

**Unitize (x)** Scales x so its vector norm equals one. The norm, or length, of a vector is the square root of the sum of the squares of the elements of the vector.

**Upcase (x)** Converts the string x to all upper case.

**Variance (x)** This function returns the sample variance for x. This is the so-called unbiased estimate of the variance; the divisor is n - 1, where n is the number of usable cases.

**Year (x)** Year of a date. The argument x must be a date.

**Zinverse (x)** Inverse of the standard normal distribution. If the value of the argument x is between 0 and 1, Zinverse returns the inverse of the standard normal distribution. That is, the value returned is the z value (standard normal value) for which the probability of a smaller value is the value of x.

**Zprob (x)** The standard normal probability of x. This function returns the probability of a value smaller than x from a standard normal distribution. In other words, this function returns the lower tail probability.

C H A P T E R

# 3

# *File Management*

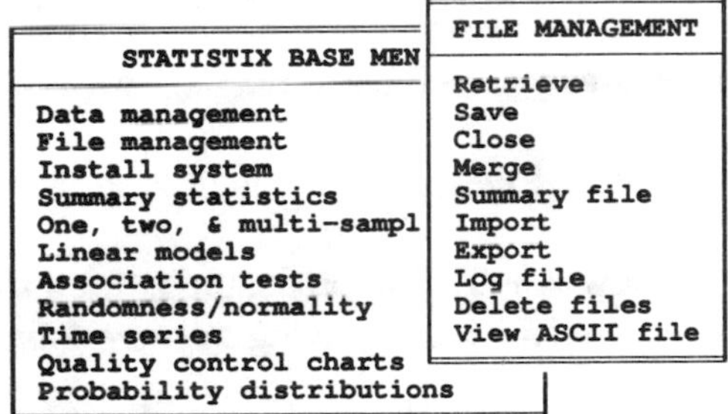


*Statistix* offers flexible and easy-to-use file management procedures. These procedures are used to manipulate data files stored on fixed disks and diskettes. You'll use the file management procedures to save, retrieve, and delete data files, import data created using other programs, and view ASCII files without leaving *Statistix*.

Data that you create using *Statistix* are temporary. Data that you enter, import, or create using transformations are not stored on disk until you explicitly create a disk file to permanently store your *Statistix* data.

The **Save** procedure is the usual method of saving *Statistix* data. It creates a high speed compact binary file representation of a *Statistix* data set. *Statistix* data files have the file name extension ".SX".

The **Retrieve** procedure is used to retrieve *Statistix* data files created previously using the Save procedure.

The **Close** procedure closes the active data set from *Statistix*. It clears the active data set from RAM, allowing you to create a new data set and start with a clean slate. It does not erase any file copies you have already created.

The **Merge** procedure combines data from your active data set and a second data set stored in a *Statistix* data file.

The **Summary File** procedure is used to create a new *Statistix* data file containing summary statistics of the active data set.

The **Import** procedure is used to read data from ASCII files (text files) and Lotus 1-2-3 files into *Statistix*.

The **Export** procedure is used to create ASCII or 1-2-3 file versions of your current *Statistix* data set so that the data can be accessed by other programs.

The **Log File** procedure is used to start recording a log of the *Statistix* procedures you will perform.

The **Delete Files** procedure is used to delete files from your disk.

The **View ASCII File** procedure is used to view the contents of a text file on the screen without having to leave *Statistix*.

## Retrieve

The **Retrieve** procedure is used to read a *Statistix* data file previously created using the **Save** procedure or the **Summary File** procedure. The file data set becomes the active *Statistix* data set. This procedure can't be used to retrieve data stored in formats other than the *Statistix* format. Use the Import procedure described later in this chapter to import data from ASCII and Lotus 1-2-3 files.

*Statistix* can only have one data set active at a time. If you already have an active *Statistix* data set, it will be replaced with the data contained in the file you retrieve. If you have not saved the active data set since it was last modified, *Statistix* will warn you with the following message:

```
Close data? | Esc Cancel  F1 Close data  Save data first
```

Press Esc to cancel and exit the retrieve procedure. Press F1 to close the active data set without saving the changes to a file. Press S to save the data before retrieving a new file. You'll be prompted for a file name.

The Retrieve options panel displays the variables of the current data set, if there are any, at the top portion of the screen. The *Statistix* data files are listed in the center of the screen.

```
                              RETRIEVE
EMPTY DATA SET



200 free variables.  1200K bytes free.
Files:
AIRLINE.SX        ALFALFA.SX        BIRTHWT.SX        BL5ED.SX          CHEMCON1.SX
CHEMCON2.SX       CHOLESTE.SX       CIRCUIT.SX        COMPUTER.SX       DOUGH1.SX
DOUGH2.SX         DREAMS.SX         E.SX              EXXON.SX          FUNGUS1.SX
HALD.SX           IBM.SX            JUICE.SX          LIZARDS.SX        LIZARDS2.SX
LIZARDS3.SX       NORTUP.SX         PAINT.SX          PISTONS.SX        ROSES.SX
SHOCKS.SX         SMALL.SX          SMIRNOV.SX        SMOKER.SX         SOYBEANS.SX
TANKDEFT.SX       VASO.SX           VISIONC.SX        VISIONT.SX

Enter a drive designator, subdirectory, or file mask for directory listing.
C:\SX\*.SX

Enter the input file name.  Press F2 to select from the list.

Esc Exit  F1 Start  F2 Select file
```

Your cursor starts at the input file name prompt at the bottom of the screen. You can enter the name of the file you want to retrieve directly, or you can press the F2 key and select a file from the list displayed. If you type in the name of a file, the disk drive and directory displayed in the panel will be assumed unless you specify a different drive and path in the file name.

You can change the drive, path, and file mask used to display a list of files. Press the up arrow key to move your cursor to the mask prompt line. Edit the drive, path, and mask displayed, or type in a new name altogether. You can use the ? and * characters to build a mask in the same manner as you do when using the DOS directory command. Use *.SX for the mask to list all the *Statistix* data files. When you press Enter, the files in your new drive, path, and mask will be displayed.

To select a file from the list, press F2 when your cursor is at the file name prompt. Then use the arrow keys and the page up and down keys to highlight the name of the file you want. Press Enter to select the highlighted file.

## Save

*Statistix* data files are ideal for saving your *Statistix* data for future *Statistix* analyses. All information about your *Statistix* data is preserved, including variable names, case omit status, missing values, value labels, and *Statistix* panel options. The **Save** takes a "snapshot" of the data set's present state for future use. *Statistix* data files store the data in a compact binary format—these files can be read and written rapidly.

```
                           SAVE SYSTEM FILE
AGE        AGECLASS  CONC       CONCLASS  STATE



5 variable(s).  30 of 30 cases selected.  1198K bytes free.
Files:
AIRLINE.SX      ALFALFA.SX      BIRTHWT.SX      BL5ED.SX        CHEMCON1.SX
DOUGH2.SX       DREAMS.SX       E.SX            EXXON.SX        FUNGUS1.SX
HALD.SX         IBM.SX          JUICE.SX        LIZARDS.SX      LIZARDS2.SX
LIZARDS3.SX     NORTUP.SX       PAINT.SX        PISTONS.SX      ROSES.SX
SHOCKS.SX       SMALL.SX        SMIRNOV.SX      SMOKER.SX       SOYBEANS.SX
TANKDEFT.SX     VASO.SX         VISIONC.SX      VISIONT.SX

Enter a drive designator, subdirectory, or file mask for directory listing.
C:\SX\*.SX
Enter the output file name.
CHOLESTE.SX
Esc Exit  F1 Start  F2 Select file
```

The variables of the current data set are listed at the top of the screen. The files for the current drive and path are listed in the center of the screen.

Your cursor starts at the output file name prompt at the bottom of the screen. You can enter the file name directly, or you can press the F2 key to select an existing file from the list displayed.

You can change the drive, path, and file mask used to display a list of files. Press the up arrow key to move your cursor to the mask prompt line and enter a new directory and/or mask.

If you enter a file name without specifying a drive or path, the drive and path displayed are assumed. After entering the file name, the file is created.

# Close

The **Close** procedure is used to close or erase the active data set from *Statistix*. This allows you to create a new data set starting from scratch.

If you have not saved the active data set since last modifying it, a warning message appears on the screen. This warning gives you an opportunity to save the active data set before erasing it from RAM.

```
You have not saved your data set since it was last modified.

Exit program? | Esc Cancel  F1 Close data  Save data first
```

Here you can press Esc to cancel the Close procedure, which returns you to the *Statistix* menus with your data intact, or you can press F1 to go ahead and close the active data set without saving your changes. You can also press S to save the active data and then close.

If you select "save data first", you'll be prompted for a file name. Enter the file name and press the Enter key. The data will be saved, and you'll be returned to the *Statistix* menus ready to create a new data set.

# Merge

The **Merge** procedure is used to combine the data of your active data set with data stored in a *Statistix* data file. New variables can be added to the active data set, or new cases can be appended to the existing variables in the active data set using the Merge.

The procedure is best explained with an example. There are actually two panels. The first panel (see below) prompts you for an input file name.

```
                              MERGE SYSTEM FILE                          AGEHTWT
 AGE        HEIGHT     WEIGHT

 3 variable(s).  37 of 37 cases selected.  1198K bytes free.
 Files:
 AIRLINE.SX       ALFALFA.SX       BIRTHWT.SX       BL5ED.SX         CHEMCON1.SX
 CHEMCON2.SX      CHOLESTE.SX      CIRCUIT.SX       COMPUTER.SX      DOUGH1.SX
 DOUGH2.SX        DREAMS.SX        E.SX             EXXON.SX         FUNGUS1.SX
 HALD.SX          HT&WT.SX         JUICE.SX         LIZARDS.SX       LIZARDS2.SX
 LIZARDS3.SX      NORTUP.SX        PAINT.SX         PISTONS.SX       ROSES.SX
 SHOCKS.SX        SMALL.SX         SMIRNOV.SX       SMOKER.SX        SOYBEANS.SX
 TANKDEFT.SX      VASO.SX          VISIONC.SX       VISIONT.SX

 Enter a drive designator, subdirectory, or file mask for directory listing.
 C:\SX\*.SX

 Enter the input file name.  Press F2 to select from the list.
 HT&WT

 Esc Exit  F1 Start  F2 Select file
```

*Statistix* displays the current variables at the top of the screen; in this example, there are three variables—AGE, HEIGHT, and WEIGHT—with 37 cases in each. The files for the current drive and path are listed in the center of the screen. Your cursor starts at the input file name prompt at the bottom of the screen. You can enter the file name directly, or you can press the F2 key to select a file from the list displayed on your screen.

To select a file from the list displayed, press F2 when your cursor is at the file name prompt. Then use the arrow keys and the page up and down keys to highlight the name of the file you want. Press Enter to select the file.

Once you've specified the name of the merge file (HT&WT in our example), a second panel (see next page) is displayed on the screen.

```
                              MERGE SYSTEM FILE                        AGEHTWT
 Current Variables:
 AGE        HEIGHT     WEIGHT




 3 variable(s).  37 of 37 cases selected.  1198K bytes free.
 File Variables:
 HEIGHT     SEX        WEIGHT




 3 variable(s).  37 cases.

 Select merge method: Append cases from matching variables. Add new variables.
 Add variables

 For "Add variables" method, list the names of the variables to add.  You may
 specify ALL or use A .. Z syntax.  Press F2 to select from list.
 SEX

 Esc Exit  F1 Start  F2 Select variable
```

*Statistix* has accessed the system file HT&WT.SX, and it has determined that HT&WT contains a data set having three variables named SEX, HEIGHT, and WEIGHT with 37 cases.

*Statistix* now presents you with two options:

1) If any variable names found in the input file match variable names in your current data set (HEIGHT and WEIGHT above), then you can select "Append cases" to append the cases from the file to your current data. Only data in matching variable names will be appended.

2) If there are variable names found in the input file that do not match variables in the current data set (SEX), then you can select "Add variables" to add the non-matching variables to your data set.

In the example shown above, the Add variables method has been selected, and you must list the variables you want to add. You can enter ALL to indicate all non-matching variables, use the A .. Z syntax to abbreviate a list, or select variables by pressing F2.

Press F1 to start the merge. Once the merge is complete, there are four variables in the current data set—AGE, HEIGHT, SEX, and WEIGHT.

Had you selected the "Append cases" option, the 37 cases from the input file would have been appended for the two variables HEIGHT and WEIGHT. Cases 38 through 74 of the variable AGE would have been filled with missing values.

The **Summary File** procedure is used to create a new *Statistix* data file containing summary statistics of your active data set. Summary statistics, such as the mean and standard deviation, can be computed for selected variables broken down by one or more grouping variables. The file will contain one case for each unique combination of values for the grouping variables. The current data set isn't modified by the procedure. Use the **Retrieve** procedure to retrieve the summary statistics for further processing.

Don't confuse this procedure with the **Save** procedure, which is used to save an exact copy of your data set.

## Specification

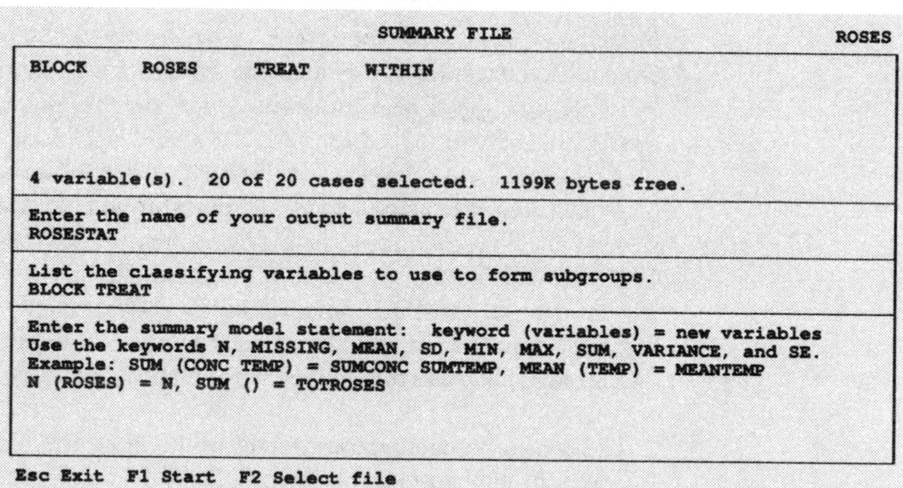

```
                         SUMMARY FILE                                  ROSES
BLOCK     ROSES     TREAT     WITHIN

4 variable(s).  20 of 20 cases selected.  1199K bytes free.
Enter the name of your output summary file.
ROSESTAT
List the classifying variables to use to form subgroups.
BLOCK TREAT
Enter the summary model statement:  keyword (variables) = new variables
Use the keywords N, MISSING, MEAN, SD, MIN, MAX, SUM, VARIANCE, and SE.
Example: SUM (CONC TEMP) = SUMCONC SUMTEMP, MEAN (TEMP) = MEANTEMP
N (ROSES) = N, SUM () = TOTROSES
Esc Exit  F1 Start  F2 Select file
```

You must first enter the name of the summary file you want to create. Because the output file is a *Statistix* data file, you must use the .SX extension. If you enter a name without an extension, the .SX extension will be added for you.

After entering the file name, list the grouping variables. The grouping variables contain discrete values that are used to identify subgroups. The grouping variables can contain numbers, dates, or strings. These variables automatically become variables in the new data file.

Enter the summary model statement. The model statement is made up of three parts: a statistical key word, a list of variables in the current data set that will be summarized (inside parentheses), and a list of variable names for the new data file.

In the example

```
MEAN (CONC) = MEANCONC, SD (CONC) = SDCONC
```

the model statement asks for the mean and standard deviation to be computed for the variable CONC and to be saved in the new file with the names MEANCONC and SDCONC. The parentheses and equals signs are required; commas are optional.

The A .. Z syntax can be used for the variable list inside the parentheses. For example,

```
MEAN (CHEM1 .. CHEM4) = M1 M2 M3 M4
```

If the same variable list is to be used for a second statistical key word, you can type an empty set of parentheses to repeat the variable list. For example,

```
N (HEIGHT WEIGHT) = NH NW, SUM () = SUMH SUMW
```

There are nine statistics that can be used with the Summary File procedure. The statistical key words can be abbreviated with as few characters as are needed to distinguish them from one another.

| | |
|---|---|
| N | number of observations in the group with non-missing values |
| Missing | number of observations in the group with missing values |
| Mean | mean |
| SD | standard deviation |
| Min | minimum value |
| Max | maximum value |
| Sum | sum |
| Variance | variance |
| SE | standard error of the mean |

## Data Restrictions

There must be at least one and no more than five grouping variables. Numeric values of grouping variables cannot exceed 99,999 and will be truncated to whole numbers. String values of a grouping variable will be truncated to ten characters.

## Example

To illustrate the summary file procedure, consider the data from a split block design where the number of saleable roses were counted (Bingham and

Fienberg, 1982). Five treatments were applied in two replicates.

| CASE | ROSES | BLOCK | TREAT | WITHIN |
|---|---|---|---|---|
| 1 | 102 | 1 | 1 | 1 |
| 2 | M | 1 | 1 | 2 |
| 3 | 84 | 1 | 2 | 1 |
| 4 | 81 | 1 | 2 | 2 |
| 5 | 67 | 1 | 3 | 1 |
| 6 | 83 | 1 | 3 | 2 |
| 7 | 71 | 1 | 4 | 1 |
| 8 | M | 1 | 4 | 2 |
| 9 | 53 | 1 | 5 | 1 |
| 10 | M | 1 | 5 | 2 |
| 11 | 71 | 2 | 1 | 1 |
| 12 | 79 | 2 | 1 | 2 |
| 13 | 76 | 2 | 2 | 1 |
| 14 | M | 2 | 2 | 2 |
| 15 | 74 | 2 | 3 | 1 |
| 16 | M | 2 | 3 | 2 |
| 17 | 51 | 2 | 4 | 1 |
| 18 | 63 | 2 | 4 | 2 |
| 19 | 63 | 2 | 5 | 1 |
| 20 | 61 | 2 | 5 | 2 |

As displayed in the example options panel above, the variables BLOCK, ROSES, and TREAT are listed as variables in the current data set. The name ROSESTAT is entered as the output file name. The variables BLOCK and TREAT are identified as the grouping variables. In the summary model statement

```
N (ROSES) = N, SUM () = TOTROSES
```

two new variables are created. N will contain the number of observations per group for ROSES, and TOTROSES will contain the group sum of ROSES.

The resulting data file ROSESTAT contains four variables with the following data:

| CASE | BLOCK | TREAT | N | TOTROSES |
|---|---|---|---|---|
| 1 | 1 | 1 | 1 | 102 |
| 2 | 1 | 2 | 2 | 165 |
| 3 | 1 | 3 | 2 | 150 |
| 4 | 1 | 4 | 1 | 71 |
| 5 | 1 | 5 | 1 | 53 |
| 6 | 2 | 1 | 2 | 150 |
| 7 | 2 | 2 | 1 | 76 |
| 8 | 2 | 3 | 1 | 74 |
| 9 | 2 | 4 | 2 | 114 |
| 10 | 2 | 5 | 2 | 124 |

# Import Comma and Quote ASCII

An ASCII file is a standard text file format commonly used to transfer data between different programs. A "Comma and Quote" ASCII file is a particular ASCII format made popular by spreadsheet and database programs. In a comma and quote file, columns of data are separated by commas, spaces, or tabs. String data, such as a person's name, is delimited with quotes (" or '). One line of text corresponds to one case in *Statistix*.

## Specification

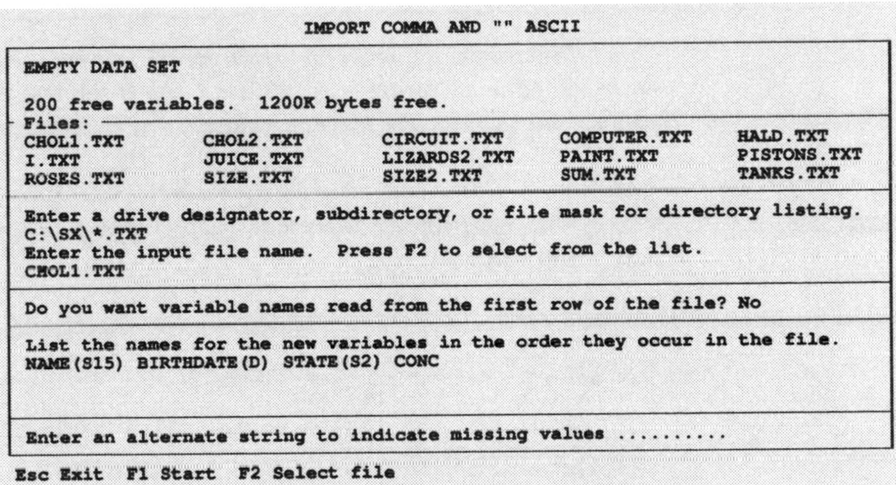


First enter the name of the input file. You can enter the file name directly, or you can press the F2 key to select a file from the list displayed. You can change the drive, path, and file mask used to display a list of files. Press the up arrow key to move your cursor to the mask prompt line and then edit or replace the file name mask.

To select a file from the list, press F2 when your cursor is at the file name prompt. Then use the arrow keys and the page up and down keys to highlight the name of the file you want. Press Enter to select the highlighted file.

The Import procedures are used to add variables to a new or existing data set. You must provide a valid variable name for each column of data you want to import. The options panel offers you the choice of listing the variable names on the panel or reading the variable names from the input file itself.

In *Statistix*, you can use integer, real, date, and string data. However, a particular column can only be used to store one type of data. You can specify the data type of variables when you list the variable names. Use the letters I, R, D, and S in parentheses after the variable names to identify integer, real, date, and string types. String types require a number after the letter S to indicate the maximum length. In the example options panel on the preceding page, the variable NAME is a string variable with a maximum length of 15. The variable BIRTHDATE is a date variable. The entry for the variable CONC does not declare a data type, so it's assigned the real data type. These data type rules apply to variable names listed on the options panel or read directly from the input file.

*Statistix* interprets the letter M and a period as a missing value. You can enter an additional string (e.g., 999 or N/A) at the last prompt on the options panel to be used to flag missing values.

### Example

The options panel on the preceding page is used to import the example ASCII file below.

```
"Fisher, E",11/02/39,"IA",228
"Haley, J",01/10/53,"IA",182
"Hickman, D",10/23/26,"IA",249
"Johnson, M",01/01/38,"IA",259
"Sellman, G",10/20/20,"IA",224
"Thorn, J",11/16/33,"IA",189
"Baur, J",12/24/73,"NE",137
"Christianson, E",10/23/47,"NE",173
"Farrow, C",10/14/58,"NE",177
"Greer, R",11/28/13,"NE",241
"Keller, G",12/13/40,"NE",225
"Lauber, R",01/10/49,"NE",223
"Neimann, P",10/07/47,"NE",190
"Price, D",11/27/33,"NE",257
"Stanley, J",12/15/28,"NE",337
"Steele, A",12/09/72,"NE",189
"Stone, O",11/26/61,"NE",140
"Swanson, D",12/15/44,"NE",196
"Taylor, E",11/20/33,"NE",262
"Thompson, B",11/09/21,"NE",261
"Tucker, T",10/26/24,"NE",356
"Williams, G",10/04/70,"NE",191
"Wright, O",11/21/35,"NE",197
```

You must enter your list of variable names in the order that the corresponding columns appear in the data file. If you can't remember the order of the columns, use the View ASCII File procedure to review the input file.

### Comment Lines

*Statistix* ignores any lines in an ASCII text file that begin with the characters "*", "$", or "#". This allows you to add comment lines to your text files.

# Import Formatted ASCII

The **Import Formatted ASCII** procedure is used to import columns of data from an ASCII text file when the data is arranged with fixed field widths. A format statement is used to specify the exact locations of data for each input variable.

The **Import Comma and Quote ASCII** procedure we discussed on page 69 is easier to use than this procedure and should be used whenever possible. Reasons for using this procedure with a format statement include:

- Columns of data are not comma or space separated.
- String data are not quote delimited.
- We want to skip unwanted columns of data.
- The data for one case requires more than one line in the input file.

## Specification

```
                         IMPORT FORMATTED ASCII
EMPTY DATA SET

200 free variables.  1200K bytes free.
Files:
CHOL1.TXT        CHOL2.TXT        CIRCUIT.TXT      COMPUTER.TXT     HALD.TXT
I.TXT            JUICE.TXT        LIZARDS2.TXT     PAINT.TXT        PISTONS.TXT
ROSES.TXT        SIZE.TXT         SIZE2.TXT        SUM.TXT          TANKS.TXT

Enter a drive designator, subdirectory, or file mask for directory listing.
C:\SX\*.TXT
Enter the input file name.  Press F2 to select from the list.
C:\SX\CHOL2.TXT

List the names for the new variables in the order they occur in the file.
NAME(S15) BIRTHDATE(D) STATE(S2) CONC

List the format statement (eg. I3, 5F5.2) or leave it blank for free format.
A15 3X A8 A4 F5

Esc Exit   F1 Start   F2 Select file
```

The variables of the current data set, if any, are listed at the top of the screen. The files for the current drive and path are listed in the center of the screen. Below that are prompts for the file name, variable list, and format statement.

Your cursor begins at the input file name prompt at the bottom of the panel. You can enter the file name directly, or press the F2 key to select a file from the list displayed.

You can change both the drive and path and the file mask used to display a list of files. Press the up arrow key to move your cursor to the mask prompt line and then edit or replace the file name mask.

Next enter a list of new variable names, one variable for each column of data. In *Statistix* you can use integer, real, date, or string data. However, a particular column can only be used to store one type of data. You can specify the data type of variables when you list the variable names. Use the letters I, R, D, and S in parentheses after the variable names to identify integer, real, date, and string types. String types require a number after the letter S to indicate the maximum length. In the example options panel on the preceding page, the variable NAME is a string variable with a maximum length of 15. The variable BIRTHDATE is a date variable. The entry for the variable CONC does not declare a data type, so it's assigned the real data type.

You can use the VAR1 .. VAR99 syntax in the variable list to abbreviate a long list of variables. Specify the data type for the entire list of variables by entering the data type at the end of the list (e.g., Q1 .. Q15(I)).

Finally, enter a format statement that details the position of the data for each variable. A single format specification consists of a letter followed by a number indicating the field width. The format statement is discussed in detail below.

Example

The options panel on the preceding page is used to import four columns of data from the text file name CHOL2.TXT. The data are arranged in fixed fields where the columns line up vertically:

```
Fisher, E            11/02/39  IA  228
Haley, J             01/10/53  IA  182
Hickman, D           10/23/26  IA  249
Johnson, M           01/01/38  IA  259
Sellman, G           10/20/20  IA  224
Thorn, J             11/16/33  IA  189
Baur, J              12/24/73  NE  137
Christianson, E      10/23/47  NE  173
Farrow, C            10/14/58  NE  177
Greer, R             11/28/13  NE  241
Keller, G            12/13/40  NE  225
Lauber, R            01/10/49  NE  223
Neimann, P           10/07/47  NE  190
Price, D             11/27/33  NE  257
Stanley, J           12/15/28  NE  337
Steele, A            12/09/72  NE  189
Stone, O             11/26/61  NE  140
Swanson, D           12/15/44  NE  196
Taylor, E            11/20/33  NE  262
Thompson, B          11/09/21  NE  261
Tucker, T            10/26/24  NE  356
Williams, G          10/04/70  NE  191
Wright, O            11/21/35  NE  197
```

The format statement is required for this example ASCII file because the string data in the first column is not quote delimited. Spaces have been inserted between columns for readability, but this isn't required when using the format statement.

The format statement in the example options panel lists a format specification for each variable. The A format specification is used for string and date data (A stands for alphanumeric). The F format is used for numerical data (F stands for floating point). The format specification 3X is used in the example to skip three spaces on the input line between the data for the variables NAME and BIRTHDATE.

If an error occurs, the input line that caused the error is displayed on the screen with the error text highlighted. An error message also appears, as shown below.

```
Month (20) out of range at case 8 for variable BIRTHDATE.
                       1         2         3         4         5         6
Column     : 123456789012345678901234567890123456789012345678901234567890
Input line: Christianson, E    20/23/47  NE  173
```

When an error is found, processing of the file stops and the new variables are not created.

## Input Format Statement

The input format statement is used to specify exactly where on an input line data for each variable are to be found. There are five format specifications that can be used for variable data. The A format (A for alphanumeric) is used for string and date variables. There are four different format specifications that can be used for integer and real variables: D - Decimal format, E - Exponential format, F - Floating point format, and I - Integer format. The differences between these types are more important when used with the **Export Formatted ASCII** procedure discussed later in this chapter. Any integer or real variable can be imported using the F format.

In all cases, enter a variable's format specification by typing the letter followed by a number representing the total field width for the variable. The field width can include blank spaces before and after the actual field of data.

In the example on options panel on page 71, the format specification A15 is used for the first variable NAME, indicating that the first 15 characters of each input line contains the string value for that variable. The last format specification—F5 for the variable CONC—includes two characters for the leading spaces and three characters for the three digit numbers.

The F format can be used to insert a decimal point into a column of numbers at a specific position. Suppose that the column of data for the variable CONC was entered as ten times the actual value, such that the number for the first case 228 represented the value 22.8. By specifying the format F5.1 instead of F5, a decimal point would be inserted one position from the right side.

If field widths repeat, we can use a shorthand notation rFw to reduce the size of the format statement. For example, the format F5.1 F5.1 F5.1 can be abbreviated as 3F5.1.

A repeat factor can be applied to a list of formats inside parentheses, too. For example, the format statement A8 I2 F8.2 A8 I2 F8.2 can be abbreviated using the statement 2(A8 I2 F8.2).

The X format is used to skip spaces between variables. The general format is rX where r indicates the number of spaces to skip. For example, we'd use 15X to skip the first 15 characters of the input line and import only the variables BIRTHDATE, STATE, and CONC.

Long records are sometimes split into several lines in an input file. Suppose you wanted to read 17 variables from a file, but the first ten variables were listed on one line and the last seven variables were listed on the following line. You would then need to use the / character in the format statement to show where the line break occurs:

```
10F8 / 7F8
```

### Importing a Single Variable

If a file contains the data for a single variable, you can use the "single" option to read all the data items, regardless of how many columns there are in the file. Just enter the word "single" in the space provided for the input format statement. The values will be read left to right, top to bottom.

### Comment Lines

*Statistix* ignores any lines in an ASCII text file that begin with the characters "*", "$", or "#". This lets you add comment lines to your text files.

# Import Lotus 1-2-3

The **Import Lotus 1-2-3** procedure is used to import data from existing 1-2-3 work sheet files into *Statistix*. It provides a convenient alternative to ASCII files for transferring data from 1-2-3 and compatible spreadsheet programs. Numbers, dates, and strings can be imported.

Lotus 1-2-3 release 3 and Quattro Pro are not directly supported. However, both these programs can save and retrieve 1-2-3 release 2 files. Simply save your spreadsheet using the .WK1 extension when preparing a 1-2-3 file for *Statistix*.

```
                    IMPORT LOTUS 1-2-3
EMPTY DATA SET

200 free variables.  1200K bytes free.
Files:
CHOL.WK1        IBM.WK1         STOCKS.WK1

Enter a drive designator, subdirectory, or file mask for directory listing.
C:\SX\*.WK?

Enter the input file name.  Press F2 to select a file from the list.
CHOL.WK1

Do you want to read variable names from first row? ......... Yes

List the range of spreadsheet columns you want to import (eg. B .. C).
Leave this space blank if you want to import all columns.

Esc Exit   F1 Start   F2 Select file
```

The variables of the current data set, if any, are listed at the top of the screen. The files for the current drive and path are listed in the center of the screen. You can change the drive, path, and file mask used to display a list of files. Press the up arrow key to move your cursor to the mask prompt line and then edit or replace the file name mask.

First enter the name of the 1-2-3 file you want to import. If you don't specify a file name extension, the extension .WK1 will be added automatically. To select a file from the list of files displayed, press F2 when your cursor is at the file name prompt. Then use the arrow keys and the page up and down keys to highlight the name of the file you want. Press Enter to select the highlighted file.

You must provide a valid variable name for each column of data you want to import. The options panel offers you the choice of listing the variable names on the panel or reading the variable names from the first row of the 1-2-3 input file.

In *Statistix* you can use integer, real, date, or string data. However, a particular column can only be used to store one type of data. You can specify the data type of variables when you list the variable names. Use the letters I, R, D, and S in parentheses after the variable names to identify integer, real, date, and string types. String types require a number after the letter S to indicate the maximum length.

If you choose to have the variable names read from the 1-2-3 file as in the example panel on the preceding page, then the variable types (real, date, string, etc.) are determined automatically by data found on the first few rows of the input file.

The last prompt on the import panel allows you to specify the range of columns to import from the 1-2-3 file. Use the standard one- or two-letter column headings (A, B, C ..., AA, AB, AC ...). You can specify a single column (e.g., B) or a range of columns (e.g., B .. G). If you don't respond to this prompt, all columns of data will be imported.

# Export Comma and Quote ASCII

An ASCII file is a standard text file format that is commonly used to transfer data between different programs. A "comma and quote" ASCII file is a particular ASCII format made popular by spreadsheet and database programs. In a comma and quote file, columns of data are separated by commas. String data, such as a person's name, are delimited with quotes.

```
                    EXPORT COMMA AND QUOTE ASCII                        CHOLESTE
 AGE      AGECLASS  BIRTHDATE CONC      CONCLASS  NAME      STATE

 7 variable(s).  30 of 30 cases selected.  1198K bytes free.

 Enter the output file name.
 CHOL2.TXT

 List the output variables.  You may specify ALL or use A .. Z syntax.
 NAME BIRTHDATE STATE CONC

 Do you want to include variable names in the file? ........... Yes
 String to use to mark missing values .........................
Esc Exit  F1 Start  F2 Select file
```

First enter the name of the output file you want to create. Then list the variables you want to export in the order you want them to appear. You can specify ALL or use A .. Z syntax (e.g., CHEM1 .. CHEM4). You can also press F2 and then select variables from the list on the screen.

Generally, *Statistix* will mark missing values using the letter M. You can enter a replacement string at the last prompt on the options panel, which you can use in place of M to flag missing values (e.g., 999 or N/A).

The first few lines of the ASCII file created using the options specified above are presented below. Note the variable names on the first line.

```
"NAME(S15)","BIRTHDATE(D)","STATE(S2)","CONC"
"Fisher, E",11/02/39,"IA",228
"Haley, J",01/10/53,"IA",182
"Hickman, D",10/23/26,"IA",249
"Johnson, M",01/01/38,"IA",259
"Sellman, G",10/20/20,"IA",224
"Thorn, J",11/16/33,"IA",189
"Baur, J",12/24/73,"NE",137
"Christianson, E",10/23/47,"NE",173
```

# Export Formatted ASCII

The **Export Formatted ASCII** procedure is used to create ASCII text files containing columns of data that line up vertically. It provides a means for transferring data to other programs, such as word processors and database management programs. A format statement can be entered to control the column widths and the number of digits displayed for numbers. Omitted cases are not exported.

## Specification

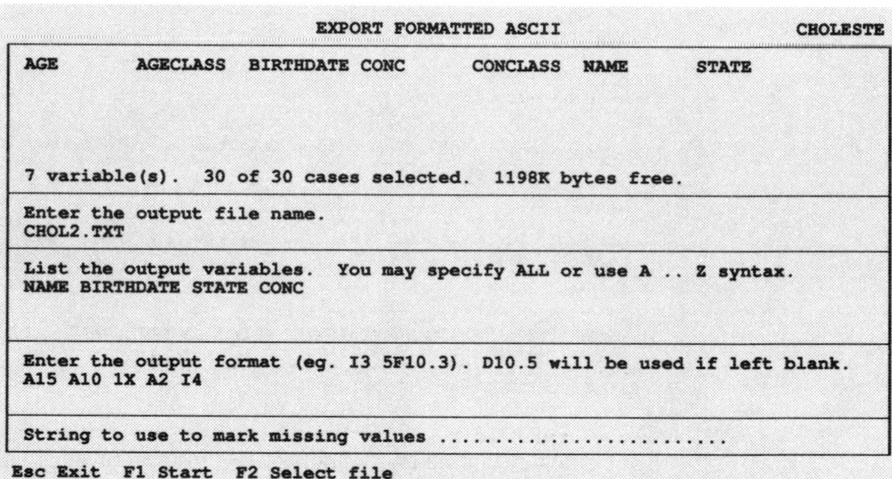

```
                    EXPORT FORMATTED ASCII                          CHOLESTE
AGE        AGECLASS   BIRTHDATE CONC       CONCLASS  NAME       STATE

7 variable(s).  30 of 30 cases selected.  1198K bytes free.

Enter the output file name.
CHOL2.TXT

List the output variables.  You may specify ALL or use A .. Z syntax.
NAME BIRTHDATE STATE CONC

Enter the output format (eg. I3 5F10.3). D10.5 will be used if left blank.
A15 A10 1X A2 I4

String to use to mark missing values ........................
Esc Exit  F1 Start  F2 Select file
```

First enter the name of the file you want to create. If you don't specify a drive or path, the current data drive and path will be assumed.

List the variables you want to export to the file in the order you want them to appear. You can specify ALL if you want all of the variables exported. You can use A .. Z syntax to abbreviate a list of variables (e.g., CHEM1 .. CHEM4). You can also press F2 and select variables from the list displayed.

You can enter a format statement to indicate how you want the data for each variable to appear. A variable format specification consists of a letter, a field width, and sometimes a number for decimal places as well. If you don't enter a format statement, *Statistix* will format your data for you; real variables will be formatted using the decimal format D10.5.

*Statistix* will usually mark missing values using the letter M. But you can enter a replacement string at the last prompt on the options panel, to use in place of M to flag missing values (e.g., 999 or N/A).

## Output Format Statement

The different format specifications are listed in the table below. In the table, "w" is the field width, "s" is the number of significant digits, "d" is the number of digits to the right of the decimal point, and "r" is the repeat factor (defined below).

| Name | General Format | Example Format | Example Appearance | Notes |
|---|---|---|---|---|
| Alphanumeric | Aw | A10 | John Smith<br>01/05/92 | |
| Decimal | Dw.s | D11.5 | 12.345<br>3.4523E-03 | s <= w - 4 |
| Exponential | Ew.s | E10.4 | 1.234E+01<br>3.452E-03 | s <= w - 4 |
| Floating point | Fw.d | F7.2 | 12.34<br>0.003 | d < w - 2 |
| Integer | Iw | I2 | 12<br>0 | |
| Space | rX | 10X | | inserts spaces |
| New line | / | / | | inserts line feed |

The A format is used for string and date variables. The D, E, F, and I formats are used for integer and real variables.

The X and / are not used as format specifications for variables but are used to insert spaces and line feeds into the output record.

Any of the format specifications can have a number in front called the repeat factor. This is used to abbreviate the format statement when several variables are to be formatted in a similar manner. A repeat factor can also be placed in front of a list of format specifications inside parentheses, as in:

```
3I5 2(I1 1X F4.2 F6.2) E10.4
```

When using format specifications, remember to make "w" large enough to account for the minus sign for negative numbers and for extra space between variables. String data are left justified, so you should always use the X format in front of a format for a string variable to insert a space.

The format statement is optional. If you don't enter a format statement, I6 will be used for integer variables, D10.5 for real variables, A9 for date variables, and 1X An for string variables of length n.

# Export Lotus 1-2-3

Use this procedure to create Lotus 1-2-3 files to export *Statistix* data to 1-2-3 or other programs that support the WK1 format. Numbers, dates, and string data can be exported.

```
                         EXPORT LOTUS 1-2-3                            CHOLESTE
 AGE       AGECLASS  CONC      CONCLASS  STATE

 5 variable(s).  30 of 30 cases selected.  1198K bytes free.
 Files:
 IBM.WK1        STOCKS.WK1

 Enter a drive designator, subdirectory, or file mask for directory listing.
 C:\SX\*.WK?

 Enter the output file name.
 CHOL.WK1

 List the output variables.  You may specify ALL or use A .. Z syntax.
 AGE CONC STATE

Esc Exit  F1 Start  F2 Select file
```

The variables of the current data set are listed at the top of the screen. The files for the current drive and path are listed in the center of the screen. You can change the drive and path and the file mask that is used to display a list of files. Press the up arrow key to move your cursor to the mask prompt line and then edit or replace the file name mask.

First enter the name of the 1-2-3 file you want to create. If you don't specify a file name extension, the extension .WK1 will be added automatically.

List the variables you want to export in the order you want them to appear in the 1-2-3 file. You can use A .. Z syntax to specify a range of variables, or specify ALL to export all variables. The variable names will appear as labels on the first row of the 1-2-3 work sheet file. Omitted cases are not exported.

# Log File

A log file is an ASCII file that lists the procedures performed during a *Statistix* session. Log files are particularly useful for verifying that a series of transformations or omit cases statements were performed as intended. A log file can be viewed and printed using the *Statistix* **View ASCII File** procedure during a *Statistix* session or printed using the DOS Print command after exiting from *Statistix* to review the work performed. Each procedure is date- and time-stamped so that log file entries can be matched with printed output.

## Specification

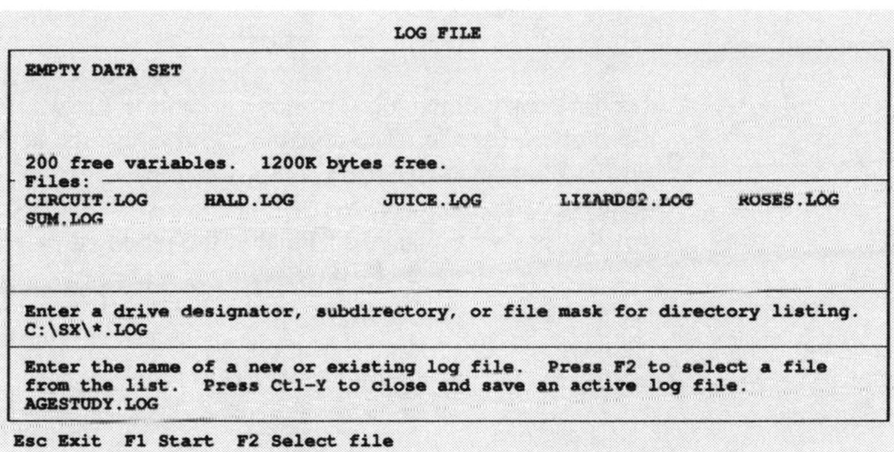


To start a log file, select the **Log File** procedure and enter a file name. If you do not enter a file name extension, the extension .LOG will be added to the file name.

If you enter the name of a file that already exists, you can choose to have new entries appended to the existing file or you can choose to erase the old file and start the log file over again.

Once you've started a log file, you can close it at any time by selecting the Log File procedure and erasing the file name from the panel. Press either Ctl-Y or Ctl-end to erase the file name.

## Example

The example log file below lists the procedures used during a short *Statistix* session.

```
LOG FILE, 05/19/92, 15:59
   C:\SX\AGESTUDY.LOG
RETRIEVE, 05/19/92, 15:59
   C:\SX\CHOLESTE.SX
TRANSFORMATIONS, 05/19/92, 16:00
   ageclass = 10 * Trunc (age / 10)
TRANSFORMATIONS, 05/19/92, 16:00
   conclass = 40 * Trunc (conc / 40)
VIEW DATA, 05/19/92, 16:01
   age ageclass conc conclass
   4I10
CROSS TABULATION, 05/19/92, 16:01
   AGECLASS CONCLASS
FREQUENCY DISTRIBUTION, 05/19/92, 16:01
   ageclass conclass
SAVE SYSTEM FILE, 05/19/92, 16:01
   C:\SX\CHOLESTE.SX
```

The first entry in the log file shows when the file was started and gives the name of the log file. The remaining entries list the activities that followed: a system file named CHOLESTE.SX was retrieved, two transformations were performed, the data were viewed, and cross tabulations and frequency distributions were obtained. Finally, the modified data set was saved.

# Delete Files

The **Delete Files** procedure allows you to delete files from your disk.

```
                              DELETE FILES
┌ Files: ─────────────────────────────────────────────────────────────┐
  AIRLINE.SX      ALFALFA.SX      BIRTHWT.SX      BL5ED.SX        CHEMCON1.SX
  CHEMCON2.SX     CHOLESTE.SX     CIRCUIT.SX      COMPUTER.SX     DOUGH1.SX
  DOUGH2.SX       DREAMS.SX       E.SX            EXXON.SX        FUNGUS1.SX
  HALD.SX         IBM.SX          JUICE.SX        LIZARDS.SX      LIZARDS2.SX
  LIZARDS3.SX     NORTUP.SX       PAINT.SX        PISTONS.SX      ROSES.SX
  ROSESTAT.SX     SHOCKS.SX       SMALL.SX        SMIRNOV.SX      SMOKER.SX
  SOYBEANS.SX     T1.SX           T2.SX           TANKDEFT.SX     VASO.SX
  VISIONC.SX      VISIONT.SX

  Enter a drive designator, subdirectory, or file mask for directory listing.
  C:\SX\*.SX

  Enter name of the file you want erased.  Press F2 to select from the list.
  LIZARDS3.SX
└─────────────────────────────────────────────────────────────────────┘
 Esc Exit  F1 Start  F2 Select file
```

Your cursor begins at the file name prompt at the bottom of the screen. If you want to delete a file, you can type the file name or you can press the F2 key to select a file from the list displayed.

You can change the drive, path, and file mask used to display a list of files. Press the up arrow key to move your cursor to the mask prompt line. You can edit the drive, path, and mask displayed, or you can type in a new name altogether. You can use the ? and * characters to build a mask in the same manner as you use the DOS commands. When you press Enter, the files in your new drive, path, and mask will be displayed.

To select a file from the list, press F2 when your cursor is at the file name prompt. Then use the arrow keys and the page up and down keys to highlight the name of the file you want. Press Enter to select the file.

Once you select a file to delete, you'll be asked to confirm it:

```
Delete C:\SX\LIZARDS3.SX (Y/N)? [ ]
```

Press Y to delete the file or N to retain it.

# View ASCII File

This procedure is used to view an ASCII text file on the screen. There are a number of ASCII files you may be interested in viewing without leaving *Statistix*. You may want to check the contents of a *Statistix* log file to refresh your memory about transformations you've made. Or you may want to review a *Statistix* report file you've saved after running an analysis of your data. You may even want to look at a text file you want to import data from.

```
                              VIEW ASCII FILE
Files:
CHOL1.TXT      CHOL2.TXT      CIRCUIT.TXT    COMPUTER.TXT   HALD.TXT
I.TXT          JUICE.TXT      LIZARDS2.TXT   PAINT.TXT      PISTONS.TXT
ROSES.TXT      SIZE.TXT       SIZE2.TXT      SUM.TXT        TANKS.TXT
VISIONC.TXT    VISIONR.TXT

Enter a drive designator, subdirectory, or file mask for directory listing.
C:\SX\40\*.TXT

Enter name of the file you want to view.  Press F2 to select from the list.
JUICE.TXT

Esc Exit  F1 Start  F2 Select file
```

Your cursor starts at the file name prompt at the bottom of the screen. You can directly enter the name of a file you want to view, or you can press the F2 key to select a file from the list displayed.

You can change the drive, path, and file mask used to display a list of files. Press the up arrow key to move your cursor to the mask prompt line. Edit the drive, path, and mask displayed, or type in a new name altogether. You can use the ? and * characters to build a mask in the same manner you use with DOS commands. When you press Enter, the files in your new drive, path, and mask will be displayed.

Once you've selected a file to view, the file is displayed on the screen. You can scroll forward and backward through the file using the arrow keys and the page up and page down keys. You can also press P to print a copy of the entire file.

CHAPTER

4

# Summary and Descriptive Statistics

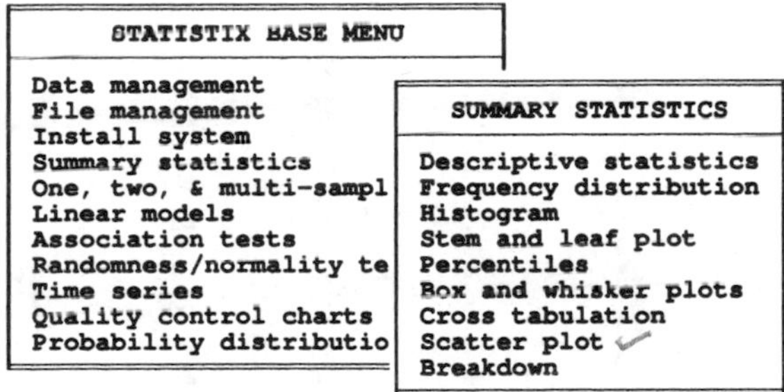


These procedures are designed to help you condense, summarize, and display data. You'll use them in the preliminary stages of analysis because they allow you to recognize general patterns and they suggest directions for further analysis. They're particularly useful for detecting "unusual" values.

The utility of these procedures isn't restricted to the preliminary stages of analysis, however. They're important tools for evaluating the results of a variety of analyses. For example, after fitting models to your data, you can use these procedures to inspect the resulting residuals.

The procedures are illustrated with example data from Snedecor and Cochran (1980, p. 386). The data are the blood serum cholesterol levels and ages of 30 women, 11 from Iowa and 19 from Nebraska. The cholesterol concentrations are in the variable CONC, and the ages are in AGE. The variable STATE indicates the state, with Iowa = 1 and Nebraska = 2. Two additional categorical variables were created using **Transformations**. The variable AGECLASS assigns the ages to ten-year age classes. For example, if a woman's age were within the range 50 to 59, the value of AGECLASS would be 50. AGECLASS is created using the transformation

```
AGECLASS = 10 * TRUNC (AGE/10)
```

CONCLASS is created in a similar manner, and assigns each case to a 40 mg/100 ml cholesterol concentration class. It's created as follows:

```
CONCLASS = 40 * TRUNC (CONC/40)
```

For example, CONCLASS is assigned the value 200 for any case for which the value of CONC is in the 200 to 239 range.

These example data are listed below. They're also distributed with the *Statistix* software in the data file CHOLESTE.SX.

| CASE | AGE | AGECLASS | CONC | CONCLASS |
|---|---|---|---|---|
| 1 | 46 | 40 | 181 | 160 |
| 2 | 52 | 50 | 228 | 200 |
| 3 | 39 | 30 | 182 | 160 |
| 4 | 65 | 60 | 249 | 240 |
| 5 | 54 | 50 | 259 | 240 |
| 6 | 33 | 30 | 201 | 200 |
| 7 | 49 | 40 | 121 | 120 |
| 8 | 76 | 70 | 339 | 320 |
| 9 | 71 | 70 | 224 | 200 |
| 10 | 41 | 40 | 112 | 80 |
| 11 | 58 | 50 | 189 | 160 |
| 12 | 18 | 10 | 137 | 120 |
| 13 | 44 | 40 | 173 | 160 |
| 14 | 33 | 30 | 177 | 160 |
| 15 | 78 | 70 | 241 | 240 |
| 16 | 51 | 50 | 225 | 200 |
| 17 | 43 | 40 | 223 | 200 |
| 18 | 44 | 40 | 190 | 160 |
| 19 | 58 | 50 | 257 | 240 |
| 20 | 63 | 60 | 337 | 320 |
| 21 | 19 | 10 | 189 | 160 |
| 22 | 42 | 40 | 214 | 200 |
| 23 | 30 | 30 | 140 | 120 |
| 24 | 47 | 40 | 196 | 160 |
| 25 | 58 | 50 | 262 | 240 |
| 26 | 70 | 70 | 261 | 240 |
| 27 | 67 | 60 | 356 | 320 |
| 28 | 31 | 30 | 159 | 120 |
| 29 | 21 | 20 | 191 | 160 |
| 30 | 56 | 50 | 197 | 160 |

# Descriptive Statistics

The **Descriptive Statistics** procedure produces a summary table of descriptive statistics for a list of variables. You can select the statistics you want tabulated from the following list: number of non-missing cases, number of missing cases, total, mean, standard deviation, standard error of the mean, 95% confidence interval of the mean, coefficient of variation, median, minimum and maximum, first and third quartiles, median absolute deviation, biased variance, skew, and kurtosis.

## Specification

```
                          DESCRIPTIVE STATISTICS                         CHOLESTE
AGE        AGECLASS  CONC       CONCLASS  STATE

5 variable(s).  30 of 30 cases selected.  1167K bytes free.

List the variables for computing descriptive statistics.  You may specify
ALL or use A .. Z syntax.  Press F2 to select variables from the list.
ALL

Enter the name of a grouping variable if
you want statistics reported by group (optional) ............

Enter a percentage coverage for mean confidence intervals ... 95.0

Check the statistics you want reported:
   [X] N                [X] SD              [ ] Median          [ ] Biased var.
   [ ] Missing          [ ] SE Mean         [X] Min/max         [ ] Skew
   [ ] Sum              [ ] Conf. int.      [ ] Quartiles       [ ] Kurtosis
   [X] Mean             [ ] C.V.            [ ] MAD

Esc Exit   F1 Start   F2 Select variable
```

List the names of the variables for which you want to compute descriptive statistics. You can enter ALL as above to indicate all variables in the data set, or you can use A .. Z syntax. You can also press F2 to select individual variables from the list displayed.

If you enter the name of a grouping variable, the summary statistics will be tabulated separately for each value found in the grouping variable.

You can change the percentage coverage for mean confidence intervals.

Select the statistics from the list of check boxes by marking them with an X. You can change the status of a check box (selected or not selected) by pressing the space bar. Use the arrow keys to move around the list of statistics.

**Data Restrictions**

The grouping variable can be of any data type. Real values will be truncated to whole numbers and must be no larger than 99,999. Strings will be truncated to ten characters.

**Example**

The data are from Snedecor and Cochran (1980, p. 386), described at the beginning of this chapter. The panel above demonstrates the use of the key word ALL to request statistics for all variables. The results are:

DESCRIPTIVE STATISTICS

| VARIABLE | N | MEAN | SD | MINIMUM | MAXIMUM |
|---|---|---|---|---|---|
| AGE | 30 | 48.566 | 16.346 | 18.000 | 78.000 |
| AGECLASS | 30 | 44.000 | 16.315 | 10.000 | 70.000 |
| CONC | 30 | 213.66 | 59.751 | 112.00 | 356.00 |
| CONCLASS | 30 | 192.00 | 60.708 | 80.000 | 320.00 |
| STATE | 30 | 1.6333 | 0.4901 | 1.0000 | 2.0000 |

If you select more than five statistics, the table is presented with the variable names along the top. For example, the report below lists all of the statistics available.

DESCRIPTIVE STATISTICS

| | AGE | AGECLASS | CONC | CONCLASS | STATE |
|---|---|---|---|---|---|
| N | 30 | 30 | 30 | 30 | 30 |
| MISSING | 0 | 0 | 0 | 0 | 0 |
| SUM | 1457 | 1320 | 6410 | 5760 | 49 |
| LO 95% CI | 42.462 | 37.907 | 191.35 | 169.33 | 1.4503 |
| MEAN | 48.566 | 44.000 | 213.66 | 192.00 | 1.6333 |
| UP 95% CI | 54.670 | 50.092 | 235.97 | 214.66 | 1.8163 |
| SD | 16.346 | 16.315 | 59.751 | 60.708 | 0.4901 |
| SE MEAN | 2.9845 | 2.9788 | 10.909 | 11.083 | 0.0894 |
| C.V. | 33.658 | 37.081 | 27.964 | 31.618 | 30.008 |
| MINIMUM | 18.000 | 10.000 | 112.00 | 80.000 | 1.0000 |
| 1ST QUARTI | 37.500 | 30.000 | 180.00 | 160.00 | 1.0000 |
| MEDIAN | 48.000 | 40.000 | 199.00 | 180.00 | 2.0000 |
| 3RD QUARTI | 59.250 | 52.500 | 251.00 | 240.00 | 2.0000 |
| MAXIMUM | 78.000 | 70.000 | 356.00 | 320.00 | 2.0000 |
| MAD | 10.000 | 10.000 | 27.500 | 20.000 | 0.0000 |
| BIASED VAR | 258.31 | 257.33 | 3451.2 | 3562.6 | 0.2322 |
| SKEW | -0.1008 | -0.1821 | 0.6711 | 0.5850 | -0.5533 |
| KURTOSIS | -0.7008 | -0.3662 | 0.2762 | -0.0783 | -1.6937 |

The median absolute deviation (MAD) is the median value of the absolute differences among the individual values and the sample median.

The biased variance is the sample variance using N rather than N - 1 as the divisor. The coefficient of skewness measures the asymmetry of a distribution. The coefficient of kurtosis measures the "peakedness" of a distribution. Snedecor and Cochran (1980, pp. 78-81) give more detail.

# Frequency Distribution

The **Frequency Distribution** procedure produces a frequency tabulation for discrete or continuous data. It computes the frequency, relative frequency (percentage of total), and cumulative and relative frequencies of data.

## Specification

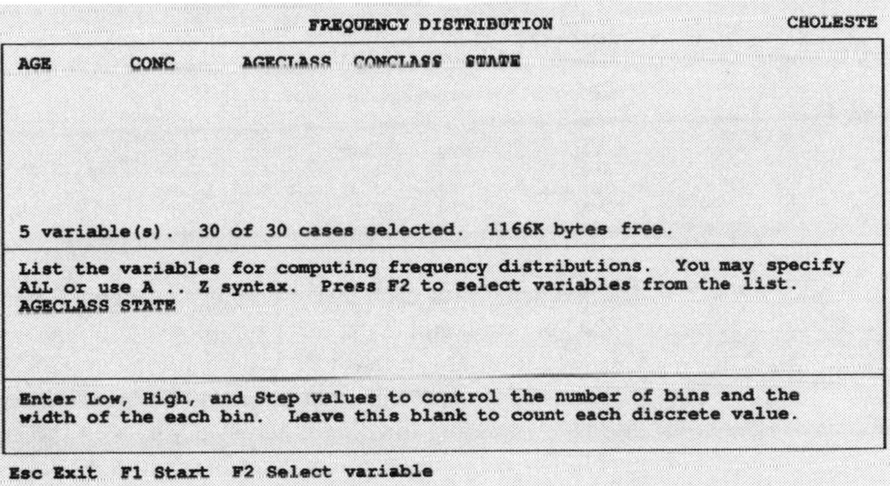


List the names of the variables for which you want to display frequency tables. You can specify ALL or use A .. Z syntax. You can also press F2 and select variables from the list displayed.

You can specify low, high, and step values to control the number of bins and the width of each bin. If you don't specify these values, frequencies are reported for each discrete value.

## Data Restrictions

Variables of any data type can be specified. There can be no more than 200 unique values for each discrete variable and no more than 200 bins if low, high, and step values are specified.

## Example

The data, from Snedecor and Cochran (1980, p. 386), are described at the beginning of this chapter. Frequencies are produced for the variable AGECLASS, which is the ten-year age class for each of the 30 female subjects, and for STATE, which indicates the state where the subject resides.

The panel on the previous page illustrates what you type in. The results are:

FREQUENCY DISTRIBUTION OF AGECLASS

| VALUE | FREQ | PERCENT | CUMULATIVE FREQ | CUMULATIVE PERCENT |
|---|---|---|---|---|
| 10 | 2 | 6.7 | 2 | 6.7 |
| 20 | 1 | 3.3 | 3 | 10.0 |
| 30 | 5 | 16.7 | 8 | 26.7 |
| 40 | 8 | 26.7 | 16 | 53.3 |
| 50 | 7 | 23.3 | 23 | 76.7 |
| 60 | 3 | 10.0 | 26 | 86.7 |
| 70 | 4 | 13.3 | 30 | 100.0 |
| TOTAL | 30 | 100.0 | | |

FREQUENCY DISTRIBUTION OF STATE

| VALUE | FREQ | PERCENT | CUMULATIVE FREQ | CUMULATIVE PERCENT |
|---|---|---|---|---|
| Iowa | 11 | 36.7 | 11 | 36.7 |
| Nebraska | 19 | 63.3 | 30 | 100.0 |
| TOTAL | 30 | 100.0 | | |

The frequencies of each discrete value for a continuous variable, such as CONC in our example data, are not of interest. For a continuous variable, you need to establish intervals that span the range of the data and then count the number of times data values fall within the bounds of the intervals. You do this by entering low, high, and step values in the bottom of the options panel. For example, you can enter the values 80 360 40 for the low, high, and step values for CONC. The results are displayed below.

FREQUENCY DISTRIBUTION OF CONC Cholesterol concentration

| LOW | HIGH | FREQ | PERCENT | CUMULATIVE FREQ | CUMULATIVE PERCENT |
|---|---|---|---|---|---|
| 80.0 | 120.0 | 1 | 3.3 | 1 | 3.3 |
| 120.0 | 160.0 | 4 | 13.3 | 5 | 16.7 |
| 160.0 | 200.0 | 10 | 33.3 | 15 | 50.0 |
| 200.0 | 240.0 | 6 | 20.0 | 21 | 70.0 |
| 240.0 | 280.0 | 6 | 20.0 | 27 | 90.0 |
| 280.0 | 320.0 | 0 | 0.0 | 27 | 90.0 |
| 320.0 | 360.0 | 3 | 10.0 | 30 | 100.0 |
| TOTAL | | 30 | 100.0 | | |

If a value falls on an interval boundary, the value is counted in the higher of the two intervals.

# Histogram

The **Histogram** procedure produces a bar graph frequency distribution for discrete or continuous variables. A histogram can summarize large amounts of data in a single visual image. You can have a normal curve superimposed over the histogram. This procedure can also produce a graph of the cumulative frequency distribution of a variable.

## Specification

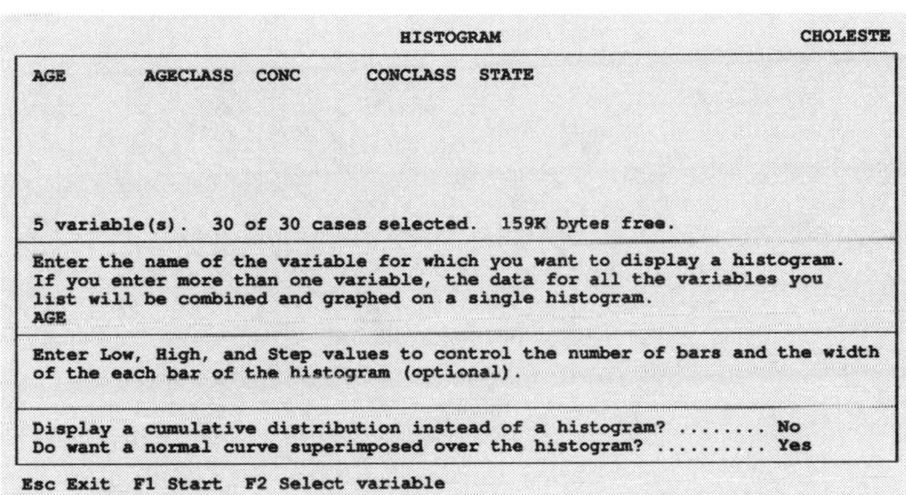

```
                              HISTOGRAM                            CHOLESTE
AGE       AGECLASS  CONC      CONCLASS  STATE

5 variable(s).  30 of 30 cases selected.  159K bytes free.

Enter the name of the variable for which you want to display a histogram.
If you enter more than one variable, the data for all the variables you
list will be combined and graphed on a single histogram.
AGE

Enter Low, High, and Step values to control the number of bars and the width
of the each bar of the histogram (optional).

Display a cumulative distribution instead of a histogram? ........ No
Do want a normal curve superimposed over the histogram? .......... Yes

Esc Exit  F1 Start  F2 Select variable
```

Enter the name of a variable you want to use to produce a histogram. You can only produce one histogram at one time. If you enter more than one variable, the values of all the variables will be combined to produce one histogram.

You can enter low, high, and step values to control the X axis scale. You can use this feature to create meaningful interval width and interval boundaries. You can also use it to limit the range of data for the specified variable in order to eliminate outliers or concentrate the plot on a particular range of values.

You can display a cumulative frequency distribution of the data instead of a bar chart histogram.

Answer YES at the final prompt if you want to superimpose a normal curve over the bars of the histogram.

Example

The data are from Snedecor and Cochran (1980, p. 386), described at the beginning of this chapter. The options panel on the previous page is used to graph a histogram for the variable AGE, the age of the 30 subjects. The results are:

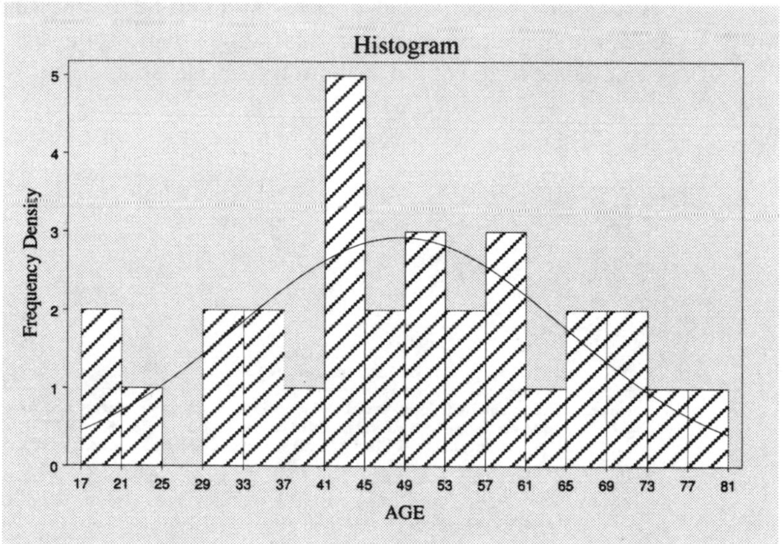


If you select the cumulative frequency distribution option, a line is plotted against percent to represent the cumulative frequency, as illustrated below.

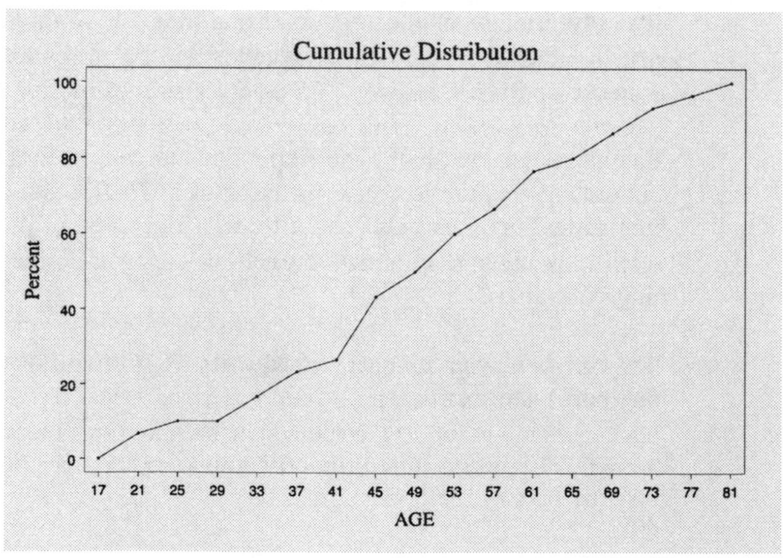

# Stem And Leaf Plot

The **Stem and Leaf Plot** is a simple but handy way to organize numerical data. The digits of the individual values are ordered in a table of "stems" and "leaves" that resembles a histogram when turned sideways. Unlike a histogram, each original measurement can be read from the plot.

## Specification

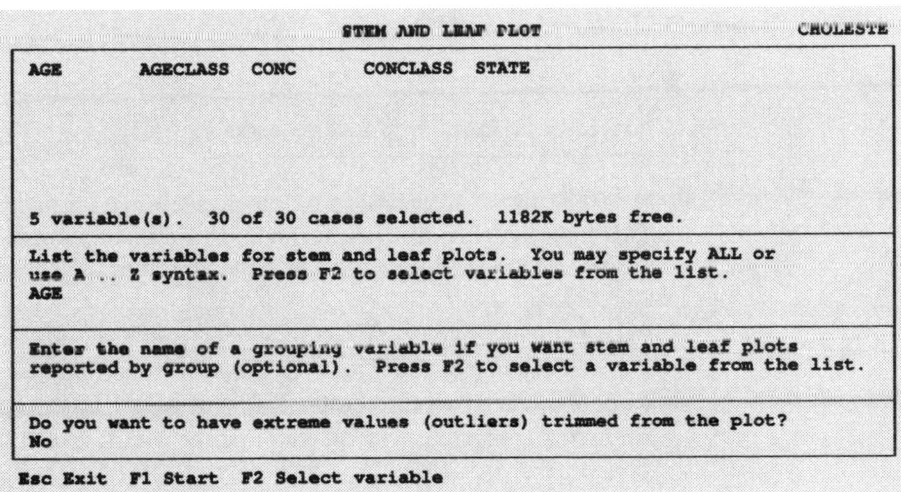


List the names of the variables from which you want to produce the stem and leaf plot. You can specify a grouping variable, in which case a separate plot is produced for each value of the grouping variable. Extreme values can affect the scale of the stem and leaf plot. If you see extreme values causing a scaling problem, answer YES to the last question on the options panel. The extreme values won't be omitted completely but will be listed individually outside the scale.

## Data Restrictions

Data values may not exceed 99,999.

## Example

The data are from Snedecor and Cochran (1980, p. 386), described at the beginning of this chapter. A stem and leaf plot will be produced for AGE, which is the age of 30 female subjects. The options panel is displayed above. The results are given on the next page.

```
STEM AND LEAF PLOT FOR AGE

   LEAF DIGIT UNIT = 1
   1  2  REPRESENTS 12.

          STEM  LEAVES
      2     1. 89
      3     2* 1
      3     2.
      7     3* 0133
      8     3. 9
     13     4* 12344
     (3)    4. 679
     14     5* 124
     11     5. 6888
      7     6* 3
      6     6. 57
      4     7* 01
      2     7. 68

30 CASES INCLUDED      0 MISSING CASES
```

This plot contains all the information of a histogram. In addition, it preserves information about the "fine structure of the data".

Each number in your data is divided into two parts, the stem and the leaf. The stem indicates the values of the most significant digits of an observation, while the leaf gives the least significant digit. Each digit in the LEAVES column is a separate leaf, so there is one leaf for each case.

For example, consider the first row of the plot "1. 89". The stem value is 1, and the leaves are 8 and 9, so you know the digits for the first subject are 1 and 8 and the digits for the second subject are 1 and 9. You don't know yet where to put the decimal point. That is, the numbers could be 1.8, 1.9, or perhaps 18, 19, or even 0.018, 0.019, etc. The message above the body of the plot "1  2  REPRESENTS 12." is telling you that a stem value of 1 and a leaf value of 2 represents the number 12. So the first two values in our example are 18 and 19.

When stems require more than one line, special characters are used to indicate the particular segment of the continued stem ("*" and "." for two line stems, and "*", "T", "F", "S", and "." for five line stems). In this example, each stem value required two lines. The * after the stem digit 3 indicates that the row is used to represent the first half of the stem for the values 30 through 34.

The first column in a stem and leaf plot is a cumulative frequency column that starts at both ends of the data and meets in the middle. The row that contains the median of the data is marked with parentheses around the count of observations for that row. For rows above the median, the number in the first column is the number of items in that row plus the number of items in all the rows above. Rows below the median are just the opposite. If the number of cases is even and the two middle values fall in different rows, there is no "median row".

Further details of how to interpret stem and leaf plots can be found in Velleman and Hoaglin (1981).

## Percentiles

The **Percentile** procedure computes the percentiles you specify for a list of variables. A percentile is a value such that a specified percent of the data falls at or below that value. The median is the 50th percentile. The lower and upper quartiles are the 25th and 75th percentiles.

### Specification

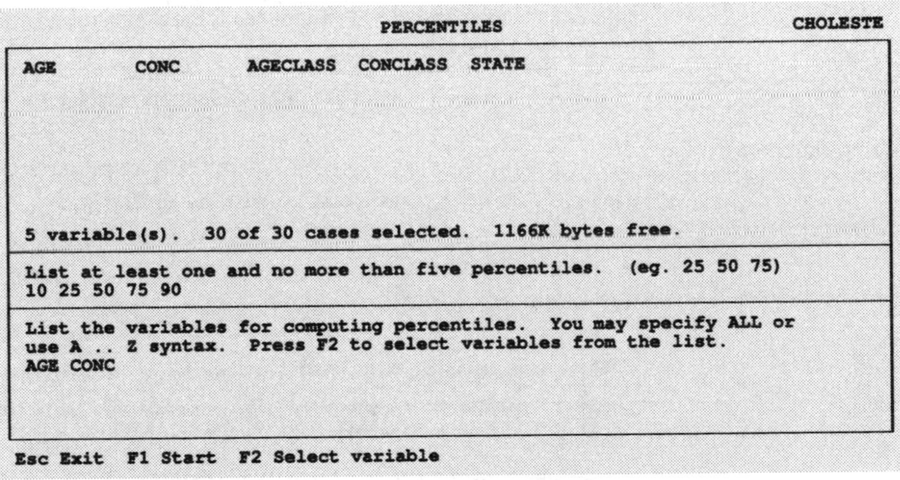


List the percentile values you want computed. You can enter up to five values. A percentile value must be greater than 0 and less than 100. Then list the variables for which you want the percentiles computed. You can specify ALL or use A .. Z syntax.

Example

The data are from Snedecor and Cochran (1980, p. 386), described at the beginning of this chapter. The 10th, 25th, 50th (the median), 75th, and 90th percentiles are computed for the variables AGE and CONC, the age and cholesterol level for a sample of female subjects. The analysis is specified in the panel on the preceding page. The results are:

PERCENTILES

| VARIABLE | CASES | 10.0 | 25.0 | 50.0 | 75.0 | 90.0 |
|---|---|---|---|---|---|---|
| AGE | 30 | 21.900 | 37.500 | 48.000 | 59.250 | 70.900 |
| CONC | 30 | 137.30 | 180.00 | 199.00 | 251.00 | 329.50 |

# Box and Whisker Plot

The **Box and Whisker Plot** procedure computes box plots that graphically present measurements of central tendency and variability. A series of box plots can be displayed side by side, which can dramatically illustrate differences between groups.

Specification

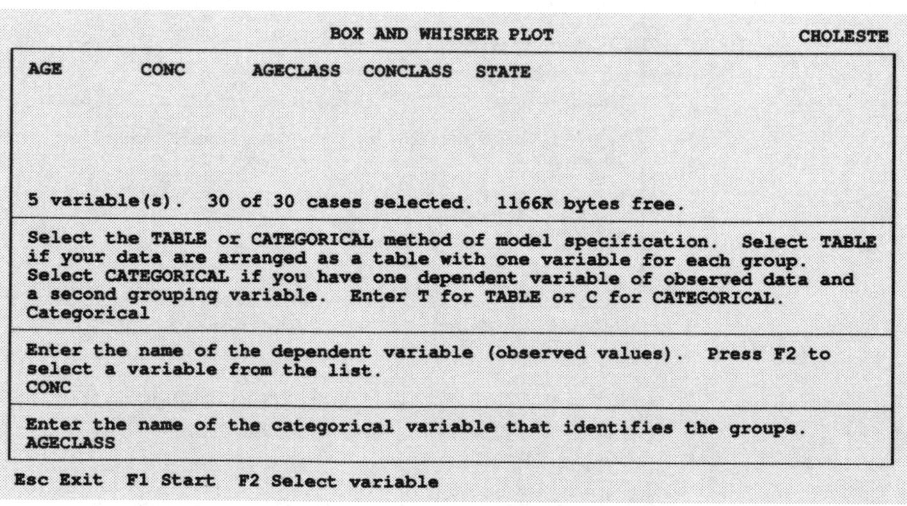
```
BOX AND WHISKER PLOT                                        CHOLESTE
AGE        CONC       AGECLASS  CONCLASS  STATE

5 variable(s).  30 of 30 cases selected.  1166K bytes free.

Select the TABLE or CATEGORICAL method of model specification.  Select TABLE
if your data are arranged as a table with one variable for each group.
Select CATEGORICAL if you have one dependent variable of observed data and
a second grouping variable.  Enter T for TABLE or C for CATEGORICAL.
Categorical

Enter the name of the dependent variable (observed values).  Press F2 to
select a variable from the list.
CONC

Enter the name of the categorical variable that identifies the groups.
AGECLASS

Esc Exit   F1 Start   F2 Select variable
```

First you select the method of specifying the analysis, using either the table method or the categorical method. If you want to plot the data of several variables side by side, select the table method and then enter the list of variable names.

If you want to plot the data of a single variable divided into groups by a second classifying variable, select the categorical method. This will produce a series of box plots, one for each level of the classifying variable.

## Data Restrictions

Data values can't exceed 99,999. No more than 20 box plots can be displayed at once. Real values for the grouping variable will be truncated to whole numbers.

## Example

The original data are from Snedecor and Cochran (1980, p. 386), described at the beginning of this chapter. The options panel on the preceding page specifies box plots for AGE grouped by CONCLASS (cholesterol concentration class). The resulting graph is displayed below.

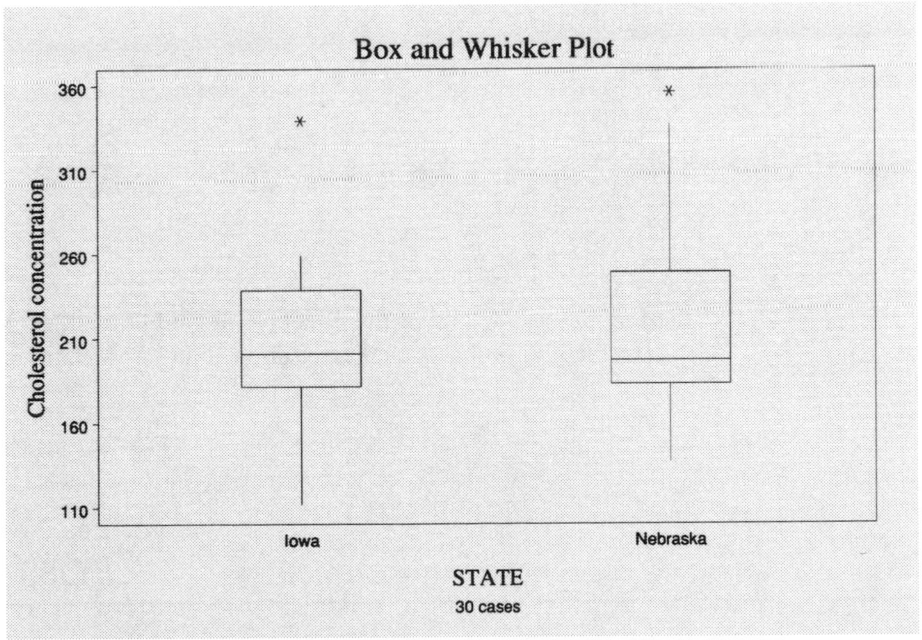


Each box plot is composed of a box and two whiskers. The box encloses the middle half of the data (the data between the first and third quartiles). The box is bisected by a line at the value for the median. The vertical lines at the top and the bottom of the box are called the whiskers, and they indicate the range of "typical" data values. Extreme values are displayed as "*" for possible outliers and "O" for probable outliers.

The box plots displayed below for cholesterol concentration (CONC) by age groups (AGECLASS) powerfully illustrate that cholesterol concentration increases with age.

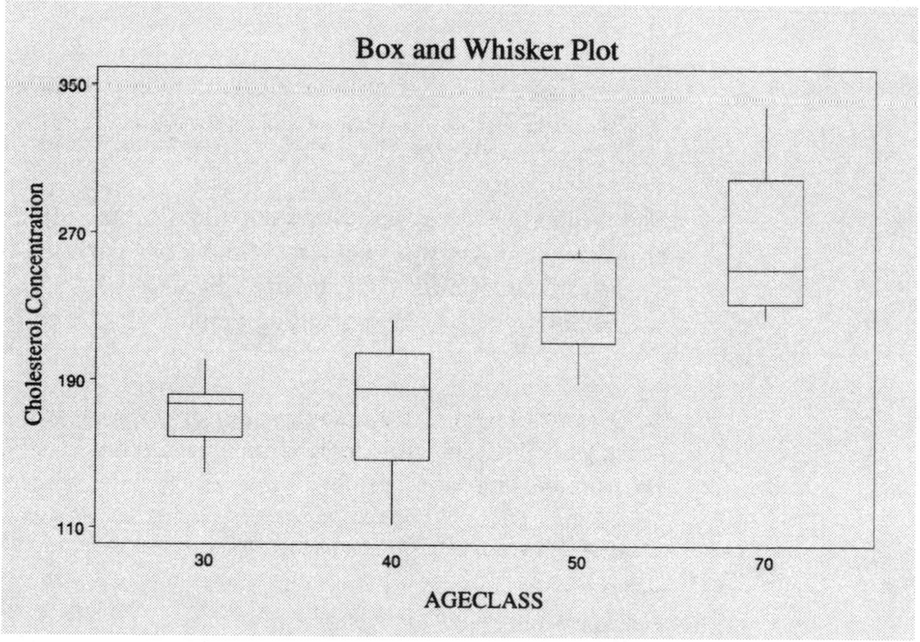


More precise details of the concepts of middle half, typical values, and possible and probable outliers can be found in Velleman and Hoaglin (1981).

# Cross Tabulation

The **Cross Tabulation** procedure forms a cross tabulation table (also called a contingency table) for up to five classifying variables. The number of classifying variables determines the dimension of the table. There's a table cell for all unique combinations of values of the classifying variables. A cross tabulation table displays the number of cases that fall into each of the cross-classified table cells. In statistical terms, such a table represents the joint frequency distribution of the classifying variables.

## Specification

```
                                CROSS TABULATION                    CHOLESTE
 AGE        CONC       AGECLASS  CONCLASS  STATE




 5 variable(s).   30 of 30 cases selected.   1166K bytes free.

 List at least two and no more than five variables for cross tabulation.
 If you list more than two variables, the last two listed will be used to
 display the primary table.   Press F2 to select variables from the list.
 ageclass conclass

 Do you want to display column percentages?
 No

 Do you want to display row percentages?
 No
 Esc Exit   F1 Start   F2 Select variable
```

To perform a cross tabulation, you simply enter a list of the classifying variables. The last variable becomes the column classifier and the second-to-last variable becomes the row classifier. If more than two variables are listed, the earlier variables become "control" variables. A separate table is produced for each unique combination of control variable values. These tables are produced in dictionary order; the levels of the right-most control variables increment most rapidly.

A cross tabulation table always contains the counts for each cell. If you want to have column and row percentages displayed for each cell as well, enter YES at the appropriate prompts.

## Data Restrictions

There can be up to five classifying variables. Each classifying variable can have up to 50 categories. Classifying variables can have any data type (real, integer, date, and string). Numerical values of classifying variables must be whole numbers no larger than 99,999.

## Example

The original data are from Snedecor and Cochran (1980, p. 386), described in the beginning of this chapter. AGECLASS indicates the age class a person was in (for example, AGECLASS = 60 means the person was in the

60 to 69 year age class). CONCLASS indicates the cholesterol concentration class a person was in (for example, CONCLASS = 160 means the person's cholesterol level was in the 160 to 199 mg/100 ml range).

The panel above illustrates how to request cross tabulation of AGECLASS by CONCLASS. The results are:

```
CROSS TABULATION OF AGECLASS BY CONCLASS

                           CONCLASS
AGECLASS     80     120    160     200     240     320

   10         0      1      1       0       0       0      2
   20         0      0      1       0       0       0      1
   30         0      2      2       1       0       0      5
   40         1      1      4       2       0       0      8
   50         0      0      2       2       3       0      7
   60         0      0      0       0       1       2      3
   70         0      0      0       1       2       1      4
              1      4     10       6       6       3     30

CASES INCLUDED 30     MISSING CASES 0
```

Note the diagonal pattern of nonzero cells in the table above. This suggests a relationship between age and cholesterol level.

# Scatter Plot

The **Scatter Plot** procedure is used to produce a bivariate scatter diagram. Pairs of numbers are plotted as points on a X-Y graph. You can also have a fitted regression line displayed.

When investigating possible relationships between variables, plotting the data should be one of your first steps. Visual inspection of the data is invaluable and often reveals features of the data that would be overlooked if you proceeded directly with your statistical analyses.

## Specification

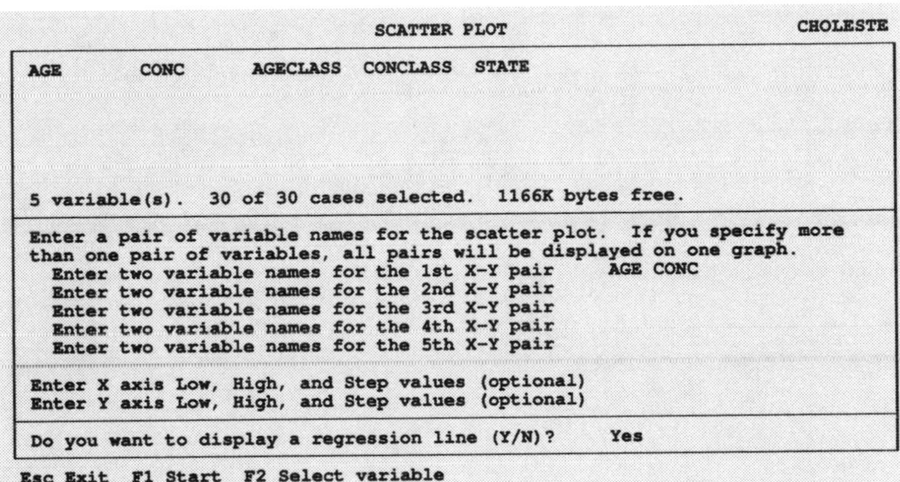

```
                         SCATTER PLOT                              CHOLESTE
AGE       CONC      AGECLASS  CONCLASS  STATE

5 variable(s).  30 of 30 cases selected.  1166K bytes free.
Enter a pair of variable names for the scatter plot.  If you specify more
than one pair of variables, all pairs will be displayed on one graph.
  Enter two variable names for the 1st X-Y pair     AGE CONC
  Enter two variable names for the 2nd X-Y pair
  Enter two variable names for the 3rd X-Y pair
  Enter two variable names for the 4th X-Y pair
  Enter two variable names for the 5th X-Y pair
Enter X axis Low, High, and Step values (optional)
Enter Y axis Low, High, and Step values (optional)
Do you want to display a regression line (Y/N)?     Yes
Esc Exit  F1 Start  F2 Select variable
```

Enter the names of the two variables at the prompt for the first pair. Enter the name of the variable to plot on the X axis first, followed by the variable for the Y axis.

You can enter additional variable name pairs. All pairs are displayed on the same graph using different symbols.

You can enter low, high, and step values to control the scales of either the X or the Y axis. If you enter low and high values for either the X or the Y axis, only points that fall between these values will be plotted. This option is useful for eliminating outliers from the plot or zooming in on a particular portion of the plot.

You can also have a fitted regression line, as selected in the panel above, drawn through the points on the scatter plot.

**Example**

The data are from Snedecor and Cochran (1980, p. 386), described at the beginning of this chapter. The options panel above is used to request a scatter plot for CONC vs. AGE, the blood cholesterol level and age of 30 female subjects. The results are:

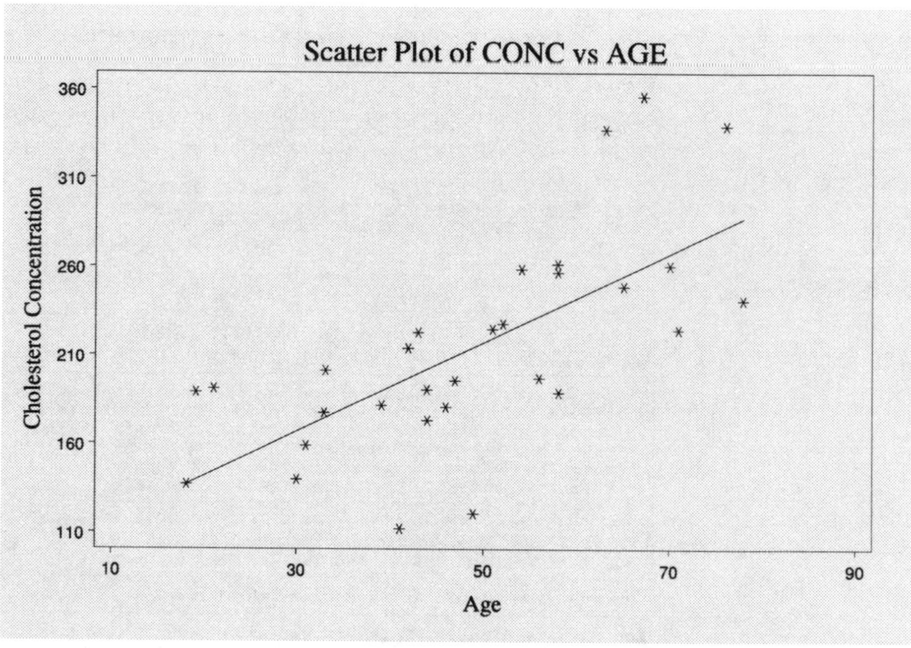


The fitted linear regression line in the graph above makes it easier to see the linear relationship between age and cholesterol concentration. A fitted line can also be useful as a reference line to spot nonlinear relationships between two variables.

**Graph Options**

Scatter plot symbols and other options that affect the scatter plot can be selected using the **Install System** procedure listed on the *Statistix* base menu. Please see Chapter 1 for details.

If you select the ASCII text printer (see **Install System**) for printing graphs, the scatter plot prints a plus sign to indicate a single point. When more than one observation is plotted in the same space, a digit representing the number of observations is displayed (e.g., 2 for two points). If ten or more points are plotted in the same place, the symbol * is printed. Clearly, the fitted line cannot be drawn using the ASCII text printer.

# Breakdown

**Breakdown** computes the sums, means, and standard deviations for the subgroups of a dependent variable. The dependent variable can be classified by up to five independent variables. The summary statistics are displayed for all levels of nesting.

## Specification

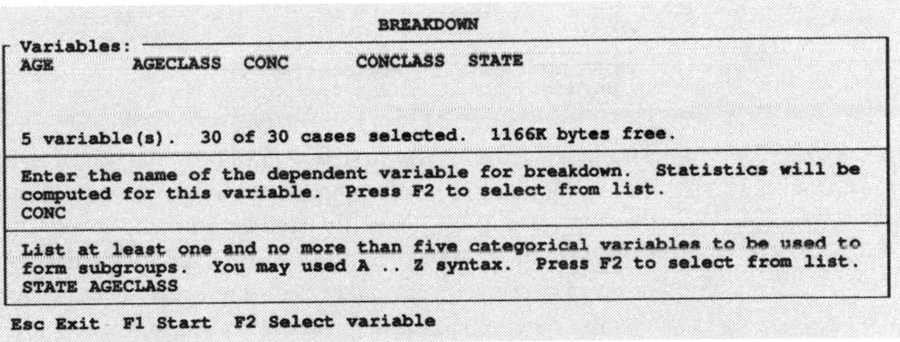


Enter the name of the variable for which you're interested in computing the summary statistics. Then list up to five classifying variables that will be used to "break down" the entire data set into groups. The order in which the classifying variables are specified determines the order of nesting, with the value of the right-most variable changing most rapidly.

## Data Restrictions

There can be up to five classifying variables. The classifying variables can be of any data type. Real values will be truncated to whole numbers and must be no larger than 99,999. Strings will be truncated to ten characters.

## Example

The original data are from Snedecor and Cochran (1980, p. 386), described at the beginning of this chapter. The dependent variable CONC is the cholesterol concentrations of 30 female subjects. The two independent variables used are STATE and AGECLASS. For example, suppose you're interested in the cholesterol concentration means by states as well as the age-specific means within states. The options given in the panel above specify that AGECLASS be nested within STATE. The results are presented below.

```
BREAKDOWN FOR CONC  Cholesterol concentration

VARIABLE     LEVEL          N        SUM        MEAN        S.D.
--------     ---------     --       ----       ------      ------
  AGECLASS   30             2        383      191.50      13.435
  AGECLASS   40             3        414      138.00      37.510
  AGECLASS   50             3        676      225.33      35.076
  AGECLASS   60             1        249      249.00
  AGECLASS   70             2        563      281.50      81.317
 STATE       Iowa          11       2285      207.72      63.795
  AGECLASS   10             2        326      163.00      36.769
  AGECLASS   20             1        191      191.00
  AGECLASS   30             3        476      158.66      18.502
  AGECLASS   40             5        996      199.20      19.791
  AGECLASS   50             4        941      235.25      30.313
  AGECLASS   60             2        693      346.50      13.435
  AGECLASS   70             2        502      251.00      14.142
 STATE       Nebraska      19       4125      217.10      58.796
OVERALL                    30       6410      213.66      59.751

CASES INCLUDED 30    MISSING CASES 0
```

The indentation of the first two columns (the variable names and their values) depict the nesting structure. Any variable X indented with respect to another variable Z means the statistics for the levels of X are nested within the levels of Z. For example, AGECLASS is nested within STATE. The order of nesting is consistent with the order in which the classifying variables are specified in response to the prompt.

Note that the outer levels of nesting summarize the inner levels. In the example above, the line labeled "Iowa" summarizes the data for the five age classes listed above it.

C H A P T E R

# 5

# One, Two, & Multi-Sample Tests

```
STATISTIX BASE MENU

Data management
File management
Install system
Summary statistics
One, two, & multi-sampl
Linear models
Association tests
Randomness/normality te
Time series
Quality control charts
Probability distributio
```

```
ONE, TWO, & MULTI-SAMPLE TESTS

Paired t test
Sign test
Wilcoxon signed rank test
Two-sample t test
Rank sum test
Median test
One-way AOV
Kruskal-Wallis one-way AOV
Friedman two-way AOV
```

*Statistix* offers a number of procedures to test hypotheses about the central values of the population distributions from which the samples are drawn. These procedures are often referred to as tests of location. Several of these tests are parametric and require the assumption that the data are normally distributed. Nonparametric tests are provided for situations where the assumption of normality is not appropriate. When their assumptions are appropriate, parametric tests are generally more powerful than their nonparametric equivalents, although nonparametric tests often compare quite well in performance. The parametric versions test hypotheses concerning the group means. The nonparametric procedures test central value hypotheses based on measures other than the mean.

The **Paired T Test** is a parametric test used to test for differences between means of two groups when the samples are made in pairs. The **Sign Test**

The **Sign Test** and **Wilcoxon Signed Rank Test** are nonparametric alternatives to the Paired T Test.

The **Two-Sample T Test** is a parametric test that tests for a difference in the means of two groups when the samples are drawn independently from two normally distributed populations.

The **Rank Sum Test** and **Median Test** are nonparametric alternatives to the Two-sample T Test.

The **One-Way AOV** is a multi-sample test that tests for differences among the means of several groups.

The **Kruskal-Wallis One-Way AOV** is a nonparametric alternative to the One-Way AOV.

The **Friedman Two-Way AOV** is a nonparametric alternative to the two-way analysis of variance. The **General AOV/AOCV** procedure, which is discussed in Chapter 6, performs parametric tests with two or more classifying attributes.

Background on the parametric tests can be found in Snedecor and Cochran (1980). Hollander and Wolfe (1973), Lehmann (1975), and Siegal (1956) are good references for the nonparametric procedures.

# Paired T Test

The **Paired T Test**, a parametric procedure, is useful for testing whether the means of two groups are different, where the samples were drawn in pairs. The test is actually testing whether the mean of the differences of thc pairs is different from zero.

## Specification

Enter the names of the two variables that contain the paired samples.

```
                         PAIRED T TEST                              TOBACCO
VIRUS1    VIRUS2

2 variable(s).  8 of 8 cases selected.  1183K bytes free.

Enter the names of two variables containing the two samples to test.
Press F2 to select variables from the list.
VIRUS1 VIRUS2
Esc Exit  F1 Start  F2 Select variable
```

## Data Restrictions

The grouping variable used with the categorical method can be of any data type (real, integer, date, or string). Real values are truncated to whole numbers and must be no larger than 99,999. Strings are truncated to ten characters.

## Example

The data for this example (Snedecor and Cochran, 1980, p. 87) concern the number of lesions produced on a tobacco leaf by the application of two different viral preparations. The halves of a leaf constitute a pair. The data for the first preparation are in variable VIRUS1, and that for the second preparation are in VIRUS2.

| CASE | VIRUS1 | VIRUS2 |
|---|---|---|
| 1 | 31 | 18 |
| 2 | 20 | 17 |
| 3 | 18 | 14 |
| 4 | 17 | 11 |
| 5 | 9 | 10 |
| 6 | 8 | 7 |
| 7 | 10 | 5 |
| 8 | 7 | 6 |

The analysis is specified on the preceding page. The results are presented below.

```
PAIRED T TEST FOR VIRUS1 - VIRUS2

MEAN          4.0000
STD ERROR     1.5236
T               2.63
DF                 7
P             0.0341

CASES INCLUDED 8    MISSING CASES 0
```

The null hypothesis being examined is that the mean of the differences is zero. If the assumption of normality is appropriate, the small p-value (0.0341) suggests that the mean of the differences is not zero, i.e., the two different viral preparations do cause lesions at different rates. (**Wilk-Shapiro/Rankit Plots** can be used to examine the assumption of normality.) The p-value is for a two-tailed test; halving it produces a one-tailed p-value.

It's possible to test a null hypothesis that the mean of the differences equals some constant other than zero. This is done by adding or subtracting some constant amount to the data, perhaps using **Transformations**. For example, suppose you're interested in testing whether the mean of the differences VIRUS1 - VIRUS2 is different from 2, rather than 0. Two is added to VIRUS2 and the t test is then specified as before.

It's not appropriate to use this test if the data are not paired. We'll call the unit from which the two members of the pair were drawn a block. For example, the blocks may be individuals and the two members of the data pair are reaction times before and after ingestion of some test medication. The advantage of a paired test is that it removes variation in the data due to blocks; the data used for the test are the pair differences within the blocks. The "noise" in the data due to the fact that some individuals have naturally faster or slower reaction times regardless of the medication would thus be eliminated. (The paired t test is a special case of a randomized block design analysis of variance.) This analysis is not very efficient if the pair members are not correlated within blocks; in this case a **Two-Sample T Test** should be considered instead. Snedecor and Cochran (1980, p. 99-102) give further detail on paired versus independent sampling.

# Sign Test

The **Sign Test** is a nonparametric alternative to the **Paired T Test**. It requires virtually no assumptions about the paired samples other than that they are random and independent. On the negative side, it's not as powerful as the **Paired T Test** or **Wilcoxon Signed Rank Test**. However, it's especially useful for situations where quantitative measures are difficult to obtain but where a member of the pair can be judged "greater than" or "less than" the other member of the pair.

As with other paired t tests, it assumes that you have two groups and that you have drawn your samples in pairs. The only information in the data which the sign test uses is whether, within a pair, the item from the first group was greater than ("+") or less than ("-") the item in the second group. If there is no consistent difference between the groups, there should be an equal number of "+"s and "-"s in the data except for random variation.

## Specification

Enter the names of the two variables that contain the paired samples.

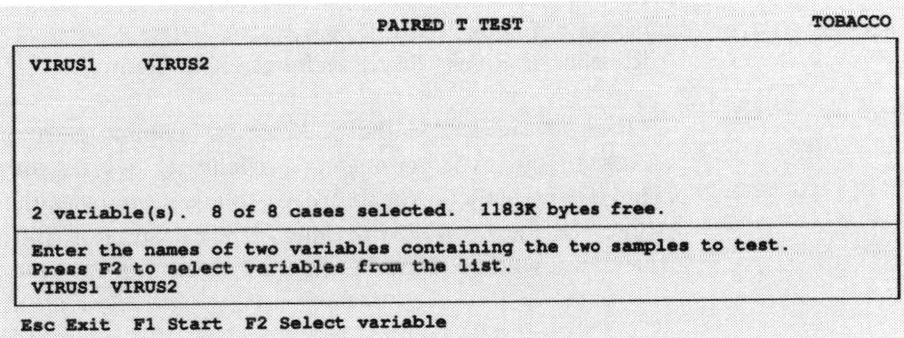


## Example

The data for this example (Snedecor and Cochran, 1980, p. 87) concern the number of lesions produced on a tobacco leaf by the application of two different viral preparations. The halves of a leaf constitute a pair. The data for the first preparation are in variable VIRUS1, and that for the second preparation are in VIRUS2.

| CASE | VIRUS1 | VIRUS2 |
|---|---|---|
| 1 | 31 | 18 |
| 2 | 20 | 17 |
| 3 | 18 | 14 |
| 4 | 17 | 11 |
| 5 | 9 | 10 |
| 6 | 8 | 7 |
| 7 | 10 | 5 |
| 8 | 7 | 6 |

The analysis is specified above. The results are displayed below.

```
SIGN TEST FOR VIRUS1 - VIRUS2

NUMBER OF NEGATIVE DIFFERENCES              1
NUMBER OF POSITIVE DIFFERENCES              7
NUMBER OF ZERO DIFFERENCES (IGNORED)        0

PROBABILITY OF A RESULT AS
OR MORE EXTREME THAN OBSERVED          0.0352

A VALUE IS COUNTED AS A ZERO IF ITS
ABSOLUTE VALUE IS LESS THAN 0.00001

CASES INCLUDED 8    MISSING CASES 0
```

The null hypothesis tested by the sign test is that the median of the differences is zero. The calculated probability is the binomial probability of observing as few or fewer of the less abundant sign, given that an individual difference is equally likely to be of either sign.

For the virus example, the calculated probability is the probability of observing one or fewer negative differences in a random sample of eight. This is a one-tailed probability; doubling it produces the correct two-tailed value. So the two-tailed p-value for the example is 0.0704, somewhat larger than the p-value observed with the **Paired T Test**.

## Computational Notes

The probability is calculated using the same routine as in the binomial function in **Probability Functions**. The parameter P is set to 0.5.

# Wilcoxon Signed Rank Test

The **Wilcoxon Signed Rank Test** is a nonparametric alternative to the **Paired T Test.** It's generally more powerful than the **Sign Test.** As with other paired tests, it assumes that you have two groups and that you have drawn your sample in pairs. Each pair contains an item from the first group and an item from the second group. This procedure tests the hypothesis that the frequency distributions for the two groups are identical. Exact p-values are computed for small sample sizes.

Specification

Enter the names of the two variables containing the paired samples.

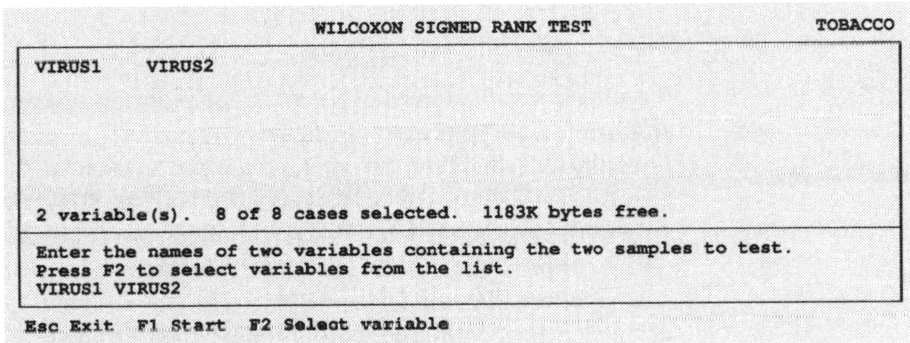


Example

The data for this example (Snedecor and Cochran, 1980, p. 87) concern the number of lesions produced on a tobacco leaf by the application of two different viral preparations. The halves of a leaf constitute a pair. The data for the first preparation are in variable VIRUS1, and that for the second preparation are in VIRUS2. See **Paired T Test** on page 107 for the data listing.

The analysis is specified above. The results are presented on the next page.

The differences are first ranked by absolute value. Differences that are near zero (absolute value less than 0.00001) are ignored. Tied values are given a mean rank (Hollander and Wolfe 1973). Differences are considered to be tied if they are within 0.00001 of one another. The ranks are given the same signs that the original differences had. The negative and positive signed ranks are then summed separately.

```
WILCOXON SIGNED RANK TEST FOR VIRUS1 - VIRUS2

SUM OF NEGATIVE RANKS                                    -2.0000
SUM OF POSITIVE RANKS                                    34.000

EXACT PROBABILITY OF A RESULT AS OR MORE
EXTREME THAN THE OBSERVED RANKS (ONE-TAILED P-VALUE)    0.0117

NORMAL APPROXIMATION WITH CONTINUITY CORRECTION          2.170
TWO-TAILED P-VALUE FOR NORMAL APPROXIMATION             0.0300

TOTAL NUMBER OF VALUES THAT WERE TIED          3
NUMBER OF ZERO DIFFERENCES DROPPED             0
MAX. DIFF. ALLOWED BETWEEN TIES          0.00001

CASES INCLUDED 8    MISSING CASES 0
```

Suppose the frequency distributions for groups one and two were the same. The frequency distribution of the differences of the pairs would then be symmetrical and have a median of zero. In this instance, the absolute values of the sums of negative and positive signed ranks would be expected to be "similar". The signed rank test tests the null hypothesis that the median of the differences equals zero.

The exact p-values for the Wilcoxon signed rank test are computed for small to moderate sample sizes (20 or fewer cases). The exact one-tailed p-value is computed; doubling this yields the exact two-tailed p-value. When ties are found to be present the "exact probability" is no longer exact but will usually be a good approximation. When sample sizes are moderate to large, the normal approximation statistic gives reliable results. The p-value for the normal approximation is two-tailed. The normal approximation includes a correction for continuity; its use is described in Snedecor and Cochran (1980, p. 142).

In the example, the exact p-value is 0.0117, which when doubled gives the two-tailed value of 0.0234. This is fairly close to the p-value of 0.0297 using the normal approximation. As with the t test, these results suggest that the preparations do produce lesions at different rates. While the paired t test is a more powerful test than the signed rank test, the difference in power is often not great. The signed rank test is a popular alternative because it requires much less restrictive assumptions about the data.

The exact p-value routine is based on the p-value routine for the **Rank Sum Test**. It exploits the fact that the null distribution of the signed rank statistic can be factored as a product of a binomial distribution and the null distribution of the rank sum statistic (Bickel and Doksum 1977).

# Two-Sample T Test

This procedure computes two-sample t tests, which test for differences between the means of two independent samples. It's applicable in situations where samples are drawn independently from two normally distributed groups. Two t tests are computed; one assumes equal group variances, and the other assumes different group variances. A test for equality of variances is also performed.

## Specification

The analysis can be specified in one of two ways, depending on how the data are stored. If the two groups were entered into *Statistix* as two variables, use the TABLE method and list the variable names. If the data from both groups are entered into a single variable and a second categorical variable is used to identify the two groups, use the CATEGORICAL method.

```
                              TWO-SAMPLE T TEST                        CHEMCON1
 CONC      METHOD




 2 variable(s).  12 of 12 cases selected.  1183K bytes free.
 Are your data arranged as a TABLE with two variables representing two
 samples, or do you have one dependent variable and one CATEGORICAL variable
 whose values determine the two samples?  Select Table or Categorical.
 Categorical
 Enter the name of the dependent variable.  Press F2 to select a variable
 from the list.
 CONC
 Enter the name of the categorical variable that identifies the two samples.
 METHOD
Esc Exit  F1 Start  F2 Select variable
```

## Data Restrictions

The grouping variable used with the categorical method can be of any data type (i.e., real, integer, date, or string). Real values are truncated to whole numbers and must be no larger than 99,999. Strings are truncated to ten characters.

## Example

The data for this example come from Snedecor and Cochran (1980). The goal is to compare the results of a standard, but slow, chemical analysis procedure with a quicker, but potentially less precise, procedure. The variable CONC is used to store the chemical concentrations determined by both methods. The variable METHOD is used to identify the method used (1 = standard, 2 = quick) to determine the concentration.

| CASE | CONC | METHOD |
|---|---|---|
| 1 | 25 | 1 |
| 2 | 24 | 1 |
| 3 | 25 | 1 |
| 4 | 26 | 1 |
| 5 | 23 | 2 |
| 6 | 18 | 2 |
| 7 | 22 | 2 |
| 8 | 28 | 2 |
| 9 | 17 | 2 |
| 10 | 25 | 2 |
| 11 | 19 | 2 |
| 12 | 16 | 2 |

The analysis is specified above. The results are as follows below.

```
TWO-SAMPLE T TESTS FOR CONC BY METHOD

                                    SAMPLE
  METHOD                  MEAN       SIZE        S.D.          S.E.
 ----------           ----------  --------   -----------   ----------
Standard                25.000       4          0.8165        0.4082
Quick                   21.000       8          4.2088        1.4880

                             T           DF           P
                         ---------   ---------   ---------
EQUAL VARIANCES            1.84        10         0.0956
UNEQUAL VARIANCES          2.59         8.0       0.0320

                             F         NUM DF      DEN DF          P
TESTS FOR EQUALITY       ---------   ---------   ---------    ---------
      OF VARIANCES        26.57          7           3          0.0106

CASES INCLUDED 12       MISSING CASES 0
```

Summary statistics for the two groups are given first, including the group means, sample sizes, standard deviations, and standard errors. The t-statistics and associated information are given next. The t test labeled EQUAL VARIANCES is testing the null hypothesis that means for the two groups are equal given that the two groups have the same variances. The t test labeled UNEQUAL VARIANCES tests the same null hypothesis except that it does not require the assumption that the variances of the two groups are equal. A discussion of such tests is given in Snedecor and Cochran (1980, p. 96-98). Note that the degrees of freedom for unequal variances are expressed as a decimal number. It's computed using Satterthwaite's approximation, described in Snedecor and Cochran. An F test for the equality of the group variances is given after the t tests.

Snedecor and Cochran use the above example to illustrate how unequal variances can influence the analysis. Evidence for a difference between two chemical analyses is considerably weaker when equal variances are assumed (p=0.0956) than when unequal variances are assumed (p=0.0320). When in doubt, it's safer to assume the variances are unequal. In our example, the F test for equality of variances lends strong support for assuming the variances are unequal (p=0.0106).

To illustrate the TABLE method of model specification, suppose that the data from the two methods were entered as two separate variables.

| CASE | STANDARD | QUICK |
|---|---|---|
| 1 | 25 | 23 |
| 2 | 24 | 18 |
| 3 | 25 | 22 |
| 4 | 26 | 28 |
| 5 | M | 17 |
| 6 | M | 25 |
| 7 | M | 19 |
| 8 | M | 16 |

The analysis is then specified as follows:

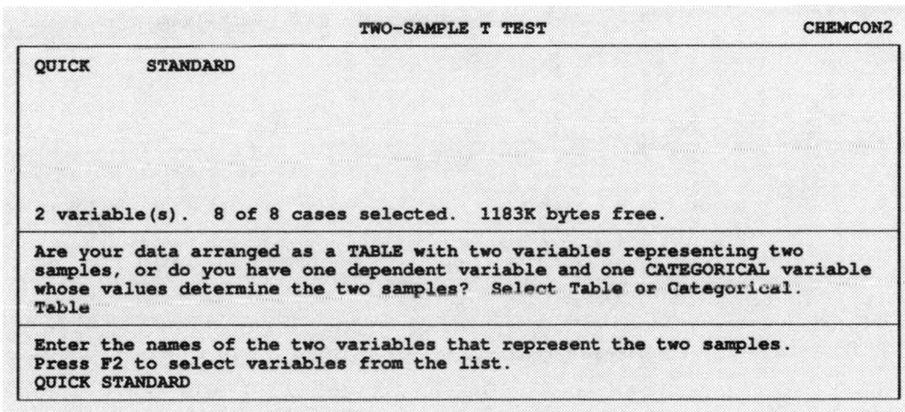
```
                         TWO-SAMPLE T TEST                          CHEMCON2
QUICK     STANDARD

2 variable(s).  8 of 8 cases selected.  1183K bytes free.

Are your data arranged as a TABLE with two variables representing two
samples, or do you have one dependent variable and one CATEGORICAL variable
whose values determine the two samples?  Select Table or Categorical.
Table

Enter the names of the two variables that represent the two samples.
Press F2 to select variables from the list.
QUICK STANDARD
```

These t tests, as well as the F-test for equality of variances, are based on the assumption that the data are normally distributed. **Wilk-Shapiro/Rankit Plots** is useful for examining this assumption. You should consider the **Median Test** or the **Rank Sum Test** if non-normality is a problem.

# Rank Sum Test

*Statistix* computes the **Rank Sum Test**, a nonparametric procedure that tests for differences in the central values of samples from two independent samples. This test can be performed with either of two statistics—the Mann Whitney U statistic or the Wilcoxon rank sum statistic. *Statistix* computes both statistics. Both of these statistics are mathematically equivalent and always lead to identical results. Exact p-values are given for small sample sizes. This test is often almost as powerful as the **Two-Sample T Test**, and is usually more powerful than the **Median Test**.

## Specification

The analysis can be specified in one of two ways, depending on how the data are stored. If the two groups are entered into *Statistix* as two variables, use the TABLE method and list the variable names. If the data from both groups are entered into a single variable and a second categorical variable is used to identify the two groups, use the CATEGORICAL method.

```
                    RANK SUM TWO-SAMPLE (MANN-WHITNEY) TEST                CHEMCON1
CONC      METHOD




2 variable(s).  12 of 12 cases selected.  1183K bytes free.

Are your data arranged as a TABLE with two variables representing two
samples, or do you have one dependent variable and one CATEGORICAL variable
whose values determine the two samples?  Select Table or Categorical.
Categorical

Enter the name of the dependent variable.  Press F2 to select a variable
from the list.
CONC

Enter the name of the categorical variable that identifies the two samples.
METHOD

Esc Exit  F1 Start  F2 Select variable
```

## Example

The data for this example come from Snedecor and Cochran (1980). The goal is to compare the results of a standard, but slow, chemical analysis procedure with a quicker, but potentially less precise, procedure. The variable CONC is used to store the chemical concentrations determined by both methods. The variable METHOD is used to identify the method used (1 = standard, 2 = quick) to determine the concentration.

| CASE | CONC | METHOD |
|---|---|---|
| 1 | 25 | 1 |
| 2 | 24 | 1 |
| 3 | 25 | 1 |
| 4 | 26 | 1 |
| 5 | 23 | 2 |
| 6 | 18 | 2 |
| 7 | 22 | 2 |
| 8 | 28 | 2 |
| 9 | 17 | 2 |
| 10 | 25 | 2 |
| 11 | 19 | 2 |
| 12 | 16 | 2 |

The analysis is specified above. The results are shown below.

```
RANK SUM TWO-SAMPLE (MANN-WHITNEY) TEST FOR CONC BY METHOD

                             SAMPLE
   METHOD        RANK SUM     SIZE       U STAT     MEAN RANK
 ------------   ----------  --------   ----------  ------------
 Standard        36.000        4        26.000         9.0
 Quick           42.000        8        6.0000         5.3
 TOTAL           78.000       12

 EXACT PROBABILITY OF A RESULT AS OR MORE EXTREME
 THAN THE OBSERVED RANKS (ONE-TAILED P-VALUE)              0.0545

 NORMAL APPROXIMATION WITH CONTINUITY CORRECTION            1.613
 TWO-TAILED P-VALUE FOR NORMAL APPROXIMATION               0.1066

 TOTAL NUMBER OF VALUES THAT WERE TIED               3
 MAXIMUM DIFFERENCE ALLOWED BETWEEN TIES       0.00001

 CASES INCLUDED 12     MISSING CASES 0
```

All the data are combined and converted to ranks. Tied scores are assigned mean ranks (Hollander and Wolfe 1973). Values are considered to be tied if they are within 0.00001 of one another. The ranks for each group are then summed to get the rank sum statistic for each group. If the distributions for the two groups are the same, the average ranks should be "similar" for each group. The null hypothesis being tested by the rank sum test is that the distributions for the two groups are the same. Rejecting this hypothesis usually leads to the conclusion that the central values for the two groups differ, although strictly you can only conclude that the distributions for the two groups differ in some way (Bradley 1968).

The Mann Whitney U statistic corresponding to the rank sum is also given. When sample sizes are small to moderate, exact p-values are calculated and displayed, eliminating the need to resort to statistical tables. (Exact p-values are computed if the product of the sample sizes for the two groups is less than or equal to 100.) The exact p-values are given as one-sided tests; doubling them gives the exact two-tailed value. When ties are present, the exact p is only approximate but should usually give a good approximation. For moderate to large samples, the traditional normal approximation statistic and associated two-tailed p-value is displayed. Snedecor and Cochran (1980, p. 144-145) describe the rank sum test and the computation of the normal approximation.

Doubling the exact p-value in the example produces 0.1090, which is quite close to the normal approximation p-value of 0.1065. These statistics may be small enough to suggest that a difference does, in fact, exist between the two chemical techniques, but it's certainly not conclusive evidence. The sample size for the standard method (METHOD = 1) is rather small (N = 4) and undoubtedly limits the power of the test.

To illustrate the TABLE method of model specification, suppose that the data from the two methods were entered as two separate variables.

| CASE | STANDARD | QUICK |
|---|---|---|
| 1 | 25 | 23 |
| 2 | 24 | 18 |
| 3 | 25 | 22 |
| 4 | 26 | 28 |
| 5 | M | 17 |
| 6 | M | 25 |
| 7 | M | 19 |
| 8 | M | 16 |

The analysis is then specified as illustrated below.

```
Are your data arranged as a TABLE with two variables representing two
samples, or do you have one dependent variable and one CATEGORICAL variable
whose values determine the two samples?  Select Table or Categorical.
Table

Enter the names of the two variables that represent the two samples.
Press F2 to select variables from the list.
QUICK STANDARD
```

## Computational Notes

Exact p-values are computed using a routine similar to Dinneen and Blakesley's (1973).

# Median Test

The **Median Test** is a nonparametric two-sample test. It tests the hypothesis that the medians for the two groups from which the samples were drawn are equal.

## Specification

The analysis can be specified in one of two ways, depending on how the data are stored. If the two groups are entered into *Statistix* as two variables, use the TABLE method and list the variable names. If the data from both groups are entered into a single variable, and a second categorical variable is used to identify the two groups, use the CATEGORICAL method.

```
                              MEDIAN TEST                              CHEMCON1
 CONC      METHOD




 2 variable(s).  12 of 12 cases selected.  1183K bytes free.

 Are your data arranged as a TABLE with two variables representing two
 samples, or do you have one dependent variable and one CATEGORICAL variable
 whose values determine the two samples?  Select Table or Categorical.
 Categorical

 Enter the name of the dependent variable.  Press F2 to select a variable
 from the list.
 CONC

 Enter the name of the categorical variable that identifies the two samples.
 METHOD

 Esc Exit  F1 Start  F2 Select variable
```

## Data Restrictions

The chi-square value is not computed for sample sizes less than ten. It is recommended that you use the **Two By Two** procedure to compute Fisher's exact method in such cases.

## Example

The data for this example come from Snedecor and Cochran (1980). The goal is to compare the results of a standard, but slow, chemical analysis procedure with a quicker, but potentially less precise, procedure. The variable CONC is used to store the chemical concentrations determined by both methods. The variable METHOD is used to identify the method used (1 = standard, 2 = quick) to determine the concentration.

| CASE | CONC | METHOD |
|---|---|---|
| 1 | 25 | 1 |
| 2 | 24 | 1 |
| 3 | 25 | 1 |
| 4 | 26 | 1 |
| 5 | 23 | 2 |
| 6 | 18 | 2 |
| 7 | 22 | 2 |
| 8 | 28 | 2 |
| 9 | 17 | 2 |
| 10 | 25 | 2 |
| 11 | 19 | 2 |
| 12 | 16 | 2 |

The analysis is specified above. The results are as follows:

```
MEDIAN TEST FOR CONC BY METHOD

                            METHOD
                     ---------------------
                     Standard      Quick       TOTAL
                     --------     -------      -----
ABOVE MEDIAN               4            2          6
BELOW MEDIAN               0            6          6
TOTAL                      4            8         12
TIES WITH MEDIAN           0            0          0

MEDIAN VALUE          23.500

CHI SQUARE   6.00    DF 1    P-VALUE 0.0143

MAX. DIFF. ALLOWED BETWEEN A TIE   0.00001

CASES INCLUDED 12     MISSING CASES 0
```

The first step is to find the median for all of the data, which for our example was 23.5. The number of values above and below the median in each sample is tallied, and the two by two table displayed above is created. The number of ties with the median is also displayed, but this information isn't used in the calculations. A value is considered to be tied with the median if it differs by no more than 0.00001.

If the medians for the two groups are equal, we would expect "similar" numbers of values within each group to fall above and below the median. The null hypothesis being tested is that the medians for the two groups are equal. The test amounts to a typical chi-square test for independence or heterogeneity, performed on the two by two table.

The chi-square value in the example is 6.00, which results in a p-value of 0.0143. This supports the idea that the chemical analysis procedures are different.

See the **Rank Sum Test** on page 118 for a description of specifying an analysis using the TABLE method.

# One-Way AOV

This procedure performs a one-way analysis of variance (Snedecor and Cochran, Chapter 12). The **One-Way AOV** provides statistics for both the fixed effects (Type I) model and the random effects (Type II) model. It also tests for equality of variances between levels, and there are options to perform pairwise comparisons of means and save fitted values and residuals.

## Specification

To use the One-Way AOV procedure, you can organize your data in one of two ways. In the TABLE method, you create one variable for each of the treatments, then enter the responses observed for each treatment in its own variable. Your second option is to create a single dependent variable and enter all of the responses observed for all of the treatments. Then create a second variable with categorical values (e.g., 1, 2, 3 ...) that represent the treatments. This is called the CATEGORICAL method. Both of these methods are illustrated below.

## Data Restrictions

Sample sizes within treatment levels can be unequal. The maximum number of treatment levels is 200. The treatment variable used with the categorical method can be of any data type. Real values are truncated to whole numbers and must be no larger than 99,999. Strings are truncated to ten characters.

## Example

The example below is from Snedecor and Cochran (1980, p. 216). The grams of fat absorbed by batches of doughnuts was measured using four types of fat. The fat absorbed is the response, the fat types are the treatments. To illustrate the TABLE method of model specification first, suppose we entered the responses using four variables, FAT1, FAT2, FAT3, and FAT4, each representing one of the four treatments.

| CASE | FAT1 | FAT2 | FAT3 | FAT4 |
|---|---|---|---|---|
| 1 | 64 | 78 | 75 | 55 |
| 2 | 72 | 91 | 93 | 66 |
| 3 | 68 | 97 | 78 | 49 |
| 4 | 77 | 82 | 71 | 64 |
| 5 | 56 | 85 | 63 | 70 |
| 6 | 95 | 77 | 76 | 68 |

The model is specified in the options panel on the next page. The TABLE method was chosen and the four variables listed. We can shorten the variable list using A .. Z syntax (i.e., FAT1 .. FAT4) or, as they're the only variables in the data set, we can simply specify ALL.

```
                              ONE-WAY AOV                              DOUGH2
FAT1        FAT2        FAT3        FAT4




4 variable(s).   6 of 6 cases selected.   1183K bytes free.

Are your data arranged as a TABLE with variables representing treatments, or
do you have one dependent variable and one CATEGORICAL variable whose values
determine the treatments?  Enter T for TABLE or C for CATEGORICAL.
Table

List the names of the variables that represent the treatments.
Press F2 to select variables from the list.
FAT1 FAT2 FAT3 FAT4

Esc Exit   F1 Start   F2 Select variable
```

The results are displayed below.

```
ONE-WAY AOV FOR: FAT1 FAT2 FAT3 FAT4

SOURCE      DF        SS            MS           F         P
-------    ----   ---------     ---------    -------   ------
BETWEEN      3     1636.50       545.500       5.41    0.0069
WITHIN      20     2018.00       100.900
TOTAL       23     3654.50

                              CHI SQ      DF         P
BARTLETT'S TEST OF            ------    ------    ------
   EQUAL VARIANCES             1.75        3      0.6258

COCHRAN'S Q                              0.4410
LARGEST VAR / SMALLEST VAR               2.9470

COMPONENT OF VARIANCE FOR BETWEEN GROUPS        74.1000
EFFECTIVE CELL SIZE                                 6.0

                             SAMPLE       GROUP
VARIABLE          MEAN        SIZE       STD DEV
---------      ---------    ------      --------
FAT1             72.000        6          13.341
FAT2             85.000        6          7.7717
FAT3             76.000        6          9.8792
FAT4             62.000        6          8.2219
TOTAL            73.750       24          10.044

CASES INCLUDED 24     MISSING CASES 0
```

A standard analysis of variance table is displayed first. Note that the F test suggests a substantial between-groups (fats) effect, with a p-value of 0.0069. The F test assumes that the within-group variances are the same for all groups. Bartlett's test for equality of variances tests this assumption; it is shown immediately below the analysis of variance table. The p-value of

0.6258 doesn't suggest that the variances are unequal. Bartlett's test is described in Snedecor and Cochran (1980, p. 252). Another test of equality of variances, Cochran's Q, is given below Bartlett's test. Cochran's Q statistic is the ratio of the largest within-group variance over the sum of all within-group variances. (See Dixon and Massey, 1957, for more details and tables.) The ratio of the largest within-group variance over the smallest has also been a popular test for equal variances and is displayed under Cochran's Q; tables are given in Pearson and Hartley (1954).

A fixed-effects model (Type I) is appropriate for these data. If a random effects model were appropriate (Type II), the component of variance for between groups may be of interest (see Snedecor and Cochran, chap. 13). The between-groups variance component and effective cell sample size are displayed below the equality of variance tests. The computation of effective cell size is described on p. 246 of Snedecor and Cochran.

The bottom portion of the report lists a table of within-group means, sample sizes, and standard deviations. The value in the standard deviation column for the TOTAL line is the pooled standard deviation.

We'll use the same analysis to illustrate the CATEGORICAL method of model specification. We now create two variables, a dependent variable FATABSORB and the treatment variable FATTYPE.

| CASE | FATABSORB | FATTYPE |
|---|---|---|
| 1 | 64 | 1 |
| 2 | 72 | 1 |
| 3 | 68 | 1 |
| 4 | 77 | 1 |
| 5 | 56 | 1 |
| 6 | 95 | 1 |
| 7 | 78 | 2 |
| 8 | 91 | 2 |
| 9 | 97 | 2 |
| 10 | 82 | 2 |
| 11 | 85 | 2 |
| 12 | 77 | 2 |
| 13 | 75 | 3 |
| 14 | 93 | 3 |
| 15 | 78 | 3 |
| 16 | 71 | 3 |
| 17 | 63 | 3 |
| 18 | 76 | 3 |
| 19 | 55 | 4 |
| 20 | 66 | 4 |
| 21 | 49 | 4 |
| 22 | 64 | 4 |
| 23 | 70 | 4 |
| 24 | 68 | 4 |

The model is specified below.

```
                         ONE-WAY AOV                                DOUGH1
FATABSORB FATTYPE




2 variable(s).  24 of 24 cases selected.  1183K bytes free.

Are your data arranged as a TABLE with variables representing treatments, or
do you have one dependent variable and one CATEGORICAL variable whose values
determine the treatments?  Enter T for TABLE or C for CATEGORICAL.
Categorical

Enter the name of the dependent variable (observed values).  Press F2 to
select a variable from the list.
FATABSORB

Enter the name of the categorical variable that identifies the treatments.
FATTYPE

Esc Exit  F1 Start  F2 Select variable
```

## One-Way AOV Results Menu

After the one-way AOV results are displayed, press Esc to view the One-Way AOV results menu:

```
 ONE-WAY AOV RESULTS

AOV table
Comparisons of means
Save residuals
Options panel
```

Select "AOV table" to have the AOV table and means displayed again. Select "Options panel" to exit the results menu and return to the original One-Way AOV options panel used to specify the model.

## Comparison of Means

The **Comparisons of Means** option is used to compare the means of the different groups. Other names for this procedure are multiple comparisons, mean separation tests, multiple range tests, and tests for homogeneity of means. Two means are said to be similar or homogeneous if they're not significantly different from one another. This procedure identifies subsets of similar (homogeneous) means.

To use the Comparisons of Means procedure, you select one of the five different comparison methods available (these different methods are

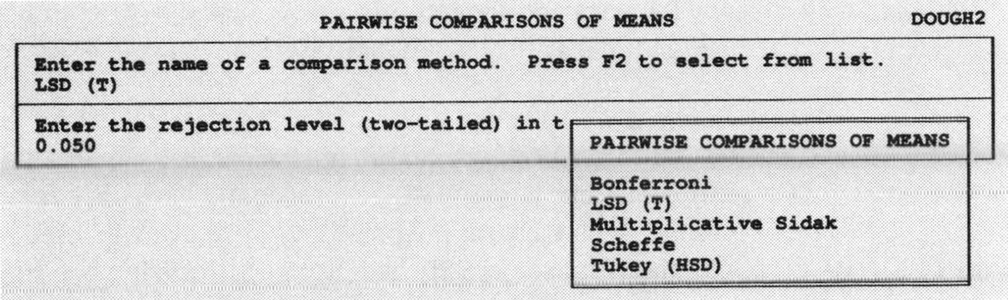


discussed at length in the **General AOV/AOCV** section in Chapter 6) and enter a value for the rejection level.

In the panel above, we've selected the Least Significant Difference method (LSD) and accepted the default rejection level of 0.05. The results for the doughnut example are displayed below.

```
LSD (T) PAIRWISE COMPARISONS OF MEANS

                                HOMOGENEOUS
VARIABLE           MEAN         GROUPS
---------       ----------      ------------
FAT2              85.000         I
FAT3              76.000         I I
FAT1              72.000        .. I I
FAT4              62.000        .... I

THERE ARE 3 GROUPS IN WHICH THE MEANS ARE
NOT SIGNIFICANTLY DIFFERENT FROM ONE ANOTHER.

CRITICAL T VALUE                      2.086    REJECTION LEVEL     0.050
CRITICAL VALUE FOR COMPARISON        12.097
STANDARD ERROR FOR COMPARISON        5.7994
```

The means are sorted in descending order so the largest one is listed in the first row. The columns of I's under the heading "Homogenous Groups" indicate which means are not significantly different from one another. There are three columns in the example because there are three groups of similar or homogenous means. The first group contains the means for FAT2 and FAT3, the second group contains the means for FAT3 and FAT1, and the third group contains the means for FAT1 and FAT4. As in the example above, it's not unusual for the groups to overlap.

If all the groups have equal sample sizes, the standard error for the comparison and the critical value of the comparison are displayed at the end of the report, as above. The standard error is computed as (2sd/n) where sd is the pooled standard deviation and n is the sample size for each group.

If the sample sizes aren't the same for all groups, the standard error of comparisons and the critical values change with each comparison. The standard error for the comparison $mean_i$ - $mean_j$ is (sd $(1/n_i + 1/n_j)$) .

Suppose we have an analysis with three means—A, B, and C—and that A > B > C. With unequal sample sizes, it's possible that A is significantly different from B but that A is not significantly different from C. The mean comparisons table on the preceding page can't be used to summarize these relationships, so *Statistix* uses a second format when this happens.

Consider the means for AGECLASS 70, 30, and 10 in the table below. The numbers in the body of the table are the Bonferroni t statistics.

```
BONFERRONI PAIRWISE COMPARISONS OF MEANS OF CONC BY AGECLASS

 AGECLASS      MEAN    60        70        50        20        40        30
    60        314.00
    70        266.25   1.61
    50        231.00   3.10      1.45
    20        191.00   2.75      1.74      0.97
    40        176.25   5.25*     3.79*     2.73      0.36
    30        171.80   5.02*     3.63*     2.61      0.45      0.20
    10        163.00   4.27*     3.08      2.19      0.59      0.43      0.27

CRITICAL T VALUE 3.413    REJECTION LEVEL 0.050
STANDARD ERRORS AND CRITICAL VALUES OF DIFFERENCES
VARY BETWEEN COMPARISONS BECAUSE OF UNEQUAL SAMPLE SIZES.
```

The mean cholesterol concentrations for these three groups are listed in decreasing order. The Bonferroni tests show a significant difference (indicated by the star) for the AGECLASS groups 70 and 30 but not for 70 and 10.

## Save Residuals

The Save Residuals procedure is used to save the fitted values and residuals in new or existing variables for later analysis. This option is only available if you use the CATEGORICAL method of model specification.

The fitted value for a particular observation in a one-way AOV is the class mean. The residuals are computed as the observed value minus the fitted value. You can compute a rankit plot of the residuals to test the assumption of normality (see Wilk-Shapiro/Rankit Plot in Chapter 8).

# Kruskal-Wallis One-Way AOV

The **Kruskal-Wallis One-Way AOV** procedure performs a nonparametric one-way analysis of variance. The Kruskal-Wallis statistic is computed as are the results of a parametric one-way analysis of variance applied to the ranks.

## Specification

To use the **Kruskal-Wallis One-Way AOV** procedure, you can organize your data in one of two ways. The TABLE method is where you enter the responses observed for each of the treatments in its own variable. The CATEGORICAL method is where you enter all of the observed responses in a single dependent variable and enter the treatment levels in a second grouping variable. Both the TABLE method and the CATEGORICAL method are illustrated in the example below.

```
                        KRUSKAL-WALLIS ONE-WAY AOV                        DOUGH2
FAT1      FAT2      FAT3      FAT4




4 variable(s).   6 of 6 cases selected.   1183K bytes free.

Are your data arranged as a TABLE with variables representing treatments, or
do you have one dependent variable and one CATEGORICAL variable whose values
determine the treatments?  Enter T for TABLE or C for CATEGORICAL.
Table

List the names of the variables that represent the treatments.
Press F2 to select variables from the list.
FAT1 .. FAT4

Esc Exit   F1 Start   F2 Select variable
```

## Data Restrictions

Sample sizes within treatments can be unequal. The maximum number of treatment levels is 200.

## Example

The example data are from Snedecor and Cochran (1980, p. 216) and are also used as example data for the **One-Way AOV** procedure. The grams of fat absorbed by batches of doughnuts were measured using four types of fat. The fat types are the treatments, and the fat absorbed is the response. We'll illustrate the TABLE method of model specification first. Suppose we enter the responses using four variables—FAT1, FAT2, FAT3, and FAT4. Each variable represents one of the four treatments.

| CASE | FAT1 | FAT2 | FAT3 | FAT4 |
|---|---|---|---|---|
| 1 | 64 | 78 | 75 | 55 |
| 2 | 72 | 91 | 93 | 66 |
| 3 | 68 | 97 | 78 | 49 |
| 4 | 77 | 82 | 71 | 64 |
| 5 | 56 | 85 | 63 | 70 |
| 6 | 95 | 77 | 76 | 68 |

The model is specified in the panel on the preceding page. The TABLE method was selected and the four variables listed using A .. Z syntax. The results are as follows:

```
KRUSKAL-WALLIS ONE-WAY NONPARAMETRIC AOV

               MEAN      SAMPLE
VARIABLE       RANK       SIZE
----------   --------   --------
FAT1           11.3          6
FAT2           19.5          6
FAT3           13.6          6
FAT4            5.7          6
TOTAL          12.5         24

KRUSKAL-WALLIS STATISTIC                               11.8322
P-VALUE, USING CHI-SQUARED APPROXIMATION                0.0080

PARAMETRIC AOV APPLIED TO RANKS

SOURCE     DF        SS           MS            F        P
-------   ----   ----------   ----------   --------   ------
BETWEEN     3     590.583      196.861       7.06     0.0020
WITHIN     20     557.416      27.8708
TOTAL      23     1148.00

TOTAL NUMBER OF VALUES THAT WERE TIED        8
MAX. DIFF. ALLOWED BETWEEN TIES        0.00001

CASES INCLUDED 24     MISSING CASES 0
```

The Kruskal-Wallis test is a generalization of the rank sum test. The data are first ranked irrespective of group. Tied values are assigned their average rank (Hollander and Wolfe 1973). Values are assumed to be tied if they are within 0.00001 of one another. If each of the groups had similar distributions, the mean ranks for all groups would be expected to be "similar". The null hypothesis being tested is that each of the groups has the same distribution. Strictly speaking, if the null hypothesis is rejected, the alternative is that the distributions for the groups differ, although in practice it's typical to assume that the differences are due to differences in the central values of the groups.

The analysis of the example is consistent with the parametric **One-Way**

**AOV**. The p-value of 0.0080 suggests that the mean ranks for the groups are dissimilar enough to conclude that the fat types differ.

Conover and Iman (1981) proposed first ranking the data and then applying the usual parametric procedure for computing a one-way analysis of variance. The results of this procedure are displayed underneath the Kruskal-Wallis test. The results are interpreted in the same way as the usual analysis of variance, comparing the within-group variance to the between-group variance. Please note that the usual F test is generally anticonservative, giving significant results more often than it should (Iman and Davenport 1976, 1980). This is perhaps the case in this example. Here the p-value is smaller than that observed with the parametric analysis of variance or the Kruskal-Wallis test.

We can use the same analysis to illustrate the CATEGORICAL method of model specification. The data are entered in two variables—a dependent variable FATABSORB and a treatment variable FATTYPE.

| CASE | FATABSORB | FATTYPE | CASE | FATABSORB | FATTYPE |
|---|---|---|---|---|---|
| 1 | 64 | 1 | 13 | 75 | 3 |
| 2 | 72 | 1 | 14 | 93 | 3 |
| 3 | 68 | 1 | 15 | 78 | 3 |
| 4 | 77 | 1 | 16 | 71 | 3 |
| 5 | 56 | 1 | 17 | 63 | 3 |
| 6 | 96 | 1 | 18 | 76 | 3 |
| 7 | 78 | 2 | 19 | 55 | 4 |
| 8 | 91 | 2 | 20 | 66 | 4 |
| 9 | 97 | 2 | 21 | 49 | 4 |
| 10 | 82 | 2 | 22 | 64 | 4 |
| 11 | 85 | 2 | 23 | 70 | 4 |
| 12 | 77 | 2 | 24 | 68 | 4 |

The model is specified as follows:

```
Are your data arranged as a TABLE with variables representing treatments, or
do you have one dependent variable and one CATEGORICAL variable whose values
determine the treatments?  Enter T for TABLE or C for CATEGORICAL.
Categorical

Enter the name of the dependent variable (observed values).  Press F2 to
select a variable from the list.
FATABSORB

Enter the name of the categorical variable that identifies the treatments.
FATTYPE
```

# Friedman Two-Way AOV

The Friedman nonparametric two-way analysis of variance is used to analyze two-way designs without replication. The results are equivalent to Kendall's coefficient of concordance (Conover 1980).

## Specification

The analysis can be specified in one of two ways, depending on how the data are arranged in the variables. A two-way analysis of variance requires that each observation of the dependent variable be classified by two factors. In the TABLE method, the levels for the one factor are represented by the variables themselves. The levels for the other factor are then represented by the cases. To specify the model, list the names of the variables that represent the column factor.

```
                    FRIEDMAN TWO-WAY AOV                        FUNGUS1
REP        TRT        Y

3 variable(s).  25 of 25 cases selected.  1183K bytes free.

Are your data arranged as a TABLE with variables representing columns and
cases representing rows, or do you have 2 CATEGORICAL variables whose values
determine the columns and rows?  Enter T for TABLE or C for CATEGORICAL.
Categorical

Enter the name of the dependent variable that contains the observed data.
Press F2 to select a variable from the list.
Y

List the names of the two categorical variables that represent factors.
TRT REP

Esc Exit   F1 Start   F2 Select variable
```

For the CATEGORICAL method, all observations of the dependent variable are in one variable. The two factors are indicated by two categorical variables.

## Data Restrictions

There can be only one observation per cell; no replication is permitted. Missing values can't be included. You can have up to 50 levels in each of the two treatment factors.

## Example

This example is a randomized block design used in Snedecor and Cochran

(1980, sect. 14.2). The same data are used for Example I in the **General AOV/AOCV** section of Chapter 6, where a parametric two-way analysis of variance is computed. The dependent variable is the number of soybeans out of 100 that failed to emerge, and the treatments were various fungicides (the first treatment level was a no-fungicide control).

To illustrate the CATEGORICAL method of model specification, we entered the observed counts into a single variable named Y. The fungicides were numbered 1 through 5 and entered into a variable named TRT. The blocks (replicates) were numbered 1 through 5 and entered into a variable named BLK.

| CASE | Y | TRT | BLK | CASE | Y | TRT | BLK |
|---|---|---|---|---|---|---|---|
| 1 | 8 | 1 | 1 | 14 | 8 | 3 | 4 |
| 2 | 10 | 1 | 2 | 15 | 10 | 3 | 5 |
| 3 | 12 | 1 | 3 | 16 | 3 | 4 | 1 |
| 4 | 13 | 1 | 4 | 17 | 5 | 4 | 2 |
| 5 | 11 | 1 | 5 | 18 | 9 | 4 | 3 |
| 6 | 2 | 2 | 1 | 19 | 10 | 4 | 4 |
| 7 | 6 | 2 | 2 | 20 | 6 | 4 | 5 |
| 8 | 7 | 2 | 3 | 21 | 9 | 5 | 1 |
| 9 | 11 | 2 | 4 | 22 | 7 | 5 | 2 |
| 10 | 5 | 2 | 5 | 23 | 5 | 5 | 3 |
| 11 | 4 | 3 | 1 | 24 | 5 | 5 | 4 |
| 12 | 10 | 3 | 2 | 25 | 3 | 5 | 5 |
| 13 | 9 | 3 | 3 | | | | |

The **Transformation** CAT function can be used to generate repetitive sequences, like those seen for TRT and BLK. After entering the 25 values for Y, we can use the **Transformation** expressions TRT = CAT (5 5) and BLK = CAT (5 1) to create these variables.

The analysis is specified on the preceding page. The results are presented on the next page.

For the first factor, which in this case is TRT, the observations are first ranked within the second factor (BLK). If there were no differences between the treatment levels, the mean ranks (averaged across blocks) for the different treatment levels would be expected to be "similar". Tied observations are given a mean rank (Hollander and Wolfe 1973). Values are considered to be tied if they are within 0.00001 of one another. "CORRECTED FOR TIES" appears in the display when the Friedman statistic is based on data that contain ties. For this example, ties within blocks were found. It appears that there are definite treatment effects because the p-value is fairly small (0.0530).

```
FRIEDMAN TWO-WAY NONPARAMETRIC AOV FOR Y = TRT REP

 FACTOR 1      MEAN    SAMPLE
   TRT         RANK     SIZE
 ---------   -------  -------
     1         4.70      5
     2         2.20      5
     3         3.40      5
     4         2.50      5
     5         2.20      5

FRIEDMAN STATISTIC, CORRECTED FOR TIES      9.3469
P-VALUE, CHI-SQUARED APPROXIMATION          0.0530
DEGREES OF FREEDOM                               4

 FACTOR 2      MEAN    SAMPLE
   REP         RANK     SIZE
 ---------   -------  -------
     1         1.80      5
     2         3.10      5
     3         3.50      5
     4         3.90      5
     5         2.70      5

FRIEDMAN STATISTIC, CORRECTED FOR TIES      5.3061
P-VALUE, CHI-SQUARED APPROXIMATION          0.2573
DEGREES OF FREEDOM                               4

MAX. DIFF. ALLOWED BETWEEN TIES   0.00001

CASES INCLUDED 25     MISSING CASES 0
```

To examine block effects, the role of the variables is reversed. The observations are now ranked within treatment levels. Ties among the observations within treatment levels were found, as indicated by the message with the Friedman statistic. There appears to be little evidence of block effects (0.2573). As with parametric analysis of variance, testing the block effect will generally not be of much interest.

To use the TABLE method, we'd choose one factor, say fungicide, to represent columns and enter the data for each fungicide into a separate variable. The cases then represent the blocks (replicates).

| CASE | CONTROL | FUNG1 | FUNG2 | FUNG3 | FUNG4 |
|---|---|---|---|---|---|
| 1 | 8 | 2 | 4 | 3 | 9 |
| 2 | 10 | 6 | 10 | 5 | 7 |
| 3 | 12 | 7 | 9 | 9 | 5 |
| 4 | 13 | 11 | 8 | 10 | 5 |
| 5 | 11 | 5 | 10 | 6 | 3 |

The order of the cases is very important with this format. The first case corresponds to the first experimental block, the second case corresponds to the second block, and so on. The model is then specified in the options panel on the next page.

```
                        FRIEDMAN TWO-WAY AOV                          FUNGUS1
CONTROL   FUNG1     FUNG2     FUNG3     FUNG4



5 variable(s).  5 of 5 cases selected.  1183K bytes free.

Are your data arranged as a TABLE with variables representing columns and
cases representing rows, or do you have 2 CATEGORICAL variables whose values
determine the columns and rows?  Enter T for TABLE or C for CATEGORICAL.
Table

List the names of the variables that represent the columns of your table.
You may enter ALL or use A .. Z syntax.  Press F2 to select variables
from the list.
CONTROL FUNG1 .. FUNG4


Esc Exit  F1 Start  F2 Select variable
```

Here the variables that represent the fungicide treatments are listed. The variable list could have been shortened using the A .. Z syntax (FUNG1 .. FUNG4).

The Friedman test is often performed as a companion analysis to the parametric two-way analysis of variance, especially when the assumption of normality in parametric analysis of variance is suspect. It's not as powerful as the parametric analysis, but it usually performs quite well.

C H A P T E R

# 6

# Linear Models

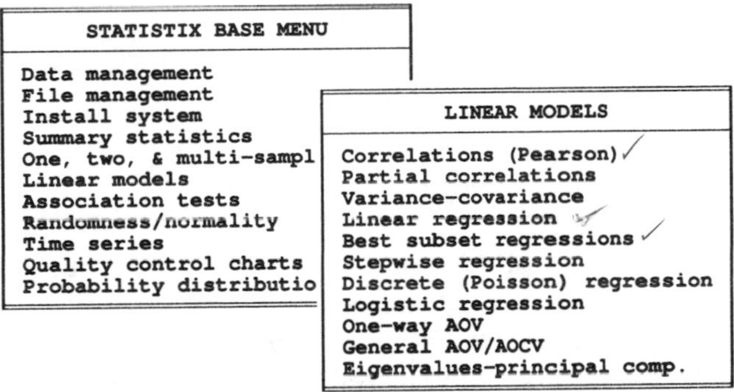


*Statistix* offers you a comprehensive selection of linear model procedures, which include regression, analysis of variance, and analysis of covariance, Linear models are among the most powerful and popular tools available for data analysis.

The **Correlations (Pearson)** procedure displays the correlation matrix for a set of variables.

The **Partial Correlations** procedure computes the correlations of a set of independent variables with a dependent variable after adjusting for the effects of another set of independent variables.

The **Variance-Covariance** procedure displays the sample variance-covariance matrix for a set of variables.

The **Linear Regression** procedure performs simple and multiple linear regression. You can compute predicted values and prediction intervals for any set of independent variable values. Extensive residual analysis options are available for model evaluation. The sensitivity of the regression coefficients to errors in the independent variables can be examined.

The **Best Subset Regressions** procedure generates a list of "best" subset models for a specified regression model.

The **Stepwise Regression** procedure performs forward and backward stepwise linear regression in search of good subset regression models.

The **Discrete (Poisson) Regression** procedure is appropriate for situations where the dependent variable consists of discrete counts.

The **Logistic Regression** procedure is appropriate for a situation where the dependent variable consists of "binary" data. Common examples of binary data are yes or no responses and success or failure outcomes. See the section titled **Analyzing Proportions and Counts** on page 181 for more background on when and why Discrete Regression and Logistic Regression are useful.

The **One-Way AOV** procedure computes a one-way analysis of variance and related statistics. While General AOV/AOCV also computes one-way analyses, One-Way AOV displays numerous statistics that are only relevant to one-way analyses and handles larger and more unbalanced problems. This procedure also appears on the One, Two, and Multi-Sample Tests menu and is discussed in detail in Chapter 5.

The **General AOV/AOCV** procedure computes analyses of variance and covariance for a wide range of experimental designs and models. Designs you can analyze include factorial designs, split-plot designs, completely nested designs, and many others. You have numerous powerful options including comparisons of means, general and polynomial contrasts, Tukey's test for nonadditivity, least squares estimation of missing values, and analysis of covariance.

The **Eigenvalues-Principle Components** procedure computes the eigenvectors and eigenvalues and the principle components for a set of variables. It's often used in regression when the independent variables are highly correlated, and it's also a useful multivariate analysis in its own right.

# Correlations (Pearson)

The **Correlations** procedure computes a correlation matrix for a list of variables. Correlations, also called Pearson or product-moment correlations, indicate the degree of linear association between variables.

## Specification

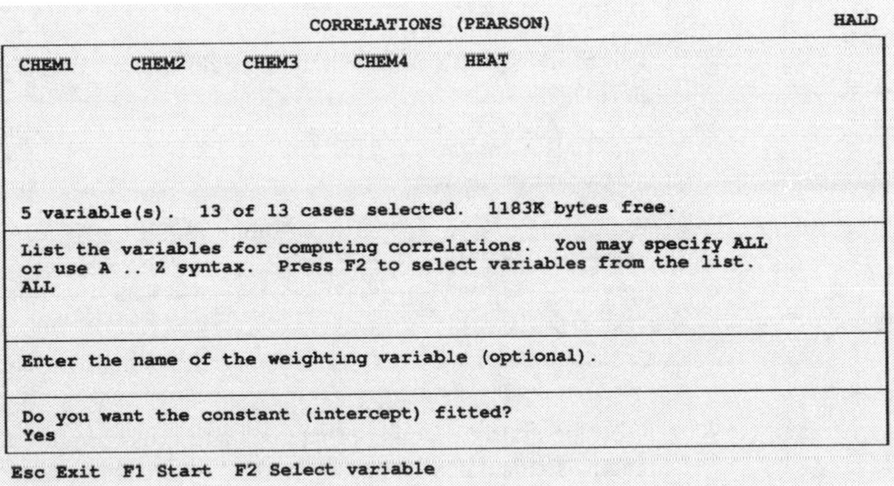


List the variables for which you want correlations computed. You can use A .. Z syntax to abbreviate the list, or simply enter ALL to specify all variables. If you want to use a weighting factor, enter the name of the variable containing the weights. You can specify a constant fitted model (YES) or a no constant (forced through the origin) model (NO).

## Data Restrictions

You can specify up to 40 variables. If a case in your data has missing values some variables, the entire case is deleted (listwise deletion). Negative weights are not allowed.

## Example

We'll use the Hald data from Draper and Smith (1981) for our example. The variable HEAT is the cumulative heat of hardening for cement after 180 days. The variables CHEM1, CHEM2, CHEM3, and CHEM4 are the percentages of four chemical compounds measured in batches of cement. The data are listed below.

| CASE | HEAT | CHEM1 | CHEM2 | CHEM3 | CHEM4 |
|---|---|---|---|---|---|
| 1 | 78.5 | 7 | 26 | 6 | 60 |
| 2 | 74.3 | 1 | 29 | 15 | 52 |
| 3 | 104.3 | 11 | 56 | 8 | 20 |
| 4 | 87.6 | 11 | 31 | 8 | 47 |
| 5 | 95.9 | 7 | 52 | 6 | 33 |
| 6 | 109.2 | 11 | 55 | 9 | 22 |
| 7 | 102.7 | 3 | 71 | 17 | 6 |
| 8 | 72.5 | 1 | 31 | 22 | 44 |
| 9 | 93.1 | 2 | 54 | 18 | 22 |
| 10 | 115.9 | 21 | 47 | 4 | 26 |
| 11 | 83.8 | 1 | 40 | 23 | 34 |
| 12 | 113.3 | 11 | 66 | 9 | 12 |
| 13 | 109.4 | 10 | 68 | 8 | 12 |

The model specification is displayed on the preceding page. The results are as follows:

CORRELATIONS (PEARSON)

| | CHEM1 | CHEM2 | CHEM3 | CHEM4 |
|---|---|---|---|---|
| CHEM2 | 0.2286 | | | |
| CHEM3 | -0.8241 | -0.1392 | | |
| CHEM4 | -0.2454 | -0.9730 | 0.0295 | |
| HEAT | 0.7307 | 0.8163 | -0.5347 | -0.8213 |

CASES INCLUDED 13    MISSING CASES 0

## Computational Notes

First, the matrix of sums of squares and cross products corrected for the means is calculated using the method of updating, also known as the method of provisional means. The results are more accurate than if the usual "computational equations" were used. If the no constant option is specified, the matrix corrected for the means is first computed and then "uncorrected".

# Partial Correlations

The **Partial Correlations** procedure computes the "residual" correlation between variables after adjustment for correlations with another set of variables. Partial correlations are often used in manual stepwise regression procedures to help you decide which variable should be included next in the regression.

## Specification

```
                          PARTIAL CORRELATION                          HALD
 CHEM1     CHEM2     CHEM3     CHEM4     HEAT

 5 variable(s).  13 of 13 cases selected.  1183K bytes free.
 Enter the name of the dependent variable.  Press F2 to select from list.
 HEAT
 List the independent variables to adjust for.  You may use A .. Z syntax.
 CHEM1 CHEM4
 List the variables for computing partial correlations. You may specify ALL.
 CHEM2 CHEM3
 Enter the name of the weighting variable (optional).

 Do you want the constant (intercept) fitted?
 Yes
Esc Exit   F1 Start   F2 Select variable
```

First enter the name of the dependent variable. Then list the independent variables for which you want the correlations adjusted. Then list the independent variables for which to compute partial correlations. If you want a weighting factor, enter the name of the variable containing the weights. You can specify a constant fitted model (YES) or a no constant (forced through the origin) model (NO). You can use A .. Z syntax to shorten either list, or you can also press F2 to select variables from the list displayed.

## Data Restrictions

The total number of independent variables can't exceed 40. Missing values or zero weights cause the entire case to be dropped. Negative weights aren't allowed.

## Example

We'll use the Hald data from Draper and Smith (1981) for our example. The variable HEAT is the cumulative heat of hardening for cement after 180 days. The variables CHEM1, CHEM2, CHEM3, and CHEM4 are the percentages of four chemical compounds measured in batches of cement. The data are listed below.

| CASE | HEAT | CHEM1 | CHEM2 | CHEM3 | CHEM4 |
|---|---|---|---|---|---|
| 1 | 78.5 | 7 | 26 | 6 | 60 |
| 2 | 74.3 | 1 | 29 | 15 | 52 |
| 3 | 104.3 | 11 | 56 | 8 | 20 |
| 4 | 87.6 | 11 | 31 | 8 | 47 |
| 5 | 95.9 | 7 | 52 | 6 | 33 |
| 6 | 109.2 | 11 | 55 | 9 | 22 |
| 7 | 102.7 | 3 | 71 | 17 | 6 |
| 8 | 72.5 | 1 | 31 | 22 | 44 |
| 9 | 93.1 | 2 | 54 | 18 | 22 |
| 10 | 115.9 | 21 | 47 | 4 | 26 |
| 11 | 83.8 | 1 | 40 | 23 | 34 |
| 12 | 113.3 | 11 | 66 | 9 | 12 |
| 13 | 109.4 | 10 | 68 | 8 | 12 |

The model specified in the options panel on the preceding page is used to compute the partial correlations for CHEM2 and CHEM3 on HEAT, adjusted for CHEM1 and CHEM4. The results are as follows:

```
PARTIAL CORRELATIONS WITH HEAT  Cumulative Heat of Hardening For Cement
CONTROLLED FOR CHEM1 CHEM4

CHEM2          0.5986
CHEM3         -0.5657

CASES INCLUDED 13    MISSING CASES 0
```

The partial correlation of CHEM2 with HEAT after the effects of CHEM1 and CHEM4 have been removed is 0.5986. The partial correlation of CHEM3 with HEAT, adjusted for CHEM1 and CHEM4, is -0.5657.

## Computational Notes

First the matrix of sums of squares and cross products corrected for the means is calculated by using the method of updating, also known as the method of provisional means. The results are more accurate than if the usual "computational equations" were used. If you specify the no constant option, the matrix corrected for the means is first computed and then "uncorrected". The matrix is ordered so that the "variables adjusted for" are on the left, and these variables are then "swept" over (Seber 1978) to produce the partial correlations.

# Variance-Covariance

The **Variance-Covariance** procedure computes the variances and covariances for a list of variables.

## Specification

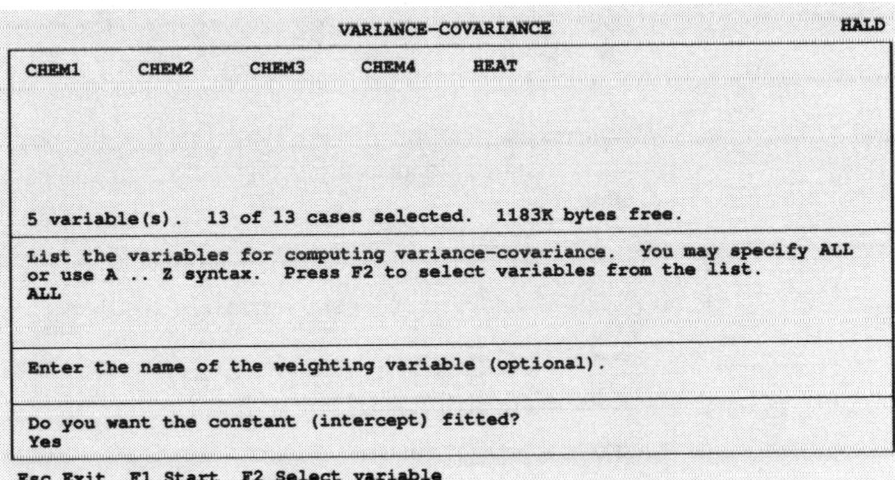
```
VARIANCE-COVARIANCE                                              HALD
CHEM1      CHEM2      CHEM3      CHEM4      HEAT

5 variable(s).  13 of 13 cases selected.  1183K bytes free.
List the variables for computing variance-covariance.  You may specify ALL
or use A .. Z syntax.  Press F2 to select variables from the list.
ALL
Enter the name of the weighting variable (optional).
Do you want the constant (intercept) fitted?
Yes
Esc Exit  F1 Start  F2 Select variable
```

List the variables for which you want variances and covariances computed. You can use A .. Z syntax to shorten the list, or simply enter ALL to specify all variables. Enter the name of a weighting variable for weighted variances-covariances. If you specify a no-constant model *Statistix* computes the sums of squares and cross products uncorrected for the means.

## Data Restrictions

Up to 40 variables can be specified. If a case in your data has missing values for any of the variables, the entire case is deleted (listwise deletion). Negative weights aren't permitted.

## Example

We'll use the Hald data from Draper and Smith (1981) for our example. The variable HEAT is the cumulative heat of hardening for cement after 180 days. The variables CHEM1, CHEM2, CHEM3, and CHEM4 are the percentages of four chemical compounds measured in batches of cement. The data are listed on the next page.

| CASE | HEAT | CHEM1 | CHEM2 | CHEM3 | CHEM4 |
|---|---|---|---|---|---|
| 1 | 78.5 | 7 | 26 | 6 | 60 |
| 2 | 74.3 | 1 | 29 | 15 | 52 |
| 3 | 104.3 | 11 | 56 | 8 | 20 |
| 4 | 87.6 | 11 | 31 | 8 | 47 |
| 5 | 95.9 | 7 | 52 | 6 | 33 |
| 6 | 109.2 | 11 | 55 | 9 | 22 |
| 7 | 102.7 | 3 | 71 | 17 | 6 |
| 8 | 72.5 | 1 | 31 | 22 | 44 |
| 9 | 93.1 | 2 | 54 | 18 | 22 |
| 10 | 115.9 | 21 | 47 | 4 | 26 |
| 11 | 83.8 | 1 | 40 | 23 | 34 |
| 12 | 113.3 | 11 | 66 | 9 | 12 |
| 13 | 109.4 | 10 | 68 | 8 | 12 |

The model is specified in the options panel on the preceding page. The variances and covariances are computed for all variables. The results are displayed below.

VARIANCE - COVARIANCE MATRIX

| | CHEM1 | CHEM2 | CHEM3 | CHEM4 | HEAT |
|---|---|---|---|---|---|
| CHEM1 | 34.6025 | | | | |
| CHEM2 | 20.9230 | 242.141 | | | |
| CHEM3 | -31.0512 | -13.8782 | 41.0256 | | |
| CHEM4 | -24.1666 | -253.416 | 3.16666 | 280.166 | |
| HEAT | 64.6634 | 191.079 | -51.5192 | -206.808 | 226.313 |

CASES INCLUDED 13 MISSING CASES 0

The values displayed on the diagonal of the matrix are the variances, the off-diagonal values are covariances.

## Computational Notes

The sums of squares and cross products matrix corrected for the means are calculated by using the method of updating, also known as the method of provisional means. The results are more accurate than if the usual "computational equations" were used. If the no constant option is specified, the matrix corrected for the means is first computed and then "uncorrected".

# Linear Regression

The **Linear Regression** procedure performs simple and multiple linear regression. Linear regression is a popular technique for examining linear relationships between a response (dependent) variable and one or more predictor (independent) variables. This procedure can perform both weighted and unweighted least squares fitting, and you can specify no-intercept models. Extensive analysis of variance and residual analysis options are available. You can also compute predicted values and prediction intervals. You can examine the sensitivity of the regression coefficients to measurement errors in the independent variables.

## Specification

```
                          LINEAR REGRESSION                                  HALD
 CHEM1     CHEM2     CHEM3     CHEM4     HEAT



 5 variable(s).  13 of 13 cases selected.  1183K bytes free.

 Enter the name of the dependent variable.  Press F2 to select from list.
 HEAT

 List the independent variables.  You may specify ALL or use A .. Z syntax.
 Press F2 to select variables from the list.
 CHEM1 CHEM2 CHEM3 CHEM4


 Enter the name of the weighting variable (optional).

 Do you want the constant (intercept) fitted?
 Yes
Esc Exit  F1 Start  F2 Select variable
```

To specify a regression model, first identify the dependent variable. Then list one or more independent variables. You can use A .. Z syntax to shorten the list or specify ALL to indicate all variables other than the dependent variable. For weighted regression, enter the name of the variable containing the weights. For a zero intercept model (no constant), enter NO at the fit constant prompt. You don't need to answer each prompt. You can make the necessary changes and then press F1 to begin computing the analysis.

## Data Restrictions

You can include up to 40 independent variables in the model. If any values within a case are missing for any of the variables in the model, the case is dropped (listwise deletion). If an independent variable is too highly correlated with a linear combination of other independent variables in the model (collinearity), it's dropped from the model. If you specify a weighting variable, cases with negative weights are treated as missing values and deleted.

## Example

We'll use the data from Hald (1952) for our example. Draper and Smith (1981) used the same data set to illustrate selecting the "best" regression equation. The variable HEAT is the cumulative heat of hardening for cement after 180 days. The variables CHEM1, CHEM2, CHEM3, and CHEM4 are the percentages of four chemical compounds measured in batches of cement. The goal is to relate the heat of hardening to the chemical composition. The data are listed below.

| CASE | HEAT | CHEM1 | CHEM2 | CHEM3 | CHEM4 |
|---|---|---|---|---|---|
| 1 | 78.5 | 7 | 26 | 6 | 60 |
| 2 | 74.3 | 1 | 29 | 15 | 52 |
| 3 | 104.3 | 11 | 56 | 8 | 20 |
| 4 | 87.6 | 11 | 31 | 8 | 47 |
| 5 | 95.9 | 7 | 52 | 6 | 33 |
| 6 | 109.2 | 11 | 55 | 9 | 22 |
| 7 | 102.7 | 3 | 71 | 17 | 6 |
| 8 | 72.5 | 1 | 31 | 22 | 44 |
| 9 | 93.1 | 2 | 54 | 18 | 22 |
| 10 | 115.9 | 21 | 47 | 4 | 26 |
| 11 | 83.8 | 1 | 40 | 23 | 34 |
| 12 | 113.3 | 11 | 66 | 9 | 12 |
| 13 | 109.4 | 10 | 68 | 8 | 12 |

The full model is specified in the options panel on the preceding page. The results are listed below.

```
UNWEIGHTED LEAST SQUARES LINEAR REGRESSION OF HEAT

PREDICTOR
VARIABLES     COEFFICIENT     STD ERROR     STUDENT'S T          P        VIF
---------     -----------     ---------     -----------     ------     -----
CONSTANT          62.4053       70.0709            0.89     0.3991
CHEM1             1.55110       0.74477            2.08     0.0708      38.5
CHEM2             0.51016       0.72378            0.70     0.5009     254.4
CHEM3             0.10190       0.75470            0.14     0.8959      46.9
CHEM4            -0.14406       0.70905           -0.20     0.8441     282.5

R SQUARED              0.9824     RESID. MEAN SQUARE (MSE)      5.98295
ADJUSTED R SQUARED     0.9736     STANDARD DEVIATION            2.44600

SOURCE          DF          SS              MS           F          P
----------     ---     ----------     ----------     ------     ------
REGRESSION       4        2667.89        666.974     111.48     0.0000
RESIDUAL         8        47.8636        5.98295
TOTAL           12        2715.76

CASES INCLUDED 13    MISSING CASES 0
```

The regression coefficient table gives the regression coefficients (slopes) associated with the independent variables and their standard errors, t-statistics, associated p-values, and variance inflation factors (VIF). You use p-values to test whether the slopes are significantly different from zero if all other variables are already in the model.

Large VIF's in a multiple regression indicate that collinearity is a problem. The VIF represents the increase in variance of a coefficient due to correlation between the independent variables. Values of 7.0 or 10.0 have been suggested for the cutoff of what constitutes a "high" value.

*Statistix* provides several other summary statistics and an analysis of variance table for the regression, including the F test and associated p-value for the significance of the overall model. In our example, the overall F is 111.48, with a p-value of 0.0000. This indicates that at least some of the independent variables are important in explaining the observed variation in HEAT.

From the coefficient column, the regression equation is found to be:

```
HEAT = 62.4 + 1.55 * CHEM1 + 0.510 * CHEM2 + 0.102 * CHEM3 -
       0.144 * CHEM4
```

However, the t tests suggest that some of the coefficients are not significantly different from zero. The high VIF's warn us that collinearity among the independent variables is a problem. Selecting the best model is discussed one page 160.

## Regression Results Menu

After you've viewed the coefficient table, press Esc to display the regression results menu shown below.

```
REGRESSION RESULTS

Coefficient table
Durbin-Watson statistic
Interval coverage
Prediction
Plots
Save residuals
Sensitivity
Stepwise AOV table
Var-covar of betas
Options panel
```

Select "Coefficient table" from the menu to redisplay the regression coefficient table. Select "Options panel" to return to the main options panel used to specify the model. The remaining options are described on the following pages.

## Durbin-Watson Test

This option computes the Durbin-Watson test for autocorrelation for a particular regression model. In the example below, the regression model was specified as HEAT = CHEM2 CHEM3. The results are as follows:

```
DURBIN-WATSON TEST FOR AUTOCORRELATION

DURBIN-WATSON STATISTIC  1.7498

P VALUES, USING DURBIN-WATSON'S BETA APPROXIMATION:
  P (POSITIVE CORR) = 0.2846,  P (NEGATIVE CORR) = 0.7154

EXPECTED VALUE OF DURBIN-WATSON STATISTIC      2.0359
EXACT VARIANCE OF DURBIN-WATSON STATISTIC     0.23450

CASES INCLUDED 13      MISSING CASES 0
```

The Durbin-Watson statistic and approximate observed significance levels (p-values) are displayed. Use the Durbin-Watson statistic to test whether the random errors about the regression line exhibit autocorrelation. In our example, there is little suggestion of either positive (p=0.2846) or negative (p=0.7154) autocorrelation.

Most tests in regression are based on the assumption that the random errors are independent. Violation of this assumption due to autocorrelation can invalidate the results of these tests. Another reason to check for autocorrelation is because it may suggest that you need additional independent variables in the model.

Autocorrelation can occur when the data have some natural sequence, i.e., the observations are ordered in time or space. You should always consider the possibility of autocorrelation in trend data, such as price or population levels over time. Positive autocorrelation results when large positive errors tend to be followed by large positive errors and large negative errors tend to be followed by large negative errors. Negative autocorrelation is less common and results when large errors tend to be followed by large errors with the opposite sign. Chatterjee and Price (1977) give more detail and some examples of the application of the Durbin-Watson test.

If there is neither positive nor negative autocorrelation, the Durbin-Watson statistic will be close to 2. A value close to 0 suggests positive autocorrelation, and a value close to 4 suggests negative autocorrelation. The observed significance levels (p-values) are calculated with the beta distribution approximation suggested by Durbin and Watson (1970). Their results indicated that this approximation usually works well even for relatively small sample sizes. (*Statistix* will not compute the test for samples with fewer than ten cases). The procedures to calculate the significance level, the expected value, and the variance are described in Durbin and Watson (1951). The beta approximation can't be used when the variance of the Durbin-Watson statistic is large, in which case, the p-values are not computed.

The **Runs Test** and **Wilk-Shapiro/Rankit Plot** procedures are also useful for examining whether the test assumptions in regression have been violated.

## Interval Coverage

By default, confidence and prediction intervals are calculated at the 95% level. The interval coverage procedure allows you to change the value.

```
                        INTERVAL COVERAGE                                HALD
 The "Prediction" and "Save residuals" options allow for computing confidence
 intervals for predicted values.  Use this procedure to change the percent
 coverage for confidence intervals.  Enter a value in the range 50.0 to 99.9.
 95.0
Esc Results menu  F1 Start
```

## Prediction

This option computes the predicted or fitted value of the dependent variable in a regression for values of the independent variable(s) you specify. The values for the independent variables can be indicated in two ways. One is simply to enter the list of desired values. The other is to enter a case number that contains the desired values for the independent variables.

```
                PREDICTION/FITTING OF DEPENDENT VARIABLE                 HALD
 Independent variables in your model:
 CHEM1     CHEM3

 You can request predicted or fitted values using two methods.  Select the
 CASE method if you want to compute a predicted value for a particular case
 in your data set.  Select the VALUE method if you want to enter a list of
 values, one number for each independent variable.  Enter C or V.
 Value method

 List 2 number(s), one for each independent variable in the order the
 variables are listed above.
 8 80

 Enter a weight value (optional).
 1.000
Esc Exit  F1 Start
```

The "Value method" is illustrated in the panel on the preceding page. The values 8 and 80 are entered for the variables CHEM1 and CHEM3. The default value of 1.0 is used for the weight, so the resulting prediction intervals are for a single future observation. If you specify a weight w, the prediction interval is for the mean of w future observations. The results are displayed below.

```
PREDICTED/FITTED VALUES OF HEAT

LOWER PREDICTED BOUND      -6.9581     LOWER FITTED BOUND      -4.7224
PREDICTED VALUE             130.40     FITTED VALUE             130.40
UPPER PREDICTED BOUND       267.77     UPPER FITTED BOUND       265.53
SE (PREDICTED VALUE)        61.649     SE (FITTED VALUE)        60.646

UNUSUALNESS (LEVERAGE)     29.9737
PERCENT COVERAGE              95.0
CORRESPONDING T               2.23

PREDICTOR VALUES: CHEM1 = 8.0000, CHEM3 = 80.000
```

The predicted value is 130.40 with a standard error of 61.649. The 95% prediction interval is -6.9581 to 267.77. This interval is expected to contain the value of a future single observation of the dependent variable HEAT 95% of the time, given that HEAT is observed at the independent variable values CHEM1 = 8, CHEM3 = 80.

The unusualness value tells you how "close" the specified independent data point is to the rest of the data. If the point isn't close to the rest of the data, then you're extrapolating beyond your data—and prediction abilities may be very poor. An unusualness value greater than 1.0 should be considered large, so the prediction results in the example above are clearly suspect.

We illustrate the "case method" for specifying values for the independent variables below.

```
PREDICTION/FITTING OF DEPENDENT VARIABLE                              HALD

Independent variables in your model:
CHEM1     CHEM3

You can request predicted or fitted values using two methods.  Select the
CASE method if you want to compute a predicted value for a particular case
in your data set.  Select the VALUE method if you want to enter a list of
values, one number for each independent variable.  Enter C or V.
Case method

Enter a case number (1-13).
7

Esc Exit   F1 Start
```

We've asked for predicted values for case number 7. The results are:

```
PREDICTED/FITTED VALUES OF HEAT

LOWER PREDICTED BOUND     61.404     LOWER FITTED BOUND     78.644
PREDICTED VALUE           87.692     FITTED VALUE           87.692
UPPER PREDICTED BOUND     113.98     UPPER FITTED BOUND     96.740
SE (PREDICTED VALUE)      11.798     SE (FITTED VALUE)      4.0609

UNUSUALNESS (LEVERAGE)    0.1344
PERCENT COVERAGE            95.0
CORRESPONDING T             2.23

CASE NUMBER 7 WAS USED TO ESTIMATE THE REGRESSION
PREDICTOR VALUES: CHEM1 = 3.0000, CHEM3 = 17.000
```

Unlike most other procedures, the prediction option lets you compute statistics for omitted cases. So you can divide the data into two subsets by omitting some cases. The regression model will be fitted using the selected cases, and you can use this procedure to see how well the model fits cases that were not used to fit the model. Points used to fit the regression shouldn't be used to validate the regression model because least squares strives to optimize the goodness-of-fit at these points, so these points give an optimistic impression of the regression's performance.

For weighted regression models, the value for the weight variable at the case specified will be used as the weight in the prediction interval calculations. A weight w causes the prediction interval to be computed for a mean of w future observations.

## Plots

*Statistix* offers four regression plots directly from the regression results menus. You can also save fitted values and residuals (page 150) and use the **Scatter Plot** procedure described in Chapter 4 to graph additional residual plots.

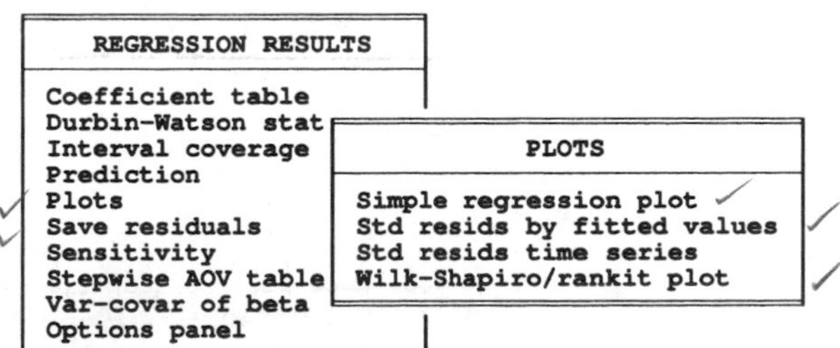


The "Simple regression" plot is only available when there is one independent variable in the model. You can see an example of this below. The observed values are displayed. The straight line in the center represents the fitted line. The inside curved lines mark the 95% confidence interval for the fitted line, the outside curves mark the 95% predicted interval.

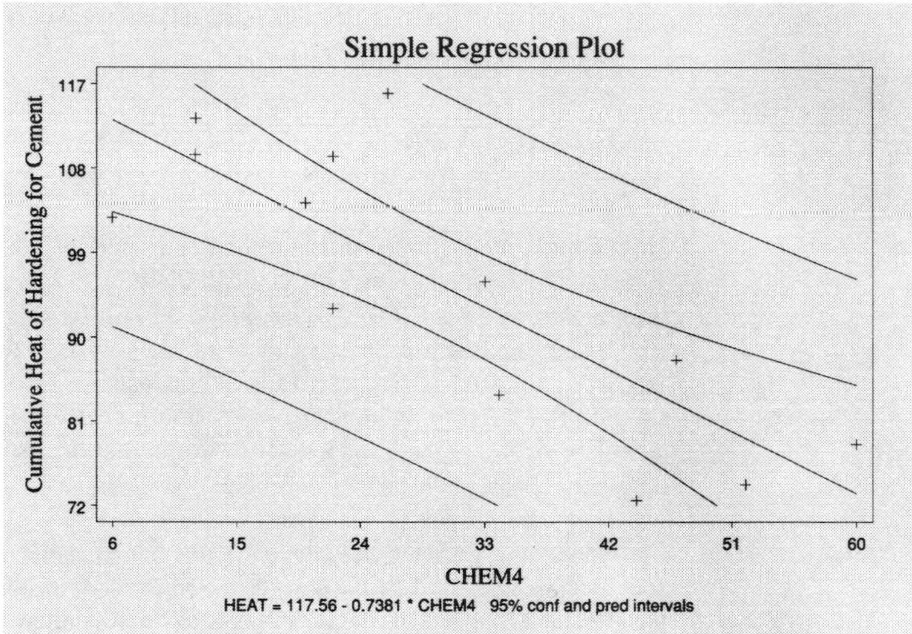


The "Std resids by fitted values" plot is a scatter plot with the standardized residuals on the Y axis and the fitted values on the X axis. You use this plot to check the assumption of constant variances.

The "Std resids time series" plot is a scatter plot with case numbers on the X axis. You'll find this plot useful when the data are sequentially ordered.

The "Wilk-Shapiro/rankit plot" is used to create a rankit plot of the standardized residuals to test the assumption of normality. The Wilk-Shapiro statistic for normality is also given (see the **Wilk-Shapiro/Rankit Plot** procedure in Chapter 8).

## Save Residuals

*Statistix* can do extensive residual analysis, which is very important for model evaluation. Systematic patterns in the residuals can suggest transformations or additional variables that would improve the model. Residuals are important for "outlier" analysis and to identify unusual observations. You can also use residuals to find those observations that are most influential in determining the values of the regression coefficient estimates. Space doesn't permit a detailed discussion here; if you're interested, consult Weisberg (1985).

```
                         SAVE RESIDUALS                                HALD
 CHEM1     CHEM2     CHEM3     CHEM4     HEAT



 5 variable(s).  13 of 13 cases selected.  1183K bytes free.

                    Residual Name            Variable

                    Fitted value             FIT
                    Residual
                    Leverage
                    Standardized residual    STDRESID
                    Distance
                    P (Distance)
                    Outlier
                    P (Outlier)
                    95.0% Pred. interval
                    95.0% Conf. interval
 Esc Results menu  F1 Start  F2 Select variable
```

Use the up and down arrow keys to move the cursor to the residual name you're interested in. Then type the name of a new or existing variable. Press F2 and select a variable from the list displayed at the top of the screen. When you've finished entering variable names, press F1 to start the computations. The results are not displayed. The residuals are stored as variables and can be examined using such procedures as Scatter Plot, Wilk-Shapiro/Rankit Plots, View Data, and Runs Test. Each of the residual options is described in more detail below.

The **Fitted value** option saves the fitted (predicted) values for the dependent variable in a new variable. You can plot these values against the dependent variable to see how well the model fits the observed values.

The **Residual** option saves the raw residuals. You use these to examine how well the model fits the data. Systematic trends indicate that data transformations may be needed or that important independent variables were not included in the model. Large residuals may indicate observations that are "outliers". The raw residual is computed as the observed value of dependent variable minus the fitted value.

The **Leverage** option saves the leverage values in a new variable. Leverage measures how influential a point is in determining the regression coefficients. Depending on the values of the independent variables, some data points are much more influential in determining the values of the regression coefficients than others. In general, the further the values of the independent variables are from their averages, the more influential these data points are in determining the regression coefficients. Points with "unusual" independent variable values have high leverage. If you're familiar with the matrix representation of multiple regression, leverage is calculated as the diagonal elements of the $X(X^TX)^{-1}X$ matrix (assuming no weights were used).

The **Standardized residual** option saves the standardized residuals in a new variable. Raw residuals are very popular for examining model fit, although they do possess at least one potential problem. Data points located at "unusual" values of the independent variables will have high leverage, which means that they tend to "attract" the regression line and seldom have large residuals. Standardized residuals adjust for this problem to some extent by standardizing each raw residual with its standard error (also known as "studentizing"). The standard error of a residual is computed as the square root of the quantity MSE*(1 - LEVERAGE), where MSE is the residual mean square for error.

The **Distance** option computes Cook's distance measure (Cook 1977, Weisberg 1985) and saves it in a new variable. It's very useful for finding influential data points, and it considers the effects of both the dependent and independent variables (LEVERAGE considers the independent variables only). Cook's distance for an observation can be thought of as a measure of how far the regression coefficients would shift if that data point was eliminated from the data set. Remember that it's a distance measure and not a test statistic. Usually, Cook's distance by itself isn't very useful because it is a function of sample size and the number of variables in the regression model. The next option, P (Distance), which "standardizes" Cook's D, is generally more useful.

**P (Distance)** calculates the "pseudo-significance level" of the confidence bound associated with the Cook's distance and saves it in a new variable. You can think of Cook's distance for an observation as a measure of how far the regression coefficients would shift if that data point were eliminated from the data set. It seems reasonable to standardize this distance by examining what level confidence bound the shifted regression coefficients would fall on. For example, if eliminating the i-th data point causes the new coefficients to shift to a position that corresponds to the edge of a 90% confidence region around the original estimates, this may be cause for concern. Again, Cook's distance isn't a test statistic but rather a distance measure, and you shouldn't think of P (Distance) as an observed significance level (hence the term "pseudo-significance") but as a standardized distance. **Note:** P (Distance) involves a good deal of computing, so it often takes a while to finish.

The **Outlier** option computes the t-statistic for the outlier test and saves it in a new variable. You may suspect an observed value of the dependent data that deviates substantially from the predicted value of being an outlier. This is usually tested with a t-statistic, which is the result of this option. The computations follow Cook (1977).

**P (Outlier)** computes the p-value for the t-statistics resulting from the outlier test and saves it in a new variable. The computed p-value is appropriate for *a priori* tests for a single outlier. In other words, it's the appropriate observed significance level if you were interested in testing one particular case that is suspected of being an outlier before the data was observed. This is a rather unusual circumstance; more often, you notice potential outliers only after inspection of the residuals.

If you suspect a case of being an outlier after inspecting the data, you must give it special consideration. Suppose there were n cases. You now need to decide whether the value of the observed t-statistic is "unusual" given that it's the "most unusual" out of n repeated t tests. If the *a priori* p-values are used, then too many cases will be detected as "outliers", so you need to somehow "inflate" the *a priori* p-values. This inflation can be easily performed with Bonferroni's inequality (Weisberg 1985).

For example, suppose there were n cases inspected for outliers. Then, Bonferroni's equality says that the actual observed significance level will bc no greater than nP, where P is the p-value returned by P (Outlier). In practice, the observed significance level may be substantially less than nP; Bonferroni's procedure has an undesirable property of becoming too conservative as n increases.

As noted earlier, you can compute Outlier and P (Outlier) for cases that were omitted and not used in the regression. Suppose m cases are used in the regression and m' are omitted. If you're interested in inspecting all m + m' cases for outliers, then you should use n = m + m'. If you're interested in just the omitted cases, then n = m'. The choice of n is your responsibility; *Statistix* always gives you the *a priori* p-value.

The **Prediction interval** option computes the half-width confidence interval for predicted values. If the original regression model didn't include a weighting variable, the results that are saved are the half-widths of the prediction intervals for **single** future observations. Otherwise, the results are the half-widths of prediction intervals for means of w future observations, were w is the value of the weight variable. Use the **Interval coverage** procedure discussed on page 147 to change the coverage level.

Suppose you save the prediction intervals in a variable called PI95, and the fitted values are saved in a variable called YHAT. Using **Transformations**, you can construct upper and lower prediction bounds as:

```
LOWER = YHAT - PI95
UPPER = YHAT + PI95
```

The **Confidence interval** computes the half-width confidence interval for fitted values.

## Treatment of Omitted Cases and Missing Y Values

*Statistix* returns values for certain residual menu options for cases that aren't used for estimation. Values are computed for predicted value, residual, leverage, outlier, and P (outlier) for omitted cases. A case that is not omitted may still not have been used for estimation if some of the values for that case are missing. If the only missing value for a case is the dependent variable, you can obtain values for predicted value and leverage.

These statistics derived from cases not used for estimation are especially useful for model validation. For omitted cases, predicted values are just what their name implies. For omitted cases, the residual option returns predicted residuals. Predicted residuals are, as you'd expect, the difference between the observed dependent variable value and predicted value (eq. 2.2.22 of Cook and Weisberg 1982). For cases that aren't used in the regression, leverage is somewhat unfortunate terminology. "Unusualness" or "generalized distance" would be a better term. For cases not used for estimation, this statistic measures how unusual the independent variable values of a case are relative to the values for cases used for estimation (see Weisberg 1985).

The interpretation of outlier is interesting and important. For cases used for estimation, outlier returns the t-statistic for the null hypothesis that the particular case conforms to the model fitted to the rest of the cases. An intuitive approach to constructing such a test is to first perform the regression without the particular case. From this regression, you can compute the predicted residual for the particular case, say e. It's fairly easy to see that the standard error of e is simply the standard error of prediction, and the resulting statistic e/SE(e) should follow a t-distribution under the null hypothesis that E[e] = 0. This leads to an alternative interpretation of outlier as a predicted Studentized residual. Since the standard error used for Studentizing was derived from a data set that didn't include the particular point of interest, Cook and Weisberg (1982) refer to this as *external* Studentizing. Note that for the m cases used for estimation, the corresponding outlier values are computed from the m different data sets that did not include the case of interest. (The usual standardized residual is *internally* Studentized, which means the set of cases used to derive the standard error included the case for the residual.)

If there were m cases used in the original regression, it would appear that m separate regressions are needed to compute outlier just for the points used for estimation. However, as Cook and Weisberg (1982) show, there are some remarkable identities that permit the calculation of these statistics from quantities obtained from only the one regression using the m points. If the regression contains p parameters, the outlier statistic for a case used for estimation has m - p - 1 degrees of freedom associated with it.

This now suggests how to handle cases not included in the regression. As before, the statistic is e/SE(e), where e is the predicted residual and SE(e) is the standard error for prediction. (The calculation of the standard error of prediction is described under Computational Notes.) For all cases not in the set of m cases used for estimation, outlier uses the same regression based on the m cases for the base comparison. (This is in contrast to the situation for Outlier for cases that were used in estimation; each such Outlier uses a different data set of m - 1 cases for base comparison.) This gains an extra case for computing the comparison regression for cases not used for estimation, so the Outlier statistic for a case not used for estimation has m - p degrees of freedom associated with it.

For cases not used for estimation, the usual standardized (internally Studentized) residuals can't be computed by definition. However, when you interpret them as predicted Studentized residuals, you can use outlier statistics for most of the purposes for which you'd want standardized residuals.

## Sensitivity

Linear regression requires the assumption that the independent variables are measured without error. The **Sensitivity** procedure determines how sensitive the estimated regression coefficients are to violations of this assumption.

The user needs to specify the expected size of the errors associated with each of the independent variables, which can be done in one of two ways.

```
                    COEFFICIENT SENSITIVITY                              HALD
 Independent variables in your model:
 CHEM1     CHEM2     CHEM3     CHEM4

 This procedure determines how sensitive the estimated regression
 coefficients are to measurement errors in the independent variables.
 There are two methods of specifying the errors:  You can enter the ERRORS
 (standard deviations) directly or specify the ROUNDING error digits.
 Enter <E> or <R>.
 Rounding

 List 4 number(s) representing the digit where you believe rounding error
 occurs.  For example, enter a 2 for 12x4.5, enter a -1 for 123.x5.
 List one number for each independent variable in the order listed above.
 1 1 1 1

Esc Results menu  F1 Start
```

If you know the standard deviations of the errors, you can enter them directly using the ERRORS method. For example, if the values for an independent variable are the readings from some instrument, the standard error of the measures may be known from calibration results. However, precise information about the errors often won't be available. Sometimes the best you can do is to say, "I trust the figures down to—but not including—the d-th digit, which may be off by plus or minus 1". Often d will point to the digit at which rounding error occurred. In this case, you specify the position of the left-most untrustworthy digit relative to the decimal point. For example, d = 2 for 9340.0 means you think the 4 may be in error. A way to model this is to assume that an additive random error is associated with 9340.0 and is uniformly distributed on the interval -5 to 5, which is exactly what *Statistix* does when treating ROUNDING error sensitivity. Negative values of d are used to indicate digits right of the decimal, for example, d = -4 points to the 8 in 0.03480. Values for d must be in the set of <u>nonzero</u> integers from 21 to -20.

We'll use the Hald data again to illustrate the procedure. Assume the regression was Y = CHEM1 CHEM2 CHEM3 CHEM4. Assume the figures are probably accurate except perhaps for rounding error in the least significant digit. *Statistix* assumes that this rounding error is uniformly distributed in the interval -0.5 to 0.5. The options are specified in the panel above. The results are presented in the table on the next page.

| COEFFICIENTS' SENSITIVITIES TO ERRORS IN INDEPENDENT VARIABLES | | | | |
|---|---|---|---|---|
| | VARIABLE IN WHICH ERROR OCCURS | | | |
| | CHEM1 | CHEM2 | CHEM3 | CHEM4 |
| ERROR SD | 0.288 | 0.288 | 0.288 | 0.288 |
| CONSTANT | 0.469 | 0.554 | 0.558 | 0.575 |
| CHEM1 | 0.829 | 0.942 | 0.922 | 0.962 |
| CHEM2 | 0.372 | 0.451 | 0.462 | 0.473 |
| CHEM3 | -0.355 | -0.250 | -0.271 | -0.229 |
| CHEM4 | -0.169 | -8.75E-02 | -7.89E-02 | -6.74E-02 |

What is the interpretation of these results? When the independent variables represent continuous quantities, they'll always have some error associated with them. The question is whether the errors are large enough to seriously influence the results.

Suppose the independent variables were "perturbed" with errors of the specified size and the regression analysis rerun. We'd be happy if the slope estimates after perturbation were similar to those from before. The sensitivity coefficients indicate just how similar the new coefficients after perturbation are expected to be to the previous ones. More specifically, sensitivity coefficients give an index of how many significant figures will agree with the coefficients. For example, the estimates 0.89768 and 0.89735 agree to 3 figures, and this degree of agreement is expected when the sensitivity coefficient is near 3. Small sensitivity coefficients are undesirable. Of course "small" is subjective, but if the values are near or less than 1, such as in the example, the analysis clearly is very sensitive to errors in the independent variables and the regression coefficients can't be trusted.

It is interesting to compare these sensitivities with those for the model Y = CHEM1 CHEM4:

| COEFFICIENTS' SENSITIVITIES TO ERRORS IN INDEPENDENT VARIABLES | | |
|---|---|---|
| | VARIABLE IN WHICH ERROR OCCURS | |
| | CHEM1 | CHEM4 |
| ERROR SD | 0.288 | 0.288 |
| CONSTANT | 2.495 | 2.865 |
| CHEM1 | 1.816 | 2.204 |
| CHEM4 | 1.918 | 2.276 |

The sensitivity coefficients have increased considerably, which means the slope coefficients are now substantially less sensitive to the errors. This makes an interesting and very important point about this data set. CHEM1, CHEM2, CHEM3, and CHEM4 are nearly collinear; for all cases, the sums of these variables are between 95 to 98. When the data are nearly collinear, the slope coefficients become very sensitive to minor changes in the independent variables. Many an hour has been wasted by researchers trying to divine the interpretation of slope coefficients that were artifacts of the interaction of near-collinearity and errors in measurement. Reducing the degree of correlation in the set of independent variables has substantially reduced the sensitivities to the influence of roundoff errors.

If you're not certain how trustworthy your independent variables are, try some "worst-case scenarios". In other words, use large potential errors.

The sensitivity calculations are described in Weisberg (1982, 1985). We display the negative log (base ten) of the relative sensitivity coefficient, which in Weisberg's notation is $-\log_{10}(g_{jk})$. When you specify a placeholder d, the standard deviation of the error is calculated by assuming the error is a uniform random variable on the interval centered at 0 of width $10^{(n - sgn(n))}$ (sgn(n)=1 if n>0, sgn(n)=0 if n<0). The standard deviation is then $10^{(n-sgn(n))}/12^{1/2}$. If the absolute value of an estimated coefficient is too small (<1.0E-06) for reliable calculations, an M is displayed.

## Stepwise AOV Table

This option produces a stepwise analysis of variance table for the specified regression model. The row order of the stepwise table reflects the order in which the independent variables are specified in the model. For the Hald example, the results are presented in the table below.

STEPWISE ANALYSIS OF VARIANCE OF HEAT

| SOURCE | INDIVIDUAL SS | CUM DF | CUMULATIVE SS | CUMULATIVE MS | ADJUSTED R-SQUARED | MALLOWS' CP | P |
|---|---|---|---|---|---|---|---|
| CONSTANT | 1.184E+05 | | | | | | |
| CHEM1 | 1450.07 | 1 | 1450.07 | 1450.07 | 0.4916 | 202.5 | 2 |
| CHEM2 | 1207.78 | 2 | 2657.85 | 1328.92 | 0.9744 | 2.7 | 3 |
| CHEM3 | 9.79386 | 3 | 2667.65 | 889.217 | 0.9764 | 3.0 | 4 |
| CHEM4 | 0.24697 | 4 | 2667.89 | 666.974 | 0.9736 | 5.0 | 5 |
| RESIDUAL | 47.8636 | 12 | 2715.76 | 226.313 | | | |

| | | | |
|---|---|---|---|
| R-SQUARED | 0.9824 | RESID. MEAN SQUARE (MSE) | 5.98295 |
| ADJUSTED R-SQUARED | 0.9736 | STANDARD DEVIATION | 2.44600 |

The table lists the individual contribution to the sums of squares, the cumulative mean squares, F test for the subset model versus the full model, and associated p-values, cumulative adjusted R-squared, and Mallows' $C_p$ statistic (see Miscellaneous Regression on the next page).

This table is useful for testing the contribution of subsets of the independent variables to the overall model. For example, you are interested in testing whether CHEM3 and CHEM4 add anything to the model once CHEM1 and CHEM2 are already included. We first find the difference between the cumulative sums of squares for the model with all independent variables in it and one with just CHEM1 and CHEM2: 2667.89 - 2657.85 = 10.04. Because we're testing the contribution of two parameters, this sum of squares has two degrees of freedom associated with it and the resulting F test is F = (10.04/2)/5.983 = 0.839 (5.983 is the residual mean square of the full model). An F statistic this small suggests that CHEM3 and CHEM4 contribute little to the model once CHEM1 and CHEM2 are already included. However, this test says little about whether the model with just CHEM1 and CHEM2 is a "good" model.

## Variance-Covariance of Betas

Select this option to obtain the variance-covariance matrix of the regression coefficient estimates. Once you've selected this option, the matrix is displayed.

**VARIANCE-COVARIANCE MATRIX FOR COEFFICIENTS**

| | CONSTANT | CHEM1 | CHEM4 |
|---|---|---|---|
| CONSTANT | 4.51130 | | |
| CHEM1 | -0.19253 | 0.01915 | |
| CHEM4 | -0.08332 | 0.00165 | 0.00236 |

The diagonal elements of the matrix are the variances of the regression coefficients. The off-diagonal values are the covariances; for example, 0.00165 is the covariance of the coefficient estimates of CHEM1 and CHEM4.

This matrix is most commonly used for constructing confidence regions about coefficient estimates, and for testing hypotheses about various functions of the coefficient estimates. More detail on these topics can be found in Weisberg (1985).

## Miscellaneous Regression Topics

Mallows' $C_p$ statistic, $R^2$, and adjusted $R^2$ are important criteria for evaluating and comparing regression models.

The **Mallows' $C_p$** statistic is useful for model selection. It's discussed in detail by Daniel and Wood (1971), Snedecor and Cochran (1980, p. 359) and Weisberg (1985). The $C_p$ statistic is based on the fact that not including an important independent variable in the model results in the fitted response values being biased. $C_p$ gives an index of this bias. "Good" models have $C_p$ values near to or less than p, where p is the number of parameters in the model. (Negative values will occasionally be observed.) This statistic is most useful for eliminating variables that contribute little to the model. However, it tells you nothing about whether you started with all of the correct independent variables in the first place.

The **$R^2$** and **adjusted $R^2$** statistics measure the goodness of fit of a regression model. $R^2$ measures the proportion of variance in the dependent data explained by the regression. It's computed as 1 - RSS/SST, where RSS is the residual sum of squares and SST is the total sum of squares. A potential problem with $R^2$ is that it always increases as new independent variables are included in the model (RSS always decreases), even if they don't possess any relationship with the dependent variable. Adjusted $R^2$ is adjusted for the number of independent variables in the model to correct for this problem, and, therefore, will often be more interesting than the unadjusted $R^2$. Adjusted $R^2$ is computed as 1 - (n - 1)RMS/SST, where RMS is the residual mean square and n is the number of cases in the regression. Clearly, adjusted $R^2$ is a monotonic function of RMS. Unlike the unadjusted $R^2$, negative adjusted $R^2$'s will occasionally be observed. Chatterjee and Price (1977), Draper and Smith (1981), and Weisberg (1985) are good references for more detail on these statistics.

$R^2$ and adjusted $R^2$ are useful for comparing models, but you must use them with caution when comparing a no-constant term model to a model having a constant term. The reason is that the total sum of squares for the no-constant model is not adjusted for the mean, which inflates it relative to the constant-term model. The result is that $R^2$ and adjusted $R^2$ are usually larger for the no-constant model. This problem is discussed by Gordon (1981).

### Best Model Selection

When there are a moderate number of independent variables, **Best Subsets Regressions** is a good way to select the best model. However, the number of subsets grows rapidly as the number of independent variables increases. If there are too many independent variables, use the **Stepwise Regression** procedure. Draper and Smith (1981) present a good description of popular stepwise procedures. The potential problem with stepwise procedures is they do not necessarily result in a model that's best when judged by adjusted $R^2$ or Mallows' $C_p$. It's generally a good idea to try at least two stepwise procedures, such as backward elimination and forward inclusion, to see if they result in the same model.

Model selection is somewhat of a craft. Regression analysis is usually performed (1) to explore possible cause-effect relations, (2) to develop some predictive relationship, or (3) some combination of these. The relative importance of each of these goals may have some bearing on the model selection strategy used. Cause-effect modeling focuses on determining the "important" independent variables. Predictive modeling focuses more on the development of a good predictor of the dependent variable than on the contribution due to any particular independent variable. Obviously, the distinction between cause-effect analysis and predictive modeling isn't a sharp one and most analyses include components of both. (As an aside, you should realize that regression analysis can't actually establish cause-effect relationships. It can examine the nature and extent of association between the dependent and potential independent variables. The interpretation of these associations as cause-effect is outside the realm of statistics, and lies in the domain of the appropriate subject-matter field.)

In addition to F tests, there are several other popular statistics for evaluating the "goodness" of a regression model. Some of these are adjusted $R^2$, Mallows' $C_p$ statistic, $R^2$ , RSS (residual sum of squares) and RMS (residual mean square). Actually, $R^2$ and RSS are equivalent in the sense that they will produce the same orderings of the models. Adjusted $R^2$ and RMS are equivalent to one another in the same sense. It's generally best to use the adjusted $R^2$ (or RMS) and Mallows' $C_p$ for model selection. $R^2$ is useful for comparing models with the same number of independent variables in them, but the adjusted $R^2$ will produce the same ordering of the models. The advantages of adjusted $R^2$ over the unadjusted $R^2$ are discussed in the previous section. There are lots of good references on the use of adjusted $R^2$ and Mallows' $C_p$ in model selection, such as Weisberg (1985), Chatterjee and Price (1977), Daniel and Wood (1971), and Snedecor and Cochran (1980, p. 358).

The job isn't over when you've found the best model, as indicated by the adjusted $R^2$ or $C_p$ statistic. Particularly in the case of cause-effect modeling, it will be of interest to examine whether all of the independent variables are significant (use the p-values from the coefficient table). No analysis is complete without an examination of the residuals. As a minimum, do the standardized residuals show any trend when plotted against the dependent variable? If they do, the model is not adequate.

The **Wilk-Shapiro/Rankit Plot** procedure is valuable for examining whether the assumption of normally distributed errors has been violated. If the errors are not normally distributed, the significance tests may be invalid. It's also a good idea to look at the correlations among the independent variables. High correlations may suggest problems with collinearity. If this is the case, the **Eigenvalues-Principal Components** procedure may be useful.

## Computational Notes

The core computations are performed using Gentleman's square root free modification of Givens' method (Seber 1978). This is one of the most accurate methods available. An interesting feature of the method is that it exploits sparseness (zeros) in the independent variables to reduce computation time. It's therefore well suited for performing analyses of (co)variance that involve dummy variables.

The error variance is estimated as $\sigma^{*2}$ = RMS, where RMS is the residual mean square from the regression. Let X be the design matrix containing all the cases used to find the coefficient estimates B*. The estimated variance of B* is $V(B^*) = \sigma^{*2} (X^T U X)^{-1}$, where U is the weight matrix if weights were used, and U = I otherwise. Suppose $x^T$ is a specific row of X, a case used for estimation. The fitted value f corresponding to case x is $f = x^T B^*$. The estimated variance of a fitted value is then $V(f) = \sigma^{*2} x^T (X^T U X)^{-1} x$.

Now assume x wasn't used for estimation. The corresponding predicted value is $p = x^T B^*$. If a weight is not specified, the prediction is for a single future observation, which has estimated variance $V(p) = \sigma^{*2} + V(f)$. If there is a weight w, then the prediction is for a mean of w future observations, which has estimated variance $V(p) = \sigma^{*2}/w + V(f)$. Let SE(f) and SE(p) be the square roots of V(f) and V(p), respectively. Then, the confidence interval for the fitted value f and the prediction interval for the predicted value p are given respectively as f  SE(f) t and p  SE(p) t, where t is the appropriate t value for the specified coverage.

If x is used for estimation, leverage is computed as $u\, x^T (X^T U X)^{-1} x$, where u is the scalar weight associated with case x. If x wasn't used for estimation, the "leverage" (unusualness) is $x^T (X^T U X)^{-1} x$. Let y be an observed value of the dependent variable (it may or may not have been used for estimation). A residual is computed as y - f, and a predicted residual is computed as y - p. An outlier t value for a case not used for estimation is (y - p) / SE(p).

# Best Subset Regressions

The **Best Subset Regressions** procedure in *Statistix* computes the best subset regression models given a full model that contains all the potential predictor variables of interest. A specified number of subset models with the highest $R^2$ are listed for each model size.

## Specification

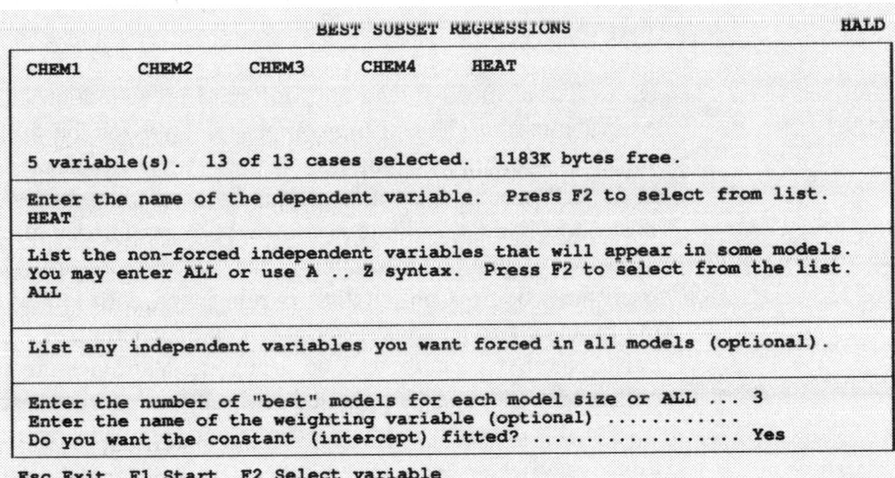

```
BEST SUBSET REGRESSIONS                                              HALD

CHEM1      CHEM2      CHEM3      CHEM4      HEAT

5 variable(s).  13 of 13 cases selected.  1183K bytes free.

Enter the name of the dependent variable.  Press F2 to select from list.
HEAT

List the non-forced independent variables that will appear in some models.
You may enter ALL or use A .. Z syntax.  Press F2 to select from the list.
ALL

List any independent variables you want forced in all models (optional).

Enter the number of "best" models for each model size or ALL ... 3
Enter the name of the weighting variable (optional) ...........
Do you want the constant (intercept) fitted? ................... Yes

Esc Exit   F1 Start   F2 Select variable
```

First enter the name of the dependent variable (response variable). Press F2 and then select the variable from the list displayed.

Enter a list of candidate independent variables underneath the "non-forced" prompt. These variables will be used in all possible combinations to form the subset regressions. Use A .. Z syntax or specify ALL to indicate all of the variables, excluding the dependent variable.

You can enter a list of independent variables you want forced in the regression models. Forced variables will appear in all of the subset models. Listing some independent variables known to be important can greatly reduce the number of subset models computed.

Enter the number of best candidate models you want listed in the results for each subset model size. You can specify as many as ten models, but this will be reduced for very large full models to limit the total number of subset models listed to 150.

To perform weighted least squares regression, enter the name of the variable containing the weights at the prompt.

You can select the more common model with a constant or intercept term (enter Yes) or force the model through the origin (enter No).

It's not necessary to respond to each prompt on the screen. Enter the variables and make the changes you want, then press F1 to begin the analysis.

## Data Restrictions

Up to a total of 40 forced and unforced independent variables can be included in the model (15 is a more practical limit for the number of unforced variables because of computation time). If any values are missing for a case in the full model, the entire case is ignored (listwise deletion) for all models. If an independent variable is too highly correlated with a linear combination of other independent variables in the full model (collinearity), it's dropped from the model. Computation is reinitiated with a new full model in which the offending independent variable has been dropped. If collinearity still exists, another variable will be dropped. Variables are dropped until such collinearity has been eliminated and reliable computations can proceed. If weighted regression is specified, the variable used for the weights cannot have negative values. Zero weights are treated as missing values.

## Example

Our example data are the Hald data from Draper and Smith (1981). The variable HEAT is the cumulative heat of hardening for cement after 180 days. The variables CHEM1, CHEM2, CHEM3, and CHEM4 are the percentages of four chemical compounds measured in batches of cement. The data are listed below.

| CASE | HEAT | CHEM1 | CHEM2 | CHEM3 | CHEM4 |
|---|---|---|---|---|---|
| 1 | 78.5 | 7 | 26 | 6 | 60 |
| 2 | 74.3 | 1 | 29 | 15 | 52 |
| 3 | 104.3 | 11 | 56 | 8 | 20 |
| 4 | 87.6 | 11 | 31 | 8 | 47 |
| 5 | 95.9 | 7 | 52 | 6 | 33 |
| 6 | 109.2 | 11 | 55 | 9 | 22 |
| 7 | 102.7 | 3 | 71 | 17 | 6 |
| 8 | 72.5 | 1 | 31 | 22 | 44 |
| 9 | 93.1 | 2 | 54 | 18 | 22 |
| 10 | 115.9 | 21 | 47 | 4 | 26 |
| 11 | 83.8 | 1 | 40 | 23 | 34 |
| 12 | 113.3 | 11 | 66 | 9 | 12 |
| 13 | 109.4 | 10 | 68 | 8 | 12 |

The goal is to relate the heat of hardening to the chemical composition. The analysis is specified in the panel on page 163. The results are presented in the table below.

```
BEST SUBSET REGRESSION MODELS FOR HEAT  Cumulative Heat of Hardening For Cement
UNFORCED INDEPENDENT VARIABLES: (A)CHEM1 (B)CHEM2 (C)CHEM3 (D)CHEM4
3 "BEST" MODELS FROM EACH SUBSET SIZE LISTED.
```

| P | CP | ADJUSTED R SQUARE | R SQUARE | RESID SS | MODEL VARIABLES |
|---|---|---|---|---|---|
| 1 | 442.9 | 0.0000 | 0.0000 | 2715.76 | INTERCEPT ONLY |
| 2 | 138.7 | 0.6450 | 0.6745 | 883.866 | D |
| 2 | 142.5 | 0.6359 | 0.6663 | 906.336 | B |
| 2 | 202.5 | 0.4916 | 0.5339 | 1265.68 | A |
| 3 | 2.7 | 0.9744 | 0.9787 | 57.9044 | A B |
| 3 | 5.5 | 0.9670 | 0.9725 | 74.7621 | A D |
| 3 | 22.4 | 0.9223 | 0.9353 | 175.738 | C D |
| 4 | 3.0 | 0.9764 | 0.9823 | 47.9727 | A B D |
| 4 | 3.0 | 0.9764 | 0.9823 | 48.1106 | A B C |
| 4 | 3.5 | 0.9750 | 0.9813 | 50.8361 | A C D |
| 5 | 5.0 | 0.9736 | 0.9824 | 47.8636 | A B C D |

Mallows' $C_p$ statistic, unadjusted and adjusted $R^2$, and residual sums of squares are produced for each model. More detail on these statistics is given in **Linear regression** under **Miscellaneous Regression Topics.**

**Note:** The number of possible subset models grows rapidly as the number of independent variables is increased. If there are M independent variables, then there are $2^{(M-1)} - 1$ subset models. For example, with 10 independent variables there are 511 subset models, while with 15 independent variables there are 16,383 subset models.

## Computational Notes

The method used to generate subset statistics is patterned after Clarke (1981). An advantage of this method is that it's very accurate without requiring extended precision computing. The first regression based on the full model is performed with the method described in **Linear Regression.**

# Stepwise Regression

The **Stepwise Regression** procedure in *Statistix* performs stepwise linear regression. You can specify an empty initial model (forward selection), a full initial model (backward elimination), or any initial model in between. Stepwise procedures are popular methods of searching for good subset models, particularly when the number of independent models is large. (See also **Best Subset Regressions** on page 163.)

## Specification

```
                         STEPWISE REGRESSION                                HALD
 CHEM1     CHEM2     CHEM3     CHEM4     HEAT

 5 variable(s).  13 of 13 cases selected.  1183K bytes free.

 Enter the name of the dependent variable ...................... HEAT

 List the non-forced independent variables for selection/elimination.
 ALL

 List any independent variables you want forced in all models (optional).

 List the starting variables.


 Enter the F needed to enter the model ......................... 4.00
 Enter the F needed to exit the model .......................... 4.00
 Select BRIEF or FULL report format (B/F) ...................... Brief
 Enter the name of the weighting variable (optional) ...........
 Do you want the constant (intercept) fitted? .................. Yes

Esc Exit   F1 Start   F2 Select variable
```

First enter the name of the dependent variable (response variable). Press F2 and then select the variable from the list displayed.

Enter a list of candidate independent variables underneath the "non-forced" prompt. These variables will be considered for selection and/or elimination. Use A .. Z syntax or specify ALL to indicate all of the variables excluding the dependent variable.

You can enter a list of independent variables you want forced in the regression model. Forced variables will appear in all steps of the stepwise procedure and will not be eliminated regardless of the elimination criteria.

Next list the "starting variables", the variables you want in the initial model. Leave this space blank for forward selection; enter ALL for backward elimination. Forced variables should not be listed since they appear in all models. You may want to enter an initial model that you have previously found of interest or an initial model that includes a variable that was overlooked in a previous stepwise regression.

A stepwise regression builds a regression model by repeating a process that adds and deletes variables from a list of candidate variables. The stepwise process stops when no variables not already in the model meet the selection criterion and no variables in the model meet the elimination criterion.

At each step in the process, the variable with the highest F value is selected to enter the model next. A variable will not be selected unless its F value is greater than the value you enter for the "F to enter" criterion. A variable's F value is the square of the variable's t value listed in *Statistix* regression coefficient tables. You can specify pure backward elimination by entering a high value (e.g., 100,000) for the "F to enter" to prevent eliminated variables from reentering the model.

The variable with the lowest F value is eliminated from the model at each step. A variable won't be eliminated unless its F value is less than the value you enter for the "F to exit" criterion. You can specify pure forward selection by entering a zero for the "F to exit" to prevent selected variables from being eliminated later.

The remaining options let you choose between brief and full report formats, enter a weighting variable for weighted regression, and specify a no-constant model.

It isn't necessary to respond to each prompt on the screen. Enter the variables and make the changes you want, then press F1 to begin the analysis.

## Data Restrictions

Up to 40 independent variables can be included in the model. If any values are missing for a case in the full model, the entire case is ignored (listwise deletion) for all models. If weighted regression is specified, the variable used for the weights can't have negative values. Zero weights are treated as missing values. Variables won't be selected that are found to be too highly correlated with variables already in the model (collinearity).

## Example

The data used in our example is the Hald data set from Draper and Smith (1981). The variable HEAT is the cumulative heat of hardening for cement after 180 days. The variables CHEM1, CHEM2, CHEM3, and CHEM4 are the percentages of four chemical compounds measured in batches of cement. The data are listed below.

| CASE | HEAT | CHEM1 | CHEM2 | CHEM3 | CHEM4 |
|---|---|---|---|---|---|
| 1 | 78.5 | 7 | 26 | 6 | 60 |
| 2 | 74.3 | 1 | 29 | 15 | 52 |
| 3 | 104.3 | 11 | 56 | 8 | 20 |
| 4 | 87.6 | 11 | 31 | 8 | 47 |
| 5 | 95.9 | 7 | 52 | 6 | 33 |
| 6 | 109.2 | 11 | 55 | 9 | 22 |
| 7 | 102.7 | 3 | 71 | 17 | 6 |
| 8 | 72.5 | 1 | 31 | 22 | 44 |
| 9 | 93.1 | 2 | 54 | 18 | 22 |
| 10 | 115.9 | 21 | 47 | 4 | 26 |
| 11 | 83.8 | 1 | 40 | 23 | 34 |
| 12 | 113.3 | 11 | 66 | 9 | 12 |
| 13 | 109.4 | 10 | 68 | 8 | 12 |

The goal is to relate the heat of hardening to the chemical composition. The analysis is specified in the panel on page 166. The results are as follows:

```
STEPWISE REGRESSION OF HEAT  Cumulative Heat of Hardening for Cement
UNFORCED VARIABLES: CHEM1 CHEM2 CHEM3 CHEM4
  F TO ENTER  4.00
  F TO EXIT   4.00
                                                    C C C C
                                                    H H H H
                                                    E E E E
                                                    M M M M
STEP    R-SQ          MSE            T              1 2 3 4

  1    0.0000       226.313                         . . . .
  2    0.6745       80.3515      -4.77 +            . . . D
  3    0.9725       7.47621      10.40 +            A . . D
  4    0.9823       5.33030       2.24 +            A B . D
  5    0.9787       5.79044      -1.37 -            A B . .

RESULTING STEPWISE MODEL
VARIABLE      COEFFICIENT     STD ERROR      STUDENT'S T        P          VIF

CONSTANT        52.5773        2.28617          23.00         0.0000
CHEM1           1.46830        0.12130          12.10         0.0000       1.1
CHEM2           0.66225        0.04585          14.44         0.0000       1.1

CASES INCLUDED     13        R-SQUARED   0.9787         MSE    5.79044
MISSING CASES       0        ADJ R-SQ    0.9744         SD     2.40633

VARIABLES NOT IN THE MODEL
              CORRELATIONS
VARIABLE     MULTIPLE   PARTIAL         T

CHEM3         0.8257     0.4113       1.35
CHEM4         0.9732    -0.4141      -1.37
```

The first part of the report is a history of the stepwise process. It lists the variables in the model for each step and presents a number of model statistics. In the example above, the intercept-only model is listed as step 0. CHEM4 is added at step 1, CHEM1 is added at step 2, CHEM3 is added at step 3, and then CHEM4 is eliminated at step 4. The $R^2$ and mean square error (MSE) are listed for each step. The t-statistic at each step is the t value for the selected variable (+) or the eliminated variable (-).

At the end of the stepwise history, a complete coefficient table and model summary statistics are presented for the final model.

The final table in the report lists the variables not in the final model. It lists the multiple and partial correlations of each variable with the final model. The column of t values lists the t value for each variable were it to be added to the final model.

The full report format differs from the brief format shown on the preceding page in the stepwise history portion of the report. The full report lists a complete coefficient table for each step. The example below displays a full format report for the backward elimination stepwise regression for the Hald data.

```
STEPWISE REGRESSION OF HEAT  Cumulative Heat of Hardening for Cement
UNFORCED VARIABLES: CHEM1 CHEM2 CHEM3 CHEM4
  F TO ENTER  4.00
  F TO EXIT   4.00

STEP    VARIABLE       COEFFICIENT         T          R-SQ         MSE
----    --------       -----------      ------       ------      -------
  1     CONSTANT          62.4053         0.89       0.9824      5.98295
        CHEM1             1.55110         2.08
        CHEM2             0.51016         0.70
        CHEM3             0.10190         0.14
        CHEM4            -0.14406        -0.20

  2     CONSTANT          71.6483         5.07       0.9823      5.33030
        CHEM1             1.45193        12.41
        CHEM2             0.41611         2.24
        CHEM4            -0.23654        -1.37

  3     CONSTANT          52.5773        23.00       0.9787      5.79044
        CHEM1             1.46830        12.10
        CHEM2             0.66225        14.44

RESULTING STEPWISE MODEL
VARIABLE      COEFFICIENT     STD ERROR      STUDENT'S T        P        VIF
--------      -----------     ---------      -----------     ------     ----
CONSTANT         52.5773        2.28617          23.00       0.0000
CHEM1            1.46830        0.12130          12.10       0.0000      1.1
CHEM2            0.66225        0.04585          14.44       0.0000      1.1

CASES INCLUDED     13         R-SQUARED   0.9787        MSE   5.79044
MISSING CASES       0         ADJ R-SQ    0.9744        SD    2.40633

VARIABLES NOT IN THE MODEL
                 CORRELATIONS
VARIABLE      MULTIPLE   PARTIAL        T
--------      --------   -------     ------
CHEM3          0.8257     0.4113      1.35
CHEM4          0.9732    -0.4141     -1.37
```

# Logistic Regression

The **Logistic Regression** procedure is used when you are interested in studying how observed proportions or rates depend on particular independent variables. A direct application of linear regression to proportions is often not satisfactory because the fitted or predicted values may be less than 0 or greater than 1 (impossibilities for proportions). There may be other shortcomings as well. Logistic regression provides a convenient alternative by examining the relationships between the logistic transformation of the proportions and linear combinations of the predictor (independent) variables. The estimation method is maximum likelihood. Numerous model diagnostic options are available.

More background on logistic regression can be found in the section titled Additional Background on Logistic and Discrete Regression on page 181. In particular, you should be familiar with likelihood ratio tests (also known as analysis of deviance tests or $G^2$ tests) to make full use of this procedure.

## Specification

```
                         LOGISTIC REGRESSION                          VASO
 LRATE     LVOL      OCCUR     RATE      VOL



 5 variable(s).  39 of 39 cases selected.  1198K bytes free.

 Enter the name of the dependent variable ..................... OCCUR
 Enter the number of trials/case or a number of trials variable . 1

 List the independent variables.  You may specify ALL or use A .. Z syntax.
 Press F2 to select variables from the list.
 LRATE LVOL


 Enter the name of the weighting variable (optional) ...........
 Do you want the constant (intercept) fitted? .................. Yes
 Enter the name of the offset variable (optional) ..............
 Enter the maximum number of iterations ........................ 10
 Enter change in deviance convergence criterion ................ 1.000E-02
Esc Exit  F1 Start  F2 Select variable
```

Enter the name of the dependent variable at the prompt (OCCUR in the example above). Enter the number of trials per case if this number is fixed. If the number of trials per case varies, you must enter the name of the variable that contains the number of trials per case. List the independent variables at the prompt. You can use A .. Z syntax to shorten the list, or press F2 and select variables from the list.

The bottom third of the model specification screen offers five options. You can enter the name of a weighting variable to specify prior case weights. You can fit the constant in the model (Yes) or have the model forced through the origin (No).

In some circumstances, the regression coefficient for a term in the model is known beforehand. Such a term is called an offset and can be "adjusted out" of the model. The offset variable is subtracted from the linear predictor, so the offset variable must be expressed on the linear predictor's scale (logit scale).

Logistic regression uses an iterative procedure (iterative reweighted least squares) to obtain its maximum likelihood results. You specify the maximum number of iterations performed before the procedure "gives up" if it hasn't converged.

Iteration stops when the absolute change in the deviance between iterations is less than the deviance convergence criterion you specify. Small values increase the estimation accuracy but may increase the number of required iterations. The value of 0.01 is usually suitable for obtaining deviances and coefficient estimates.

## Data Restrictions

Up to 40 independent variables can be included in the model. If any values within a case are missing, the case is dropped (listwise deletion). If an independent variable is too highly correlated with a linear combination of other independent variables in the model (collinearity), it's dropped from the model. Computation is reinitiated with a new model in which the offending independent variable has been dropped. Variables are dropped until such collinearity has been eliminated and reliable computations can proceed. For each case, the ratio of the dependent variable to the number of trials (success/trials) must always be bounded by 0 to 1. If weighted regression is specified, the weight variable cannot contain negative weights. Zero weights are treated as missing values.

## Example

The logit transformation is ln(p/(1-p)), where p is a proportion. The ratio p/(1-p) is often interpreted as "odds"; for example, if p is the probability of success, then 1-p is the probability of failure and p/(1-p) is the odds for success. By relating ln(p/(1-p)) to a linear combination of predictors, we are assuming that the predictors act in a multiplicative fashion to influence the odds p/(1-p). Remember that logistic regression is relating the linear combination of predictors to ln(p/(1-p)) and not to p, as the analysis specification may suggest.

Finney's data from Pregibon (1981) are used for this example. The response was whether or not vasoconstriction occurred in the skin of the digits; variable OCCUR takes the values 1 or 0. There are two quantitative predictor variables—the rate and volume of air inspired by the subject. For analysis, log rate and log volume were used, variables LRATE and LVOL, respectively. The data are said to be ungrouped; each case is based on a single trial, so you enter a 1 for the number of trials per case. The logistic regression is specified on page 170.

Convergence is reached after the sixth cycle, and the coefficient table is displayed as follows:

```
UNWEIGHTED LOGISTIC REGRESSION OF OCCUR

PREDICTOR
VARIABLES      COEFFICIENT     STD ERROR        COEF/SE          P
---------      -----------     ---------      ----------      ------
CONSTANT         -2.87494       1.30649          -2.20        0.0278
LRATE             4.56100       1.81790           2.51        0.0121
LVOL              5.17862       1.84313           2.81        0.0050

DEVIANCE                 29.23
P-VALUE                 0.7807
DEGREES OF FREEDOM          36

CASES INCLUDED 39    MISSING CASES 0
```

The p-value of 0.7807 suggests this model fits the data fairly well.

Maybe it's not necessary to include both terms LVOL and LRATE in the model. When we run the analysis using only LRATE, we find that the deviance is 48.86 (p=0.0918). When LVOL is specified alone, the resulting deviance is 47.06 (p=0.1243).

Finally, perhaps only the intercept is needed. For this model, *Statistix* must be tricked into analyzing an intercept-only model. In **Transformations**, you create a variable ONE = 1; it has the value 1 for all cases. You then perform the logistic regression using ONE as the only independent variable and enter No at the "fit constant" option to prevent *Statistix* from automatically including an intercept. The resulting deviance is 54.04 (p=0.0440).

The following analysis of deviance table summarizes the results (I = intercept, R = log rate, V = log volume):

| Model | Deviance | Difference | DF | Component | P-Value |
|---|---|---|---|---|---|
| I | $d_I = 54.04$ | $d_I - d_{IVR} = 24.81$ | 2 | V and R | 0.000 |
| I+R | $d_{IR} = 48.86$ | $dI_R - d_{IRV} = 19.63$ | 1 | V | 0.000 |
| I+V | $d_{IV} = 47.06$ | $d_{IV} - d_{IRV} = 17.83$ | 1 | R | 0.000 |
| I+R+V | $d_{IRV} = 29.23$ | | | | |

The column labeled Component shows which terms are being tested. The first row tests whether LVOL and LRATE improve the intercept-only model. The deviance for this test is the difference of the deviances for model I and model I+R+V, which is 54.04 - 29.23 = 24.81. The associated value for the degrees of freedom is the difference in the number of independent variables in the two models. The p-value displayed in the last column is computed using the chi-square function in **Probability Distributions** (see Chapter 11). The second row tests whether LVOL improves the model when I and LRATE are already in the model. The deviance for this test is the difference of the deviances for model I+R and model I+R+V, which is 48.86 - 29.23 = 19.63. The LRATE term is tested in a similar manner in the third row. The conclusion from this analysis of deviance table is that both LVOL and LRATE are needed in the model.

Before accepting this model, you should examine the regression diagnostics. You should examine the standardized residuals and Cook's D (or p-value) routinely. Use **Wilk-Shapiro/Rankit Plot** to plot the standardized residuals.

## Logistic Regression Results Menu

After you've viewed the coefficient table, press Esc to display the regression results menu.

```
REGRESSION RESULTS

Coefficient table
Hosmer-Lemeshow statistic
Odds ratios
Save residuals
Var-covar of betas
Options panel
```

Select "Coefficient table" from the menu to redisplay the regression coefficient table. Select "Options panel" to return to the main options panel used to specify the model. Logistic regression offers the options of saving various residual- and model-diagnostic statistics and examining the variance-covariance matrix of the regression coefficients. These options are performed in the same manner as in **Linear Regression** (page 150).

## Hosmer-Lemeshow Statistic

The Hosmer-Lemeshow statistics are goodness-of-fit tests suitable for models with a large number of covariate patterns (unique combinations of values for the independent variables). These tests are illustrated here using data from Hosmer and Lemeshow (1989, p. 92), a study whose object was to identify risk factors for low birth weights of babies. The response variable is LOW: 0 = normal birth weight, 1 = low birth weight. The table below shows the tests for the model found on page 101, Hosmer and Lemeshow.

**HOSMER-LEMESHOW GOODNESS-OF-FIT TESTS FOR LOW**

| | | DECILE OF RISK | | | | | | | | | | |
|---|---|---|---|---|---|---|---|---|---|---|---|---|
| | | 1 | 2 | 3 | 4 | 5 | 6 | 7 | 8 | 9 | 10 | |
| LOW | | 0.07 | 0.09 | 0.16 | 0.21 | 0.28 | 0.33 | 0.42 | 0.49 | 0.61 | 0.94 | TOTAL |
| 1 | OBS | 0 | 1 | 4 | 2 | 6 | 6 | 6 | 10 | 9 | 15 | 59 |
| | EXP | 0.9 | 1.6 | 2.4 | 3.5 | 5.0 | 5.6 | 6.8 | 8.6 | 10.5 | 14.1 | 59 |
| 0 | OBS | 19 | 18 | 15 | 17 | 14 | 12 | 12 | 9 | 10 | 4 | 130 |
| | EXP | 18.1 | 17.4 | 16.6 | 15.5 | 15.0 | 12.4 | 11.2 | 10.4 | 8.5 | 4.9 | 130 |
| | TOTAL | 19 | 19 | 19 | 19 | 20 | 18 | 18 | 19 | 19 | 19 | 189 |

| | |
|---|---|
| HOSMER-LEMESHOW STATISTIC (C) | 4.78 |
| P-VALUE | 0.7804 |
| DEGREES OF FREEDOM | 8 |

| | | FIXED CUT POINTS | | | | | | | | | | |
|---|---|---|---|---|---|---|---|---|---|---|---|---|
| LOW | | 0.10 | 0.20 | 0.30 | 0.40 | 0.50 | 0.60 | 0.70 | 0.80 | 0.90 | 1.00 | TOTAL |
| 1 | OBS | 2 | 5 | 8 | 9 | 11 | 9 | 7 | 5 | 2 | 1 | 59 |
| | EXP | 2.7 | 4.5 | 8.3 | 8.7 | 10.7 | 8.8 | 6.5 | 5.3 | 1.7 | 1.9 | 59 |
| 0 | OBS | 38 | 25 | 25 | 16 | 13 | 7 | 3 | 2 | 0 | 1 | 130 |
| | EXP | 37.3 | 25.5 | 24.7 | 16.3 | 13.3 | 7.2 | 3.5 | 1.7 | 0.3 | 0.1 | 130 |
| | TOTAL | 40 | 30 | 33 | 25 | 24 | 16 | 10 | 7 | 2 | 2 | 189 |

| | |
|---|---|
| HOSMER-LEMESHOW STATISTIC (H) | 6.17 |
| P-VALUE | 0.6281 |
| DEGREES OF FREEDOM | 8 |

The tables are constructed by grouping the observations into ten groups based on the values of the fitted values (estimated probabilities). Two grouping methods are used as follows:

The first method groups the data based on percentiles of the fitted values, resulting in a table with ten "deciles of risk". The test statistic C = 4.78 is computed from the observed and expected frequencies within each decile of risk for each outcome. The p-value 0.7804 is computed from the chi-square distribution with 8 degrees of freedom.

The value above each of the columns in the deciles-of-risk table represent the highest fitted value for the column. Observations with the same covariate pattern are forced into the same decile, which can result in some columns with zero observed frequencies. In these cases, the statistic isn't computed.

The second grouping method bases the groups on fixed cut points of the fitted values. Both the C and H statistics indicate a good fit. See Hosmer and Lemeshow (1989) for a detailed discussion.

## Odds Ratios

Select "Odds ratios" from the results menu to obtain odds ratios and 95% confidence intervals. The table of odds ratios from the logistic regression of the birth weight data from Hosmer and Lemeshow (1989, p. 94) follows:

LOGISTIC REGRESSION ODDS RATIOS FOR LOW

| PREDICTOR VARIABLES | 95% C.I. LOWER LIMIT | ODDS RATIO | 95% C.I. UPPER LIMIT |
|---|---|---|---|
| AGE | 0.91 | 0.97 | 1.05 |
| LWT | 0.97 | 0.98 | 1.00 |
| RACE1 | 1.26 | 3.54 | 9.91 |
| RACE2 | 1.00 | 2.37 | 5.59 |
| SMOKE | 1.15 | 2.52 | 5.51 |
| PTL | 0.87 | 1.72 | 3.39 |
| HT | 1.62 | 6.26 | 24.23 |
| UI | 0.87 | 2.14 | 5.25 |

The odds ratios reported in *Statistix* give the change in the odds for an increase in one unit of the independent variable. For the dichotomous variable SMOKE, the odds of a low birth weight baby are 2.52 greater for a mother who smokes (SMOKE = 1) than for a mother who doesn't smoke (SMOKE = 0). The odds ratio of 0.97 for the continuous variable AGE is for an increase of one year in age.

## General Notes

If fitted values are saved, the resulting values are the estimates of expected number of successes E[N]. If you want estimates of p, first save the fitted values and then divide them by the total number of trials per case. Estimates for the logits ln(p/(1-p)) can be obtained from the estimated p's.

Probit regression is a method very similar to logistic regression. *Statistix* does not perform probit regression. For the vast majority of data sets, logistic and probit analyses will return virtually identical results. We prefer logistic regression because it can be calculated more efficiently and the logit transform has a simple interpretation as the log of the odds ratio.

# Discrete (Poisson) Regression

The **Discrete (Poisson) Regression** procedure performs Poisson regression using the maximum likelihood estimation method. It's used when you're interested in examining how observed counts depend on particular independent variables. A direct application of linear regression to counts often isn't satisfactory because the fitted or predicted values may be negative; this is impossible for counts. There may be other shortcomings as well. Poisson regression provides a convenient alternative. It examines the relationships between the log transformed counts and linear combinations of the predictor (independent) variables.

More background on Poisson regression can be found in Additional Background on Logistic and Discrete Regression on page 181. In particular, you should be familiar with likelihood ratio tests (also known as analysis of deviance tests or G2 tests) to make full use of this procedure.

## Specification

```
                     DISCRETE (POISSON) REGRESSION                          DREAMS
 A1         A2         A3         A4         AGE        BOYS       DUMMYV
 R1         R2         R3         RATING     RXA


 12 variable(s).  20 of 20 cases selected.  1198K bytes free.

 Enter the name of the dependent variable.  Press F2 to select from list.
 BOYS

 List the independent variables.  You may specify ALL or use A .. Z syntax.
 Press F2 to select variables from the list.
 R1 .. R3 A1 .. A4


 Enter the name of the weighting variable (optional) ...........
 Do you want the constant (intercept) fitted? ................... Yes
 Enter the name of the offset variable (optional) ...............
 Enter the maximum number of iterations ......................... 10
 Enter change in deviance convergence criterion ................. 1.000E-02
Esc Exit  F1 Start  F2 Select variable
```

The data set variables are listed at the top of the panel. Enter the name of the dependent variable that contains the counts. List the independent variables at the prompt. You can specify ALL, use A .. Z syntax, or press F2 and select variables from the list displayed.

As with Linear Regression, you can specify a weight variable for prior case weights and force the model through the origin (No to the constant prompt).

In some circumstances, the regression coefficient for a term in the model is known beforehand. Such a term is called an offset, and the offset option allows it to be "adjusted out" of the model. The offset variable is subtracted from the linear predictor, so the offset variable must be expressed on the linear predictor's scale (i.e., natural log of counts).

Discrete regression uses an iterative procedure (iterative reweighted least squares) to obtain the maximum likelihood estimates. You can specify the maximum number of iterations performed before the procedure "gives up" if it hasn't converged.

Iteration stops when the absolute change in the deviance between iterations reaches the deviance convergence criterion. Decreasing the criterion will increase the estimation accuracy but may increase the number of iterations required. The default value of 0.01 is usually suitable for obtaining deviances and coefficient estimates. Decreasing the criterion appears to improve the accuracy of coefficient standard errors and the regression diagnostics.

## Data Restrictions

Up to 40 independent variables can be included in the model. If any values within a case are missing, the case is dropped (listwise deletion). If an independent variable is too highly correlated with a linear combination of other independent variables in the model (collinearity), it's dropped from the model. Computation is reinitiated with a new model in which the offending independent variable has been dropped. Variables are dropped until such collinearity has been eliminated and reliable computations can proceed. If a prior weight variable is specified, the weight variable cannot contain negative weights. Zero weights are treated as missing values.

## Example

Maxwell's data, presented in Nelder and Wedderburn (1972), are used. The analysis treats a 5 x 4 contingency table giving the number of boys (BOYS) with four different ratings for disturbed dreams in five different age categories:

| | | RATING | | | |
|---|---|---|---|---|---|
| Age group | AGE | 4 | 3 | 2 | 1 |
| 5 - 7 | 1 | 7 | 3 | 4 | 7 |
| 8 - 9 | 2 | 13 | 11 | 15 | 10 |
| 10 - 11 | 3 | 7 | 11 | 9 | 23 |
| 12 - 13 | 4 | 10 | 12 | 9 | 28 |
| 14 - 15 | 5 | 3 | 4 | 5 | 32 |

AGE has the values 1 - 5, and RATING the values 1 - 4. We're interested in whether there's a linear x linear interaction of AGE and RATING.

First we create dummy variables for the main effects as if we were using linear regression (see, for example, Weisberg 1985). There are 4 main effect degrees of freedom for AGE and 3 main effect degrees of freedom for RATING. The main effect dummy variables R1, R2, and R3 for RATING and the dummy variables A1, A2, A3, and A4 for AGE are created in **Transformations**:

```
DUMMY (RATING 1 2 3) R1 R2 R3
DUMMY (AGE 2 3 4 5) A1 A2 A3 A4
```

The RATING X AGE interaction is computed as:

```
RXA = RATING * AGE
```

The data are listed below.

| CASE | BOYS | AGE | RATING | A1 | A2 | A3 | A4 | R1 | R2 | R3 | RXA | DUMMYV |
|---|---|---|---|---|---|---|---|---|---|---|---|---|
| 1 | 7 | 1 | 4 | 0 | 0 | 0 | 0 | 0 | 0 | 0 | 4 | 0 |
| 2 | 3 | 1 | 3 | 0 | 0 | 0 | 0 | 0 | 0 | 1 | 3 | 0 |
| 3 | 4 | 1 | 2 | 0 | 0 | 0 | 0 | 0 | 1 | 0 | 2 | 0 |
| 4 | 7 | 1 | 1 | 0 | 0 | 0 | 0 | 1 | 0 | 0 | 1 | 0 |
| 5 | 13 | 2 | 4 | 1 | 0 | 0 | 0 | 0 | 0 | 0 | 8 | 0 |
| 6 | 11 | 2 | 3 | 1 | 0 | 0 | 0 | 0 | 0 | 1 | 6 | 0 |
| 7 | 15 | 2 | 2 | 1 | 0 | 0 | 0 | 0 | 1 | 0 | 4 | 0 |
| 8 | 10 | 2 | 1 | 1 | 0 | 0 | 0 | 1 | 0 | 0 | 2 | 0 |
| 9 | 7 | 3 | 4 | 0 | 1 | 0 | 0 | 0 | 0 | 0 | 12 | 0 |
| 10 | 11 | 3 | 3 | 0 | 1 | 0 | 0 | 0 | 0 | 1 | 9 | 0 |
| 11 | 9 | 3 | 2 | 0 | 1 | 0 | 0 | 0 | 1 | 0 | 6 | 0 |
| 12 | 23 | 3 | 1 | 0 | 1 | 0 | 0 | 1 | 0 | 0 | 3 | 0 |
| 13 | 10 | 4 | 4 | 0 | 0 | 1 | 0 | 0 | 0 | 0 | 16 | 0 |
| 14 | 12 | 4 | 3 | 0 | 0 | 1 | 0 | 0 | 0 | 1 | 12 | 0 |
| 15 | 9 | 4 | 2 | 0 | 0 | 1 | 0 | 0 | 1 | 0 | 8 | 0 |
| 16 | 28 | 4 | 1 | 0 | 0 | 1 | 0 | 1 | 0 | 0 | 4 | 0 |
| 17 | 3 | 5 | 4 | 0 | 0 | 0 | 1 | 0 | 0 | 0 | 20 | 0 |
| 18 | 4 | 5 | 3 | 0 | 0 | 0 | 1 | 0 | 0 | 1 | 15 | 0 |
| 19 | 5 | 5 | 2 | 0 | 0 | 0 | 1 | 0 | 1 | 0 | 10 | 0 |
| 20 | 32 | 5 | 1 | 0 | 0 | 0 | 1 | 1 | 0 | 0 | 5 | 1 |

We'll fit two models—one without the interaction and one with the interaction. The main effects only model is computed first. The model is specified in the options panel on page 176. The results are presented in the coefficient table on the next page.

The deviance for this model is 32.46 with 12 degrees of freedom; this main effects only model appears to fit poorly (p = 0.0012).

Next we fit the main effects plus linear interaction model by adding the RXA term. This model fits much better (deviance = 14.08, df = 11, p = 0.2288). The contribution to the deviance due to the interaction RXA is

UNWEIGHTED DISCRETE (POISSON) REGRESSION OF BOYS

| PREDICTOR VARIABLES | COEFFICIENT | STD ERROR | COEF/SE | P |
|---|---|---|---|---|
| CONSTANT | 1.32623 | 0.26102 | 5.08 | 0.0000 |
| R1 | 0.91629 | 0.18707 | 4.90 | 0.0000 |
| R2 | 0.04879 | 0.22092 | 0.22 | 0.8252 |
| R3 | 0.02469 | 0.22223 | 0.11 | 0.9115 |
| A1 | 0.84729 | 0.26081 | 3.25 | 0.0012 |
| A2 | 0.86750 | 0.26003 | 3.34 | 0.0008 |
| A3 | 1.03301 | 0.25410 | 4.07 | 0.0000 |
| A4 | 0.73966 | 0.26522 | 2.79 | 0.0053 |

| | |
|---|---|
| DEVIANCE | 32.46 |
| P-VALUE | 0.0012 |
| DEGREES OF FREEDOM | 12 |

CASES INCLUDED 20 MISSING CASES 0

32.46 - 14.08 = 18.38, which is clearly significant (it is treated as a chi-square statistic with 1 df). From the coefficient table, the estimated linear x linear interaction is -0.2051. Nelder and Wedderburn conclude "that the data are adequately described by a negative linear x linear interaction (indicating that the dream rating tends to decrease with age)".

If we look at the regression diagnostics, Cook's distance calls attention to the cell in the lower right; the count in AGE = 5, RATING = 1 is a bit high, and Cook's distance indicates this is a rather influential case. Let's see what happens when this point is fitted separately. To do this, a new variable is created as:

```
IF AGE=5 AND RATING=1 THEN DUMMYV = 1 ELSE DUMMYV = 0
```

When the model: BOYS = R1 R2 R3 A1 A2 A3 A4 RXA DUMMYV is fitted, the new deviance is 9.58 (10 degrees of freedom, p = 0.4781). The RXA interaction slope is now -0.13758. The change in deviance due to the DUMMYV term is 4.50 = 14.08 - 9.58, which can be treated as a chi-square statistic with 1 df. The p-value of 0.034 (from Probability Distributions) is small enough to make you suspect that the lower right corner does require special attention. This is not the definitive analysis of this data set; the point is just to show the value of using the regression diagnostics to gain a better understanding of the data.

We could have fitted the main effects only model a little easier using the **Log Linear Models** procedure in Chapter 7. Log Linear Models is especially suited for fitting models with only qualitative predictors; the drawback of using Poisson regression is that you must manually create the dummy variables. However, Log Linear Models can't deal with quantitative predictors and so, for example, they could not compute the linear x linear interaction RXA. Poisson regression must be used when you need the standard errors of the coefficients.

### Discrete Regression Results Menu

After you have viewed the coefficient table, press Esc to display the regression results menu.

```
REGRESSION RESULTS
Coefficient table
Save residuals
Var-covar of betas
Options panel
```

Select "Coefficient table" from the menu to redisplay the regression coefficient table. Select "Options panel" to return to the main options panel used to specify the model. Discrete regression offers the options of saving various residual- and model-diagnostic statistics and examining the variance-covariance matrix of the regression coefficients. These options are performed in the same manner as in **Linear Regression** (page 150).

### General Comments

By relating ln(Y) to a linear combination of predictors, we're assuming that the predictors act in a multiplicative fashion to influence the counts Y. Remember that Poisson regression is relating the linear combination of predictors to ln(Y) and not Y, as the analysis specification might suggest.

# Additional Background on Logistic and Discrete Regression

## Analyzing Proportions and Counts

For those unfamiliar with logistic and Poisson regression, the following sections give you a brief background on why and when these procedures should be used.

The analysis of counts and proportions is the objective of discrete, or categorical, data analysis. The theory of analysis of variance and regression is more mature than methods for discrete data analysis. So it's natural that many of the techniques for discrete data analysis are based on ideas from analysis of variance and regression.

The typical application of least squares procedures [analysis of (co)variance or regression] usually involves the assumption that the dependent variable is some quantity that can be measured on a continuous scale, such as millimeters or grams. It's also usually assumed that the random errors in the dependent variable are independent normal random variables with identical variances, perhaps after suitable transformations or weightings. The goal of analysis, then, is to examine whether the dependent variable is influenced by the independent variables of interest.

Problems arise when least squares is applied to data sets where the dependent variable is discrete counts or proportions that arose from discrete counts. Suppose you were to fit a simple linear regression model $p = a + bx$ to a data set, where the p's are proportions. You can always find values of x where p is less than 0 or greater than 1, a clearly undesirable situation for a model of proportions. Likewise, if you fit the model $c = a + bx$ where now c is discrete count data, you can find values of x that result in negative predicted counts, also undesirable.

You can avoid these problems by transforming the dependent data. For example, when the data are proportions, the logistic transformation $\ln [p/(1-p)]$ creates a new variable that ranges from $-\infty$ to $+\infty$. With count data, you can achieve a similar scaling by converting the data to the log scale. We are then interested in how a linear combination of the independent variables is related to the transformed data. This involves estimating the slope coefficients and testing their significance. However, even after the data have been transformed, the usual application of least squares for estimation often doesn't work very well because the errors do not closely approximate the usual assumption of identical variances.

The application of least squares to transformed discrete data can be improved by using various weighting schemes to adjust for unequal variances. A classic example of such a procedure is minimum logit $C^2$, described in Snedecor and Cochran (1980). These techniques should be viewed as approximations to the preferred method of estimation, which is maximum likelihood (ML) estimation. These approximate methods work well in some situations and poorly in others. The appeal of the approximate methods has been that they are easy to calculate with traditional methods.

Efficient general algorithms for ML estimation of linear models fitted to transformed discrete data are now available and are part of a larger body of theory known as generalized linear models, or GLM's. *Statistix* uses these procedures to make it possible to perform ML estimation with no more effort than required for a traditional least squares analysis. If you have count data, we suggest you use the appropriate ML procedure. This may require some background reading if you're not familiar with ML procedures, especially likelihood ratio tests. If you understand how F tests are performed in the usual regression situation, likelihood ratio tests are easy. The ML procedures always work as well as the approximate weighted least squares procedures. More important, the ML procedures will work well in situations where least squares fails dismally.

If you're interested in proportions, **Logistic Regression** is the appropriate procedure. If you have count data, consider either **Discrete (Poisson) Regression** or **Log-Linear Models**. If you have count data and your independent variables include continuous variables ("covariates"), use Discrete (Poisson) Regression. More detail to help you decide which to use is found within each of the respective descriptions.

There are many good references on discrete data analysis. Bishop et al. (1975) give a thorough treatment of discrete analysis for categorical designs, the discrete analogs to analysis of variance. Fienberg (1977) gives a concise, readable account of such models. McCullagh and Nelder (1983) consider a broader class of models, including those with continuous variates, the analogs to regression or analysis of covariance. Cox (1970) and Hosmer and Lemeshow (1989) are good references for the logistic model. The references in these books can direct you to more specific areas of interest.

## Generalized Linear Models

The procedures for **Logistic Regression** and **Discrete (Poisson) Regression** are based on the theory of generalized linear models (McCullagh and Nelder 1983), or GLM's. The class of models included in GLM's is quite rich;

multiple, logistic, and Poisson regression are the most commonly encountered members of GLM's, but many others are included.

Many of the statistics in linear regression have generalized analogs in GLM's. A distinction is that many of the statistics for GLM's in general are justified by large sample approximations, while the statistics for normal theory linear regression are "exact". The performance of these approximations is an active field of investigation.

First we'll discuss the statistics displayed on the coefficient table. The standard measure of GLM fit is the deviance, also known as the $G^2$ statistic. Under the null hypothesis of the specified model, the deviance asymptotically follows a chi-square distribution. The deviance plays a role similar to that of the residual error in linear regression. You can think of it as a "distance measure" between the fitted model and the actual data—the smaller, the better. When used as an overall goodness-of-fit measure, the corresponding p-value should be interpreted with caution; it is best viewed as simply a convenient way to standardize the deviance for comparison purposes. A more traditional goodness-of-fit measure is Pearson's chi-square, which *Statistix* does not display (it's easy to compute from residual results if desired). Pearson's chi-square has the same asymptotic distribution as the deviance (under the null hypothesis); the reason for preferring the deviance is that the deviance can be used to construct a stepwise analysis of deviance table similar to the stepwise analysis of variance table displayed in linear regression. Pearson's chi-square doesn't lend itself as readily to this use.

Stepwise analysis of variance tables and their uses are described in **Linear Regression**. Analogous analysis of deviance tables can be constructed for **Logistic** and **Discrete (Poisson) Regression** (see examples). Understanding the construction and interpretation of such tables is essential to performing regression analyses properly. *Statistix* doesn't automatically generate analysis of deviance tables because the structure of these tables often depends on the goals of the investigation imposed by the subject matter. However, such tables are easy to construct by hand from the displayed results.

In addition to the model deviance, COEF/SE statistics and associated p-values are displayed on the coefficient table. Again, these are justified by large sample theory. Better tests for the individual contributions of independent variables can be constructed as 1 degree of freedom tests using the deviance (see examples).

Direct analogies exist for most of the residual diagnostics you can select from the residuals and fitted values menu in linear regression. The computation of leverage is as described in McCullagh and Nelder (1983) and Pregibon (1981). The standardized residual, r, is described in McCullagh and Nelder (eq. 11.1); we describe its calculation at the end of this section on page 185. Leverage values, h, are the diagonal elements of the H matrix described by McCullagh and Nelder (sect. 11.3).

If you're interested in Pearson (chi-square) residuals rather than standardized residuals, you can calculate them as $r(1 - h)^{1/2}$ using **Transformations.** If you square the Pearson residuals and then sum them, you'll obtain the Pearson chi-square goodness-of-fit statistic for the model. Cook's distance is computed as described in McCullagh and Nelder (1983) and Pregibon (1981). Computing the "p-value" for Cook's D should simply be regarded as converting D to an alternate scale that may help make influential points more easily recognizable. The method for computing the "p-value" of Cook's D is the same as that used in linear regression. The outlier t-statistic and its p-value should be regarded as experimental; at this point, a cautious interpretation of these statistics is that they are monotonic transforms of the standardized residuals (Weisberg 1985) and should be sensitive to outliers.

### Aliasing

Parameters being estimated are said to be aliased if the associated independent variables are (nearly) linear combinations of other independent variables. Another name for this is collinearity. As in linear regression, aliased independent variables in logistic and Poisson regression are successively detected and dropped until the remaining independent variables constitute a linearly independent set.

Some special considerations come into play when this variable-dropping technique is used for logistic and Poisson regression. The first is what is called "saw-toothing". As the iterative fitting process used for GLM's proceeds, it occasionally happens that the information in a parameter diminishes to the point that the procedure detects it as being aliased, even though it really isn't. Saw-toothing can be recognized as occurring when a variable is dropped sometime after the first fitting cycle, along with a substantial increase in the deviance to the next cycle. When this is observed, the deviance from the cycle immediately before the one in which the variable is dropped should be used.

There is a related issue that you should be aware of. This is the potential interaction of dropping aliased variables and missing values. A case is not included in the analysis if any of the values for any of the variables (dependent, independents, or weight) used in the analysis are missing values. Thus, if an independent variable with missing values is detected as being aliased and is dropped, new cases may be pulled into the analysis in the next cycle. This makes use of all of the available data, but it also means the deviance may be based on an expanded set of cases as iteration continues and hence is not truly comparable from cycle to cycle. This will usually not be of concern, but it's a point you need to know. If this behavior influences the results, it can be controlled by using **Omit/Restore Cases** to select case subsets for analysis.

## Infinite Parameter Estimates

A potential problem with the logistic transformation occurs when the estimate of p is very near to 0 or 1. The fitted logit ln[p/(1-p)] then approaches minus or plus infinity, which can obviously cause computational problems. A similar problem occurs in Poisson regression when the fitted count is very near 0; the fitted log count approaches minus infinity. In these cases, the parameter estimates in the linear predictors approach infinity. *Statistix* prevents potential computational problems in such cases by enforcing an upper bound on the absolute value of the fitted values of the linear predictors.

This approach appears to work quite well, and biases are generally small. However, when it's known in advance that some parameter estimates are infinite, it's better to drop the corresponding data cases from the analysis. An example would be to delete all rows and columns in two-way contingency tables that have marginal sums of zero. The major negative consequence of not deleting such cases is that the deviance may be distorted downward relative to the degrees of freedom.

## Equations for Linear, Logistic, and Poisson Regression

The following section outlines some of the equations used for various quantities in multiple, logistic, and Poisson regression. The matrix X represents the design matrix of predictor variable values. The prior weights are the weights specified by the weighting variable option. RMS stands for residual mean square. In logistic regression, p is the expected proportion, or E[p] (the expected logit is ln [p/(1-p)]). The various terms are described in more detail in McCullagh and Nelder (1983). The number of cases used for estimation is n. The number of parameters in the linear model is m (m includes the intercept, if present).

| Description | Linear | Logistic | Poisson |
|---|---|---|---|
| prior weight | w | w | w |
| s = scale parameter | $\sigma^2$<br>$\sigma^2$ = E[RMS] | 1 | 1 |
| f = variance function | 1 | $n\pi(1 - \pi)$<br>$\pi$ = E[p] | M<br>M= expected count |
| q = iterative weight = fw | w | $n\pi(1 - \pi)w$ | Mw |
| v = variance of an observation = sf/w | $\sigma^2/w$ | $n\pi(1 - \pi)/w$ | M/w |

Let $C = (X^TQX)^{-1}$

variance of estimated coefficients V(B*) = sC

variance of a fitted value of the linear predictor $V(f) = sx^TCx$

h = leverage = $q\, x^TCx$
("unusualness" or "distance" is $fx^TCx$)

Let e = raw residual (observation minus fitted or predicted value)

Studentized residual = $r = e[((sf) / w)(1 - h)]^{-1/2}$

outlier t-statistic = $r\, [(n - m - 1) / (n - m - r^2)]^{-1/2}$

Cook's D = $(r^2 / m)\,(h / (1 - h))$

# General AOV/AOCV

The **General AOV/AOCV** procedure is a flexible procedure you can use to analyze many analysis of variance and covariance designs, including ones that are moderately unbalanced. Many options are available—pairwise comparisons of means, general and polynomial contrasts, mean estimation, Tukey's test for nonadditivity, least squares estimation of missing values, and residuals.

## Specification

The General AOV/AOCV procedure requires that the *Statistix* data set be arranged in a particular manner. The observed data (the dependent variable data) have to be stored in a single variable. You also need two or more independent variables (factors) whose values are used to identify each case uniquely. If replication occurs, it must be indicated by its own variable. Please look at the examples starting on page 192 for example data sets.

```
                GENERAL ANALYSIS OF VARIANCE/COVARIANCE                  ROSES
 BLK        LOC        ROSES      TRT        WITHIN




 5 variable(s).  20 of 20 cases selected.  1199K bytes free.

 Enter the name of the dependent variable.  Press F2 to select from list.
 ROSES

 List the variables to be used as main effects and all interaction terms
 (eg. BLOCK*TREATMENT) in your AOV model. Indicate which terms are to be used
 as error terms by typing (E) after the term. Press F2 to select from list.
 TRT BLK TRT*BLK TRT*BLK*WITHIN(E)

 For analysis of covariance, list the variables to be used as covariables.
 LOC

Esc Exit  F1 Start  F2 Select variable
```

The data set variables are listed at the top of the panel. Enter the name of the dependent variable. The dependent variable contains the observed data.

Models are specified in a manner similar to the usual algebraic expression of analysis of variance models, such as those illustrated in Snedecor and Cochran (1980). Use the factor variables to list the terms in your model. The terms are main effects, which are entered as a single variable, and interaction terms, which are listed as a group of factor variables combined using stars (e.g., BLK∗TRT). The high order interaction term is assumed to be an error term. Other interaction terms can be indicated as an error term by typing (ERROR) or (E) after the term (see the split-plot example below).

For analysis of covariance, list the names of thc variables you want to use as covariates. Take special care in interpreting the results of analysis of variance. See Interpreting Analysis with Missing Values or Covariates on page 191.

Press F1 to begin the analysis. You'll be offered additional options once the analysis is specified and computed.

## Example Model Statements

Model specification (list of main effects and interaction terms) is very flexible and best illustrated by example. The variables X1 X2 ... XN represent the treatments (factors or explanatory variables). (Hint: The CAT function in the **Transformations** procedure often provides a convenient way to generate treatment variables).

Example 1: One-Way AOV. TREAT identifies the treatments, REP the replication within each treatment. The model is specified as:

```
TREAT TREAT*REP
```

Example 2: Two-way AOV without replication (additive model). X1 and X2 represent two factors.

```
X1 X2 X1*X2
```

Example 3: Two-way AOV with replication (interaction model). Replicates are indexed by variable X3.

```
X1 X2 X1*X2 X1*X2*X3
```

Example 4: Completely nested design with four levels.

```
X1 X1*X2 X1*X2*X3 X1*X2*X3*X4
```

Example 5: Split-plot design. X1 designates main plot treatments, X2 designates replication, and X3 indicates subplot treatments.

```
X1 X2 X1*X2(E) X3 X2*X3(E) X1*X3 X1*X2*X3(E)
```

Example 6. Five-way factorial design. The ALL terms syntax is described below.

```
ALL (X1 X2 X3 X4 X5)
```

Example 7: Repeated measures design. TRT identifies the treatment, SUB the subject, and REP replication within subject.

```
TRT SUB TRT*SUB*REP
```

The most common mistake in specifying a model is to omit the factor for within-cell replication and the error term using that variable. For the one-way model, you may want to simply enter the treatment factor for the model (e.g., TRT). But the model requires the error term as well (e.g., TRT TRT*REP). Replication variables can easily be created using the Transformation CAT function.

In most situations, neither the order in which terms are specified in the model nor the order in which variables are specified within terms has any influence on the analysis. The only exception occurs in certain models with multiple error terms, which are described next.

## Error Term Specification

The (ERROR) modifier behind a term indicates that the term is to be used as a error term for computing F tests. Note that multiple error terms can be specified, as in Example 5 on the preceding page. When multiple error terms are specified, an F test for an effect or interaction is based on the lowest order error term that includes the effect or interaction being tested. If the highest order interaction is not explicitly listed in the model, it's automatically added and is an error term. For instance, in Example 2, the results would be exactly the same if the model had been specified as X1 X2.

Occasionally, there will be error terms of equal order that contain the term for which a test is desired. For example, consider the split-plot model:

```
X1 X2 X1*X2(ERROR) X3 X2*X3(ERROR) X1*X3 X1*X2*X3(ERROR)
```

The second order error terms X1*X2 and X2*X3 both contain X2; which term will be used to construct the F test for X2? *Statistix* scans the model from left to right. When it encounters the first factor (X1), it assigns it the name "A". The next factor encountered (X2) is assigned the name "B", and so on. The error terms X1*X2 and X2*X3 are represented as AB and BC, respectively. To decide which term to use, *Statistix* always uses the one with the lowest dictionary order, AB in this case. Actually, at least in this particular example, it's moot what error term is used since X2 is probably a block factor and not very interesting to test. *Statistix* can't judge whether testing particular terms against one another makes sense; that's your responsibility.

### ALL Term Specification

The ALL modifier is provided to simplify model specifications when you want all subset interactions. For example, the model

```
X1 ALL (X2 X3 X4)
```

is equivalent to

```
X1 X2 X3 X4 X2*X3 X2*X4 X3*X4 X2*X3*X4
```

### Data Restrictions

Up to five treatment variables and five covariates can be included in a model. There can be 50 levels within each treatment. Up to 20 missing values are allowed. The treatment variables can have any data type (real, integer, date, string). When using real variables, treatment levels should always be given as whole numbers.

The combinations of treatment levels must be unique and exhaustive. For example, suppose that the model is Y = X1 X2; that X1 has four levels (1,2,3,4) associated with it; and that X2 has three levels (1,2,3) associated with it. Then there must be exactly 12 cases, and the only pairs of levels for X1, X2 that can appear are 1,1; 1,2; 1,3; 2,1; 2,2; 2,3; 3,1; 3,2; 3,3; 4,1; 4,2; 4,3. If all possible combinations are not present or if some are duplicated, an error message is given.

If a data set contains missing values, the case still must be represented. Include a case using the level for each factor in the model as well as an M for the dependent variable.

If a design includes replication, a variable representing this replication must be included in the model. Compare Examples 2 and 3 on page 188 if this is unclear.

### Pooling of Sums of Squares

Internally, the AOV is initially treated as if it's a full factorial design; sums of squares are computed for all possible terms. Then if a term isn't included in a model, the sums of squares calculated for that term is pooled in the lowest order interaction that contains that term as a subset. For example, in the model A B C A*B*C, the sums of squares for A*B, A*C and B*C are pooled with the ABC sums of squares.

### Treatment of Missing Values

Before the procedure computes the analysis of covariance statistics, the missing values in the data are located and replaced with their least squares estimates. For a given model and a particular pattern of missing values, it may be impossible to derive estimates of the missing values. In this case, you're notified and the computations are terminated. Situations where missing values can't be estimated do not reflect a flaw in the calculation procedures; any procedure that computes missing value estimates under these circumstances would be incorrect. Be careful in interpreting the results when missing values are estimated.

## Interpreting Analyses with Missing Values or Covariates

When missing values and/or covariates are present in an analysis, the treatment sums of squares reported by *Statistix* will only be approximate. The resulting F tests in the analysis of variance table are approximate, and they will generally be too liberal, i.e., rejecting the hypothesis when the exact test would not. So if the approximate F test isn't significant, the exact F test usually won't be either. In general, don't rely on the approximate F tests reported by *Statistix*; it's easy to construct exact F tests by hand for most hypotheses of interest.

Even if missing values and/or covariates are present in an analysis, the error sum of squares is always exact—and orthogonal to the other sums of squares. This provides a very convenient way to obtain nearly any exact F test. The general approach involves sequentially fitting models with different terms of interest deleted. The exact sums of squares are obtained by subtracting error sums of squares for different models. The particular models and order in which they're fitted will depend on the particular hypotheses of interest. The wide variety of hypotheses that you may be interested in preclude *Statistix* from automatically constructing these exact F tests. If you are working with missing values or covariates, you should understand how to construct such exact F tests or else you are liable to make serious misinterpretations of your data. This isn't a flaw in *Statistix*, but rather a general feature of analyses of covariance (balanced designs or otherwise) and unbalanced analyses of variance. The basic ideas are discussed in Snedecor and Cochran (1980) and Bingham and Fienberg (1982).

Constructing exact F tests for most hypotheses in nonorthogonal analyses is simple. The first step is always to fit the model with all terms in it, including terms that are hypothesized to be zero. This model is referred to as the full, or alternate, model. The next step is to fit the model in which the terms that are hypothesized to be zero are deleted. This is the reduced, or null, model. As mentioned, the error sums of squares are exact, even with missing values or covariates. The difference of the error sums of squares for the two models is the so-called sum of squares due to the hypothesis. The hypothesis sum of squares is the sum of squares due to the terms that are hypothesized to be zero after adjusting for all other terms in the model. This hypothesis sum of squares is found by subtraction: hypothesis SS = reduced error SS - full error SS. The degrees of freedom are found in a similar manner: hypothesis DF = reduced error DF - full error DF. The hypothesis mean square (MS) is: hypothesis SS / hypothesis DF. The F test is then constructed as: hypothesis MS / full MSE. (MSE stands for mean square for error.)

A detailed example is given in example III below. The general approach used in this example is relevant to any analyses of variance with missing values and analyses of covariance with or without missing values.

This method of sequentially fitting models can be used to obtain any SAS type 1 and type 2 sums of squares. In general, you can't obtain SAS type 3 and type 4 sums of squares from *Statistix*. Types 3 and 4 sums of squares are only necessary if you want to test for effects that are also present in higher order interactions and you aren't willing to assume that these higher order interactions containing the effects are zero. An alternative approach that many prefer is to test the interactions first; if insignificant, they're assumed to be zero for future testing. This approach, which Bingham and Fienberg (1982) refer to as the hierarchical approach, can always be performed with *Statistix* (see Example III on page 195).

## Example I: Two-Way Analysis of Variance

Example I is a randomized block design from Snedecor and Cochran (1980, sect. 14.2). The dependent variable is the number of soybeans out of 100 that failed to emerge, and the treatments are various fungicides (the first treatment level was a no-fungicide control). The variable names are Y for the dependent variable, BLK for replication (block), and TRT for treatment.

| CASE | Y | TRT | BLK | CASE | Y | TRT | BLK |
|---|---|---|---|---|---|---|---|
| 1 | 8 | 1 | 1 | 14 | 8 | 3 | 4 |
| 2 | 10 | 1 | 2 | 15 | 10 | 3 | 5 |
| 3 | 12 | 1 | 3 | 16 | 3 | 4 | 1 |
| 4 | 13 | 1 | 4 | 17 | 5 | 4 | 2 |
| 5 | 11 | 1 | 5 | 18 | 9 | 4 | 3 |
| 6 | 2 | 2 | 1 | 19 | 10 | 4 | 4 |
| 7 | 6 | 2 | 2 | 20 | 6 | 4 | 5 |
| 8 | 7 | 2 | 3 | 21 | 9 | 5 | 1 |
| 9 | 11 | 2 | 4 | 22 | 7 | 5 | 2 |
| 10 | 5 | 2 | 5 | 23 | 5 | 5 | 3 |
| 11 | 4 | 3 | 1 | 24 | 5 | 5 | 4 |
| 12 | 10 | 3 | 2 | 25 | 3 | 5 | 5 |
| 13 | 9 | 3 | 3 | | | | |

You can use the **Transformations** CAT function to generate repetitive sequences, such as those seen for TRT and BLK. After entering the 25 values for Y, we can use the **Transformation** expressions TRT = CAT (5,5) and BLK = CAT (5,1) to create these variables. The model is specified in the options panel below.

```
GENERAL ANALYSIS OF VARIANCE/COVARIANCE                          SOYBEANS

BLK        TRT        Y

3 variable(s).   25 of 25 cases selected.   1199K bytes free.

Enter the name of the dependent variable.   Press F2 to select from list.
Y

List the variables to be used as main effects and all interaction terms
(eg. BLOCK*TREATMENT) in your AOV model. Indicate which terms are to be used
as error terms by typing (E) after the term. Press F2 to select from list.
BLK TRT BLK*TRT

For analysis of covariance, list the variables to be used as covariables.

Esc Exit   F1 Start   F2 Select variable
```

The results are as follows:

ANALYSIS OF VARIANCE TABLE FOR Y

| SOURCE | DF | SS | MS | F | P |
|---|---|---|---|---|---|
| BLK (A) | 4 | 49.8400 | 12.4600 | 2.30 | 0.1032 |
| TRT (B) | 4 | 83.8400 | 20.9600 | 3.87 | 0.0219 |
| A*B | 16 | 86.5600 | 5.41000 | | |
| TOTAL | 24 | 220.240 | | | |
| GRAND AVERAGE | 1 | 1413.76 | | | |

The treatment effect is significant at the 5% level (p = 0.0219). Because this is a randomized block design, the test for block effects (BLK) won't usually be of interest.

The variables in this analysis are BLK and TRT. In the SOURCE column, these variables are assigned a letter designator. The letter in the parentheses behind the variable name in the source column indicates which letter has been assigned to the variable name. For example, A is assigned to BLK and B is assigned to TRT. When interaction terms are given in the source column, they're represented only by the letter tags. The interaction term in the SOURCE column represented as A∗B is the interaction BLK∗TRT.

## Example II: Split-plot Analysis of Variance

The following example is a split-plot design from Section 16.15 of Snedecor and Cochran (1980). TONS is the yield of alfalfa in tons per acre. VAR is the variety of alfalfa. BLK is the so-called main plot. DATE is the time in days between the second and third cuttings. The second cutting was on July 27. The third cuttings were on September 1, September 20, and October 7. One treatment wasn't cut a third time. We assigned this group the date November 10, intending to reflect the end of the growing season. The values for DATE are 36, 55, 72, and 106. VAR and BLK are qualitative factors, and the actual values of them have meaning only as labels. When possible, factors, such as DATE, should be represented quantitatively because response surfaces can then be examined with polynomial contrasts (see Polynomial Contrasts on page 213).

A partial listing of the data is presented in the table below.

| CASE | TONS | VAR | BLK | DATE |
|---|---|---|---|---|
| 1 | 2.17 | 1 | 1 | 106 |
| 2 | 1.58 | 1 | 1 | 35 |
| 3 | 2.29 | 1 | 1 | 54 |
| 4 | 2.23 | 1 | 1 | 71 |
| 5 | 1.88 | 1 | 2 | 106 |
| 6 | 1.26 | 1 | 2 | 35 |
| 7 | 1.60 | 1 | 2 | 54 |
| 8 | 2.01 | 1 | 2 | 71 |
| 9 | 1.62 | 1 | 3 | 106 |
| 10 | 1.22 | 1 | 3 | 35 |
| 11 | 1.67 | 1 | 3 | 54 |
| 12 | 1.82 | 1 | 3 | 71 |
| . . . | | | | |
| 72 | 1.33 | 3 | 6 | 71 |

The split-plot model is specified in the options panel below.

```
                    GENERAL ANALYSIS OF VARIANCE/COVARIANCE                ALFALFA
BLK          DATE          TONS          VAR

4 variable(s).   72 of 72 cases selected.   1197K bytes free.

Enter the name of the dependent variable.   Press F2 to select from list.
TONS

List the variables to be used as main effects and all interaction terms
(eg. BLOCK*TREATMENT) in your AOV model. Indicate which terms are to be used
as error terms by typing (E) after the term. Press F2 to select from list.
VAR BLK VAR*BLK(E) DATE BLK*DATE(E) VAR*DATE BLK*VAR*DATE(E)

For analysis of covariance, list the variables to be used as covariables.

Esc Exit   F1 Start   F2 Select variable
```

The results are presented in the analysis of variance table below.

ANALYSIS OF VARIANCE TABLE FOR TONS   Tons of alfalfa

| SOURCE | DF | SS | MS | F | P |
|---|---|---|---|---|---|
| VAR (A) | 2 | 0.17801 | 0.08901 | 0.65 | 0.5412 |
| BLK (B) | 5 | 4.14982 | 0.82996 | 6.09 | 0.0077 |
| A*B | 10 | 1.36234 | 0.13623 | | |
| DATE (C) | 3 | 1.96247 | 0.65415 | 17.84 | 0.0000 |
| B*C | 15 | 0.55013 | 0.03667 | | |
| A*C | 6 | 0.21055 | 0.03509 | 1.49 | 0.2166 |
| A*B*C | 30 | 0.70840 | 0.02361 | | |
| TOTAL | 71 | 9.12176 | | | |
| GRAND AVERAGE | 1 | 183.584 | | | |

The interaction term A∗B (VAR∗BLK) is used as the error term to compute the F test for VAR. The p-value of 0.5412 suggests little difference between the varieties. The term B∗C (BLK∗DATE) is used as the error term to test C (DATE); DATE appears to be very significant (p = 0.0000).

## Example III: Analysis of Covariance with Missing Values

Missing values are a common cause for unbalanced, or nonorthogonal, analysis of variance designs. Analysis of covariance designs are nearly always nonorthogonal regardless of whether they have missing values or not.

Nonorthogonal analyses require special consideration. If you ignore non-orthogonality and use the "usual" procedure appropriate only for orthogonal designs, the conclusions drawn will be suspect at best. Fortunately, the correct technique for nonorthogonal designs is easy. It can be applied equally regardless of the cause of nonorthogonality—analysis of covariance, missing values in analysis of variance, or analysis of covariance with missing values. This example uses an analysis of covariance with missing values.

The main effects and interactions sums of squares given in the analysis of variance table are only approximations when the design is nonorthogonal. In general, the "more nonorthogonal" the design is, the worse the approximations become. These approximate sums of squares will generally be larger than the exact sums of squares. This example shows that the error can be quite substantial. The general approach illustrated here for computing exact sums of squares is equally applicable to analyses of variance with missing values and analyses of covariance (with or without missing values).

The data set comes from Bingham and Fienberg (1982) and was originally from Federer (1957). The dependent variable is the number of saleable flowers that open in one month (ROSES). Five different treatments (TRT) were applied to the roses. The treatments were unequally replicated within two randomized blocks (BLK). The factor WITHIN indicates the within-block replication. The covariate is the location on the greenhouse bench, represented by LOC.

The data set is listed in the table below.

| CASE | ROSES | TRT | BLK | WITHIN | LOC |
|---|---|---|---|---|---|
| 1 | 102 | 1 | 1 | 1 | 15 |
| 2 | M | 1 | 1 | 2 | M |
| 3 | 71 | 1 | 2 | 1 | 10 |
| 4 | 79 | 1 | 2 | 2 | 11 |
| 5 | 84 | 2 | 1 | 1 | 9 |
| 6 | 81 | 2 | 1 | 2 | 7 |
| 7 | 76 | 2 | 2 | 1 | 14 |
| 8 | M | 2 | 2 | 2 | M |
| 9 | 67 | 3 | 1 | 1 | 5 |
| 10 | 83 | 3 | 1 | 2 | 4 |
| 11 | 74 | 3 | 2 | 1 | 2 |
| 12 | M | 3 | 2 | 2 | M |
| 13 | 71 | 4 | 1 | 1 | 11 |
| 14 | M | 4 | 1 | 2 | M |
| 15 | 51 | 4 | 2 | 1 | 4 |
| 16 | 63 | 4 | 2 | 2 | 5 |
| 17 | 53 | 5 | 1 | 1 | 2 |
| 18 | M | 5 | 1 | 2 | M |
| 19 | 63 | 5 | 2 | 1 | 8 |
| 20 | 61 | 5 | 2 | 2 | 7 |

The goal of the analysis is to test for a treatment (TRT) effect as well as to examine the importance of bench location (LOC). The first step is to fit the full model containing all main effects and interactions. This model is specified in the options panel below.

```
GENERAL ANALYSIS OF VARIANCE/COVARIANCE                              ROSES
BLK        LOC        ROSES       TRT        WITHIN

5 variable(s).  20 of 20 cases selected.  1199K bytes free.

Enter the name of the dependent variable.  Press F2 to select from list.
ROSES

List the variables to be used as main effects and all interaction terms
(eg. BLOCK*TREATMENT) in your AOV model. Indicate which terms are to be used
as error terms by typing (E) after the term. Press F2 to select from list.
TRT BLK TRT*BLK TRT*BLK*WITHIN(E)

For analysis of covariance, list the variables to be used as covariables.
LOC
Esc Exit  F1 Start  F2 Select variable
```

The resulting statistics are shown below.

```
ANALYSIS OF VARIANCE TABLE FOR ROSES

SOURCE          DF       SS          MS           F      P
-------------   --   ---------   ---------    ------  ------
TRT (A)          4    1339.30     334.825       5.84  0.0579
BLK (B)          1    266.450     266.450       4.64  0.0974
A*B              4    410.050     102.512       1.79  0.2939
WITHIN (C)
A*B*C            4    229.500     57.3750
-------------   --   ---------
TOTAL           13    2245.30
GRAND AVERAGE    1    94668.8

COVARIATE SUMMARY TABLE

COVARIATE
VARIABLES     COEFFICIENT    STD ERROR    STUDENT'S T       P
---------     -----------    ---------    -----------    ------
LOC               1.50000      3.78731           0.40    0.7123

RESIDUAL SS IGNORING COVARIATES           238.500
RESIDUAL SS ADJUSTED FOR COVARIATES       229.500
REDUCTION IN SS DUE TO COVARIATES         9.00000
F TEST FOR COVARIATES   0.16       P (F, 1, 4)   0.7123

CASES INCLUDED 15    MISSING CASES 5
```

As mentioned, the statistics given in the analysis of variance table are approximations except for the error line, i.e., the A∗B∗C interaction. The statistics given on the covariate summary table are always exact. As you'll see, you could be seriously misled if you based the F test for TRT on the approximate TRT SS of 1339.30.

To test for TRT effect, we use the hierarchical approach discussed by Bingham and Fienberg (1982). With this approach, the higher order interaction terms involving the term of interest are assumed to be zero. The first step, which examines how reasonable this assumption is, requires testing the TRT∗BLK interaction term. To do this, we fit the reduced, or null, model, which does not include the TRT∗BLK interaction. This is specified as:

```
Enter the name of the dependent variable.  Press F2 to select from list.
ROSES

List the variables to be used as main effects and all interaction terms
(eg. BLOCK*TREATMENT) in your AOV model. Indicate which terms are to be used
as error terms by typing (E) after the term. Press F2 to select from list.
TRT BLK TRT*BLK*WITHIN

For analysis of covariance, list the variables to be used as covariables.
LOC
```

The resulting statistics are displayed below.

```
ANALYSIS OF VARIANCE TABLE FOR ROSES

SOURCE          DF      SS          MS          F       P
-----------     --   ---------   ---------   -----   ------
TRT (A)          4    979.396     244.849     3.90   0.0482
BLK (B)          1    264.703     264.703     4.21   0.0742
WITHIN (C)
A*B*C            8    502.531     62.8163
-----------     --   ---------
TOTAL           13    1746.63
GRAND AVERAGE    1    92300.1

COVARIATE SUMMARY TABLE

COVARIATE
VARIABLES    COEFFICIENT    STD ERROR   STUDENT'S T      P
---------    -----------    ---------   -----------   ------
LOC              1.55991      0.81980          1.90   0.0936

RESIDUAL SS IGNORING COVARIATES          729.966
RESIDUAL SS ADJUSTED FOR COVARIATES      502.531
REDUCTION IN SS DUE TO COVARIATES        227.435
F TEST FOR COVARIATES  3.62       P (F, 1, 8)  0.0936

CASES INCLUDED 15   MISSING CASES 5
```

The exact sum of squares for TRT∗BLK are found by subtracting the error sum of squares for the full model from the error sum of squares for the reduced model: 502.531 - 229.500 = 273.031. This sum of squares is said to be adjusted for the BLK and TRT main effects. Notice how inflated the approximate SS of 410.050 is. With 4 degrees of freedom, the exact mean square (MS) is 273.031 / 4 = 68.2578. The F test uses the error MS from the full model in the denominator: 68.2578 / 57.3750 = 1.19. FPROB (1.19, 4, 4) is specified in **Probability Distributions**, and the p-value for this test is found to be 0.4351. This gives little reason to suspect the assumption that the TRT∗BLK interaction is zero, so we'll proceed on the basis of this assumption.

The next model we need omits both the TRT and TRT∗BLK terms:

```
Enter the name of the dependent variable.  Press F2 to select from list.
ROSES

List the variables to be used as main effects and all interaction terms
(eg. BLOCK*TREATMENT) in your AOV model. Indicate which terms are to be used
as error terms by typing (E) after the term. Press F2 to select from list.
BLK TRT*BLK*WITHIN

For analysis of covariance, list the variables to be used as covariables.
LOC
```

The resulting statistics are shown below.

```
ANALYSIS OF VARIANCE TABLE FOR ROSES

SOURCE              DF        SS            MS              F        P
---------------   ----   -----------   -----------   --------  ------
BLK (A)              1     514.161       514.161          5.27  0.0405
TRT (B)
WITHIN (C)
A*B*C               12    1170.45        97.5381
---------------   ----   -----------
TOTAL               13    1684.61
GRAND AVERAGE        1   84464.6

COVARIATE SUMMARY TABLE

COVARIATE
VARIABLES    COEFFICIENT    STD ERROR    STUDENT'S T       P
---------    -----------    ---------    -----------    ------
LOC              1.95831      0.65179           3.00    0.0110

RESIDUAL SS IGNORING COVARIATES            2050.92
RESIDUAL SS ADJUSTED FOR COVARIATES        1170.45
REDUCTION IN SS DUE TO COVARIATES          880.470
F TEST FOR COVARIATES   9.03        P (F,  1, 12)   0.0110

CASES INCLUDED 15    MISSING CASES 5
```

We need to compute the sum of squares for TRT adjusted for BLK assuming the TRT∗BLK interaction is zero. This is done by subtracting the error SS for this second reduced model from the error SS for the first reduced model: 1170.45 - 502.531 = 667.919. The mean square is 166.98, and the resulting F test is 166.98 / 57.375 = 2.91. The p-value is found by specifying FPROB (2.91, 4, 4), and is 0.1628. If we'd used the approximate SS of 1339.30, the p-value would be 0.0579. The discrepancy between the exact and approximate tests will often not be this large, but obviously you should not put too much trust in the approximate tests. Approximate F tests will generally be too large and will result in too many significant tests.

The covariate summary table allows you to assess the importance of the covariates. All statistics given in the covariate summary table are exact. This table shares several similarities with the coefficient table produced by **Linear Regression**. Student's t tests are performed to test the hypothesis that the regression coefficients for the covariates are zero, given that all other analysis of variance and covariance terms are in the model. The bottom line of the covariate summary table gives an F test that tests the overall significance of all covariates in the model. This F test examines the null hypothesis that the regression coefficients for all covariates are simultaneously zero, given that all of the analysis of variance terms are in the model. If there is only one covariate, the test based on Student's t and the test based on the F statistic are equivalent.

It's rather difficult to assess the importance of LOC in the example. Its importance appears to depend greatly on the model. LOC doesn't appear to be very important in the full model (p = 0.7123). In the second reduced model, it appears to be substantially more important (p = 0.0110). It's likely that the apparent importance of LOC in the second reduced model is due to the fact that LOC is confounded to some extent with TRT, which is not included in the model. The increasing denominator degrees of freedom would tend to increase the power of the test.

## Large AOV's

Occasionally, a data set is encountered for which there are more than the maximum of 50 levels for each factor, especially for factors corresponding to replication. In many cases, you can still analyze such a data set using the General AOV/AOCV procedure. Suppose the factor with too many levels has L levels. IF L can be factored into a product of two terms less than or equal to 50, then pseudofactors can be used to perform the analysis.

Suppose you have a 2 X 2 factorial design, with 80 within-cell replications for a total of 320 samples. Call the dependent variable BIRTHWT, the two factors SMOKER and JOGGER, and the replication factor REP. Assuming the birth weights were entered in smoker jogger order, the factors can be created using the following transformations:

```
SMOKER = CAT (2, 160)
JOGGER = CAT (2, 80)
REP = CAT (80, 1)
```

However, if you tried to run the General AOV/AOV using the model:

```
JOGGER SMOKER JOGGER*SMOKER JOGGER*SMOKER*REP
```

you would be told that REP has too many levels. The solution is to partition REP into pseudofactors, using pseudofactors REP1 with 10 levels and REP2 with 8 levels. The key to constructing pseudofactors is that for every unique level of the original factor, you now construct a unique combination of levels with the pseudofactors. You can create REP1 and REP2 using the Transformations:

```
REP1 = CAT (10, 8)
REP2 = CAT (8, 1)
```

Now we replace each reference to REP in the original model with the interaction REP1*REP2 in the model using pseudofactors. The new model is:

```
JOGGER SMOKER JOGGER*SMOKER JOGGER*SMOKER*REP1*REP2
```

The resulting AOV table is:

```
ANALYSIS OF VARIANCE TABLE FOR BIRTHWT

SOURCE              DF        SS            MS              F        P
JOGGER (A)           1     3.12160       3.12160         9.09   0.0028
SMOKER (B)           1     57.8046       57.8046       168.30   0.0000
A*B                  1     1.04294       1.04294         3.04   0.0824
REP1 (C)
REP2 (D)
A*B*C*D            316     108.534       0.34346

TOTAL              319     170.503
GRAND AVERAGE        1     10104.7
```

This general approach is quite flexible, and you can use it for many problems that would otherwise be much too large. In general, any factor that has too many levels can be replaced by an interaction of pseudofactor terms. The crux of the matter is to be able to factor the number of levels of the original factor into a product of terms that have no more than 50 levels each. See Oliver (1967) for more information on using pseudofactors in analysis of variance.

## AOV Results Menu

After the initial analysis of variance is completed and displayed, the following options can be selected.

```
AOV RESULTS

AOV table
Comparisons of means
General contrasts
Means and std errors
Nonadditivity
Polynomial contrasts
Save residuals
Options panel
```

Select "AOV table" from the menu to redisplay the initial AOV results. Select "Options panel" to return to the main General AOV options panel used to specify the model. The remaining results options are described below.

## Comparisons of Means

You will often be interested in comparing means for different levels of a main effect. This is the function of **Comparisons of means**. Other names for this procedure are multiple comparisons, mean separation tests, multiple range tests, and tests for homogeneity of means. Two means are said to be similar, or homogeneous, if they're not significantly different from one another. This procedure identifies groups (subsets) of similar, or homogeneous, means. Use of the procedure is first illustrated with an example, and then some details of its application are discussed.

We'll use Example I, where the treatment factor TRT was the type of fungicide applied to batches of 100 soybeans. TRT has five levels; the first is a no-fungicide control, and the remaining four are different types of fungicide. The dependent variable Y is the number of beans out of 100 that failed to sprout.

```
                    PAIRWISE COMPARISONS OF MEANS                    SOYBEANS
 Dependent variable: Y
 Factors:               BLK TRT

 Enter the variable name of the main effect for pairwise comparisons.
 TRT
 Enter the name of a co | PAIRWISE COMPARISONS OF MEANS | ect from list.
 LSD (T)                |                               |
                        | Bonferroni                    |
 Enter the rejection le | LSD (T)                       | to 0.100
 0.050                  | Multiplicative Sidak          |
                        | Scheffe                       |
                        | Tukey (HSD)                   |
```

First enter the name of the factor you want comparisons for (TRT in the example above). Next select a comparison method. Press F2 to display the menu of the five comparison methods. We've selected the Least Significant Difference method (LSD). The default value for the rejection level of 0.05 is what you want, so press F1 to start. The following results are then displayed:

```
LSD (T) PAIRWISE COMPARISONS OF MEANS OF Y BY TRT

                             HOMOGENEOUS
     TRT          MEAN       GROUPS
 ----------    ----------   -----------
      1          10.800       I
      3          8.2000       I I
      4          6.6000      .. I
      2          6.2000      .. I
      5          5.8000      .. I

THERE ARE 2 GROUPS IN WHICH THE MEANS ARE
NOT SIGNIFICANTLY DIFFERENT FROM ONE ANOTHER.

CRITICAL T VALUE                      2.120    REJECTION LEVEL    0.050
CRITICAL VALUE FOR COMPARISON        3.1185
STANDARD ERROR FOR COMPARISON        1.4710

ERROR TERM USED: BLK*TRT, 16 DF
```

The second column of the results shows the means of Y for the levels of the factor TRT. The means have been sorted in descending order so the largest one is listed in the first row, the next to largest in the second row, and so on. The first column displays the treatment levels and shows how the sorting has reordered the means. For example, the first treatment level has the largest mean, the third treatment level has the next largest mean, and so on.

The columns of I's under the heading "Homogenous Groups" indicate which means are not significantly different from one another. There are two columns in the example since there are two groups of similar or homogenous means. The first group contains the means for TRT levels 1 and 3, and the second group contains the means for TRT levels 2, 3, 4, and 5. As you see in this example, it's not unusual for the groups to overlap, although they need not. The row of .'s after some means serve as "ruler lines" to help you identify the mean with its appropriate homogeneous subset(s).

It's easy to construct confidence intervals for the differences of any two means. Suppose you were interested in 95% confidence bounds around the difference of the best and worst fungicides—treatment levels 3 and 5. The difference is 8.2 - 5.8 = 2.4. The confidence interval is 2.4   3.1185 = -0.72 to 5.52. The value 3.1185 is the critical value for the comparison. Note that the confidence interval contains zero, which is expected since treatments 3 and 5 were both members of the second homogenous subset.

## Multiple Comparison Procedures

It's important you understand the difference between (1) the hypotheses being tested by the overall F test for a main treatment effect in analysis of variance and (2) the hypotheses being tested by pairwise comparisons procedures. A contrast is any linear combination of treatment means such that the linear coefficients sum to zero (see General Contrasts on page 208). A pairwise comparison of two means is a special case of a contrast where the contrast coefficients are 1 and -1 for the means being compared, and 0 for all other means.

The overall F test for a treatment effect in AOV is testing the hypothesis that all of the means are equal. You can think of it as a test of whether all possible contrasts are zero. If the overall F is significant, it means that there is <u>some</u> contrast that's significant, but it doesn't guarantee that any pairwise comparison is particularly important. The set of pairwise comparisons is a small subset of the entire set of all possible contrasts. The F test has to be a conservative test because it must guard against type 1 errors (rejecting a null hypothesis when it's true) over the entire set of all possible contrasts, not just the smaller subset of pairwise comparisons. If you're interested only in the set of pairwise comparisons, you can construct a more powerful test than the overall F test over this restricted space.

If you're interested in a single comparison of two means, the most powerful procedure is the T test. For a single such comparison, the probability of falsely rejecting a true null hypothesis (type 1 error) is whatever the significance level of the T test is. Suppose that there are two comparisons of interest to you. Suppose you test each one at the level $\alpha$ with a T test. The probability of making a type 1 error in each comparison is $\alpha$, so the probability of making at least one type 1 error over both comparisons is greater than $\alpha$. As the number of comparisons grows, the probability of making at least one type 1 error grows toward 1. This probability of making at least one type 1 error for all comparisons is called the experimentwise error rate, in contrast to the comparisonwise error rate. The T test controls the comparisonwise error rate at $\alpha$ but allows the experimentwise error rate to increase as the number of comparisons increases. (Experimentwise error rate refers to the maximum experimentwise error rate under a complete or partial null hypothesis. Under a complete null hypothesis, all the population means are equal; under a partial null hypothesis, only some of the population means are equal.)

If there are P means, there are m = P(P-1)/2 pairwise comparisons, so the number of comparisons grows rapidly as the number of means increases. Some control over the experimentwise error rate is desirable. Numerous methods have been proposed for this, and there is some disagreement as to the best procedures. The following discussion describes the procedures available in *Statistix*.

First, some terminology: Suppose $M_i$ and $M_j$ are two means. The comparison between means i and j is $L_{ij} = M_i - M_j$. For a complete, balanced AOV, the standard error of $L_{ij}$ is $SE(L_{ij}) = (2*MSE/n)^{1/2}$, where MSE is the mean square for error and n is the number of samples present at a level of the factor of interest. For the comparison $L_{ij}$ to be significant, its absolute value must exceed some critical value C, where C depends on the method of comparison being used. Confidence intervals for a comparison are computed as $L_{ij}$ C.

The most powerful (least conservative) comparison procedure is the **LSD**, or Least Significant Difference method. The critical value for a comparison is $SE(L_{ij})$ T, where T is Student's t-statistic for the degrees of freedom associated with MSE. This method is also called the T method. LSD controls the comparisonwise error rate at $\alpha$ but allows the experimentwise error rate to increase as the number of comparisons increases. Some advocate using this method only if the overall F test is significant, leading to what has sometimes been called the PSD, or Protected Significant Difference. Contrary to what has sometimes been claimed, the PSD method does not control the experimentwise error rate if there are more than three levels for the factor of interest.

As we noted earlier, the overall F test is testing a much broader range of hypotheses than a multiple comparison test and so it must be more conservative. If the set of pairwise comparisons are of primary interest, then the so-called protected approach (proceeding only if the overall F is significant) can be refuted to some extent regardless of the comparison method because the F test sacrifices power to test hypotheses that are not of direct interest. However, such cases are probably exceptions rather than the rule.

You should use the LSD method if there are a few preplanned comparisons that are of primary interest. However, inspecting the means for large differences before deciding which comparisons to make invalidates its use. The LSD procedure is the most powerful pairwise comparison procedure, but it will generally have the highest experimentwise error rate. We mentioned earlier that the LSD approach controls the comparisonwise error rate at $\alpha$. If you use the LSD method and report significant comparisons, you should be prepared to justify why you didn't find it necessary to control the experimentwise error rate.

The LSD procedure can be modified to prevent the experimentwise error from growing as the number of comparisons increases. The general idea is to make it more difficult to reject as the number of comparisons increases, which can be done by increasing the critical value of T as the number of comparisons increases. Suppose T(p) is the T value corresponding to a two-tailed significance level of p for Student's t. For the LSD procedure, p is the constant $\alpha$. To control the experimentwise error rate, p should be some decreasing function of m, where m is the number of comparisons. Two common methods for this are **Bonferroni's** and **Sidak's**. Bonferroni's—probably the more popular of the two—uses the function $p = \alpha/m$, and Sidak's uses the function $p = 1 - (1 - \alpha)^{1/m}$. Using either of these methods results in an experimentwise error rate of less than $\alpha$. The problem with these procedures is they rapidly grow conservative as m increases; in effect, the experimentwise error rate is reduced too much and real differences do not get detected (test power is lost). Bonferroni's is generally more conservative than Sidak's. Because of rapidly decreasing power, these procedures are not recommended for general use although they can be useful when the number of means, and hence the number of comparisons, is small.

**Tukey's** method is the most useful pairwise comparison procedure *Statistix* performs. It controls the experimentwise error rate, yet still retains good power. It's based on the Studentized range statistic. Suppose there are P means for the factor of interest, with $X_{(1)}$ being the smallest and $X_{(P)}$ being the largest. The standard error of a mean is $(MSE/n)^{1/2}$, where MSE is the mean square for error and n is the number of samples within each level. (In terms of $SE(L_{ij})$, which is displayed by *Statistix*, the standard error of a mean is $SE(Lij)/(2^{1/2})$.) Under the usual assumptions, the statistic $(X_{(1)}-X_{(P)})$ / $(MSE/n)^{1/2}$ then has a Studentized range distribution if there are no differences between the population means. The critical value for a comparison $L_{ij}$ is $C = (MSE/n)^{1/2}\, Q(P,DF)$, where Q(P,DF) is the Studentized range value for P means and DF degrees of freedom (degrees of freedom associated with MSE) at the desired rejection level $\alpha$. Tukey's procedure may find significant comparisons even if the overall F test is not significant because Tukey's test restricts itself to the pairwise comparison subset of contrast space. This is mentioned because it helps in deciding whether to use Tukey's procedure or Scheffe's procedure.

Basically, **Scheffe's** procedure treats pairwise comparisons as "just another contrast". Suppose you've just observed a significant overall F. Clearly you'd be interested in investigating the pattern(s) among the means that produced this result. In this context, pairwise comparisons are just one of any number of contrasts that may interest you; you are interested in general "data-snooping". Scheffe's procedure controls the experimentwise error rate, but here the "experiment" is not just the m = P(P-1)/2 comparisons but all possible contrasts. The price you pay for such general protection is that Scheffe's procedure is more conservative than Tukey's; it will not detect some differences between means that Tukey's will. If the overall F test was not significant, Scheffe's comparisons will never be significant either. The critical value for Scheffe's is $C = SE(L_{ij})\, [(P-1)\, F(P-1, DF)]^{1/2}$, where F(P-1, DF) is the appropriate F value.

Two comparison procedures that are very popular in the natural sciences and other areas are **Duncan's New** method and the **Student-Newman-Keuls**, or SNK, method. These procedures are not recommended for general use, and *Statistix* doesn't compute them. Duncan's New method controls the comparisonwise error rate at $\alpha$ and generally gives results similar to the LSD procedure. The LSD procedure is easier to explain and compute than Duncan's, and we prefer it. The SNK procedure doesn't control the experimentwise error rate under a partial null hypothesis and cannot be recommended (Einot and Gabriel 1975). There are a number of procedures more powerful than Tukey's that still control the experimentwise error rate (Ryan 1960, Einot and Gabriel 1975, Welsch 1977, Begun and Gabriel 1981). Like Duncan's New and SNK, these procedures are multiple stage tests, which means the critical value doesn't remain constant for all comparisons but rather varies as the homogenous subsets are constructed. The disadvantages of such multiple-stage procedures are that they're more complex to explain and compute and, in particular, do not permit the construction of confidence intervals, which is often useful when you present your results.

The basis for deciding which procedure to use is somewhat subjective and philosophical. Conceivably, two researchers with exactly the same data could apply different comparison methods and reach different conclusions about the means, both of which could be justified, depending on the researchers' assumptions. If you're not certain which procedure to use, try several, keeping their various interpretations in mind.

## Comparisons of Means - Missing Values

If you have missing values, the comparison of means results are only approximate and the quality of the approximation deteriorates as the number of missing values increases. You can't use this procedure when covariates are present because when a design isn't orthogonal, the standard errors of the comparisons vary from comparison to comparison. Suppose you have the means A>B>C>D. In a nonorthogonal design, it's possible that B and C are significantly different but A and D are not. A and D belong to a homogenous subset, but B and C do not belong in a homogenous subset, even though the values of B and C fall between the values of A and D.

## Comparisons of Means - Computational Notes

*Statistix* computes quantiles for Student's t distribution using a procedure patterned after Hill (1970). Quantiles for the F distribution are found by finding the inverse of the corresponding beta distribution using Newton's method. The algorithm used to perform this is similar to Majumder and Bhattacharjee's (1973), although a different procedure, described in Probability Distributions (Chapter 11), is used to compute the cumulative distribution function of the beta distribution. The quantiles for the Studentized range distribution are computed with a procedure patterned after Lund and Lund (1983).

## General Contrasts

This powerful option computes any linear contrast for any effect or interaction. Linear contrasts are linear combinations of the means for any effect or interaction, and they're valuable for examining the "fine structure" of the data after the overall F test indicates that the effect or interaction is significant.

Suppose, in Example I, you're interested in whether the mean for the control (no fungicide) is different from the mean of the four treatments (fungicides applied). To make this comparison, you enter "4 -1 -1 -1 -1" for the contrast coefficients. For example:

```
                    GENERAL LINEAR CONTRASTS                         SOYBEANS
Dependent variable: Y
Factors:            BLK TRT

Enter the main effect or interaction term for computing contrasts.
TRT

If you would like contrasts computed for each level of a different model
variable, enter the name of the model variable here (see manual).

List the 5 coefficients for contrast number 1.
4 -1 -1 -1 -1
List the 5 coefficients for contrast number 2.

List the 5 coefficients for contrast number 3.

List the 5 coefficients for contrast number 4.

List the 5 coefficients for contrast number 5.

Esc Results menu  F1 Start
```

First specify the main effect or interaction for which you want to construct contrasts—TRT in our example. You can specify up to five contrasts at once. The coefficients entered must sum to 0, but their absolute values don't matter. The coefficients can be entered as integer or real values. The ordering of the coefficients is determined by the values used to represent the levels of the factors. In the example above, the no-fungicide control is represented in the variable TRT as 1, the four fungicides are represented as 2, 3, 4, and 5. The list of coefficients in the example above can be shortened using a repeat factor: 4 4(-1).

The results are presented on the next page.

Scheffe's F method of significance testing for arbitrary simultaneous contrasts is used to test the hypothesis that the contrast is zero. The contrast in the above example is seen to be significant at the 5% level (p = 0.0453).

```
AOV CONTRASTS OF Y BY TRT

CONTRAST COEFFICIENTS: 4 -1 -1 -1 -1

CONTRAST             16.400          SS (CONTRAST)         67.240
SCHEFFE'S F            3.11          P (SCHEFFE'S F)       0.0453
T-STATISTIC            3.53          P (T-STATISTIC)       0.0028
SE (CONTRAST)        4.6510

ERROR TERM USED: BLK*TRT, 16 DF
```

Scheffe's procedure is appropriate for any number of a posteriori contrasts, which means it can be used to test hypotheses that arise after the data are collected and inspected. It protects you from making too many type 1 errors (rejecting a correct null hypothesis) during such "data-snooping". In the example output above, the sum of squares due to contrast is computed in the usual way, as illustrated in Sections 12.7 and 12.8 of Snedecor and Cochran (1980). If there are missing values or covariates, it is approximate, and the usual orthogonal decompositions are no longer orthogonal. The contrast is always the correct least squares estimate. The standard error and Scheffe's F (and resulting p-value) are exact if there are no missing values, even if covariates are present. The computational methods used are discussed in Section 6.4 of Scheffe (1959).

The statistic SCHEFFE'S F is computed as SSC/(DF∗MSE), which is equivalent to $L^2/(DF*SE(L)^2)$, where SSC is the sum of squares due to the contrast, MSE is the mean square for error, L is the value of the contrast, SE(L) is the standard error of the contrast, and DF is the degrees of freedom associated with the contrast. The same error term is used as would be used for the F test in the original AOV table. Scheffe's F will not be computed for contrasts of interaction terms in models that have multiple error terms; neither will it be computed for terms used as error terms in the model.

In addition to Scheffe's F method, Student's t test is performed. Student's t test is appropriate for a priori tests (contrasts that had been planned before the data were inspected). Student's t test doesn't control the experimentwise error rate, as we discussed in the comparisons of means section (page 203). Student's t-statistic is computed as L/SE(L).

It's possible to compute contrasts for a term in the model as shown on the preceding page, but at each level of another variable in the model. Using the same example, we'll compute the contrast for TRT at each level for BLK. This is specified in the options panel presented on the next page.

```
Enter the main effect or interaction term for computing contrasts.
TRT

If you would like contrasts computed for each level of a different model
variable, enter the name of the model variable here (see manual).
BLK

List the coefficients for contrast number 1.
4 -1 -1 -1 -1
```

The results are as follows:

```
AOV CONTRASTS OF Y BY TRT FOR BLK

CONTRAST COEFFICIENTS: 4 -1 -1 -1 -1

FOR BLK = 1
CONTRAST              14.000          SS (CONTRAST)         9.8000

FOR BLK = 2
CONTRAST              12.000          SS (CONTRAST)         7.2000

FOR BLK = 3
CONTRAST              18.000          SS (CONTRAST)         16.200

FOR BLK = 4
CONTRAST              18.000          SS (CONTRAST)         16.200

FOR BLK = 5
CONTRAST              20.000          SS (CONTRAST)         20.000
```

The no-fungicide - fungicide contrast is 14.0 for block 1, 12.0 for block 2, and so on. The F test and t test are not performed in this particular example because the error term is BLK∗TRT.

## Means and Standard Errors

You can compute means for any combinations of factors. You need to specify the effect or interaction for which you want means computed. For instance, suppose you're interested in the means for VAR (variety) and VAR∗DATE (variety by cutting date interaction) in Example II (page 194). The means are requested as follows:

```
                    AOV MEANS AND STANDARD ERRORS                    ALFALFA

Dependent variable: TONS
Factors:            VAR BLK DATE

List the main effects and interaction terms for computing means and standard
errors.  You may use the "all terms" syntax (eg. ALL (BLOCK TREATMENT).
VAR VAR*DATE

Esc Results menu  F1 Start
```

The results are as follows:

```
GRAND MEAN     1.5968

MEANS OF TONS FOR VAR

    VAR            MEAN         SS (MEAN)
 ___________    ___________    ___________
       1         1.6662          3.6371
       2         1.5716          3.5179
       3         1.5525          1.7886

OBSERVATIONS PER CELL                    24
STD ERROR OF AN AVERAGE              0.0753
STD ERROR (DIFF OF 2 AVE'S)          0.1065
ERROR TERM USED: VAR*BLK, 10 DF

MEANS OF TONS FOR VAR*DATE

    VAR           DATE           MEAN          SS (MEAN)
 ___________   ___________   ___________    ___________
       1            35         1.3066           0.3023
       1            54         1.6633           0.8275
       1            71         1.8200           0.8266
       1           106         1.8750           0.5015
       2            35         1.3016           0.4394
       2            54         1.5766           0.6453
       2            71         1.6433           1.0655
       2           106         1.7650           0.6749
       3            35         1.4133           0.3393
       3            54         1.4833           0.3287
       3            71         1.6100           0.2510
       3           106         1.7033           0.5683

OBSERVATIONS PER CELL                     6
STD ERROR OF AN AVERAGE              0.0627
ERROR TERM USED: VAR*BLK*DATE, 30 DF
```

As this example illustrates, means for several terms can be computed at once. Note that the grand mean is always displayed.

In some circumstances, you may want to compute means for all of the main effects and interaction terms that are subsets of some higher-order interaction term. You can do this easily with the ALL option. For example, entering ALL (BLK VAR DATE) produces means for BLK, VAR, DATE, BLK∗VAR, BLK∗DATE, VAR∗DATE, and BLK∗VAR∗DATE.

The standard error of an average uses the MSE from the error term associated with it on the original AOV table. The standard error for the difference of two averages won't be computed for interaction terms in multiple error term models; neither will it be given for terms used as errors in the model.

The means are computed after missing values have been estimated and the data have been adjusted for covariates. The resulting means are the correct least squares estimates. The actual within-cell sums of squares and theoretical standard deviation based on the MSE are displayed. These are used to examine whether the assumption of constant variances seems reasonable.

## Nonadditivity

Tukey's one degree of freedom test for nonadditivity is useful when the experimental design only permits an additive model to be fitted to the data but you suspect that interaction is present. Its most common application is with a two-way strictly additive model, such as Example I (Snedecor and Cochran, 1980, sect. 15.8 & 15.9), although it can be applied in many other situations. To perform this procedure, you simply specify which error term you want to use.

In Example I, it would be appropriate to apply Tukey's nonadditivity test to the BLK∗TRT term. To specify the analysis, you enter:

```
          TUKEY'S 1 DEGREE OF FREEDOM TEST FOR NONADDITIVITY        FUNGUS1
 Dependent variable: Y
 Factors:            BLK TRT

 Enter the interaction term for computing Tukey's test for nonadditivity.
 BLK*TRT

Esc Exit  F1 Start
```

The results are:

```
TUKEY'S 1 DEGREE OF FREEDOM TEST FOR NONADDITIVITY
FOR Y BY BLK*TRT

SOURCE         DF       SS          F       P
------------- ----  ----------  ------  ------
NONADDITIVITY   1     1.49568     0.26  0.6150
REMAINDER      15    85.0643
```

There's little suggestion of nonadditivity (p = 0.6150). Otherwise, you'd probably want to examine the residuals to determine the nature of the departure from additivity. You can do this by saving the residuals with the **Save Residuals** option and then inspecting them with the **Scatter Plot** procedure. If nonadditivity is present, you should consider transforming your data in an effort to remove it. Tukey's procedure assumes that if interaction exists, it's multiplicative in nature. Even if this assumption isn't strictly correct, Tukey's model can often serve as a useful approximation.

## Polynomial Contrasts

This option computes the polynomial decomposition of the sums of squares for any effect or interaction. This is very useful for determining the existence and nature of trends in the treatment level means.

In Example II, we're interested in examining the trends of yield TONS as a function of cutting date DATE.

```
                    AOV POLYNOMIAL CONTRASTS                     ALFALFA
Dependent variable: TONS
Factors:            VAR BLK DATE

Enter the main effect or interaction term for computing polynomial contrasts.
DATE

Enter the maximum degree for the polynomial contrasts.
3
```

By specifying polynomials up to degree 3 be computed, you will get sums of squares for linear (degree 1), quadratic (degree 2), and cubic (degree 3) trends due to DATE. The results:

```
POLYNOMIAL CONTRASTS OF TONS BY DATE

 DEGREE         SS           F        P
 ------     ---------     -----    ------
   1           1.7003     46.36    0.0000
   2           0.2594      7.07    0.0178
   3        2.721E-03      0.07    0.7890

ERROR TERM USED: BLK*DATE, 15 DF
```

Strong support exists for a linear trend with DATE (p = 0.0000) in the example. Inspection of the means using **Means and standard errors** reveals that the TONS increase with increasing DATE. There also appears to be some evidence of a quadratic trend in addition to the linear trend (p = 0.0178). Perhaps this indicates that a date before November 10 should have been used as the end of the effective growing season. For example, if you use October 15 instead (DATE = 80 instead of 106), the linear trend is stronger and the quadratic trend disappears (p = 0.4842).

Polynomial contrasts can be computed for any term, even if that term doesn't appear in the model. For example, if the model were Y = X1 X2 X3 X1*X2*X3, a polynomial decomposition for X1*X3 could be requested. The sums of squares that result are orthogonal one degree of freedom contrasts that are pooled within X1*X2*X3 in the summary AOV table. Thus, the AOV table could be entirely decomposed into one degree of freedom contrasts.

Remember that the actual spacings of the treatment levels are used to compute polynomial contrasts. Because calculating unequally spaced polynomials can be quite tedious, researchers commonly ignore the unequal spacing of levels and treat them as equally spaced, even though this can result in substantial errors. As the above example shows, the choice of level spacings can have considerable influence on the results. Because of the ease with which this option can handle unequal spacings, there is little excuse for not using them.

If missing values are estimated or if covariates are used, the resulting sums of squares are not orthogonal and the F tests are only approximations. This is discussed thoroughly in Bingham and Fienberg (1982).

## Save Residuals

Select "Save Residuals" to compute the residuals, fitted values, or adjusted data for a particular model and store them for later examination.

To compute the residuals or fitted values, you need to specify the interaction term to base the residuals and fitted values on. The specified interaction term will generally be one used as an error term in the model, although you're permitted to compute residuals for any term in the model.

```
                              SAVE RESIDUALS                          ALFALFA
Dependent variable: TONS
Factors:            VAR BLK DATE

BLK      DATE      TONS      VAR


4 variable(s).  72 of 72 cases selected.  1197K bytes free.

Enter the name of a new or existing variable to store the fitted values.
FIT

Enter the name of a new or existing variable to store the residuals.
MAINRES

Enter the name of a new or existing variable to store the adjusted data.


Enter the error term to use to compute residuals.
VAR*BLK*DATE

Esc Results menu   F1 Start   F2 Select variable
```

To illustrate how this option works, suppose we wanted the main plot residuals and fitted values for the split-plot design analyzed in Example II.

In the options panel on the preceding page, the variable name MAINFIT is entered for the fitted values variable and MAINRES is entered for the residuals variable. The main plot error term is specified as VAR*BLK.

The residuals are used to evaluate how well a model fits the data. A residual is defined as the difference between the actual observed response and that predicted by the fitted model. In the example just given, the residual indicates how well the additive model VAR + BLK fits the data. Residuals can help detect bad values (outliers) and can also help suggest more appropriate models or transformations to apply. Consult Daniel (1976) for more detail.

You'd only be interested in the adjusted data if you had missing values or covariates; otherwise, the saved data will be the same as the original data. The data are adjusted in the sense that missing values have been filled in with their least squares estimates and the data have been corrected for covariates.

## General AOV/AOCV - Computational Notes

**General AOV/AOCV** uses Oliver's (1967) generalization of Yates' algorithm (Daniel 1976, Snedecor and Cochran 1980, p. 317-318) and Rubin's (1972) missing value estimation methods. Oliver's method requires orthonormal matrices, which are generated as transpose Helmert matrices.

Analysis of covariance methods are used to estimate the missing values (Seber 1978). In general, analyses of covariance can be performed by first performing analyses of variance on the covariates, generating residuals, and then performing a multiple regression on these residuals to estimate the covariate coefficients. Oliver's method of obtaining residuals was used. Rubin's method avoids the need to save all the residuals and results directly in the cross-product matrix for the residuals. The multiple regression solution is obtained from this cross-product matrix. This is performed with a square-root free modification of Cholesky's factorization (Martin et al. 1965). Missing values for the dependent variable are filled in first. If covariates are specified, it's necessary to fill in corresponding missing value estimates (Seber 1978, p. 300). After the missing values are dealt with, any covariates are treated. Like the missing values, the covariates are first residualized. The resulting residuals are accumulated, and a multiple regression is then performed on them using Gentleman's square-root free modification of Given's method (Gentleman 1973). The fact that all the residuals for the covariates must be stored is why the upper limit on the number of covariates is substantially less than the permissible maximum number of missing values.

(The main factor determining the maximum allowable number of missing cases is speed consideration.) If the residualized covariates show substantial multicollinearity during the regression, the procedure is aborted. Otherwise, the estimated covariate coefficients are used to adjust the dependent variable data, and the analysis of variance is then performed. An algorithm similar to Cooper's (1968) is used to generate orthogonal polynomials.

# Eigenvalues-Principal Components

The **Eigenvalues-Principal Components** procedure displays the eigenvectors and eigenvalues for a list of variables. You can also save principal components as new variables.

## Specification

```
                    EIGENVALUES/PRINCIPAL COMPONENTS                    HALD
CHEM1     CHEM2     CHEM3     CHEM4     HEAT

5 variable(s).  13 of 13 cases selected.  1199K bytes free.

List the variables for computing eigenvalues.  You may specify ALL
or use A .. Z syntax.  Press F2 to select variables from the list.
CHEM1 .. CHEM4

Enter the name of the weighting variable (optional).

Compute analysis using correlation matrix (CORR) or covariance matrix (COV)?
Correlation

Esc Exit  F1 Start  F2 Select variable
```

List the variables you want to analyze. You can specify ALL or use A .. Z syntax. To weight the analysis, enter the name of the variable that contains the values to be used as weights. The eigenvalues can be based on the correlation matrix or the covariance matrix. Press F1 to begin the analysis.

## Data Restrictions

Up to 40 variables can be specified. If there are missing values for any of the variables for a case, the entire case is deleted (listwise deletion). Negative weights are not allowed.

## Example

We use the Hald data from Draper and Smith (1981) for this example. The same data are used to illustrate **Linear Regression**. The variables CHEM1, CHEM2, CHEM3, and CHEM4 are the percentages of four chemical compounds measured in batches of cement. The data are listed below.

| CASE | HEAT | CHEM1 | CHEM2 | CHEM3 | CHEM4 |
|---|---|---|---|---|---|
| 1 | 78.5 | 7 | 26 | 6 | 60 |
| 2 | 74.3 | 1 | 29 | 15 | 52 |
| 3 | 104.3 | 11 | 56 | 8 | 20 |
| 4 | 87.6 | 11 | 31 | 8 | 47 |
| 5 | 95.9 | 7 | 52 | 6 | 33 |
| 6 | 109.2 | 11 | 55 | 9 | 22 |
| 7 | 102.7 | 3 | 71 | 17 | 6 |
| 8 | 72.5 | 1 | 31 | 22 | 44 |
| 9 | 93.1 | 2 | 54 | 18 | 22 |
| 10 | 115.9 | 21 | 47 | 4 | 26 |
| 11 | 83.8 | 1 | 40 | 23 | 34 |
| 12 | 113.3 | 11 | 66 | 9 | 12 |
| 13 | 109.4 | 10 | 68 | 8 | 12 |

The analysis is specified on the preceding page. The results are presented in the table below.

EIGENVALUES/EIGENVECTORS BASED ON CORRELATION MATRIX

| | EIGENVALUES | PERCENT OF VARIANCE | CUMULATIVE PERCENT OF VARIANCE |
|---|---|---|---|
| 1 | 2.23570 | 55.9 | 55.9 |
| 2 | 1.57606 | 39.4 | 95.3 |
| 3 | 0.18660 | 4.7 | 100.0 |
| 4 | 0.00162 | 0.0 | 100.0 |

| FACTOR | VECTORS 1 | 2 | 3 | 4 |
|---|---|---|---|---|
| CHEM1 | 0.4760 | 0.5090 | 0.6755 | 0.2411 |
| CHEM2 | 0.5639 | -0.4139 | -0.3144 | 0.6418 |
| CHEM3 | -0.3941 | -0.6050 | 0.6377 | 0.2685 |
| CHEM4 | -0.5479 | 0.4512 | -0.1954 | 0.6767 |

Eigenvalue analysis is interesting in its own right as a way to analyze multivariate data structure (Morrison 1977, chap. 8). It's also an important supplement to multiple regression analysis (Chatterjee and Price 1977).

## Principal Components

After viewing the resulting eigenvalues and eigenvectors, press Esc to display the principle components panel. You're prompted to enter variable names for the principal components.

```
                         PRINCIPAL COMPONENTS                         HALD
 CHEM1     CHEM2     CHEM3     CHEM4     HEAT




 5 variable(s).  13 of 13 cases selected.  1199K bytes free.
 Original variables:
 CHEM1     CHEM2     CHEM3     CHEM4



 List the new variable names for the principal components.
 Press <ESC> to return the linear models menu.
 PCHEM1 PCHEM2 PCHEM3

Esc Exit  F1 Start  F2 Select variable
```

The options panel above results in the first three principal components being saved with the variable names PCHEM1, PCHEM2, and PCHEM3, respectively. The principal component with the largest eigenvalue (variance component) comes first, the next largest second, and so on.

Press Esc to exit if you don't want to save any principal components.

In some regression data sets, the independent variables may be highly correlated with one another. When such collinearity exists, estimates of the regression coefficients may be unstable and can lead to erroneous inferences. If this is the case, it's sometimes useful to perform the regression on a set of principal components. The computational advantage of using principal components rather than the original data is that they're all uncorrelated (they're said to be orthogonal). Chatterjee and Price (1977) give a nice example of the application of this method.

Typically, the principal components corresponding to the largest eigenvalues (i.e., largest variance components) are used for the regression. Jolliffe (1982) makes the point that this is not always a wise approach.

Generally, it's best to use the correlation matrix to compute the eigenvalues because in effect this assigns equal weight to each variable. If the covariance matrix is used, the results depend on the scales on which the original variables were measured.

## Computational Notes

The correlation or covariance matrix is first computed using the method of updating (see **Correlations**). The resulting matrix is converted to tridiagonal form using Householder reductions. The eigenvalues and eigenvectors are then extracted using the QL decomposition. Details on these methods are described by Martin et al. (1968) and Bowdler et al. (1968).

In matrix notation, the principal components are calculated as XU, where X is an n x p matrix derived from the original data and U is a p x m matrix of eigenvectors. The number of usable cases is n, the number of variables in the original variable list is p, and m is the number of eigenvectors retained. If the calculations were based on the correlation matrix, the data in X are the original data after Studentization (the means subtracted from the values and then divided by their standard deviations). If the calculations are based on the covariance matrix, X is the original data with the means subtracted.

CHAPTER

7

# Association Tests

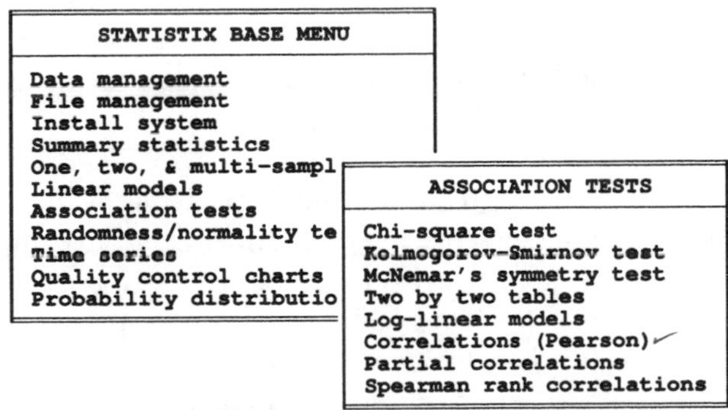


*Statistix* offers many association tests that can be used to examine the similarity or association among two or more variables.

The **Chi-Square Test** computes the traditional chi-square goodness-of-fit test for two-way tables. Two hypotheses can be examined with this test: (1) whether the row and column classifying variables are independent and (2) whether the relative frequency distributions for each of the rows or columns are the same. The first hypothesis is referred to as the hypothesis of independence, and the second is referred to as the hypothesis of homogeneity.

The **Kolmogorov-Smirnov Test** is useful for comparing the similarity of the distributions of samples from two populations. Inexperienced analysts often use a chi-square test when the two-sample Kolmogorov-Smirnov test would be more appropriate. If there is an intrinsic ordering to the categories, the Kolmogorov-Smirnov test is usually better because it can exploit the information in the ordering while the chi-square analysis cannot.

The **McNemar's Symmetry Test** is a goodness-of-fit test that's often useful for measuring change. It's used to analyze square contingency tables; often the rows represent classifications before some event, while the columns represent the same classes after some event. "Individuals" (whatever is being classified) may be in one class before the event but in another class after the event. However, if the table is symmetric about the diagonal from the upper left to the lower right, there will be no net shift in the row and column proportions before and after. McNemar's test examines whether the table is in fact symmetric.

The **Two by Two Tables** procedure computes a variety of tests of association for two by two contingency tables. A typical example of a two by two table is where a number of individuals are cross-classified by two dichotomous variables, such as treated-not treated and survived-died. The tests include Fisher's exact test, Pearson chi-square, log odds ratio, and others, along with standard errors.

The **Log-Linear Models** procedure is a powerful tool for analyzing discrete multidimensional categorical data. Log-linear models are the discrete data analogs to analysis of variance. If a set of discrete data has more than two classifying variables, you may be tempted to analyze such data as a series of two-way tables with traditional chi-square tests. However, the danger of such an approach is that collapsing the data over some categorical variables results in these variables becoming confounded with the remaining two categorical variables. Log-linear models allows all dimensions of multidimensional contingency tables to be treated simultaneously and so avoids such potential confounding.

The **Correlations** procedure measures the degree of linear association between two variables.

The **Partial Correlations** procedure allows you to examine the degree of linear association between two variables after the effect of other variables have been "adjusted out". Correlations and Partial Correlations appear on the Linear Models menu as well as the Association Tests menu and are discussed in detail in Chapter 6.

The **Spearman Rank Correlations** procedure produces nonparametric correlation coefficients that are suitable for examining the degree of association when the samples violate the assumption of bivariate normality.

## Chi-Square Test

The **Chi-Square Test** procedure is used to analyze two-dimensional tables of discrete data. Two hypotheses can be examined; the hypothesis of independence examines whether the row-classifying variable acts independently of the column-classifying variable, and the hypothesis of homogeneity tests whether the relative frequency distributions for each of the rows or columns are the same. The appropriate hypothesis choice depends on how the sampling was performed. The calculations involved are identical for the two tests.

### Specification

```
          CHI-SQUARE TEST FOR HETEROGENEITY OR INDEPENDENCE         VISIONC
 COUNTS    LEFT       RIGHT


 3 variable(s).  16 of 16 cases selected.  1167K bytes free.
 Are your data arranged as a TABLE with variables representing columns and
 cases representing rows, or do you have 2 CATEGORICAL variables whose values
 determine the columns and rows?  Enter T for TABLE or C for CATEGORICAL.
 CATEGORICAL
 If you have a variable that contains a count for each case, enter its name
 here.  If each case represents one observation, leave this field blank.
 COUNTS
 Enter the name of the variable whose values represent rows.
 LEFT
 Enter the name of the variable whose values represent columns.
 RIGHT
 Esc Exit  F1 Start  F2 Select variable
```

The analysis can be specified in two ways, depending on how you choose to enter the data. If you enter the data in columns using two categorical variables to identify the rows and columns, use the CATEGORICAL method and identify the two classifying variables and, optionally, a dependent variable containing counts. You can also enter the data in as a two-dimensional table, with variables identifying the columns and cases identifying the rows. This is called the TABLE method.

Select either the CATEGORICAL or the TABLE method that fits the way your data have been entered. Using the categorical method, enter the classifying variables that identify the rows and columns of the contingency table. If each case represents one observation, don't enter a counts variable. If the data are summarized, enter the variable that contains the counts for each case.

Using the table method, list the variables that will represent the columns of the contingency table.

## Data Restrictions

No more than 50 row categories and 50 column categories are allowed. Missing values are not permitted. The count data should be non-negative integer values.

## Example

We use the data from Table 8.2-1 in Bishop, Fienberg, and Holland (1975) for our example. The data are the results of vision tests for 7,477 women. The variables LEFT and RIGHT are the scores for the left and right eyes, respectively. Each eye was assigned a score 1, 2, 3, or 4. The counts that fall in each of the cells of the contingency table are in the variable COUNTS.

| CASE | COUNTS | LEFT | RIGHT |
|---|---|---|---|
| 1 | 1520 | 1 | 1 |
| 2 | 234 | 1 | 2 |
| 3 | 117 | 1 | 3 |
| 4 | 36 | 1 | 4 |
| 5 | 266 | 2 | 1 |
| 6 | 1512 | 2 | 2 |
| 7 | 362 | 2 | 3 |
| 8 | 82 | 2 | 4 |
| 9 | 124 | 3 | 1 |
| 10 | 432 | 3 | 2 |
| 11 | 1772 | 3 | 3 |
| 12 | 179 | 3 | 4 |
| 13 | 66 | 4 | 1 |
| 14 | 78 | 4 | 2 |
| 15 | 205 | 4 | 3 |
| 16 | 492 | 4 | 4 |

The analysis is specified above. The results are displayed on the next page.

In each cell, the original observed value, the value expected under the hypothesis of independence or homogeneity, and the cell contribution to the overall chi-square are displayed. In this example, the hypothesis of

```
CHI-SQUARE TEST FOR HETEROGENEITY OR INDEPENDENCE
FOR COUNTS = LEFT RIGHT

                                          RIGHT
LEFT                    1          2          3          4

1       OBSERVED      1520        234        117         36      1907
        EXPECTED    503.98     575.39     626.40     201.23
    CELL CHI-SQ    2048.32     202.55     414.25     135.67

2       OBSERVED       266       1512        362         82      2222
        EXPECTED    587.22     670.43     729.87     234.47
    CELL CHI-SQ     175.72    1056.38     185.41      99.15

3       OBSERVED       124        432       1772        179      2507
        EXPECTED    662.54     756.43     823.48     264.55
    CELL CHI-SQ     437.75     139.14    1092.53      27.66

4       OBSERVED        66         78        205        492       841
        EXPECTED    222.26     253.75     276.25      88.75
    CELL CHI-SQ     109.86     121.73      18.38    1832.37

                      1976       2256       2456        789      7477

OVERALL CHI-SQUARE     8.097E+03
P VALUE                0.0000
DEGREES OF FREEDOM          9

CASES INCLUDED 16     MISSING CASES 0
```

independence is appropriate. If either the row or the column totals had been predetermined before the sample was taken, the hypothesis of homogeneity would have been appropriate. The calculations are the same for either hypothesis.

In our example, the large differences between the expected values and the observed values indicate that the model of independence is not an acceptable model for this data set (p-value = 0.0000). This seems quite reasonable; one might reasonably expect the vision score for one eye to have a positive association with that for the other eye.

It's more convenient in some situations to store the column categories as separate variables. For example, the data listed on the preceding page can rearranged using the TABLE format. The variables RIGHT1, RIGHT2, RIGHT3, and RIGHT4 contain the data for columns 1 through 4 of the table. Each variable has four cases, and the order of the cases represent rows 1 through 4 of the table (left eye scores 1 through 4).

| CASE | RIGHT1 | RIGHT2 | RIGHT3 | RIGHT4 |
|---|---|---|---|---|
| 1 | 1520 | 234 | 117 | 36 |
| 2 | 266 | 1512 | 362 | 82 |
| 3 | 124 | 432 | 1772 | 179 |
| 4 | 66 | 78 | 205 | 492 |

The analysis for this data configuration is specified in the panel below.

```
              CHI-SQUARE TEST FOR HETEROGENEITY OR INDEPENDENCE          VISIONT
 RIGHT1     RIGHT2     RIGHT3     RIGHT4


 4 variable(s).  4 of 4 cases selected.  1167K bytes free.

 Are your data arranged as a TABLE with variables representing columns and
 cases representing rows, or do you have 2 CATEGORICAL variables whose values
 determine the columns and rows?  Enter T for TABLE or C for CATEGORICAL.
 TABLE

 List the names of the variables that represent the columns of your table.
 You may enter ALL or use A .. Z syntax.  Press F2 to select variables
 from the list.
 RIGHT1 RIGHT2 RIGHT3 RIGHT4
```

The most common problem in applying the chi-square test is that it becomes unreliable when numerous expected cell values are near zero. Snedecor and Cochran (1980, p. 77) give the following general rules:

1) No expected values should be less than one.
2) Two expected values may be close to one if most of the other expected values exceed five.
3) Classes with expectations less than one should be combined to meet 1) and 2).

If your contingency table is a two by two table (two categories in both the rows and columns), use the **Two by Two Tables** procedure (page 232).

## Computational Notes

You should consult Snedecor and Cochran (sec. 10.11) for more detail on this test. We don't use the correction for continuity; we believe that the arguments given by Fienberg (1980) for not using the correction are compelling.

# Kolmogorov-Smirnov Test

The **Kolmogorov-Smirnov Test** procedure examines whether two samples have the same distribution. You must order the categories within the samples. The test, which is also known as the Smirnov test, is sensitive to any differences between the distributions, including differences in means and variances. It's generally preferable to a chi-square test because it exploits the information in the ordering of the categories.

## Specification

The sample counts for one distribution are one variable, and the counts for the other distribution are in a second variable. It's assumed that the ordering of the cases in the two variables reflects the ordering of the categories.

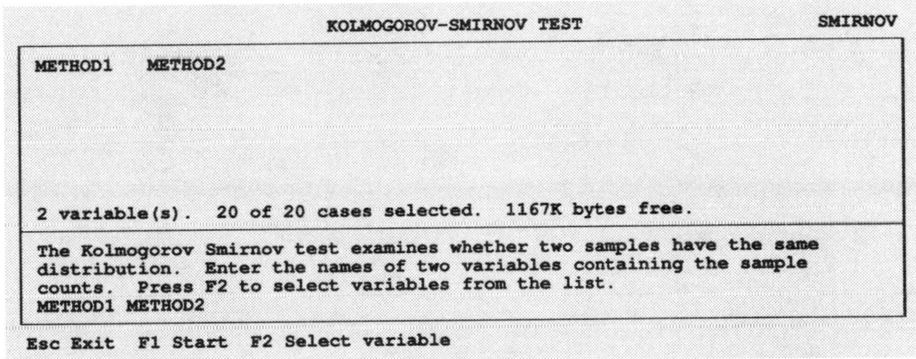


Enter the names of the two variables containing the samples. The order of the variables isn't important, except that the signs of the resulting one-tailed statistics are reversed.

## Data Restrictions

The data must be non-negative whole numbers and can't exceed 99,999. There must be at least five cases.

## Example

The data for our example are fabricated. Suppose you want to examine whether students' test scores are the same under two teaching methods. The variables METHOD1 and METHOD2 represent the number of students receiving a particular grade. There are 20 questions on the test, so there are 20 categories corresponding to the total number of possible scores. The data are listed in the table on the next page.

| CASE | METHOD1 | METHOD2 |
|---|---|---|
| 1 | 1 | 7 |
| 2 | 0 | 5 |
| 3 | 0 | 7 |
| 4 | 1 | 5 |
| 5 | 1 | 6 |
| 6 | 0 | 8 |
| 7 | 6 | 6 |
| 8 | 12 | 7 |
| 9 | 18 | 7 |
| 10 | 30 | 4 |
| 11 | 24 | 5 |
| 12 | 20 | 7 |
| 13 | 21 | 8 |
| 14 | 8 | 9 |
| 15 | 2 | 5 |
| 16 | 1 | 5 |
| 17 | 0 | 6 |
| 18 | 0 | 7 |
| 19 | 0 | 5 |
| 20 | 1 | 7 |

The analysis is specified on the preceding page. The results are as follows:

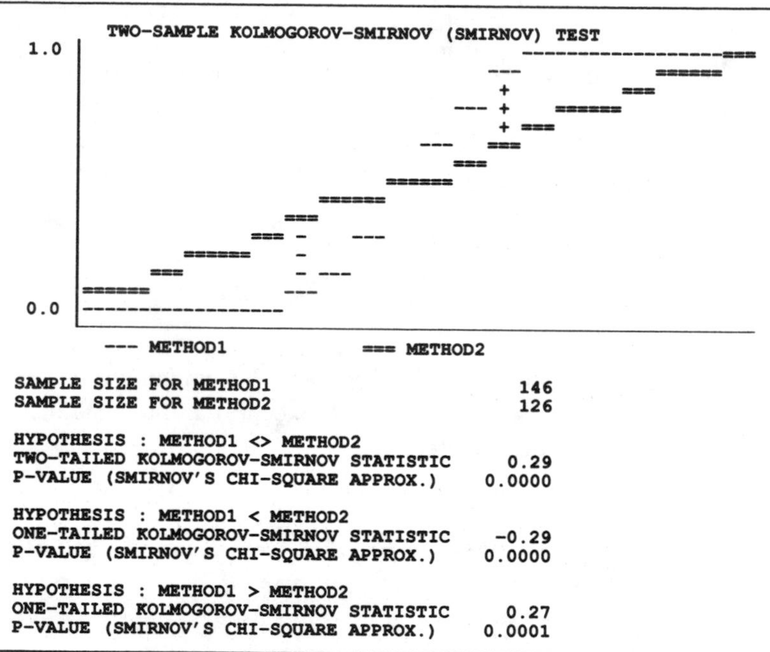


The graph at the top of the output displays the sample cumulative distribution functions. The Kolmogorov-Smirnov two-sample test is based on the maximum difference between the cumulative distribution functions. The location of the greatest negative difference between the two curves is shown by the column of "-"s. The greatest positive difference is located at the column of "+"s. The two-tailed test, which tests the hypothesis that the two curves are different, is based on the difference with the greatest absolute value, 0.29 in the example. The very small p-value indicates that the distributions are indeed different. One-tailed tests are also computed to test (1) whether the largest positive difference is greater than expected by chance if the two distributions are identical, and (2) whether the smallest negative difference is smaller than expected. Note that in this example both one-tailed tests are significant. The p-values are based on Smirnov's (1939) approximation using the chi-square distribution. P-values are computed only if the sum of the observations in the variables both exceed 15.

See Lehmann (1975) and Hollander and Wolfe (1973) for more detail.

## McNemar's Symmetry Test

The **McNemar's Symmetry Test** procedure tests whether a square contingency table is symmetric about the diagonal running from the upper left to the lower right. It is actually a generalized version of McNemar's test developed by Bowker (1948).

### Specification

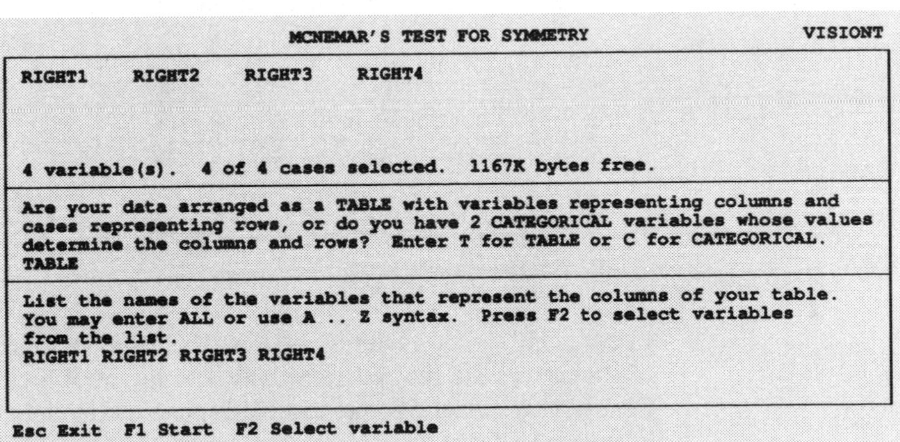

```
MCNEMAR'S TEST FOR SYMMETRY                                VISIONT
RIGHT1     RIGHT2     RIGHT3     RIGHT4

4 variable(s).  4 of 4 cases selected.  1167K bytes free.
Are your data arranged as a TABLE with variables representing columns and
cases representing rows, or do you have 2 CATEGORICAL variables whose values
determine the columns and rows?  Enter T for TABLE or C for CATEGORICAL.
TABLE
List the names of the variables that represent the columns of your table.
You may enter ALL or use A .. Z syntax.  Press F2 to select variables
from the list.
RIGHT1 RIGHT2 RIGHT3 RIGHT4
Esc Exit   F1 Start   F2 Select variable
```

The analysis can be specified in two ways, depending on how you decide to enter the data. If you enter the data in columns using two categorical variables to identify the rows and columns, then you use the CATEGORI-

CAL method and identify the two classifying variables and, optionally, a dependent variable containing counts. You can also enter the data as a two-dimensional table, with variables identifying the columns and cases identifying the rows. This is called the TABLE method.

Select whichever method fits the way your data were entered. Using the categorical method, enter the name of the variable containing the counts and the names of the two classifying variables that identify the rows and columns of the contingency table.

Using the table method, list the variables that will represent the columns of the contingency table.

## Data Restrictions

The contingency table must be square, i.e., the number of rows and columns must be equal. No more than 50 row and column categories are allowed. Missing values aren't permitted. The count data should be non-negative integer values.

## Example

We use the data from Table 8.2-1 in Bishop, Fienberg, and Holland (1975) for our example. The data are the results of vision tests for 7,477 women. The variables LEFT and RIGHT are the scores for the left and right eyes, respectively. Each eye was assigned a score 1, 2, 3, or 4. The data were entered in the TABLE format (see the **Chi-Square Test** in this chapter for an example of the CATEGORICAL method).

| CASE | RIGHT1 | RIGHT2 | RIGHT3 | RIGHT4 |
|---|---|---|---|---|
| 1 | 1520 | 234 | 117 | 36 |
| 2 | 266 | 1512 | 362 | 82 |
| 3 | 124 | 432 | 1772 | 179 |
| 4 | 66 | 78 | 205 | 492 |

The analysis of the vision test data is specified on the preceding page. The results are presented on the next page.

In each cell, the original observation, the value expected under the hypothesis of symmetry, and the cell contribution to the overall chi-square are displayed. Clearly, this model fits the data better than the model of independence examined in **Chi-Square Test**, but there's still a significant lack of fit (p-value = 0.0040). By examining the cell chi-squares, you'll see that the left and right pairs on the diagonal running from the lower left to the upper right are primarily responsible for the lack of symmetry.

MCNEMAR'S TEST FOR SYMMETRY

| CASE | | VARIABLE RIGHT1 | RIGHT2 | RIGHT3 | RIGHT4 | |
|---|---|---|---|---|---|---|
| 1 | OBSERVED | 1520 | 234 | 117 | 36 | 1907 |
| | EXPECTED | 1520.00 | 250.00 | 120.50 | 51.00 | |
| | CELL CHI-SQ | 0.00 | 1.02 | 0.10 | 4.41 | |
| 2 | OBSERVED | 266 | 1512 | 362 | 82 | 2222 |
| | EXPECTED | 250.00 | 1512.00 | 397.00 | 80.00 | |
| | CELL CHI-SQ | 1.02 | 0.00 | 3.09 | 0.05 | |
| 3 | OBSERVED | 124 | 432 | 1772 | 179 | 2507 |
| | EXPECTED | 120.50 | 397.00 | 1772.00 | 192.00 | |
| | CELL CHI-SQ | 0.10 | 3.09 | 0.00 | 0.88 | |
| 4 | OBSERVED | 66 | 78 | 205 | 492 | 841 |
| | EXPECTED | 51.00 | 80.00 | 192.00 | 492.00 | |
| | CELL CHI-SQ | 4.41 | 0.05 | 0.88 | 0.00 | |
| | | 1976 | 2256 | 2456 | 789 | 7477 |

| | |
|---|---|
| OVERALL CHI-SQUARE | 19.11 |
| P-VALUE | 0.0040 |
| DEGREES OF FREEDOM | 6 |

CASES INCLUDED 16 MISSING CASES 0

The most common problem in the application of McNemar's test is that it becomes unreliable when numerous expected cell values are near zero. The guidelines usually given for the chi-square test for independence and homogeneity are also applicable to McNemar's test. Snedecor and Cochran (1980, p. 77) give the following general rules:

1) No expected values should be less than one.
2) Two expected values may be close to one if most of the other expected values exceed five.
3) Classes with expectations less than one should be combined to meet 1) and 2).

When classes for one table margin are combined, the corresponding classes for the other table margin must also be combined to preserve the "squareness" of the table.

## Computational Notes

Consult Bishop, Fienberg, and Holland (1975) for more detail on this test and example.

# Two By Two Tables

The **Two By Two Tables** procedure computes several measures and tests of association for two by two contingency tables.

## Specification

When the two by two tables procedure is selected, an empty two by two table is displayed, with the cursor positioned in the upper left cell:

**TWO BY TWO TABLES**

| | |
|---|---|
| ■ 0 | 0 |
| 0 | 0 |

Simply enter the number you want in this cell and press Enter. The cursor then moves to the next cell, and the process is repeated until all four cells have been filled. You can use the up and down arrow keys to move from cell to cell to change values. Press F1 to start.

## Data Restrictions

The cell values must be non-negative integers. All row and column totals must be greater than zero. The individual cell values can't exceed 99,999.

## Example

Suppose 30 people are selected at random and asked two questions. The first question is whether they favor increasing the budget for space research, and the second is whether they favor increasing the defense budget. The responses are as follows:

| | | Increase the space research budget? Yes | No |
|---|---|---|---|
| Increase the defense budget? | Yes | 11 | 3 |
| | No | 6 | 10 |

The goal of the analysis is to examine whether the responses to the two questions are related. That is, if a person favors increasing space research, would he or she also favor increased defense spending? The results of the analysis are shown below.

```
                         TWO BY TWO TABLES

                    +---------+---------+
                    |   11    |    3    |    14
                    +---------+---------+
                    |    6    |   10    |    16
                    +---------+---------+
                        17        13         30

FISHER EXACT TESTS:  LOWER TAIL 0.0279   UPPER TAIL 0.0051   TWO TAILED 0.0329

PEARSON'S CHI-SQUARE          5.13      YULE'S Q                0.72
  P (PEARSON'S)             0.0235        SE (Q)              0.2009
YATES' CORRECTED CHI-SQ       3.59        SE (HO: Q = 0)      0.3692
  P (YATES)                 0.0580      YULE'S Y                0.42
LOG ODDS RATIO              1.8101        SE (Y)              0.1704
  SE (LOR)                  0.8312        SE (HO: Y = 0)      0.1846
  SE (HO: LOR = 0)          0.7385      C MAX                   0.63
CROSS PRODUCT RATIO         6.1111      PHI                     0.41
CONTINGENCY COEFF             0.38      PHI MAX                 0.82
```

Descriptions of most of these measures can be found in Bishop et al. (1975) and the BMDP-83 manual. Notice that where standard errors are reported for a measure, two types of standard errors are given—unrestricted and restricted. The restricted standard error is appropriate for constructing hypothesis tests that the measure equals zero. The unrestricted measure is appropriate for constructing confidence intervals around the measure if the hypothesis that the measure equals zero is rejected. Brown and Benedetti (1977) should be consulted for more detail. Large sample theory can be used to test whether a measure differs from zero. If the samples are "large enough", the measures should be nearly normally distributed. Under the null hypothesis, a measure divided by its restricted standard error should have a Z, or standard normal distribution. For example, to test whether the log odds ratio is different from zero, we compute Z = 1.8101 / 0.7385 = 2.451. When we calculate the p-value for Z = 2.451 with the Z2TAIL procedure (see **Probability Functions** chapter), we find that p = 0.014, suggesting that the log likelihood ratio is different from zero. Approximate 95% confidence intervals around the log odds ratio would be constructed as 1.8101   1.96 * 0.8312 using the unrestricted standard error.

The results of this analysis suggest that there is, in fact, a relationship between the responses to the two questions.

If the total number of samples is less than or equal to 25, only the results of

Fisher's exact tests are displayed because the other measures may be misleading for such small sample sizes. If the sample size is greater than 35, results for Fisher's exact tests aren't displayed. If the sample size is between 25 and 35, all statistics are displayed.

### Computational Notes

The procedure for determining the upper- and lower-tail probabilities for Fisher's exact test is described in Bradley (1968).

## Log-Linear Models

The **Log-Linear Models** procedure fits a hierarchical log-linear model to the data in a multidimensional contingency table and computes several goodness-of-fit statistics. You can also save the expected values and residuals.

### Specification

```
                        LOG-LINEAR MODELS                                NESTS
COUNTS    DIAMETER  HEIGHT    SPECIES

4 variable(s).  8 of 8 cases selected.  1167K bytes free.

Enter the name of the dependent variable containing the count data.
COUNTS

Enter the name of the variable containing starting values (optional).

Enter log-linear model configurations using the variables that cross-
classify the data.  Use a "*" to show interaction (eg. HEIGHT*SPECIES).
SPECIES*HEIGHT SPECIES*DIAMETER

Enter the maximum number of iterations.
25

Enter a value for the termination convergence difference criterion.
0.100

Esc Exit  F1 Start
```

Enter the name of the dependent variable, which contains the discrete count data. You can specify starting values for the estimated cell counts by entering the name of the variable that contains the starting values. This isn't necessary normally. Starting values are discussed in detail on page 238.

Log-linear model configurations are specified in a manner quite similar to the traditional approach of Bishop, Fienberg, and Holland (1975) and Fienberg (1980). Some examples are given below. The variables X1, X2, ..., and XN represent the categorical variables by which the data in Y are cross-classified. The Xi's should be integers; decimal values are truncated. (Hint: the CAT function in **Transformations** is often very useful for generating the classifying variables.)

Example 1: Two-way table. Model for complete independence.

```
X1 X2
```

Example 2: Three-way table. Conditional independence of X1 and X2 given X3.

```
X1*X3 X2*X3
```

Example 3: Four-way table. Model includes a three-way interaction.

```
X1 X2*X3*X4
```

Variables within the same interaction term are separated by "*". Interaction terms are set off from other interaction terms by spaces. The order in which the terms are specified in the model doesn't matter, and neither does the order of variables within the interaction terms.

Log-Linear Models is based on a procedure called iterative proportional fitting (IPF), which is described in the references mentioned above. Three aspects of the IPF procedure can be controlled by the user: (1) starting values for the estimated expected values, (2) maximum number of iterations, and (3) estimated expected value convergence criterion, or tolerance. You should specify these only if you're certain the defaults are unacceptable. The defaults are appropriate for the majority of applications. The details of changing the defaults follow.

The starting values for the estimated expected values default to 1.0 unless they're specified otherwise. This is appropriate for most log-linear analyses (but see Specifying Starting Values on page 238). To override the default, a variable containing the starting values must be supplied. These initial values don't need to be integers.

The IPF algorithm continues until one of two termination criteria is satisfied. These criteria are (1) the number of iterations and (2) the maximum absolute difference in the cell estimates from one iteration to the next, which is called the tolerance. The default value for the tolerance is 0.01; if none of the absolute differences in the estimated expected cell counts from one iteration to the next exceeds the tolerance value, satisfactory convergence is assumed to have occurred. If the maximum allowable number of iterations is reached, it's assumed that the procedure didn't converge satisfactorily and no results will be given. The default for the maximum allowable number of iterations is 25.

Decreasing the size of the tolerance often increases the required number of iterations. The default tolerance value will usually be satisfactory.

### Data Restrictions

The maximum number of classifying variables that are allowed in one model is five. Within each classifying variable, the maximum number of classes permitted is 50. The combinations of cross-classifications must be unique and exhaustive. For example, suppose the model is Y = X1 X2 and that X1 has four classes (1,2,3,4) associated with it and X2 has three classes (1,2,3) associated with it. This requires a total of 12 cases; the only pairs of classes for X1,X2 that may appear are 1,1; 1,2; 1,3; 2,1; 2,2; 2,3; 3,1; 3,2; 3,3; 4,1; 4,2; and 4,3. If all possible cross-classifications are not present or if some are duplicated, an error message is given. No missing values are allowed in the cell data.

### Example

The data in the multidimensional contingency table may have been generated by either a Poisson, multinomial, or product multinomial sampling scheme. Consult Bishop et al. (1975) for more detail. It's assumed that the model to be fitted is hierarchical; all lower-order interactions that are subsets within the specified configurations are always included in the model.

The example is from Table 3-2 of Fienberg (1980). The variable COUNTS contains the counts for two species of tree-dwelling lizards. The object of the analysis is to examine how the height of a perch, the diameter of a perch, and the species of lizard influence perch selection. The categorical variable SPECIES indicates which species a count is for. (SPECIES = 1 and SPECIES = 2 for the two species, respectively.) There are two perch-diameter classes recorded in the variable DIAMETER. Likewise, there are two perch-height classes in HEIGHT. A variety of models could be fitted to this data. Refer to Bishop et al. (1975) and Fienberg (1980) for strategies for finding the "best" models.

The results for a model of conditional independence are shown. That is, suppose it's hypothesized that, given the species of a lizard, the diameter of the perch it selects is independent of the height of the perch. The model is specified in the options panel on page 234. The results are displayed below:

```
LOG-LINEAR MODEL ANALYSIS ON COUNTS

CONFIGURATION 1   SPECIES*HEIGHT
CONFIGURATION 2   SPECIES*DIAMETER

GOODNESS-OF-FIT SUMMARY STATISTICS

  STATISTIC         CHI-SQ       DF         P

PEARSON               6.11        2    0.0471
LIKELIHOOD            4.88        2    0.0871
FREEMAN-TUKEY         3.99        2    0.1360

NUMBER OF NEAR ZERO EXPECTED CELLS          0
NUMBER OF ITERATIONS PERFORMED              2
TERMINATION CRITERION DIFFERENCE         0.10
```

The Pearson, likelihood ratio, and Freeman-Tukey goodness-of-fit statistics are discussed in Bishop et al. (1975). In this example, it's difficult to decide whether the model of conditional independence fits the data; the Pearson chi-square would lead to the rejection of this model at the 5% significance level, while the other two goodness-of-fit statistics would not. In an actual analysis, it's often desirable to look at the results for all feasible models.

The degrees of freedom are computed as the total number of cells in the multi-dimensional table minus the number of independent parameters that were estimated. This is appropriate for a "complete" table that has no zero marginals. (See Bishop et al. for the definition of complete tables.) Incomplete tables or zero marginals will require special treatment. The number of near zero cell estimates are displayed to indicate when the degrees of freedom need to be adjusted.

### Log-Linear Results Menu

After you've viewed the log-linear results, press Esc to display the log-linear results menu.

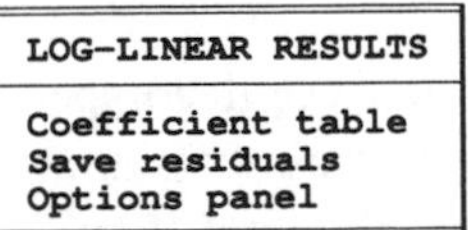


Select "Coefficient table" to redisplay the log-linear results table. Select "Options panel" to return the log-linear options panel used to specify the model. The "Save residuals" options is discussed below.

## Save Residuals

The **Save residuals** command is used to save residuals and expected values as new variables. You can save standardized, maximum likelihood, Freeman-Tukey, or raw residuals. You save residuals by entering variable names in the panel below.

```
                          SAVE RESIDUALS                          LIZARDS3
 COUNTS    DIAMETER  HEIGHT    SPECIES

 4 variable(s).  8 of 8 cases selected.  1167K bytes free.

               Option Name                        Variable
               Expected values
               Freeman-Tukey residuals
               Maximum likelihood residuals
               Raw residuals
               Standardized residuals             STDRESID

 Esc Exit  F1 Start  F2 Select variable
```

Use the arrow keys to move the cursor to the desired residual or expected value, then enter the name of a new or existing variable. You can select as many options as you like, and you can also return and edit variable names already given for options. When you've entered all the names you want, press F1 to start.

Residuals are useful for diagnosing why a model doesn't fit the data well, which in turn may suggest models that will fit well. When the model is correct, the Freeman-Tukey and standardized residuals are approximately normally distributed with a mean of zero and a variance slightly less than one.

## Specifying Starting Values

Occasionally, it's useful to specify starting values for the estimated cell counts. One such circumstance is when the cell counts follow a Poisson distribution and the counts have been taken from different reference populations. Haberman (1978) and Heisey (1985) give some examples of such analyses; the starting values will often be non-integer values.

Heisey (1985) gives an example where the goal is to examine factors affecting the preferences shown by white-tailed deer for different habitat types. Frequent use of a habitat may result from a preference for that habitat or from that habitat just being common, so it's desirable to adjust for the areas of habitats available to the animals. In Heisey's study, the categorical variable indicating the habitat type was called HABITAT and the areas of the different habitats in the study area were called AREA. The categorical variables ("factors") were DEER and TIME—the animal under observation and the time of day, respectively. The number of times a deer was found in a particular habitat was USE. The best model was found to be:

```
Enter the name of the dependent variable containing the count data.
USE

Enter the name of the variable containing starting values (optional).
AREA

Enter log-linear model configurations using the variables that cross-
classify the data.  Use a "*" to show interaction (eg. HEIGHT*SPECIES).
HABITAT*TIME TIME*DEER
```

The main point of interest is that AREA was adjusted for by using it as the starting values for the estimated expected cell frequencies. Consult Heisey (1985) for more detail.

Another situation where the user will want to specify initial values is for models of quasi-independence; the starting values will be either zero or one (Fienberg 1980). Quasi-independence is often of interest for tables that by definition must include empty cells, or so-called structural zeros. Incomplete tables are handled in a similar way; missing cells are given a starting value of zero. A note is given in the results when initial values are specified.

## Computational Notes

Iterative proportional fitting is used to estimate the expected cell frequencies. The program was generally patterned after Haberman (1972), although the actual implementation is substantially different.

# Spearman Rank Correlations

The **Spearman Rank Correlations** procedure computes the Spearman rank correlation coefficient matrix for a list of variables. Typical significance tests for simple correlations usually require that the samples follow a bivariate normal distribution. This is often a difficult assumption to justify, especially for ordinal data, i.e., ranks. Spearman rank correlations are suitable for examining the degree of association when the samples violate the assumption of bivariate normality.

## Specification

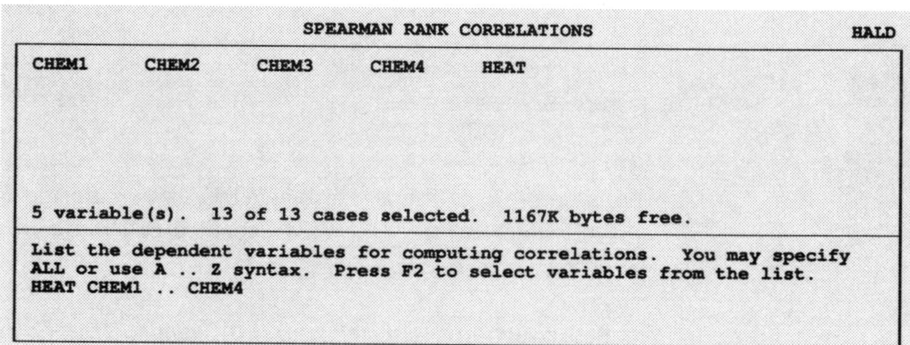


List the variables for which you want to compute rank correlations. You can specify ALL or use A .. Z syntax.

## Data Restrictions

Up to 40 variables can be specified. If a case in your data has missing values for any variable, the entire case is deleted (listwise deletion). Some of the variable data storage area is required to temporarily store the ranks.

## Example

We use the data of Hald (1952) used in Draper and Smith (1981) for our example. This data set is also used for the example for the **Correlations** procedure in Chapter 6. The variable HEAT is the cumulative heat of hardening for cement after 180 days. The variables CHEM1, CHEM2, CHEM3, and CHEM4 are the percentages of four chemical compounds measured in batches of cement. The data are listed on the next page.

| CASE | HEAT | CHEM1 | CHEM2 | CHEM3 | CHEM4 |
|---|---|---|---|---|---|
| 1 | 78.5 | 7 | 26 | 6 | 60 |
| 2 | 74.3 | 1 | 29 | 15 | 52 |
| 3 | 104.3 | 11 | 56 | 8 | 20 |
| 4 | 87.6 | 11 | 31 | 8 | 47 |
| 5 | 95.9 | 7 | 52 | 6 | 33 |
| 6 | 109.2 | 11 | 55 | 9 | 22 |
| 7 | 102.7 | 3 | 71 | 17 | 6 |
| 8 | 72.5 | 1 | 31 | 22 | 44 |
| 9 | 93.1 | 2 | 54 | 18 | 22 |
| 10 | 115.9 | 21 | 47 | 4 | 26 |
| 11 | 83.8 | 1 | 40 | 23 | 34 |
| 12 | 113.3 | 11 | 66 | 9 | 12 |
| 13 | 109.4 | 10 | 68 | 8 | 12 |

The analysis is specified on the preceding page. The results are as follows:

SPEARMAN RANK CORRELATIONS, CORRECTED FOR TIES

| | HEAT | CHEM1 | CHEM2 | CHEM3 |
|---|---|---|---|---|
| CHEM1 | 0.7912 | | | |
| CHEM2 | 0.7373 | 0.3301 | | |
| CHEM3 | -0.4488 | -0.7186 | 0.0527 | |
| CHEM4 | -0.7521 | -0.3320 | -0.9903 | -0.0806 |

MAXIMUM DIFFERENCE ALLOWED BETWEEN TIES 0.00001

CASES INCLUDED 13 MISSING CASES 0

The Spearman correlation coefficient is the usual (Pearson product moment) correlation coefficient computed from the rank scores of the data rather than the original data. If ties are found when the data are ranked, the average rank is assigned to the tied values, as suggested by Hollander and Wolfe (1973). Values are considered to be tied if they are within 0.00001 of one another. A message "corrected for ties" is displayed in the first line of the report when ties are found.

A similar nonparametric correlation coefficient is Kendall's tau. In most cases, inference based on Kendall's tau will produce results nearly identical to that based on Spearman's rho (Conover 1980).

## Computational Notes

The ranks are first computed for the data. The correlations are then computed with the same procedures used to produce the Pearson correlations. See **Correlations (Pearson)** in Chapter 6 for more detail.

C H A P T E R

# 8

# Randomness / Normality Tests

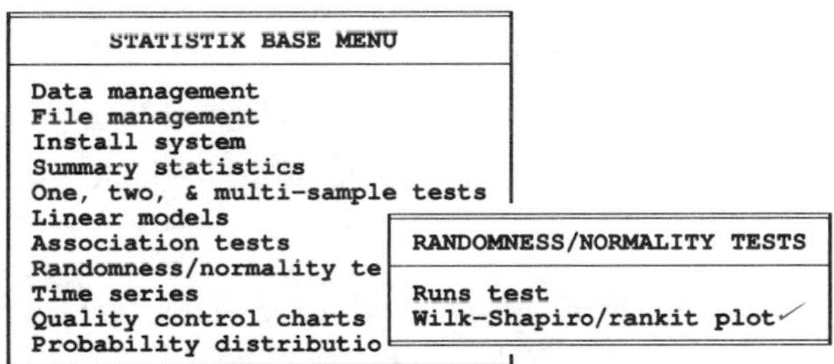


*Statistix* offers two procedures for testing data for randomness and normality.

The **Runs Test** is useful for examining whether samples have been drawn at random from a single population. It can detect patterns that often result from autocorrelation.

The **Wilk-Shapiro/Rankit Plot** procedure is used to examine whether data conform to a normal distribution.

Although these procedures have numerous other applications, both are useful for analyzing residuals resulting from regression and analysis of variance, where it's assumed that the random errors are independent and normally distributed. The **Durbin-Watson** statistic computed in Linear Regression is also an important tool for examining possible correlations among residuals.

# Runs Test

The **Runs Test** procedure examines whether the number of runs found in a variable are consistent with the hypothesis that the samples are order-independent. A run is defined as consecutive samples that are either consistently above or below the sample median. Autocorrelation often results in more or fewer runs than if the samples are independent.

## Specification

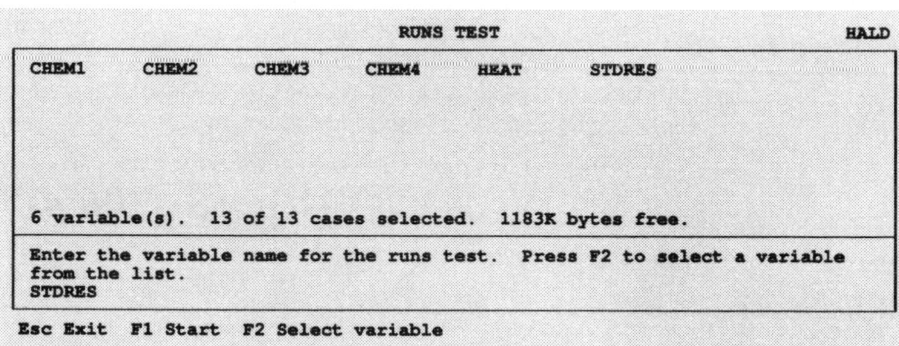


Simply enter the name of the variable that you want to test for runs.

## Example

We'll apply the runs test to residuals resulting from a linear regression analysis. The data—the Hald data from Draper and Smith (1981)—are used for the example data set in **Linear Regression**. Standardized residuals were computed for the regression model HEAT = CHEM1 CHEM4 and stored in the variable STDRES. The runs test is specified by entering the variable name as shown above. The results are presented below.

```
RUNS TEST FOR STDRES

MEDIAN                          0.0552
VALUES ABOVE THE MEDIAN              6
VALUES BELOW THE MEDIAN              6
VALUES TIED WITH THE MEDIAN          1
RUNS ABOVE THE MEDIAN                4
RUNS BELOW THE MEDIAN                4
TOTAL NUMBER OF RUNS                 8
EXPECTED NUMBER OF RUNS            7.0

PROBABILITY OF GETTING 8 OR FEWER RUNS  0.8247

A VALUE WAS COUNTED AS A TIE WITH THE MEDIAN IF
ITS ABSOLUTE VALUE WAS WITHIN  0.00001

CASES INCLUDED 13     MISSING CASES 0
```

In residual analysis, you're more likely to see too few runs rather than too many. Too few runs result from runs generally being too long, which indicates positive autocorrelation. When observed in residuals, this could be because you didn't include important explanatory variables in the model. The p-value of 0.8247 indicates that there is no evidence for too few runs in these residuals.

Too many short runs is less common, and results from negative autocorrelation. An example where negative autocorrelation can be expected is in a situation where a process is being constantly monitored and adjusted, and there's a tendency toward over-compensation when adjustments are made. The probability of more than eight runs in our example is 1 - 0.8247 = 0.1753, which again is no cause for alarm.

The **Durbin-Watson** statistic in Linear Regression is also very important for diagnosing autocorrelation in regression residuals.

## Computational Notes

The equations used to calculate the runs probabilities can be found in Bradley (1968, p. 254). These exact equations are used unless the number of values above or below the median exceeds 20, in which case normal approximations are used (p. 262).

The **Wilk-Shapiro/Rankit Plot** procedure examines whether a variable conforms to a normal distribution. A rankit plot of the variable is produced, and an approximate Wilk-Shapiro normality statistic, the **Shapiro-Francia** statistic, is calculated.

## Specification

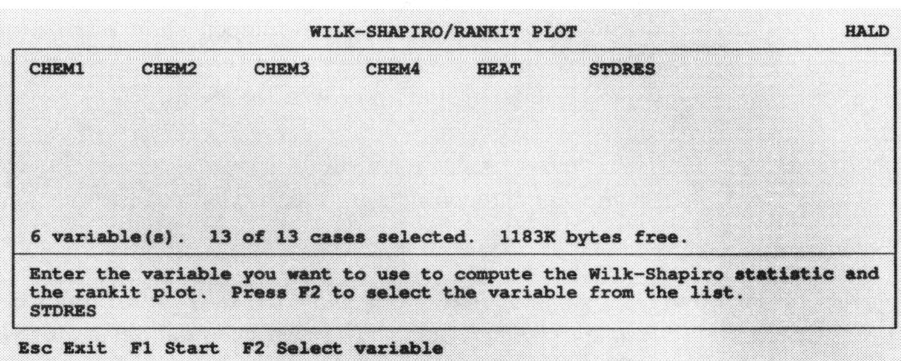


Simply enter the name of the variable you want to test for normality.

## Example

We'll apply the Wilk-Shapiro/Rankit Plot procedure to residuals resulting from a linear regression analysis. The data—the Hald data from Draper and Smith (1981)—are used for the example data in **Linear Regression**. Standardized residuals were computed for the regression model HEAT = CHEM1 CHEM4 and stored in the variable STDRES. Wilk-Shapiro/Rankit Plot is specified by entering the variable name as shown above. The results are presented on the next page.

If the assumptions of linear regression are met, the standardized residuals should be approximately normally distributed with mean 0 and variance 1. The i-th rankit is defined as the expected value of the i-th order statistic for the sample, assuming the sample was from a normal distribution. The order statistics of a sample are the sample values reordered by their rank. If the sample conforms to a normal distribution, a plot of the rankits against the order statistics should result in a straight line, except for random variation.

The approximate Wilk-Shapiro statistic calculated is the square of the linear

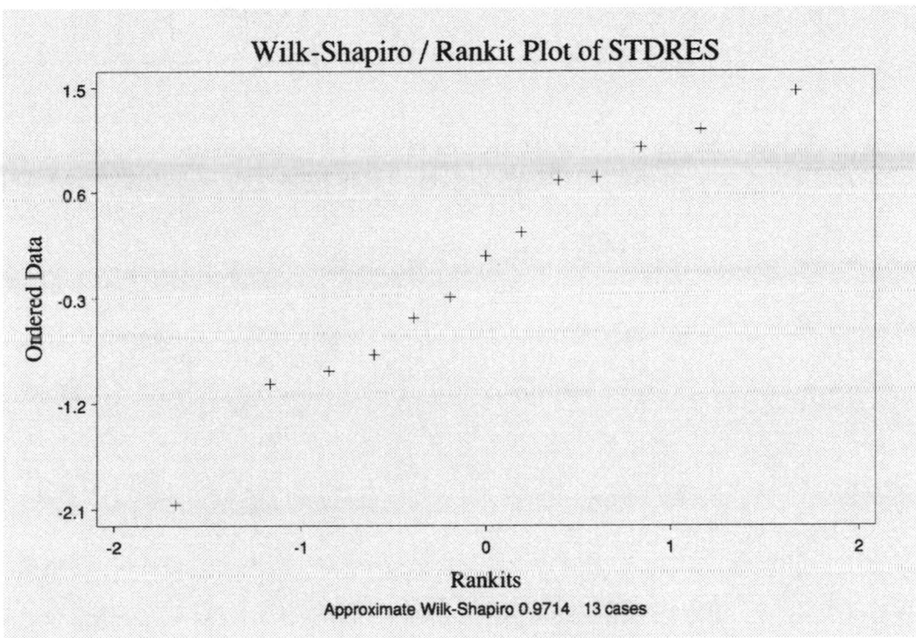


correlation between the rankits and the order statistics (Shapiro and Francia 1972).

Systematic departure of the rankit plot from a linear trend indicates non-normality, as does a small value for the Wilk-Shapiro statistic. The above example shows no evidence of non-normality. Tables for the approximate Wilk-Shapiro statistic can be found in Shapiro and Francia (1972). One or a few points departing from the linear trend near the extremes of the plot are indicative of outliers. Consult Daniel and Wood (1971), Daniel (1976), and Weisberg (1985) for more detail.

## Computational Notes

Rankits are computed with an algorithm similar to Royston's (1982) NSCOR2. The procedure for calculating the required percentage points of the normal distribution is patterned after Beasley and Springer (1977).

C H A P T E R

# 9

# *Time Series*

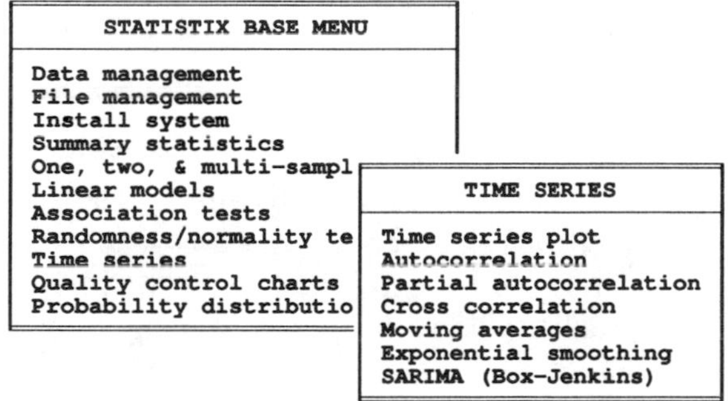


A time series is a list of observations collected sequentially, usually over time. Common time series subjects are stock prices, population levels, product sales, rainfall, and temperature. It's assumed that the observations are taken at uniform time intervals, such as every day, month, or year. Not all time series occur over time. For example, a list of diameters taken at every meter along a telephone cable is a legitimate time series.

Observations in a time series are often sequentially dependent. For example, population levels in the future often depend on levels at present and in the past. The goal of time series analysis is to model the nature of these dependencies, which in turn allows you to predict, or forecast, observations that have not yet been made.

The **Time Series Plot** procedure is used to create a time series plot for one or more variables.

The **Autocorrelation Plot** procedure is used to create an autocorrelation plot for a specified variable.

The **Partial Autocorrelation Plot** procedure is used to create a partial autocorrelation plot for a specified variable.

The **Cross Correlation** procedure is used to create a cross correlation plot for two variables.

The **Moving Averages** procedure is used to compute forecasts for time series data based on moving averages.

The **Exponential Smoothing** procedure computes forecasts for time series data using exponentially weighted averages.

The **SARIMA** procedure allows you to fit a variety of models to data, including both nonseasonal and multiplicative, and nonmultiplicative seasonal models.

## Model Building

The methods described by Box and Jenkins (1976) are a popular tool for modeling time series. The Box-Jenkins approach assumes that the time series can be represented as an ARIMA process, which stands for AutoRegressive Integrated Moving Average.

Box and Jenkins advocate an iterative three-step approach to model building:

1) Identification of terms to be included in the model
2) Parameter estimation
3) Model evaluation

Model term identification relies on the use of Time Series Plots, Autocorrelation Plots, and Partial Autocorrelation Plots. These plots are examined to suggest what transformations, differencing operators, AR terms, and MA terms should be included in the model.

Once a tentative model has been identified, parameter estimation is accomplished with the SARIMA procedure, which uses the unconditional least squares method (sometimes called the backcasting method) to fit the identified model to the series.

Model evaluation is accomplished by examining the results of the SARIMA fitting. If the model isn't adequate, a new tentative model is identified and the process repeated until a good model is found. A good model can then be used to forecast future observations. Box and Jenkins (1976) should be consulted for more details.

The forecasting procedures Exponential Smoothing and Moving Averages are easier to use and understand than ARIMA models.

### Treatment of Missing or Omitted Cases

Time series data sets can't have embedded missing values or omitted cases. There can be blocks of missing or omitted cases at the beginning and end of the data set. *Statistix* time series procedures use the first continuous block of data that doesn't contain missing values or omitted cases for the series.

# Time Series Plot

The **Time Series Plot** procedure is used to create a time series plot for one or more variables. The values of the variables are plotted in case order.

## Specification

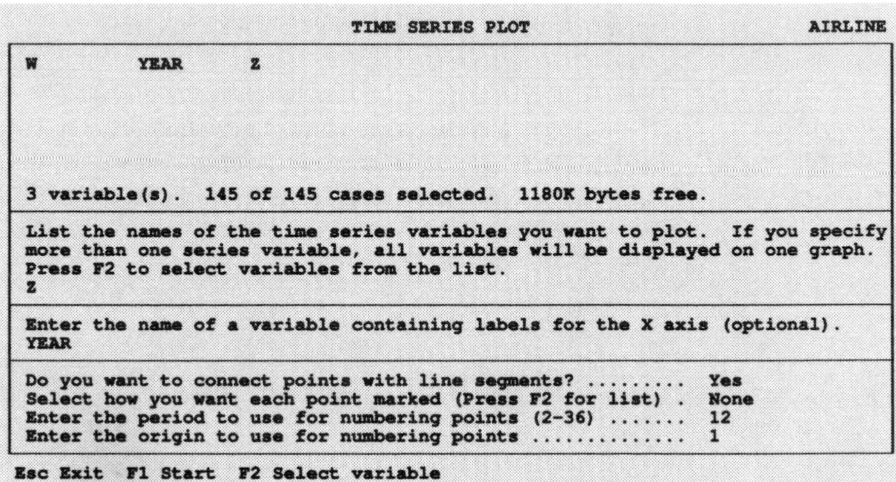

```
                         TIME SERIES PLOT                          AIRLINE
W          YEAR       Z

3 variable(s).  145 of 145 cases selected.  1180K bytes free.
List the names of the time series variables you want to plot.  If you specify
more than one series variable, all variables will be displayed on one graph.
Press F2 to select variables from the list.
Z
Enter the name of a variable containing labels for the X axis (optional).
YEAR
Do you want to connect points with line segments? ........  Yes
Select how you want each point marked (Press F2 for list) .  None
Enter the period to use for numbering points (2-36) ......  12
Enter the origin to use for numbering points .............  1
Esc Exit  F1 Start  F2 Select variable
```

Enter the name of one or more time series variables. If you enter more than one name, all the variables will be plotted on a single time series plot using different line patterns and point symbols.

Normally, the points along the X axis are labeled as case numbers starting with 1. You can customize the X axis labels specifying a second variable containing the labels. The label variable can be a string, date, integer, or real variable. Strings are truncated to ten characters.

Additional options are available to control the appearance and labeling of the plot. Points on a time series plot are usually connected by line segments. You can have the individual points marked with a circle, a digit, or no mark at all. If you don't have points marked ("none"), you should have the points connected by line segments.

Use the origin option to change the starting case number. For example, if you have annual data starting with 1955, enter 1955 at the origin prompt to have the axis labeled 1955, 1956, and 1957 instead of 1, 2, and 3.

Numbering the points using digits is useful for identifying seasonal trends.

You should enter a value for period that reflects the frequency of data collection. For example, enter 4 for quarterly data or a 12 for monthly data. A seasonal trend stands out clearly when the same digit appears in either peaks or valleys.

The period also affects how often the X axis is labeled. The example panel on the preceding page specifies a period of 12, which is suitable for labeling monthly data. The X axis will be labeled every 12 cases.

### Example

The example data are the natural logs of monthly passenger totals (in thousands) in international air travel for 12 years from January 1949 to December 1960 (Box and Jenkins 1976, p. 304). A total of 144 cases are in the variable named Z. The variable YEAR was created to annotate the X axis of our example plot—the year was entered for every 12th case. The panel on the preceding page is used to obtain the time series plot below.

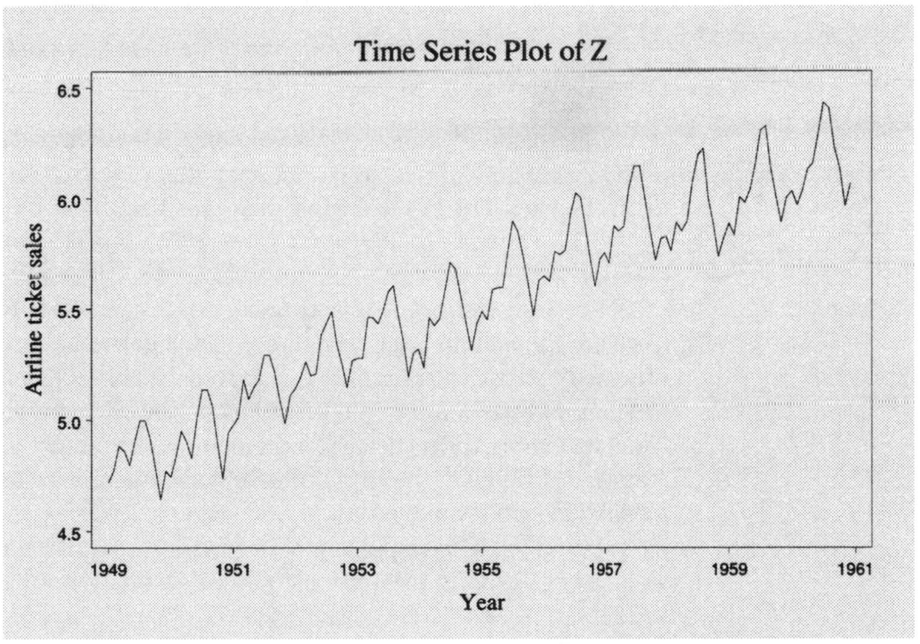


### ASCII Text Printer

If you have selected the ASCII printer for your graphics printer, single variable time series plots will always be drawn using numbers without line segments. Multiple variable plots will be drawn using the letters A for the first variable, B for the second variable, and so on.

# Autocorrelation

The **Autocorrelation Plot** procedure is used to create an autocorrelation plot for the specified variable. Approximate 95% confidence intervals are also shown.

## Specification

```
                          AUTOCORRELATION                                AIRLINE
W         Z




3 variable(s).  144 of 144 cases selected.  1180K bytes free.

Enter the name of a time series variable.  Press F2 to select a variable
from the list.
W

Enter the lag (optional).  If you do not enter a lag, the maximum lag will
be used (calculated as the square root of the sample size plus 5).
0

Esc Exit   F1 Start   F2 Select variable
```

Enter the name of a time series variable. You can specify a lag. If you don't specify a lag (left as 0), the maximum lag is used, which is calculated as the square root of the sample size plus five.

## Example

We use the data from Box and Jenkins (1976, p. 304) for our example. The data are the natural logs of monthly passenger totals (in thousands) in international air travel for 12 years from January 1949 to December 1960. A total of 144 cases are in a variable named Z. The variable W is created by first seasonally differencing Z and then nonseasonally differencing the seasonal difference. Using **Transformations** in Data Management, W is created in two steps by:

```
W = Z - LAG (Z, 12)
W = W - LAG (W)
```

That is, $W = DD^{12}Z$, where D is the differencing operator.

The options screen above shows the entries for the differenced airline data. A specific lag is not specified, so the maximum lag is used. The results are presented in the autocorrelation plot on the next page.

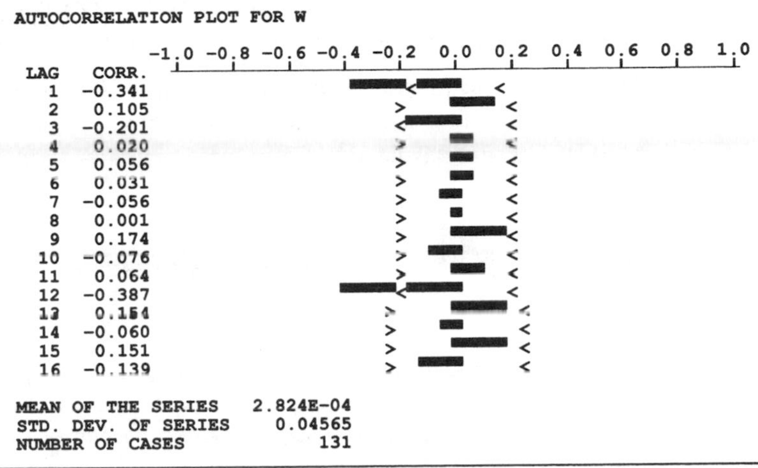


The first column indicates the lag for which the autocorrelation is computed. The next column displays the value of the autocorrelation. The autocorrelation is displayed graphically as a horizontal bar. Approximate 95% confidence bounds are indicated with angled brackets (< >). The direction in which the confidence bounds point indicates where the observation lies relative to the confidence bound. For example, with a lag of 3, the autocorrelation is -0.201, which lies outside of the confidence bound to the left.

The confidence intervals for the lag p are based on the assumption that autocorrelations for lags p and greater are zero.

## Computational Notes

Computations follow those outlined in Box and Jenkins (1976).

# Partial Autocorrelation

The **Partial Autocorrelation Plot** procedure is used to create a partial autocorrelation plot for the specified variable. Approximate 95% confidence intervals are also displayed.

## Specification

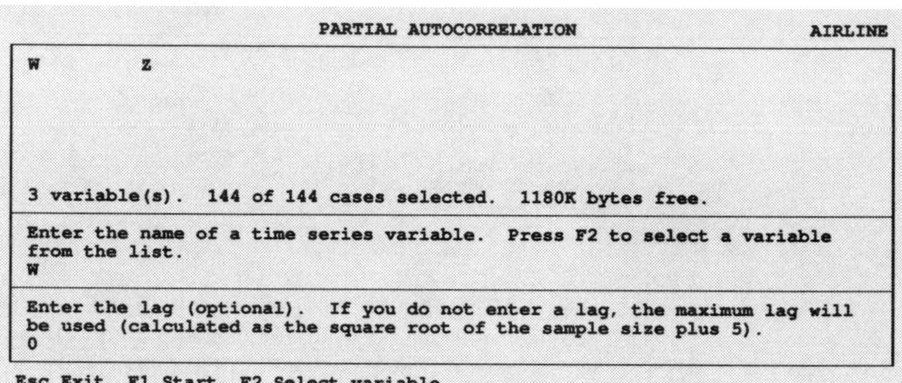


Enter the name of a time series variable. You may specify a lag. If you don't (left as 0), the maximum lag is used, calculated as the square root of the sample size plus five.

## Example

We use the data from Box and Jenkins (1976, p. 304) for our example. The data are the natural logs of monthly passenger totals (in thousands) in international air travel for 12 years from January 1949 to December 1960. The options panel above shows the entries for the differenced airline data in the variable W (page 254). A specific lag isn't specified, so the maximum lag is used. The resulting partial autocorrelation plot is shown on the next page.

The first column indicates the lag for which the partial autocorrelation is computed. The next column displays the value of the partial autocorrelation. The partial autocorrelation is displayed graphically as a horizontal bar. Approximate 95% confidence bounds are indicated with angled brackets (< >). The direction in which the confidence bounds point indicates where the observation lies relative to the confidence bound.

The confidence intervals for lag p are based on the assumption that the series results from an autoregressive process of order p - 1.

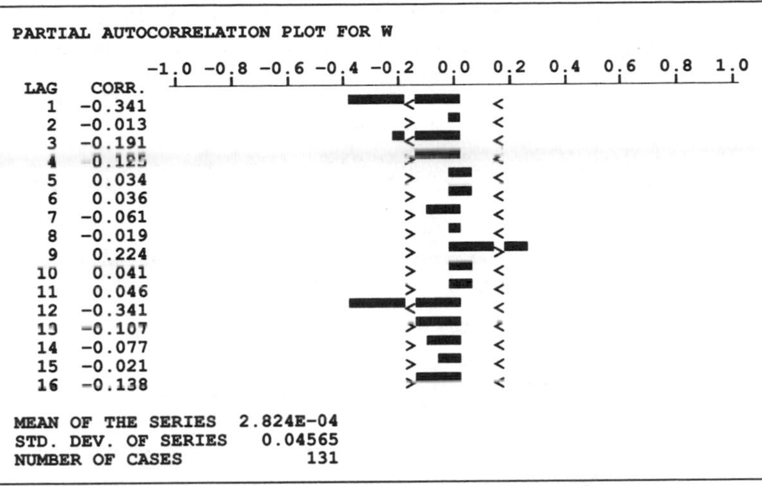

```
PARTIAL AUTOCORRELATION PLOT FOR W

              -1.0 -0.8 -0.6 -0.4 -0.2  0.0  0.2  0.4  0.6  0.8  1.0
 LAG   CORR.
  1  -0.341
  2  -0.013
  3  -0.191
  4  -0.125
  5   0.034
  6   0.036
  7  -0.061
  8  -0.019
  9   0.224
 10   0.041
 11   0.046
 12  -0.341
 13  -0.107
 14  -0.077
 15  -0.021
 16  -0.138

MEAN OF THE SERIES   2.824E-04
STD. DEV. OF SERIES    0.04565
NUMBER OF CASES            131
```

## Computational Notes

Computations follow those outlined in Box and Jenkins (1976).

# Cross Correlation

The **Cross Correlation** procedure is used to create a cross correlation plot for two variables.

## Specification

```
                         CROSS CORRELATION                        AIRLINE
 EVENT1    EVENT2    W        Z

 4 variable(s).  144 of 144 cases selected.  1179K bytes free.

 Enter the names of two time series variables for the cross correlation plot.
 Press F2 to select variables from the list.
 EVENT1 EVENT2

 Enter the lag (optional).  If you do not enter a lag, the maximum lag will
 be used (calculated as the square root of the sample size plus 5).
 10

 Esc Exit  F1 Start  F2 Select variable
```

Enter the names of the two time series variables. Unless a lag is explicitly specified, the maximum absolute value of the lag is used, computed as the square root of the sample size plus five.

## Example

To demonstrate cross correlation, we'll fabricate some data. The variable EVENT1 is created simply as a list of uniform random numbers. We then create the variable EVENT2 as a moving average process of EVENT1. These two variables are generated in **Transformations** as:

```
EVENT1 = RANDOM

EVENT2 = EVENT1 + LAG (EVENT1) / 2 + LAG (EVENT1, 2) / 3 +
LAG (EVENT1, 6) / 4
```

The options panel displayed above is used to find the cross correlations for EVENT1 and EVENT2 for 10 lags. The results are presented below in the cross correlation plot.

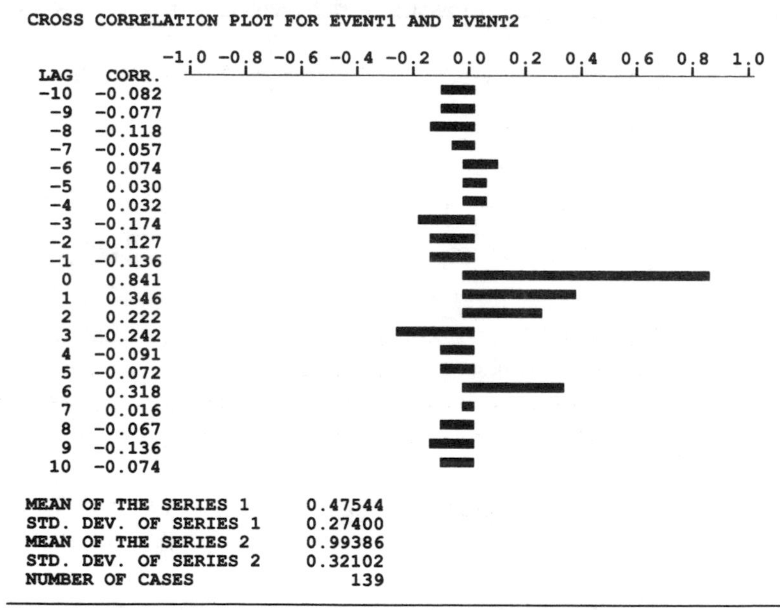

```
CROSS CORRELATION PLOT FOR EVENT1 AND EVENT2

              -1.0 -0.8 -0.6 -0.4 -0.2  0.0  0.2  0.4  0.6  0.8  1.0
 LAG   CORR.
 -10  -0.082
  -9  -0.077
  -8  -0.118
  -7  -0.057
  -6   0.074
  -5   0.030
  -4   0.032
  -3  -0.174
  -2  -0.127
  -1  -0.136
   0   0.841
   1   0.346
   2   0.222
   3  -0.242
   4  -0.091
   5  -0.072
   6   0.318
   7   0.016
   8  -0.067
   9  -0.136
  10  -0.074

MEAN OF THE SERIES 1       0.47544
STD. DEV. OF SERIES 1      0.27400
MEAN OF THE SERIES 2       0.99386
STD. DEV. OF SERIES 2      0.32102
NUMBER OF CASES                139
```

## Computational Notes

Computations follow those outlined in Box and Jenkins (1976).

# Moving Averages

The **Moving Averages** procedure is used to compute forecasts for time series data. Both single and double moving averages techniques are available. Use single moving averages when there is no trend in the time series data. Use double moving averages when there is a trend in the data,

## Specification

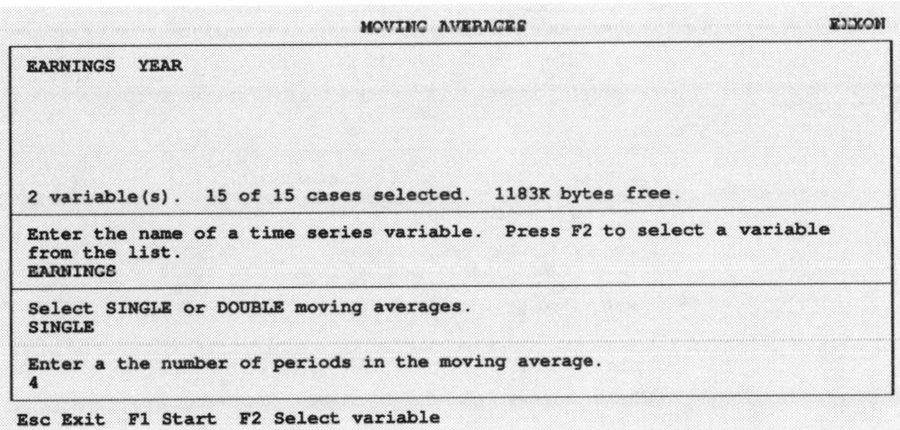


Enter the name of a time series variable. Then select single or double moving averages.

Enter a value for the number of periods in the moving average(s). In general you can select a value for the period that minimizes the maximum absolute deviation (MAD) or the mean squares of the forecast errors (MSE). The number of periods in the moving average is sometimes selected to remove seasonal effect; 4 is used for quarterly data, 12 for monthly data, and so on.

When using double moving averages, you can also specify the number of future periods for which you want to compute forecasts.

## Data Restrictions

There must be enough cases in the time series to compute the moving averages. The minimum number depends on the value you enter for the length of the moving averages. If the number of periods you specify for the moving averages is n, there must be at least n + 1 cases for single moving averages and 2 x n cases for double moving averages.

## Example

We illustrate single moving averages using earnings per share for Exxon for the years 1962 to 1976. The data are presented below.

| YEAR | EARNINGS | YEAR | EARNINGS |
|---|---|---|---|
| 1962 | 1.94 | 1970 | 2.96 |
| 1963 | 2.37 | 1971 | 3.39 |
| 1964 | 2.44 | 1972 | 3.42 |
| 1965 | 2.41 | 1973 | 5.45 |
| 1966 | 2.53 | 1974 | 7.02 |
| 1967 | 2.77 | 1975 | 5.60 |
| 1968 | 2.97 | 1976 | 5.90 |
| 1969 | 2.89 | | |

The options panel on the preceding page shows the moving averages options selected for the Exxon data. The results are:

```
SINGLE MOVING AVERAGES FOR EARNINGS

MOVING AVERAGE LENGTH  4

SUM OF SQUARED ERRORS (SSE)             17.2542
MEAN SQUARED ERROR (MSE)                1.56856
STANDARD ERROR (SE)                     1.25242
MEAN ABSOLUTE DEVIATION (MAD)           0.82386
MEAN ABS PERCENTAGE ERROR (MAPE)          16.84
MEAN PERCENTAGE ERROR (MPE)               16.84

              95% C.I.                    95% C.I.
LEAD       LOWER BOUND     FORECAST     UPPER BOUND
----       -----------     --------     -----------
   1           3.53774      5.99250         8.44725
```

The results list a number of summary statistics that are useful for checking the adequacy of the model. The forecast for the year 1977 is displayed with a 95% confidence interval.

## Moving Averages Results Menu

After viewing the coefficient table, press Esc to display a menu of results options.

```
MOVING AVERAGES RESULTS

Coefficient table
Forecast table
Save residuals
Options panel
```

Selecting "Coefficient table" from the menu will redisplay the results presented above. Selecting "Options panel" from the menu will return you to the Moving Averages options panel used to generate these results.

## Forecast Table

The "Forecast table" lists the actual value, moving average, forecast, and forecast error for each time period in the data.

SINGLE MOVING AVERAGES FORECAST TABLE FOR EARNINGS

| TIME | ACTUAL VALUE | MOVING AVERAGE | FORECAST | FORECAST ERROR |
|---|---|---|---|---|
| 1 | 1.94000 | | | |
| 2 | 2.37000 | | | |
| 3 | 2.44000 | | | |
| 4 | 2.41000 | 2.29000 | | |
| 5 | 2.53000 | 2.43750 | 2.29000 | 0.24000 |
| 6 | 2.77000 | 2.53750 | 2.43750 | 0.33250 |
| 7 | 2.97000 | 2.67000 | 2.53750 | 0.43250 |
| 8 | 2.89000 | 2.79000 | 2.67000 | 0.22000 |
| 9 | 2.96000 | 2.89750 | 2.79000 | 0.17000 |
| 10 | 3.39000 | 3.05250 | 2.89750 | 0.49250 |
| 11 | 3.42000 | 3.16500 | 3.05250 | 0.36750 |
| 12 | 5.45000 | 3.80500 | 3.16500 | 2.28500 |
| 13 | 7.02000 | 4.82000 | 3.80500 | 3.21500 |
| 14 | 5.60000 | 5.37250 | 4.82000 | 0.78000 |
| 15 | 5.90000 | 5.99250 | 5.37250 | 0.52750 |

## Save Residuals

Use the Save Residuals procedure to save the fitted values (forecasts) and/or residuals (forecast errors) in new or existing variables for later analysis.

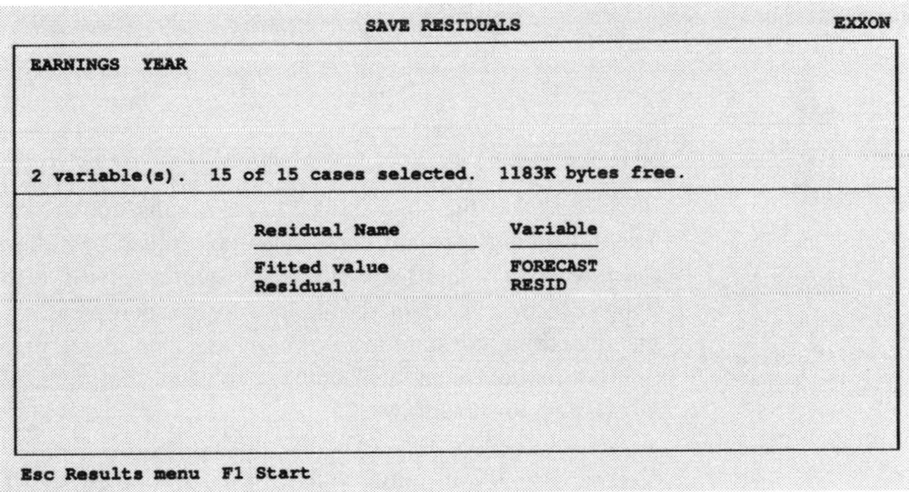


## Computational Notes

Computations follow those described in Hanke and Reitsch (1989) and Mercier (1987).

# Exponential Smoothing

The **Exponential Smoothing** procedure computes forecasts for time series data using exponential weighted averages. Use single exponential smoothing when no trend exists in the data. Use double exponential smoothing when there is a linear trend in the data.

## Specification

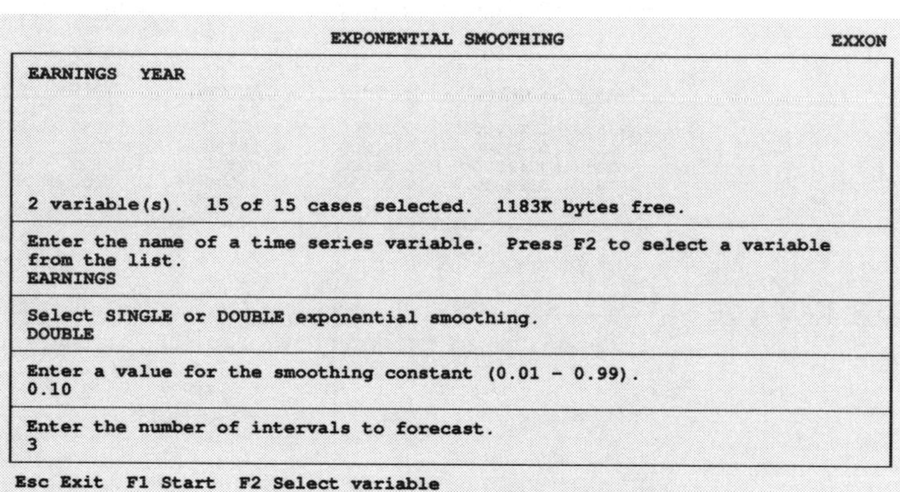


First enter the name of a time series variable and then select either single or double exponential smoothing. Enter a value for the smoothing constant. The smoothing constant determines how much past observations influence the forecast. A small smoothing constant results in a slow response to new values; a large constant results in a fast response to new values. Values for the smoothing constant are normally selected in the range 0.05 to 0.60. For the best model, select a smoothing constant that minimizes the mean squares of the forecast errors (MSE).

You can specify an initial value for the smoothed statistic (exponential average) with single exponential smoothing. For double exponential smoothing, you may specify the number of forecasts to compute.

## Example

Double exponential smoothing is illustrated using earnings per share data for Exxon for the years 1962 to 1976. The data are listed on the next page.

| YEAR | EARNINGS | YEAR | EARNINGS |
|---|---|---|---|
| 1962 | 1.94 | 1970 | 2.96 |
| 1963 | 2.37 | 1971 | 3.39 |
| 1964 | 2.44 | 1972 | 3.42 |
| 1965 | 2.41 | 1973 | 5.45 |
| 1966 | 2.53 | 1974 | 7.02 |
| 1967 | 2.77 | 1975 | 5.60 |
| 1968 | 2.97 | 1976 | 5.90 |
| 1969 | 2.89 | | |

The options panel on the preceding page shows the exponential smoothing options selected for the Exxon data. The results are:

```
DOUBLE EXPONENTIAL SMOOTHING FOR EARNINGS

SMOOTHING CONSTANT    0.10

SUM OF SQUARED ERRORS (SSE)             9.47381
MEAN SQUARED ERROR (MSE)                0.63158
STANDARD ERROR (SE)                     0.79472
MEAN ABSOLUTE DEVIATION (MAD)           0.59165
MEAN ABS PERCENTAGE ERROR (MAPE)          16.57
MEAN PERCENTAGE ERROR (MPE)               -1.81

             95% C.I.                     95% C.I.
LEAD      LOWER BOUND    FORECAST      UPPER BOUND
----      -----------    --------      -----------
   1        4.60534       6.16300        7.72066
   2        4.91179       6.47742        8.04305
   3        5.21789       6.79184        8.36579
```

The coefficient table above lists a number of summary statistics that are useful for checking the adequacy of the model (Hanke and Reitsch 1989). You can also use the residuals (see Save Residuals on the next page) to examine the model fit.

The forecasts for the years 1977 to 1979 are displayed with their 95% confidence intervals.

### Exponential Smoothing Results Menu

After viewing the coefficient table, press Esc to view the menu of additional results options.

```
EXPONENTIAL SMOOTHING RESULTS
-----------------------------
Coefficient table
Forecast table
Save residuals
Options panel
```

Select "Coefficient table" from the menu to redisplay the results presented above. Select "Options panel" from the menu to return to the Exponential

Smoothing options panel used to generate these results.

## Forecast Table

The forecast table lists the actual value, first and second exponential averages, slope, forecast, and forecast error for each time period in the data.

**DOUBLE EXPONENTIAL FORECAST TABLE FOR EARNINGS**

| TIME | ACTUAL VALUE | 1ST EXP AVERAGE | 2ND EXP AVERAGE | SLOPE | FORECAST | FORECAST ERROR |
|---|---|---|---|---|---|---|
| 0 | | -1.62107 | -4.38728 | 0.30735 | | |
| 1 | 1.94000 | -1.26496 | -4.07505 | 0.31223 | 1.45250 | 0.48750 |
| 2 | 2.37000 | -0.90146 | -3.75769 | 0.31735 | 1.85735 | 0.51264 |
| 3 | 2.44000 | -0.56732 | -3.43865 | 0.31903 | 2.27211 | 0.16788 |
| 4 | 2.41000 | -0.26958 | -3.12175 | 0.31690 | 2.62305 | -0.21305 |
| 5 | 2.53000 | 0.01037 | -2.80853 | 0.31321 | 2.89948 | -0.36948 |
| 6 | 2.77000 | 0.28633 | -2.49905 | 0.30948 | 3.14249 | -0.37249 |
| 7 | 2.97000 | 0.55470 | -2.19367 | 0.30537 | 3.38120 | -0.41120 |
| 8 | 2.89000 | 0.78823 | -1.89548 | 0.29819 | 3.60845 | -0.71845 |
| 9 | 2.96000 | 1.00540 | -1.60539 | 0.29008 | 3.77013 | -0.81013 |
| 10 | 3.39000 | 1.24386 | -1.32047 | 0.28492 | 3.90629 | -0.51629 |
| 11 | 3.42000 | 1.46147 | -1.04227 | 0.27819 | 4.09312 | -0.67312 |
| 12 | 5.45000 | 1.86033 | -0.75201 | 0.29026 | 4.24342 | 1.20657 |
| 13 | 7.02000 | 2.37629 | -0.43918 | 0.31283 | 4.76293 | 2.25706 |
| 14 | 5.60000 | 2.69866 | -0.12539 | 0.31378 | 5.50461 | 0.09538 |
| 15 | 5.90000 | 3.01880 | 0.18902 | 0.31442 | 5.83652 | 0.06348 |

## Save Residuals

Use the "Save residuals" procedure to save the fitted values (forecasts) and/or residuals (forecast errors) in new or existing variables for later analysis. Simply enter variable names at the prompts for fitted values and/or residuals.

## Computational Notes

Computations follow those described in Abraham and Ledolter (1983). If you don't specify an initial value for single exponential smoothing, the arithmetic average of the series will be used. The initial values for the two smoothed statistics for double exponential smoothing are computed from the intercept and slope of simple least squares regression.

# SARIMA

The **SARIMA** procedure allows you to fit a variety of models to data, including both nonseasonal and multiplicative, and nonmultiplicative seasonal models. SARIMA stands for Seasonal AutoRegressive Integrated Moving Average. It's a procedure for modeling time series popularized by Box and Jenkins (1976). MA and AR terms need not be sequential, so nonsignificant terms don't need to be included in the model.

Output includes parameter estimates, approximate significance levels, and several statistics useful for diagnosing model fit. You can also obtain forecasts with confidence intervals. You can save fitted values and residuals to evaluate model adequacy.

Estimation is based on unconditional least squares, also known as the backcasting method.

## Specification

```
                     SARIMA (BOX-JENKINS)                          AIRLINE

          Variable ..................... Z
          Lags for AR model terms .......
          Nonseasonal d ................ 1
          Lags for MA model terms ...... 1
          Lags for SAR model terms ......
          Seasonal D ................... 1
          Lags for SMA model terms ..... 1
          Season length ................ 12
          Include constant in model? ... No
          Marquardt criterion .......... 0.010
          Nelder-Mead simplex search? .. Yes
          Nelder-Mead criterion ........ 0.010
          Maximum iterations ........... 20
          Iterations until query ....... 10

 List the initial values (optional).
 AR
 MA
 SAR
 SMA
 Constant

Esc Exit   F1 Start
```

First enter the name of your time series variable. Next you specify the ARIMA model by responding to the relevant prompts. You can also specify the Marquardt and Nelder-Mead criteria, the maximum number of iterations, and initial values. You can move up and down the options panel to edit the model specifications using the arrow keys. Press F1 to begin the analysis.

For example, the panel above fits the ARIMA model $(0, 1, 1)X(0, 1, 1)_{12}$ to the airline data described on page 267.

A description of each of the options panel fields is listed below:

**Variable**: Variable name for the time series variable
**AR model terms:** Lags of nonseasonal autoregressive terms in model
**Nonseasonal d:** Order of nonseasonal differencing
**MA model terms:** Lags of nonseasonal moving average terms in model
**SAR model terms:** Seasonal lags of seasonal autoregressive terms in model
**Seasonal D:** Order of seasonal differencing
**SMA model terms:** Seasonal lags of seasonal moving average terms in model
**Season length:** Period of seasonality
**Include constant:** Should model include a constant term?
**Marquardt criterion:** Criterion to stop nonlinear least squares
**Nelder-Mead search:** Perform simplex search after nonlinear least squares?
**Nelder-Mead criterion:** Criterion to stop Nelder-Mead simplex search
**Maximum iterations:** Number of iterations allowed
**Iterations until query:** Iterations before being prompted to stop or continue
**Initial values:** List of starting values for any of the model parameters

Most of these fields are self-explanatory. Estimation is initially performed with Marquardt's nonlinear least squares procedure. After each iteration, the changes in the parameter estimates are checked. If all parameters have changed less in absolute value than the "Marquardt criterion", the procedure terminates and is assumed to have converged successfully. If you enter "Yes" for the "Nelder-Mead simplex search", a Nelder-Mead simplex search is performed after the Marquardt procedure in an attempt to further reduce the unconditional sums of squares. Unlike the Marquardt criterion, the Nelder-Mead criterion is based on the reduction of the unconditional sums of squares. After each iteration, the reduction in the unconditional sums of squares is checked. If the reduction is less than the number specified for the "Nelder-Mead criterion", the procedure terminates and convergence is assumed. Both Marquardt and Nelder-Mead stop when the number of iterations equals "Maximum iterations" if convergence hasn't occurred. When the number of iterations reaches "Iterations until query", you'll be asked whether you want iteration to continue. If you don't want to be asked, be sure that "Iterations until query" is larger than "Maximum iterations".

**Note:** When specifying AR, MA, SAR, or SMA terms, **all** lags must be specified. For example, to specify an AR(3) model, you would enter "1 2 3", not "3". The latter specification is appropriate if you want the AR coefficients for lags 1 and 2 constrained to zero.

Example

We use the data from Box and Jenkins (1976, p. 304) for our example. The data in the variable Z are the natural logs of monthly passenger totals (in thousands) in international air travel for 12 years from January 1949 to December 1960. The variable W is created by first seasonally differencing Z and then nonseasonally differencing the seasonal difference. Using **Transformations** in Data Management, W is created in two steps by:

```
W = Z - LAG (Z, 12)
W = W - LAG (W)
```

That is, $W = DD^{12}Z$, where D is the differencing operator. The panel on page 265 specifies the ARIMA model $(0, 1, 1)X(0, 1, 1)_{12}$.

At each iteration, the current parameter estimates are displayed. The lag at which the backcasts have died out to effectively zero is also displayed (large lags indicate estimation difficulties).

```
ITERATION      TOTAL SS        MA  1       SMA 1     BACK LAG
     1        0.23906268      0.100       0.100        -11
     2        0.20797849      0.201       0.250        -11
     3        0.18830643      0.278       0.400        -11
     4        0.17742828      0.348       0.550        -11
     5        0.17601103      0.391       0.618        -11
     6        0.17600232      0.393       0.613        -11

Marquardt reduction done; starting simplex search.

ITERATION      TOTAL SS        MA  1       SMA 1     BACK LAG
     1        0.17600232      0.393       0.613        -11
     2        0.17603164      0.393       0.623        -11
```

The results are summarized in the coefficient table below.

```
UNCONDITIONAL LEAST SQUARES SARIMA MODEL FOR Z

NONSEASONAL DIFFERENCING OF ORDER    1
SEASONAL DIFFERENCING OF ORDER    1, PERIOD  12
NOTE: NO CONSTANT TERM IN MODEL

  TERM         COEFFICIENT     STD  ERROR     COEF / SE          P
 -------       -----------     ----------     ---------      ---------
  MA  1          0.39308         0.08032         4.89          0.0000
  SMA 1          0.61262         0.06941         8.83          0.0000

MS (BACKCASTS EXCLUDED)        0.00133
DF                                 129
SS (BACKCASTS EXCLUDED)        0.17212    SS DUE TO BACKCASTS        0.00387
N BEFORE DIFFERENCING              144
N AFTER DIFFERENCING               131
MARQUARDT CRITERION OF 0.010 WAS MET.
SIMPLEX CRITERION OF    0.010 WAS MET.
LJUNG-BOX PORTMANTEAU LACK-OF-FIT DIAGNOSTICS
LAG (DF)    =        12(      10)         24(      22)          36(      34)          48(      46)
CHI-SQ (P)  =    9.31(0.5027)     25.41(0.2780)     35.39(0.4023)     44.05(0.5541)
```

Parameter significance can be judged with the t-like statistic COEF / SE. The p-value for this statistic assumes a standard normal distribution. Overall model fit can be judged with the Ljung-Box statistic (Ljung and Box 1978), which is calculated for lags at multiples of 12. Small p-values indicate that the model fit is poor. In the example on the preceding page, the p-values are large enough to suggest lack of fit isn't a problem.

As noted, model terms don't need to be sequential. As an example, we'll fit a nonmultiplicative seasonal model to the airline data set. The model we've already used is $DD^{12}z_t = (1 - \Phi B)(1 - \Theta B^{12})a_t$ (D is the differencing operator; other terms are explained in Box and Jenkins 1976). When expanded, this model is $DD^{12}z_t = a_t - \Phi a_{t-1} - \Theta a_{t-12} + \Phi\Theta a_{t-13}$. The more general nonmultiplicative model is $DD^{12}z_t = a_t - \Phi_1 a_{t-1} - \Phi_{12}\, a_{t-12} - \Phi_{13}\, a_{t-13}$.

This model is specified in the panel below.

```
                         SARIMA (BOX-JENKINS)                          AIRLINE

          Variable ...................... Z
          Lags for AR model terms .......
          Nonseasonal d ................. 1
          Lags for MA model terms ....... 1 12 13
          Lags for SAR model terms ......
          Seasonal D .................... 1
          Lags for SMA model terms ......
          Season length ................. 12
          Include constant in model? .... No
          Marquardt criterion ........... 0.010
          Nelder-Mead simplex search? ... Yes
          Nelder-Mead criterion ......... 0.010
          Maximum iterations ............ 20
          Iterations until query ........ 10

 List the initial values (optional).
 AR
 MA
 SAR
 SMA
 Constant

Esc Exit  F1 Start
```

While this model has a smaller MS (0.00127) than the multiplicative model, it also requires an additional parameter. Box and Jenkins (1976, p. 324) briefly consider how to examine whether such models are improvements over their multiplicative counterparts.

## SARIMA Results Menu

After viewing the coefficient table, press Esc to display a menu of additional SARIMA results options.

```
SARIMA RESULTS
Coefficient table
Forecasts
Save residuals
Variance-covariance matrix
Options panel
```

Select "Coefficient table" from the menu to redisplay the results presented above. Select "Options panel" from the menu to return to the SARIMA options panel used to generate these results.

## Forecasts

The forecast procedure lets you forecast future observations. It also gives confidence intervals for the forecasts.

```
FORECAST                                                    AIRLINE
Enter the lead time (number of future lags, 1-100).
12
Enter a percentage coverage for forecast confidence intervals (50.0-99.9).
95.0
```

First enter the lead time, which is the number of future time intervals you want to forecast. You can also specify the interval coverage for confidence levels.

The first 12 forecasts for our airline ticket sales example are presented below.

| LEAD | 95% C.I. LOWER BOUND | FORECAST | 95% C.I. UPPER BOUND |
|---|---|---|---|
| 1 | 6.03778 | 6.10938 | 6.18097 |
| 2 | 5.97162 | 6.05537 | 6.13912 |
| 3 | 6.08325 | 6.17760 | 6.27195 |
| 4 | 6.09433 | 6.19821 | 6.30208 |
| 5 | 6.11795 | 6.23055 | 6.34315 |
| 6 | 6.24756 | 6.36825 | 6.48894 |
| 7 | 6.37619 | 6.50446 | 6.63273 |
| 8 | 6.36544 | 6.50087 | 6.63631 |
| 9 | 6.18287 | 6.32510 | 6.46733 |
| 10 | 6.05869 | 6.20741 | 6.35614 |
| 11 | 5.90897 | 6.06391 | 6.21885 |
| 12 | 6.00841 | 6.16933 | 6.33025 |

## Save Residuals

Use the Save Residuals procedure to save the fitted values (forecasts) and/or residuals (forecast errors) for later analysis. Because of differencing and lagging, the residuals may have fewer cases than the original series.

## Variance - Covariance Matrix

The Variance-covariance matrix menu selection displays the variance-covariance matrix of the estimated model coefficients.

```
VARIANCE-COVARIANCE MATRIX FOR COEFFICIENTS

                  MA  1       SMA 1
  MA  1        0.00645
  SMA 1     -3.165E-04     0.00481
```

## Computational Notes

Computations generally follow those outlined in Box and Jenkins (1976). Initial values for the nonseasonal AR parameters are computed as described on page 499. These, along with the mean of the series, are used to construct an initial estimate of the constant (Box and Jenkins 1976, p. 500) if the model contains one. All other parameters are initially set to 0.1. The Marquardt procedure follows Box and Jenkins (1976) with modifications suggested by Nash (1979). Numerical derivatives use "Nash's compromise" (Nash, 1979, eq. 18.5). The Nelder-Mead procedure is patterned after Nash's outline.

C H A P T E R

# 10

# *Quality Control*

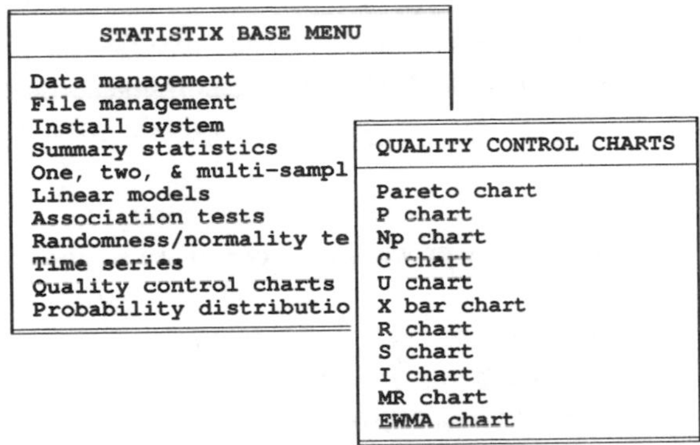


*Statistix* offers a number of quality control or statistical process control (SPC) procedures. SPC methods are used to improve the quality of a product or service by examining the process employed to create the product or service.

The **Pareto Chart** procedure produces a Parteo chart, which is used in SPC to identify the most common problems or defects in a product or service. It is a histogram with the bars sorted by decreasing frequency.

A control chart plots a measurement sampled from a process by sample number over time. A center line is drawn to represent the average value of the quality characteristic when the process is stable, that is, "in control".

Two lines are drawn on the control chart to represent the upper and lower control limits (UCL and LCL). A point that falls outside the control limits is evidence that the process is "out of control". *Statistix* uses "3-sigma" control limits that are computed as the center line value plus or minus three times the standard deviation of the process statistic being plotted.

A quality characteristic that can't be measured on a quantitative scale but can be classified as conforming or nonconforming, is called an *attribute*. Consider a cardboard juice container as an example: Either the seams are conforming (will not leak) or nonconforming (will leak). *Statistix* computes four attributes control charts—the p chart, np chart, c chart, and u chart.

The **P Chart** procedure plots the fraction nonconforming. The **NP Chart** procedure plots the number nonconforming.

The **C Chart** procedure plots the number of nonconformities per inspection unit (e.g., flaws on the finish of a television set). The **U Chart** procedure plots the average number of nonconformities per unit.

A quantitative quality characteristic, such as the diameter of piston rings, is called a *variable*. *Statistix* computes six control charts for variables—the X bar chart, R chart, S chart, I chart, MR chart, and EWMA chart.

The **X Bar Chart** procedure plots the average of samples; it's used to control the process average of a variable.

The **R Chart** procedure plots the sample range. The **S Chart** procedure plots the sample standard deviation. These plots are used to control the variability of a process.

The **I Chart** procedure plots individuals—variables with a sample size of one. The **MR Chart** procedure plots the moving range of individuals.

The **EWMA Chart** procedure plots an exponentially weighted moving average. It can be used to control the process mean using individuals or sample averages.

See Montgomery (1991) for computational details for all the procedures discussed in this chapter.

**Printer Installation**

All of the charts on the Quality Control menu produce high-resolution graphs. Your computer, therefore, must have a graphics monitor. Before printing a graph you must select a graphics printer. To do so, select "Install system" from the *Statistix* base menu then select "Printers" (see Chapter 1 for more details).

**Graph Options**

Various characteristics of graphs can be controlled using the options listed on the "Graphics options" installation panel discussed in Chapter 1. For example, the samples on a control chart are normally marked using a circle. The symbol can be changed to something else (square, triangle, etc.) by selecting an alternate symbol for "sequential plot symbol #1".

**ASCII Text Printer**

If you have selected the ASCII printer for your graphics printer, observations on control charts can't be connected with line segments. Points are marked on the charts using plus signs when the charts are printed.

# Pareto Chart

The **Pareto Chart** is used to identify the most frequent causes of defects. It displays a histogram with the bars ordered by frequency.

## Specification

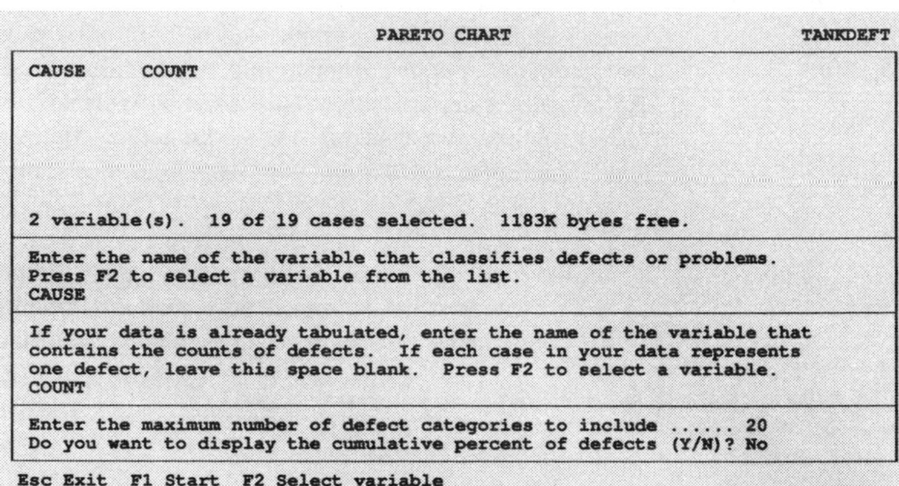

```
                              PARETO CHART                         TANKDEFT
 CAUSE     COUNT




 2 variable(s).  19 of 19 cases selected.  1183K bytes free.

 Enter the name of the variable that classifies defects or problems.
 Press F2 to select a variable from the list.
 CAUSE

 If your data is already tabulated, enter the name of the variable that
 contains the counts of defects.  If each case in your data represents
 one defect, leave this space blank.  Press F2 to select a variable.
 COUNT

 Enter the maximum number of defect categories to include ...... 20
 Do you want to display the cumulative percent of defects (Y/N)? No
 Esc Exit  F1 Start  F2 Select variable
```

First enter the name of the variable that contains the defect classifications. This variable can be of any type—real, integer, date, or string. Strings are truncated to ten characters.

You can enter your data one defect at a time, so that each case in your data set represents one defect. These types of data are often tabulated as they are collected, in which case it's more convenient to enter the data in two columns, one for the defect cause and one for the count of defects. In this case you must enter the name of the variable containing the counts of defects for each cause.

Enter Yes at the last prompt on the panel to have a cumulative distribution curve drawn on the Pareto chart.

## Example

We use data from Montgomery (1991, p. 119) for our example. The various reasons that aircraft tank were classified defective were collected over several months. The data were entered into *Statistix* using two variables. The variable CAUSE is used to identify the defect cause, and the variable COUNT records the count for each cause.

| CASE | CAUSE | COUNT |
|---|---|---|
| 1 | Adhesive | 6 |
| 2 | Alignment | 2 |
| 3 | Alodine | 1 |
| 4 | Cast voids | 2 |
| 5 | Damaged | 34 |
| 6 | Delam comp | 2 |
| 7 | Dimensions | 36 |
| 8 | Fairing | 3 |
| 9 | Film | 5 |
| 10 | Machining | 29 |
| 11 | Masking | 17 |
| 12 | Out order | 4 |
| 13 | Paint dam | 1 |
| 14 | Paint spec | 2 |
| 15 | Primer dam | 1 |
| 16 | Procedure | 1 |
| 17 | Rusted | 13 |
| 18 | Salt spray | 4 |
| 19 | Wrong part | 3 |

The variable names have been entered in the appropriate spaces in the options panel on the preceding page. The results are as follows:

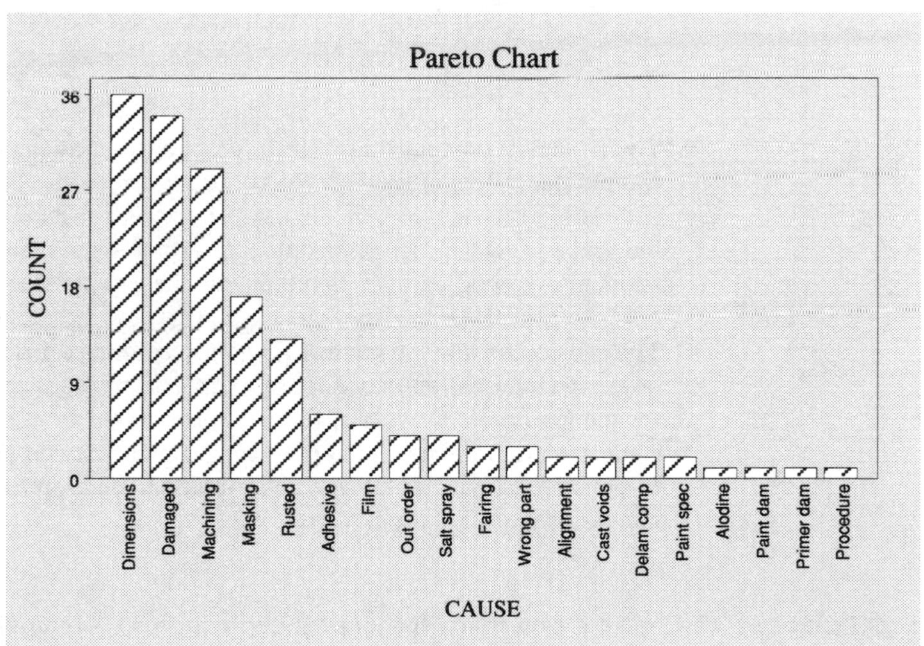

# P Chart

The **P Chart** is the control chart for the fraction of a sample that is nonconforming. P charts are used for attributes—quality characteristics that can be classified as conforming or nonconforming.

## Specification

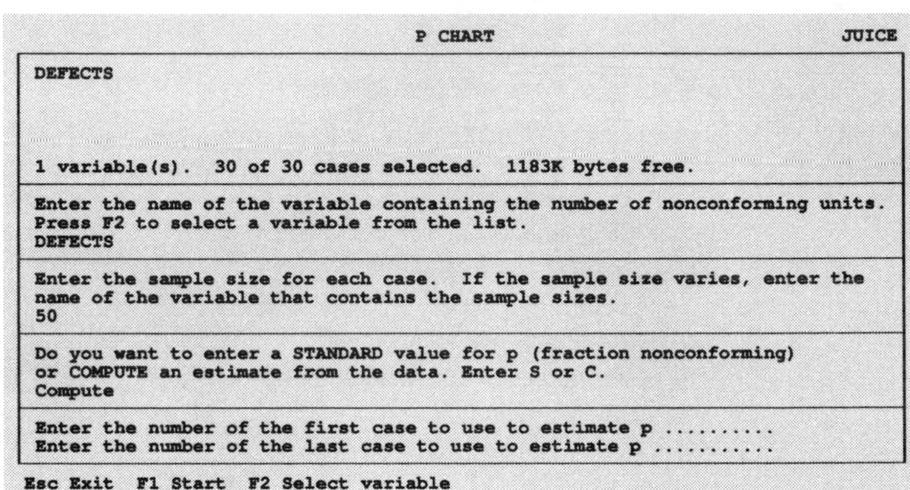

```
P CHART                                                         JUICE
DEFECTS

1 variable(s).  30 of 30 cases selected.  1183K bytes free.
Enter the name of the variable containing the number of nonconforming units.
Press F2 to select a variable from the list.
DEFECTS
Enter the sample size for each case.  If the sample size varies, enter the
name of the variable that contains the sample sizes.
50
Do you want to enter a STANDARD value for p (fraction nonconforming)
or COMPUTE an estimate from the data. Enter S or C.
Compute
Enter the number of the first case to use to estimate p .........
Enter the number of the last case to use to estimate p ..........
Esc Exit  F1 Start  F2 Select variable
```

The p chart is computed both from the number of defects per sample and the sample size. First enter the name of the variable that contains the counts of defects for each sample. If the sample size is constant, enter the number in the space provided. If the sample size is not always the same, enter the name of a second variable that contains the sample size for each case.

The center line and the control limits are computed from p, the fraction nonconforming. You may choose to enter a standard or historical value for p for this purpose. You can also have p computed from the data. When p is estimated from the data, you may specify the first and last case number used in order to compute p. If these case numbers are left blank as in the panel above, all cases are used.

## Example

We use data from Montgomery (1991, p. 151) for our example. Cardboard cans being manufactured for orange juice concentrate were sampled from the machine at half-hour intervals. Each sample contained 50 cans. The number of cans with defective seams were recorded for each sample.

| CASE | DEFECTS | CASE | DEFECTS |
|---|---|---|---|
| 1 | 12 | 16 | 8 |
| 2 | 15 | 17 | 10 |
| 3 | 8 | 18 | 5 |
| 4 | 10 | 19 | 13 |
| 5 | 4 | 20 | 11 |
| 6 | 7 | 21 | 20 |
| 7 | 16 | 22 | 18 |
| 8 | 9 | 23 | 24 |
| 9 | 14 | 24 | 15 |
| 10 | 10 | 25 | 9 |
| 11 | 5 | 26 | 12 |
| 12 | 6 | 27 | 7 |
| 13 | 17 | 28 | 13 |
| 14 | 12 | 29 | 9 |
| 15 | 22 | 30 | 6 |

The p chart model is specified in the options panel on the preceding page. The results are shown in the figure below.

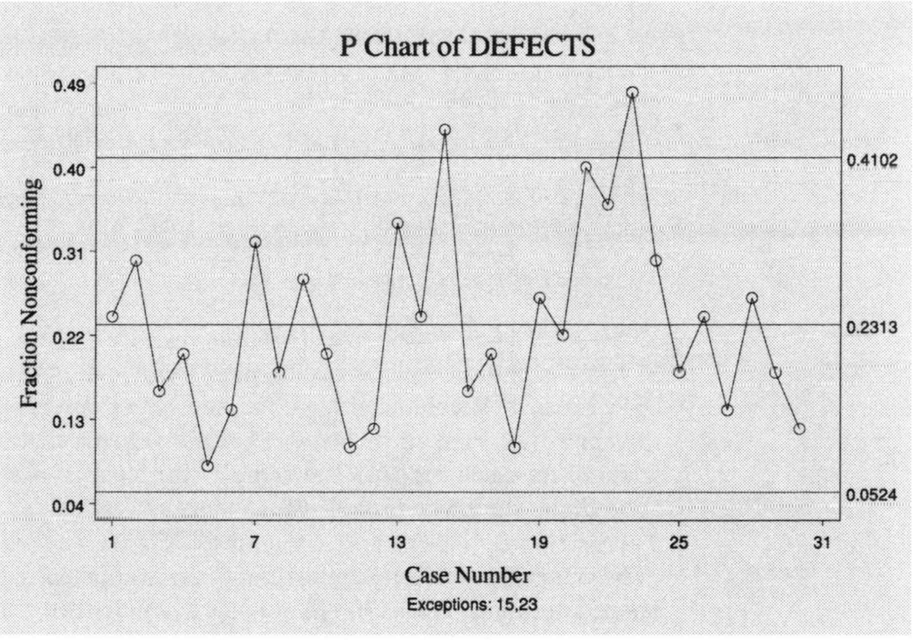


The fraction of defective cans is plotted for each sample. The center line is plotted at the average value for p which is 0.2313. The 3-sigma control limits are labeled on the right side: UCL = 0.4102, LCL = 0.0524. Two values exceed the UCL, indicating that the process is out of control. These case numbers (15 and 23) are noted at the bottom of the chart.

# NP Chart

The **Np Chart** is the control chart for the number of nonconforming units. Np charts are used for attributes—quality characteristics that can be classified as conforming or nonconforming. The np chart gives the same results as the p chart discussed earlier (page 276), the only difference is the units of the vertical axis.

## Specification

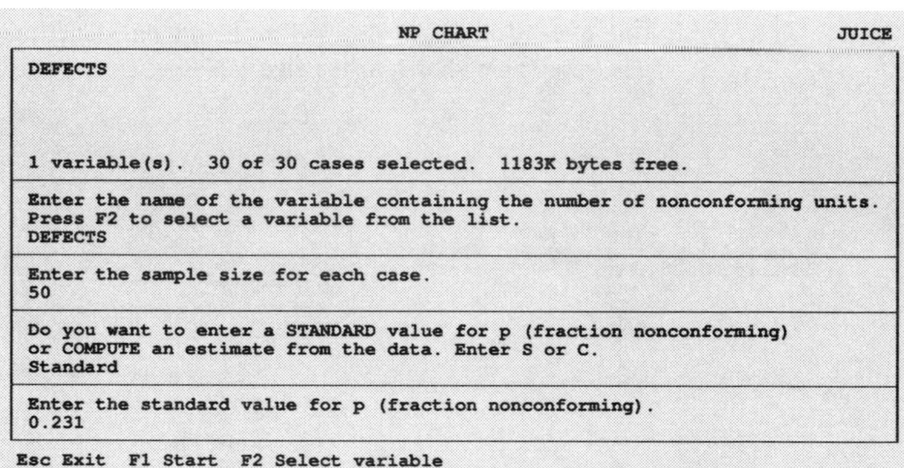

```
NP CHART                                                    JUICE
DEFECTS



1 variable(s).  30 of 30 cases selected.  1183K bytes free.

Enter the name of the variable containing the number of nonconforming units.
Press F2 to select a variable from the list.
DEFECTS

Enter the sample size for each case.
50

Do you want to enter a STANDARD value for p (fraction nonconforming)
or COMPUTE an estimate from the data. Enter S or C.
Standard

Enter the standard value for p (fraction nonconforming).
0.231

Esc Exit  F1 Start  F2 Select variable
```

The np chart is computed from the number of defects per sample and the sample size. First enter the name of the variable that contains the counts of defects for each sample. The sample size must be a constant. Enter the number in the space provided for the sample size.

The center line and the control limits are computed from p, the fraction nonconforming. You can either enter a standard or historical value for p or have p computed from the data. When p is estimated from the data, you can specify the first and last case numbers to use to compute p. If these case numbers are left blank, all cases are used.

## Example

We use data from Montgomery (1991, p. 151) for our example. Cardboard cans being manufactured for orange juice concentrate were sampled from the machine at half-hour intervals. Each sample contained 50 cans. The number of cans with defective seams were recorded for each sample.

| CASE | DEFECTS | CASE | DEFECTS |
|---|---|---|---|
| 1 | 12 | 16 | 8 |
| 2 | 15 | 17 | 10 |
| 3 | 8 | 18 | 5 |
| 4 | 10 | 19 | 13 |
| 5 | 4 | 20 | 11 |
| 6 | 7 | 21 | 20 |
| 7 | 16 | 22 | 18 |
| 8 | 9 | 23 | 24 |
| 9 | 14 | 24 | 15 |
| 10 | 10 | 25 | 9 |
| 11 | 5 | 26 | 12 |
| 12 | 6 | 27 | 7 |
| 13 | 17 | 28 | 13 |
| 14 | 12 | 29 | 9 |
| 15 | 22 | 30 | 6 |

The np chart model is specified in the options panel on the preceding page. The results are shown in the figure below.

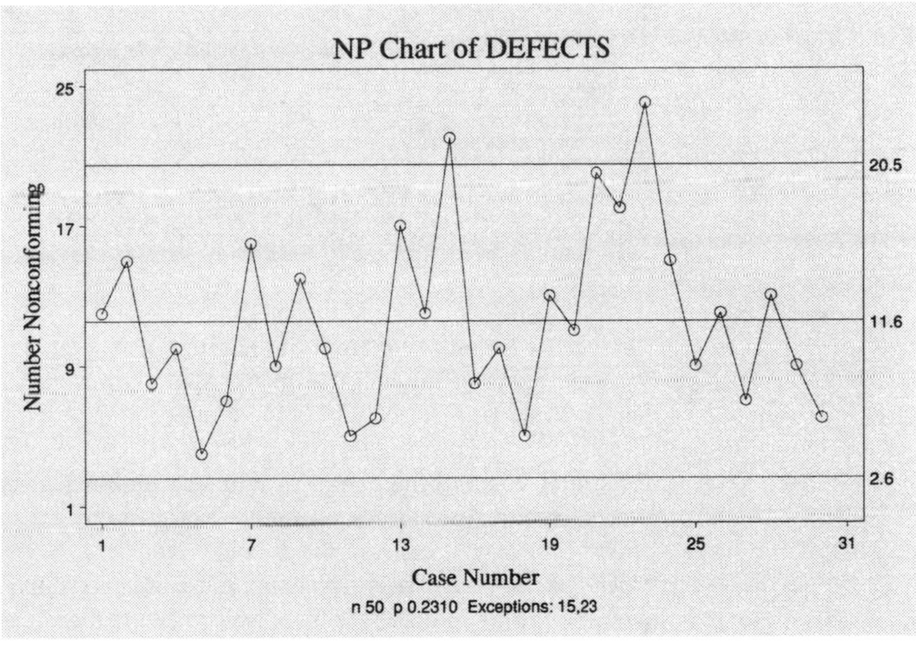


The number of defective cans is plotted for each sample. The center line is plotted at the historical value for np, 50 $*$ 0.231 = 11.6. The 3-sigma upper and lower control limits are labeled on the right side at 20.5 and 2.6. Two values exceed the UCL at cases 15 and 23, which are noted at the bottom of the chart.

# C Chart

The **C Chart** is the control chart for nonconformities (defects). A product may contain one or more defects and not be considered defective. If, for example, a television cabinet has a flaw in the finish, we wouldn't necessarily want to reject the television. In these situations we're more interested in the number of defects per inspection unit.

## Specification

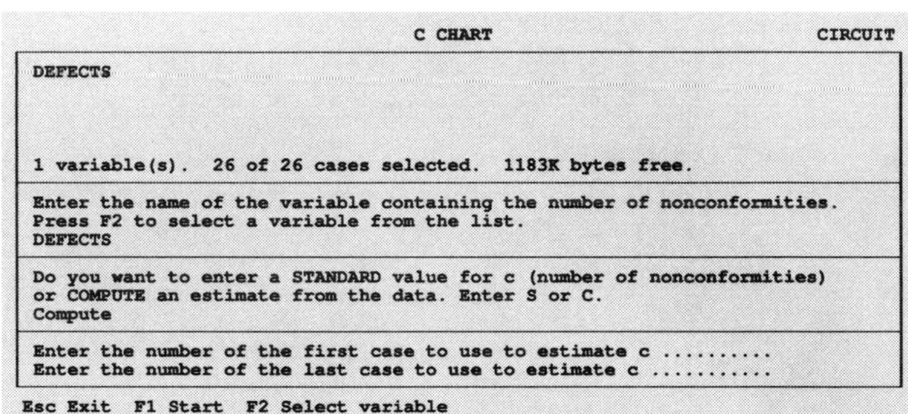


The c chart is computed from the number of defects per inspection unit. Enter the name of the variable that contains the counts of defects for each inspection unit.

The center line and the control limits are computed from c, the number of nonconformities per inspection unit. You can enter a standard or historical value for c, or you can use the average value of c computed from the data. When c is estimated from the data, you can specify the first and last case number used to compute the average value. If these case numbers are left blank, as in the panel above, all cases are used.

## Example

We use data from Montgomery (1991, p. 173) for our example. Printed circuit boards were inspected for defects. The inspection unit was defined as 100 circuit boards.

The number of defects per 100 circuit boards for 26 samples are listed below.

| CASE | DEFECTS | CASE | DEFECTS |
|---|---|---|---|
| 1 | 21 | 14 | 19 |
| 2 | 24 | 15 | 10 |
| 3 | 16 | 16 | 17 |
| 4 | 12 | 17 | 13 |
| 5 | 15 | 18 | 22 |
| 6 | 5 | 19 | 18 |
| 7 | 28 | 20 | 39 |
| 8 | 20 | 21 | 30 |
| 9 | 31 | 22 | 24 |
| 10 | 25 | 23 | 16 |
| 11 | 20 | 24 | 19 |
| 12 | 24 | 25 | 17 |
| 13 | 16 | 26 | 15 |

The resulting c chart for the variable DEFECTS is illustrated below.

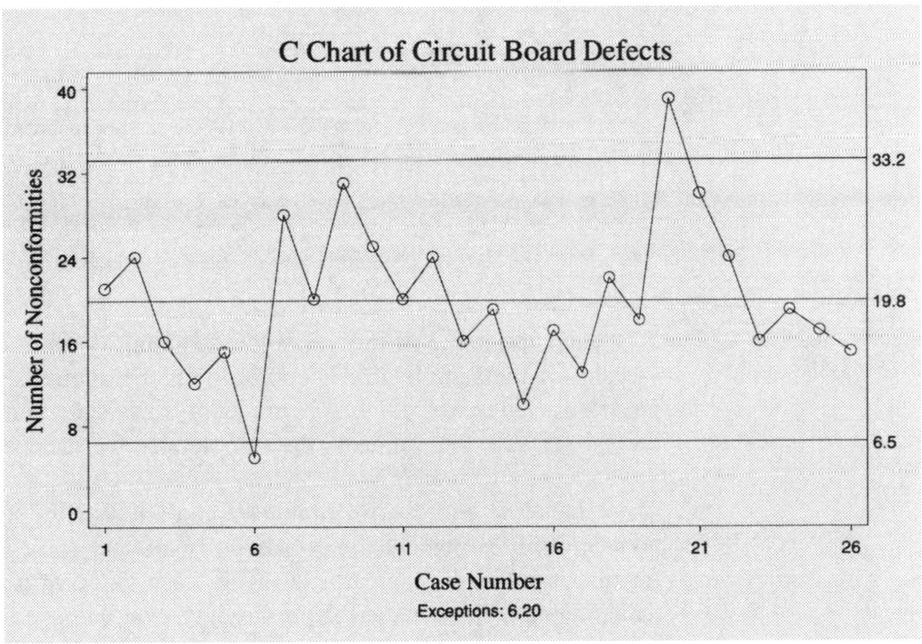


The number of nonconformities is plotted for each inspection unit (100 printed circuit boards). The center line is plotted at the average value for c 19.8. The 3-sigma upper and lower control limits are labeled on the right side at 33.2 and 6.5. The value at case 6 is below the LCL, and the value at case 20 is above the UCL. The process in not in control.

# U Chart

The **U Chart** is the attributes control chart for nonconformities per unit. It is used in controlling the nonconformities per unit when the sample size is not one inspection unit. The c chart discussed earlier (page 280) is used when the sample size is one.

## Specification

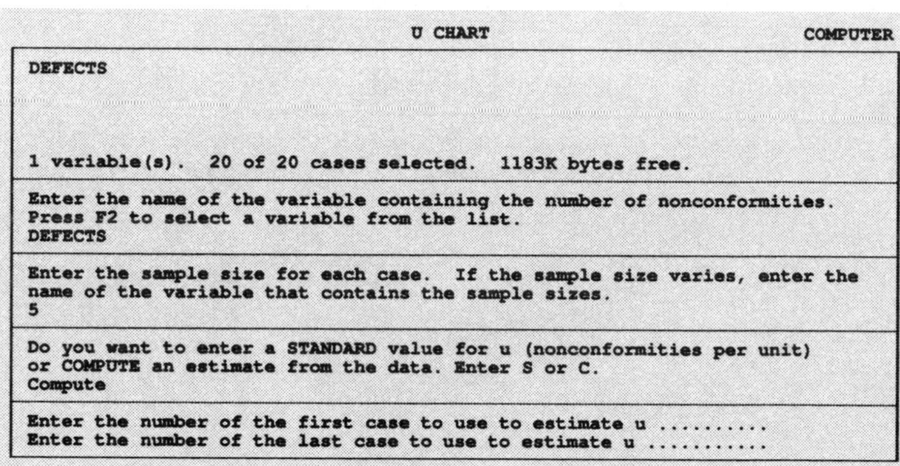


First enter the name of the variable containing the number of defects for each sample. If the sample size is constant, enter the number in the space provided. If the sample size is not always the same, enter the name of a second variable that contains the sample size for each case.

The center line and control limits are computed from u, the number of nonconformities per unit. You can enter a standard or historical value for u for this purpose, or you can use the average value of u computed from the data. When u is estimated from the data, you can specify the first and last case number to use to compute the average value. If these case numbers are left blank, as in the panel above, all cases are used.

## Example

We use data from Montgomery (1991, p. 181) for our example. Five personal computers were periodically sampled from the final assembly line and inspected for defects. The inspection unit was one computer. The sample size was five.

The total number of defects for each sample of five computers are listed below.

| CASE | DEFECTS | CASE | DEFECTS |
|---|---|---|---|
| 1 | 10 | 11 | 9 |
| 2 | 12 | 12 | 5 |
| 3 | 8 | 13 | 7 |
| 4 | 14 | 14 | 11 |
| 5 | 10 | 15 | 12 |
| 6 | 16 | 16 | 6 |
| 7 | 11 | 17 | 8 |
| 8 | 7 | 18 | 10 |
| 9 | 10 | 19 | 7 |
| 10 | 15 | 20 | 5 |

The variable for the defect counts and the sample size are entered in the u chart options panel on the preceding page. The results are presented in the figure below.

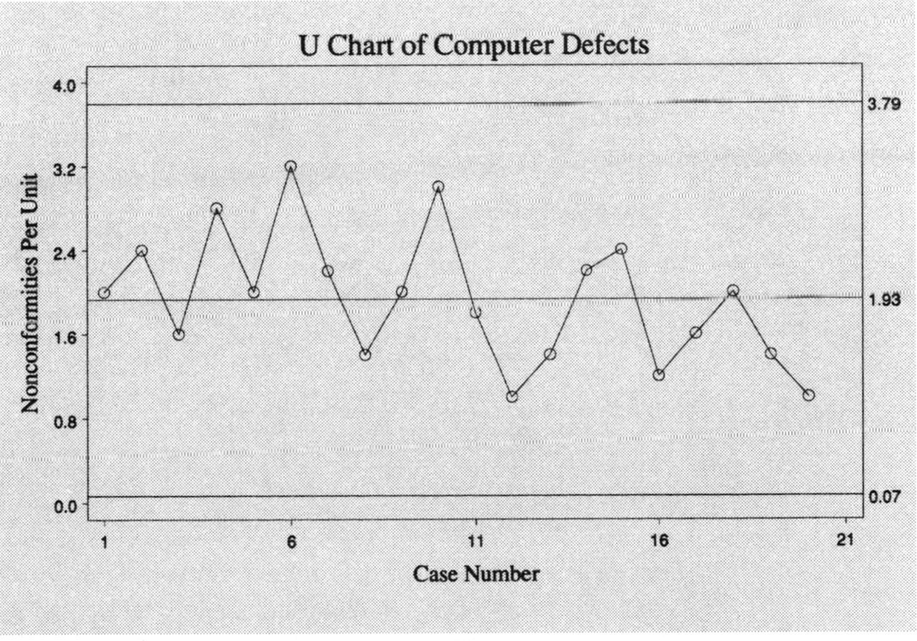


The process appears to be in control.

# X Bar Chart

The **X Bar Chart**, which plots sample averages, is used to control the process average of a variable. A quantitative quality characteristic, such as the diameter of a piston ring, is called a variable. This chart is normally used in conjunction with either the R chart or the S chart to control the variability in the process.

## Specification

The X bar chart requires that the quality characteristic is sampled with a sample size of at least two (use the I chart when the sample size is one). The data must be arranged in a *Statistix* data set so each case represents one sample and the individual measurements of a sample are recorded in separate variables (see the example data on the next page). If your data are presented in a single column, you can use the Stack/unstack command to rearrange (unstack) the data (see Chapter 2).

```
                              X Bar Chart                             PISTONS
X1        X2        X3        X4        X5



5 variable(s).  40 of 40 cases selected.  1182K bytes free.

List the variables containing the samples for the X bar chart.  You may
enter ALL or use A .. Z syntax.  Press F2 to select variables.
X1 .. X5

Do you want to enter STANDARD values for mu and sigma or COMPUTE estimates
from the data.  Enter S or C to indicate your choice.
Compute

Estimate sigma using R bar or S bar ............................. R bar
Enter the first case number to use to estimate mu and sigma ...... 1
Enter the last case number to use to estimate mu and sigma ....... 25

Perform tests for specific causes? .............................. Yes

Esc Exit  F1 Start  F2 Select variable
```

List the names of the variables containing the individual measurements of the quality characteristic. You must list at least two variables, but no more than 20.

The center line and control limits are computed from the mean (mu) and standard deviation (sigma) of the process. You can choose to enter standard or historical values for mu and sigma, or you can have estimates computed from the data. If you select STANDARD, you'll be asked to enter standard values for both mu and sigma.

If you select COMPUTE, you must also select a method for estimating sigma—the R-bar or S-bar method. You should choose the method that corresponds to the control chart you're using to control the process variability, either the R chart or the S chart. You can also specify the first and last case numbers to use to compute mu and sigma. If these case numbers are left blank, all cases are used.

Use the last option on the X bar chart panel to have eight tests for special causes performed. These tests are described below.

## Example

We use data from Montgomery (1991, p. 206) for our example. Automotive piston rings were sampled from a forge. Five rings were taken per sample. The inside diameter of the piston ring—listed below—was recorded.

| CASE | X1 | X2 | X3 | X4 | X5 |
|---|---|---|---|---|---|
| 1 | 74.030 | 74.002 | 74.019 | 73.992 | 74.008 |
| 2 | 73.995 | 73.992 | 74.001 | 74.011 | 74.004 |
| 3 | 73.988 | 74.024 | 74.021 | 74.005 | 74.002 |
| 4 | 74.002 | 73.996 | 73.993 | 74.015 | 74.009 |
| 5 | 73.992 | 74.007 | 74.015 | 73.989 | 74.014 |
| 6 | 74.009 | 73.994 | 73.997 | 73.985 | 73.993 |
| 7 | 73.995 | 74.006 | 73.994 | 74.000 | 74.005 |
| 8 | 73.985 | 74.003 | 73.993 | 74.015 | 73.988 |
| 9 | 74.008 | 73.995 | 74.009 | 74.005 | 74.004 |
| 10 | 73.998 | 74.000 | 73.990 | 74.007 | 73.995 |
| 11 | 73.994 | 73.998 | 73.994 | 73.995 | 73.990 |
| 12 | 74.004 | 74.000 | 74.007 | 74.000 | 73.996 |
| 13 | 73.983 | 74.002 | 73.998 | 73.997 | 74.012 |
| 14 | 74.006 | 73.967 | 73.994 | 74.000 | 73.984 |
| 15 | 74.012 | 74.014 | 73.998 | 73.999 | 74.007 |
| 16 | 74.000 | 73.984 | 74.005 | 73.998 | 73.996 |
| 17 | 73.994 | 74.012 | 73.986 | 74.005 | 74.007 |
| 18 | 74.006 | 74.010 | 74.018 | 74.003 | 74.000 |
| 19 | 73.984 | 74.002 | 74.003 | 74.005 | 73.997 |
| 20 | 74.000 | 74.010 | 74.013 | 74.020 | 74.003 |
| 21 | 73.988 | 74.001 | 74.009 | 74.005 | 73.996 |
| 22 | 74.004 | 73.999 | 73.990 | 74.006 | 74.009 |
| 23 | 74.010 | 73.989 | 73.990 | 74.009 | 74.014 |
| 24 | 74.015 | 74.008 | 73.993 | 74.000 | 74.010 |
| 25 | 73.982 | 73.984 | 73.995 | 74.017 | 74.013 |
| 26 | 74.012 | 74.015 | 74.030 | 73.986 | 74.000 |
| 27 | 73.995 | 74.010 | 73.990 | 74.015 | 74.001 |
| 28 | 73.987 | 73.999 | 73.985 | 74.000 | 73.990 |
| 29 | 74.008 | 74.010 | 74.003 | 73.991 | 74.006 |
| 30 | 74.003 | 74.000 | 74.001 | 73.986 | 73.997 |
| 31 | 73.994 | 74.003 | 74.015 | 74.020 | 74.004 |
| 32 | 74.008 | 74.002 | 74.018 | 73.995 | 74.005 |
| 33 | 74.001 | 74.004 | 73.990 | 73.996 | 73.998 |
| 34 | 74.015 | 74.000 | 74.016 | 74.025 | 74.000 |
| 35 | 74.030 | 74.005 | 74.000 | 74.016 | 74.012 |
| 36 | 74.001 | 73.990 | 73.995 | 74.010 | 74.024 |
| 37 | 74.015 | 74.020 | 74.024 | 74.005 | 74.019 |
| 38 | 74.035 | 74.010 | 74.012 | 74.015 | 74.026 |
| 39 | 74.017 | 74.013 | 74.036 | 74.025 | 74.026 |
| 40 | 74.010 | 74.005 | 74.029 | 74.000 | 74.020 |

The parameters for the X bar chart are specified in the options panel above. Note that cases 1 through 25 have been entered as the cases (or samples) to use to estimate mu and sigma. The results are presented below.

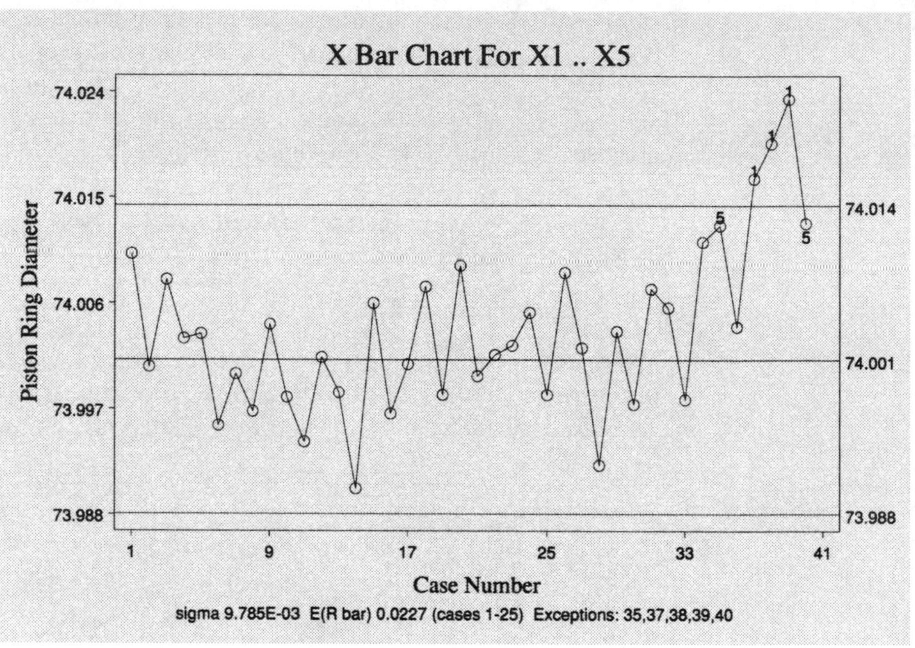


The sample averages are plotted for each case. The values for the center line and the 3-sigma control limits are labeled on the right side. The estimates for sigma and expected R bar computed from the first 25 cases are given in the footnote.

Note the upward drift in the process mean, starting around case 34. The points at cases 37, 38, and 39 exceed the UCL. The points at cases 36 and 40 are marked with a 5. This means that these points failed test number 5: two out of three consecutive points in zone A (beyond the 2-sigma limits).

## Tests for Special Causes

A "special cause", or "assignable cause", is signaled on control charts when a point is plotted outside the 3-sigma control limits. In addition to a point outside the UCL and LCL, there are other tests based on patterns of more than one point that can be applied to the X bar and I charts. These tests are summarized by Nelson (1984).

When these tests are selected, *Statistix* will indicate an out of control point using a digit indicating the test that caused the signal. If a point fails more than one test, the lowest digit is used to mark the point.

Test #1: A point outside the 3-sigma control limits.

Test #2: Nine points in a row on one side of the center line.

Test #3: Six points in a row, either all increasing or all decreasing.

Test #4: Fourteen points in a row, alternating up and down.

Tests #5 through #8 refer to zones A, B, and C. Zone A is the area of the chart between the 2- and 3-sigma lines. Zone B is the area between the 1- and 2-sigma lines. Zone C is the area between the center line and the 1-sigma line.

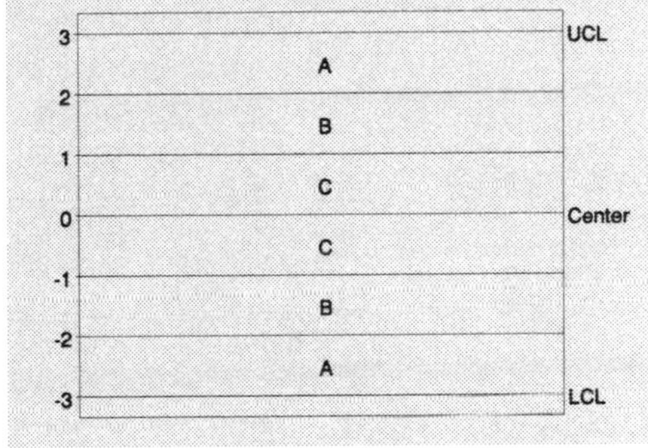


Test #5: Two out of three points in a row in zone A or beyond on one side of the center line.

Test #6: Four out of five points in a row in zone B or beyond on one side of the center line.

Test #7: Fifteen points in a row in zone C on either side on the center line.

Test #8: Eight points in a row on either side of the center line, but none of them in zone C.

By using a number of these tests at once, you increase the sensitivity of the control chart. But you also increase the chance of a false alarm. The probability of getting a false alarm using test #1 alone is about 3 in 1000. Using tests #1-4, the probability increases to 1 in 100.

# R Chart

The **R Chart**, which plots sample ranges, is used to control the process variability of a variable. A quantitative quality characteristic, such as the diameter of a piston ring, is called a variable. The S chart is an alternative control chart for process variability.

## Specification

The R chart requires that the quality characteristic is sampled with a sample size of at least two (use the MR chart when the sample size is one). The data must be arranged in a *Statistix* data set such that each case represents one sample and the individual measurements of a sample are recorded in separate variables. If your data are presented in a single column, you can use the Stack/unstack command to rearrange (unstack) the data (see Chapter 2).

```
                              R Chart                              PISTONS
X1         X2         X3         X4         X5



5 variable(s).  40 of 40 cases selected.  1182K bytes free.

List the variables containing the samples for the R Chart.  You may
enter ALL or use A .. Z syntax.  Press F2 to select variables.
X1 .. X5

Do you want to enter a STANDARD value for sigma or COMPUTE an estimate
from the data.  Enter S or C to indicate your choice.
Compute

Enter the first case number to use to estimate mu and sigma ......
Enter the last case number to use to estimate mu and sigma .......
Esc Exit  F1 Start  F2 Select variable
```

List the names of the variables containing the individual measurements of the quality characteristic. You must list at least two variables, but no more than 20.

The center line and control limits are computed from the standard deviation (sigma) of the process. You can choose to enter a standard or historical value for sigma, or you can have an estimate computed from the data. If you select COMPUTE, you can specify the first and last case numbers to compute sigma. If these case numbers are left blank, all cases are used.

**Example**

We use example data from Montgomery (1991, p. 206) for our example. Automotive piston rings were sampled from a forge. Five rings were selected per sample. The inside diameter of each piston ring was measured. This data set is also used as the X Bar Chart example and is listed on page 285.

The R chart model is specified in the options panel on the preceding page. The results are presented below.

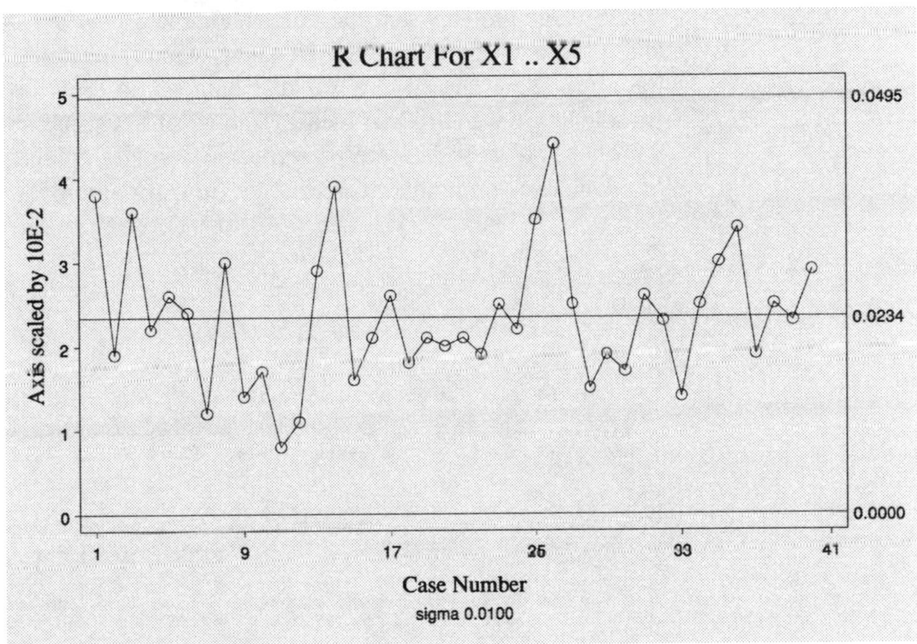


The sample ranges are plotted for each case. The values for the center line and the 3-sigma control limits are labeled on the right side. The value used for sigma, in this case estimated from the data, is given at the bottom of the R chart.

# S Chart

The **S Chart**, which plots sample standard deviations, is used to control the process variability of a variable. A quantitative quality characteristic, such as the diameter of a piston ring, is called a variable. The R chart discussed earlier is another control chart for process variability.

## Specification

The S chart requires that the quality characteristic is sampled with a sample size of at least two (use the MR chart when the sample size is one). The data must be arranged in a *Statistix* data set so each case represents one sample and the individual measurements of a sample are recorded in separate variables. If your data are presented in a single column, you can use the Stack/unstack command to rearrange (unstack) the data.

```
                              S Chart                                PISTONS
X1        X2        X3        X4        X5


5 variable(s).  40 of 40 cases selected.  1182K bytes free.

List the variables containing the samples for the S chart.  You may
enter ALL or use A .. Z syntax.  Press F2 to select variables.
X1 .. X5

Do you want to enter a STANDARD value for sigma or COMPUTE an estimate
from the data.  Enter S or C to indicate your choice.
Compute

Enter the first case number to use to estimate mu and sigma ......
Enter the last case number to use to estimate mu and sigma .......

Esc Exit  F1 Start  F2 Select variable
```

First list the names of the variables containing the individual measurements of the quality characteristic. You must use a minimum of two variables, but no more than 20.

The center line and control limits are computed from the standard deviation (sigma) of the process. You can choose to enter a standard or historical value for sigma, or you can have an estimate computed from the data. If you select COMPUTE, you can specify the first and last case number to be used to compute sigma. If these case numbers are left blank, all cases are used.

## Example

We use data from Montgomery (1991, p. 206) for our example. Automotive piston rings were sampled from a forge, five rings per sample. The inside diameter of the piston ring was the quality characteristic of interest. This data set was also used as the X Bar Chart example and is listed on page 285.

The S chart model is specified in the options panel on the preceding page. The results are displayed below.

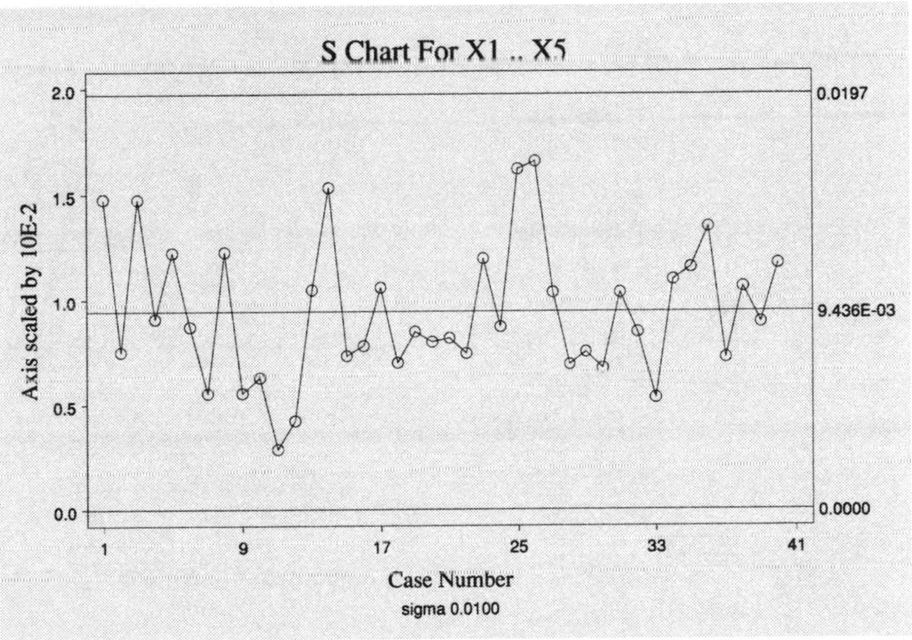


The sample standard deviations are plotted for each sample. The values for the center line and the 3-sigma control limits are labeled on the right side. The value used for sigma, in this case estimated from the data, is given at the bottom of the S chart.

# I Chart

The **I Chart** is the control chart for individuals used to control the process mean. This chart is sometimes called the X chart. The process variability is estimated from the moving range, which is the difference between two successive observations. The MR chart is the companion chart used to control the process variability.

## Specification

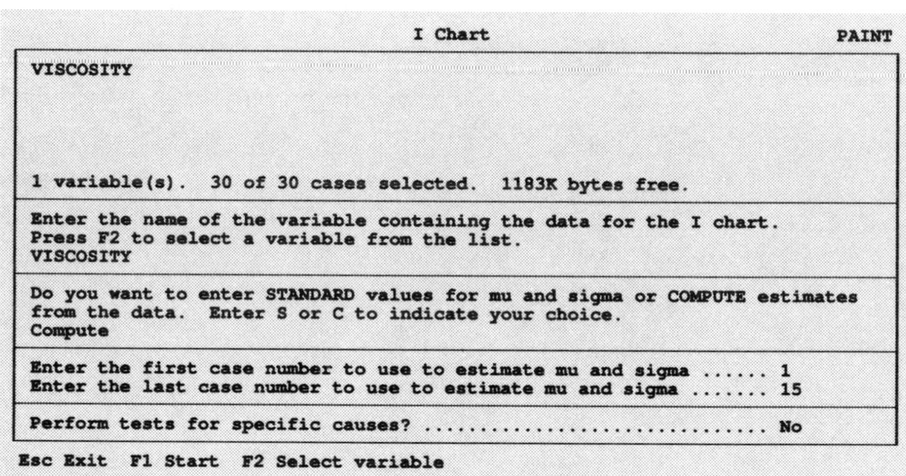

```
I Chart                                                        PAINT
VISCOSITY

1 variable(s).  30 of 30 cases selected.  1183K bytes free.

Enter the name of the variable containing the data for the I chart.
Press F2 to select a variable from the list.
VISCOSITY

Do you want to enter STANDARD values for mu and sigma or COMPUTE estimates
from the data.  Enter S or C to indicate your choice.
Compute

Enter the first case number to use to estimate mu and sigma ...... 1
Enter the last case number to use to estimate mu and sigma ....... 15

Perform tests for specific causes? ............................. No

Esc Exit  F1 Start  F2 Select variable
```

Enter the name of the variable that contains the individual observations.

The center line and control limits are computed from the mean (mu) and standard deviation (sigma) of the process. You can choose to enter standard or historical values for mu and sigma, or you can have estimates computed from the data. If you select COMPUTE, you can specify the first and last case number to be used in computing mu and sigma. If these case numbers are left blank, all cases are used.

Use the last option on the panel to have eight tests for special causes performed. These tests are described on page 286.

## Example

We use data from Montgomery (1991, p. 242) for our example. The viscosity of batches of aircraft paint primer was measured. Because it takes several hours to make one batch of primer, it wasn't practical to accumulate samples of more than one batch. The data from 30 batches of primer are listed on the next page.

| CASE | VISCOSITY | CASE | VISCOSITY |
|---|---|---|---|
| 1 | 33.75 | 16 | 33.50 |
| 2 | 33.05 | 17 | 33.25 |
| 3 | 34.00 | 18 | 33.40 |
| 4 | 33.81 | 19 | 33.27 |
| 5 | 33.46 | 20 | 34.65 |
| 6 | 34.02 | 21 | 34.80 |
| 7 | 33.60 | 22 | 34.55 |
| 8 | 33.27 | 23 | 35.00 |
| 9 | 33.49 | 24 | 34.75 |
| 10 | 33.20 | 25 | 34.50 |
| 11 | 33.62 | 26 | 34.70 |
| 12 | 33.00 | 27 | 34.29 |
| 13 | 33.54 | 28 | 34.61 |
| 14 | 33.12 | 29 | 34.49 |
| 15 | 33.84 | 30 | 35.03 |

The options panel on the preceding page specifies the I chart model. Cases 1-15 are used to estimate the process mean and standard deviation. The results are as follows:

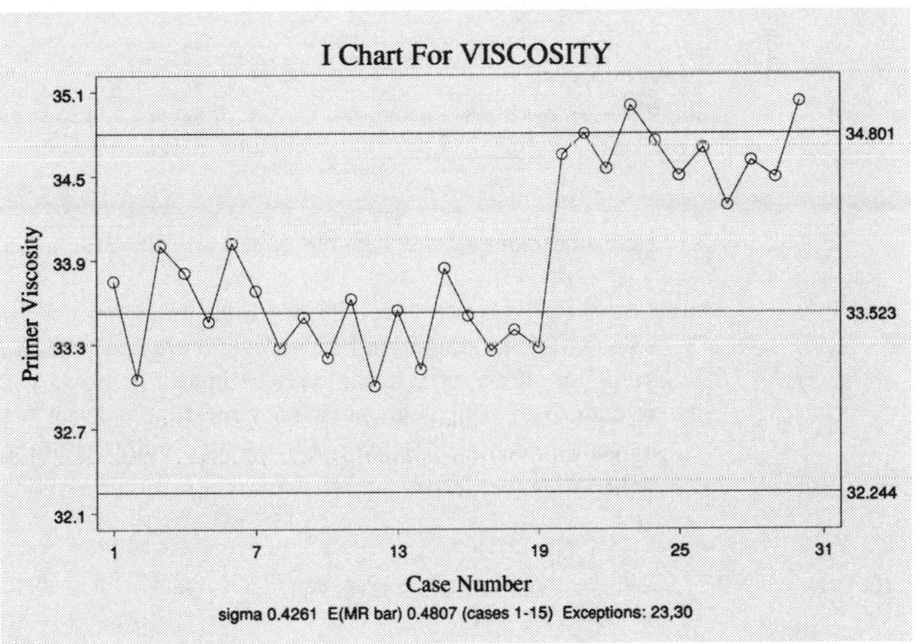


The individual observed values of primer viscosity are plotted for each case. The center line and 3-sigma UCL and LCL are labeled on the right side. The estimate for sigma and expected MR bar, based on the first 15 cases, are given in the footnote. Note the shift in the process mean at case 20. Two points are plotted above the UCL. This process is clearly out of control.

# MR Chart

The **MR Chart** is the control chart for individuals used to control process variability. The process variability is estimated from the moving range, the difference between two successive observations: MR = $|x_i - x_{i-1}|$.

## Specification

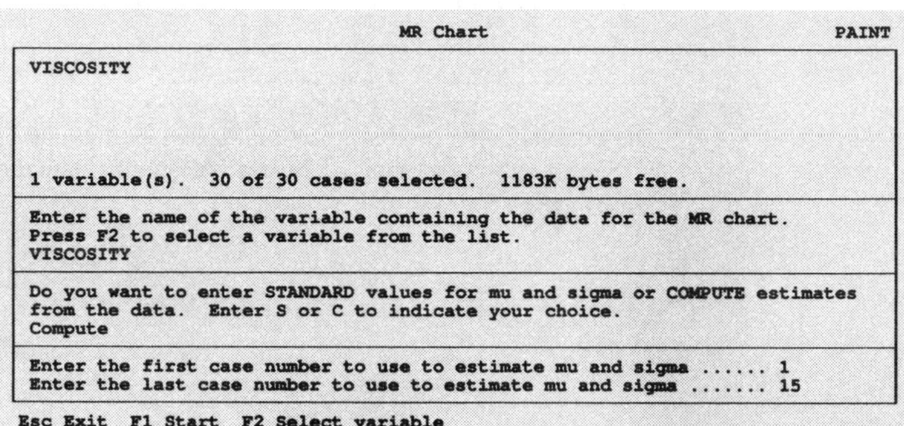
MR Chart PAINT
VISCOSITY
1 variable(s). 30 of 30 cases selected. 1183K bytes free.
Enter the name of the variable containing the data for the MR chart.
Press F2 to select a variable from the list.
VISCOSITY
Do you want to enter STANDARD values for mu and sigma or COMPUTE estimates
from the data. Enter S or C to indicate your choice.
Compute
Enter the first case number to use to estimate mu and sigma ...... 1
Enter the last case number to use to estimate mu and sigma ....... 15
Esc Exit F1 Start F2 Select variable

Enter the name of the variable containing the individual observations.

The center line and upper control limit are computed from the process standard deviation (sigma). You can choose to enter a standard or historical value for sigma, or you can have estimates computed from the data. If you select COMPUTE, you can specify the first and last case numbers to be used to compute mu and sigma. If these case numbers are left blank, all cases are used.

## Example

We use data from Montgomery (1991, p. 242) for our example. The viscosity of batches of aircraft paint primer was measured. Because it takes several hours to make one batch of primer, it wasn't practical to accumulate samples of more than one batch. The example uses 30 batches of primer. This data set was also used for the I Chart example and is listed on the preceding page.

The options panel above specifies the MR chart model. Cases 1-15 are used to estimate the process standard deviation. The results are presented on the next page.

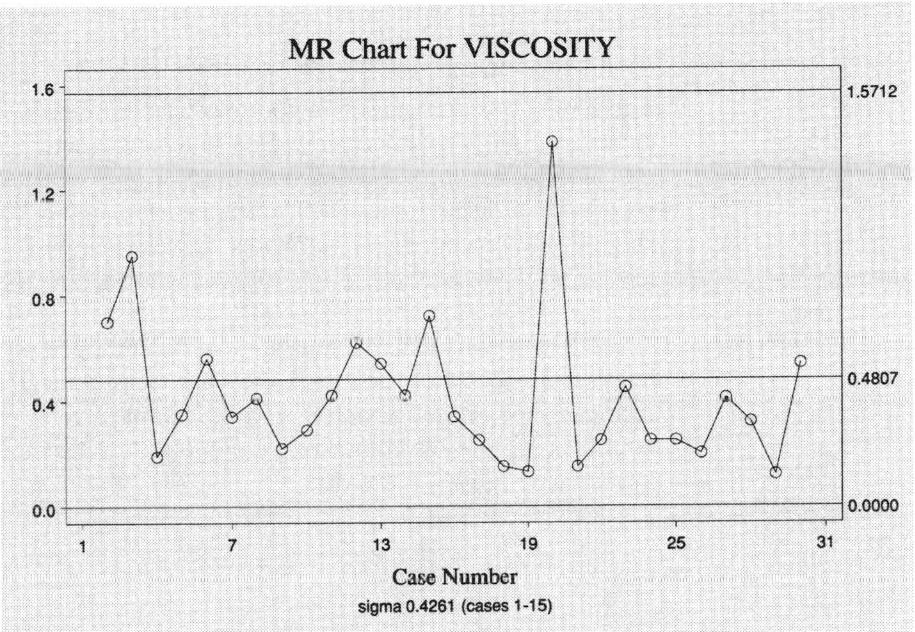


The moving ranges are plotted for each case, starting with the second case. The center line and 3-sigma UCL are labeled on the right side. The estimate for sigma and expected MR bar, based on the first 15 cases, are given in the footnote.

The spike at case 20 signals the shift in the process mean observed in the example I chart shown on page 293.

Montgomery (1991) warns that caution should be used when examining patterns in MR charts. Because the moving ranges are correlated, runs and patterns arise naturally in the charts.

# EWMA Chart

The **EWMA Chart** chart is a control chart for variables used to control the process mean. The value plotted on the chart is an exponentially weighted moving average incorporating data from all previous samples as well as the sample mean itself. This chart reacts faster than the X bar chart to small shifts in the process mean but reacts slower to large shifts.

## Specification

The EWMA chart requires that the data be arranged so that each case represents one sample and the individual measurements of a sample are recorded in separate variables. If your sample size is greater than one but your data are presented in a single column, use the Stack/unstack command to rearrange (unstack) the data.

```
                              EWMA Chart                                PISTONS
X1        X2        X3        X4        X5



5 variable(s).  40 of 40 cases selected.  1182K bytes free.

List the variables containing the samples for the EWMA Chart.  You may
enter ALL or use A .. Z syntax.  Press F2 to select variables.
X1 .. X5

Do you want to enter STANDARD values for mu and sigma or COMPUTE estimates
from the data.  Enter S or C to indicate your choice.
Compute

Estimate sigma using R bar or S bar ............................ R bar
Enter the first case number to use to estimate mu and sigma ...... 1
Enter the last case number to use to estimate mu and sigma ....... 25

Enter the EWMA weight (0.1 - 1.0) .......................... 0.15
Esc Exit  F1 Start  F2 Select variable
```

List the names of the variable(s) containing the individual measurements of the quality characteristic. The number of variables entered equals the sample size, which must be constant.

The center line and control limits are computed from the mean (mu) and standard deviation (sigma) of the process. You can choose to enter standard or historical values for mu and sigma, or you can have estimates computed from the data. If you select STANDARD, you'll be asked to enter standard values for mu and sigma.

If you select COMPUTE, you must also select a method for estimating sigma, either the R bar or S bar method. You can also specify the first and last case numbers to be used to estimate mu and sigma.

The EWMA chart requires a weight that determines the extent to which past observations influence the exponentially weighted moving average plotted on the chart. A small weight results in a slow response to new values; a large weight results in a fast response to new values. Values used for the weight are normally in the range 0.05 - 0.25.

## Example

We use data from Montgomery (1991, p. 206) for our example. Automotive piston rings were sampled from a forge, five rings per sample. The inside diameter of the piston ring was recorded. These data were also used for the X Bar Chart example and are listed on page 285.

The EWMA chart is specified in the options panel on the preceding page. The results are as follows:

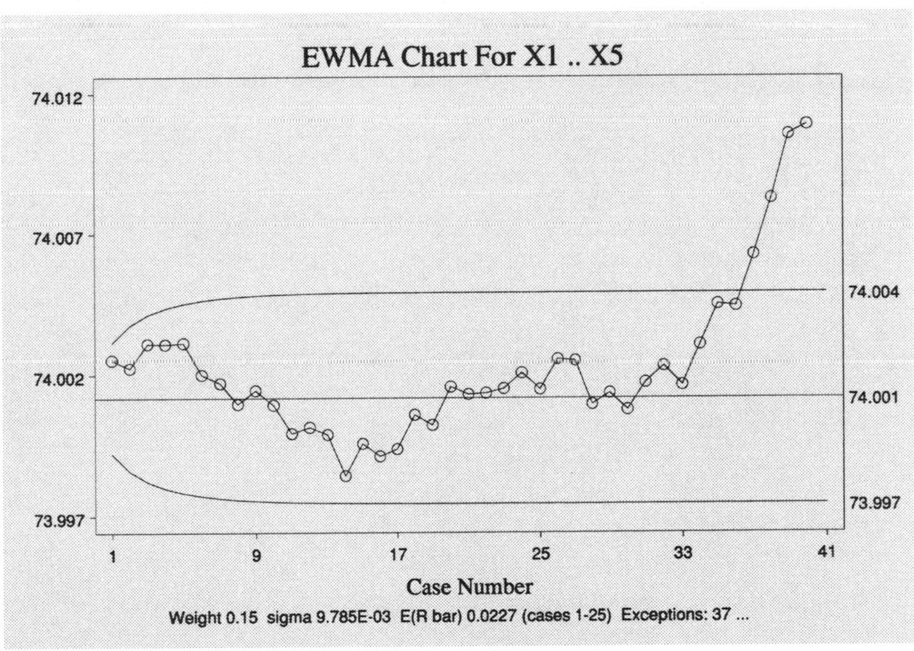


The process mean and 3-sigma control limits are reported on the right, and the process standard deviation (sigma) is reported at the bottom.

C H A P T E R

# 11

# Probability Distributions

*Statistix* offers a number of useful procedures to calculate the probabilities for various probability distributions and the inverse functions for the standard normal, the t-distribution, and the F-distribution. The function names and arguments are displayed at the top of the panel shown below, which appears when **Probability Distributions** is selected from the base menu.

```
                        PROBABILITY DISTRIBUTIONS

BEta (x, a, b)           BInomial (x, n, p)            CHisquare (x, df)
COrrelation (x, n)       FInverse (p, dfnum, dfden)    FProb (x,dfnum,dfden)
HYper (x1,x2,n1,n2)      NEgbin (n+x, n, p)            POisson (x, lambda)
T1tail (x, df)           T2tail (x, df)                TInverse (p, df)
Z1tail (x)               Z2tail (x)                    ZInverse (p)

                       Function ID: FPROB
                       x          : 2.98
                       df num     : 3
                       df den     : 19

                 Z1TAIL (1.96)                      0.02500
                 Z2TAIL (1.96)                      0.05000
                 T1TAIL (1.96, 20)                  0.03204
                 T2TAIL (1.96, 20)                  0.06408
                 ZINVERSE (0.95)                       1.64
                 FPROB (2.98, 3, 19)                0.05732

Esc Exit   Alt-P Print   Alt-F File
```

First enter the name of a probability function or inverse function. You only need enter the first two letters of the name. Once you've selected a function, the prompts for the arguments appear. Enter numbers for each of the arguments displayed. In the list of function names, the position of the random variable is usually represented as an X, although there are some minor variations on this which are described below. Parameters are indicated on the panel with logical abbreviations. After you've entered all of the values, the probability will be computed and displayed.

Once you correctly enter the command for a function, your input values remain displayed. This makes it convenient to compute a number of probabilities for the same function.

As you enter functions, the results accumulate in the bottom portion of the screen. Once the 8 lines in the results area fills up, the first results computed scroll off the top of the screen.

Press Alt-P to print the results. Press Alt-F to save the results to a file. The entire list of results will be printed or saved, not just the most recent 8 lines.

The distributions are described in detail below. We use standard notation to describe the region of the distribution for which the probability is being calculated. For example, the expression "Pr (y ≤ X)" represents the probability of a value of a random variable y equal to or less than some specified value X. The inverse functions compute the test statistic for a lower-tail probability.

## BETA (X, A, B)
## Lower-Tail Beta Probability Distribution

This function computes Pr (y ≤ X) for a beta random variable y with parameters A and B. The beta distribution is very flexible. The parameters A and B control the shape of the distribution, the mean of the distribution is given by A / (A + B). The beta distribution is sometimes used itself for tests and several other important distributions are easily derived from it, such as the t- and F-distributions (Kennedy and Gentle 1980).

The values permitted for X range from 0 to 1. A and B must be positive, but they don't need to be integer values. The beta distribution can be used to compute probability values for generalized t and F random variables with non-integer degrees of freedom—T1TAIL, T2TAIL, and FPROB require integer degrees of freedom.

## BINOMIAL (X, N, P)
### Lower-Tail Binomial Probability Distribution

This function computes Pr (y ≤ X) for a random variable y from a binomial distribution with N trials and parameter P. In many situations, the random variable is thought of as the number of "successes" out of N independent trials (i.e., there were N-X "failures"). The parameter P is the probability of a success on a particular trial. In other words, BINOMIAL computes the probability of observing X or fewer successes out of N trials when the success rate per trial is P.

X and N must be specified as integers. The parameter P must be between zero and one. To find the upper-tail distribution, you can use the relationship Pr (y > X) = 1 - Pr (y ≤ X).

## CHISQUARE (X, DF)
### Upper-Tail Chi-Square Probability Distribution

This function computes Pr (y ≥ X) for a random variable y from a central chi-square distribution with DF degrees of freedom. In other words, it computes the probability of a value equal to or larger than X. The typical chi-square tests in goodness-of-fit analyses use the upper-tail probabilities. Use the relationship Pr (y < X) = 1 - Pr (y ≥ X) if you want a lower-tail probability.

X must be a positive number and the degrees of freedom must be a positive integer.

## CORRELATION (X, N)
### Two-Tailed Probability Distribution for the Correlation Coefficient

This function computes Pr (|y| ≥ |X|) for a random variable y, where y is a simple (Pearson) correlation coefficient computed from N pairs of data. This distribution is appropriate for testing the null hypothesis that the correlation coefficient is equal to zero; the distribution being computed assumes the true correlation coefficient is zero. Snedecor and Cochran (1980, sect. 10.5) discuss the application of this procedure and the assumptions required. This procedure is equivalent to testing the hypothesis that the slope of the line is equal to zero in simple linear regression; the assumptions required are the same.

The values permitted for X range between -1 and 1. The number of pairs N must be a positive integer greater than two.

### FPROB (X, DFNUM, DFDEN)
### Upper-Tail F Probability Distribution

This function computes Pr (y ≥ X) for a random variable y from a central F-distribution with DFNUM numerator degrees of freedom and DFDEN denominator degrees of freedom. In other words, it computes the probability of a value equal to or larger than the observed X. The typical F tests in regression and analysis of variance use the upper-tail probabilities. Use the relationship Pr (y < X) = 1 - Pr (y ≥ X) if you want a lower-tail probability.

X must be a positive number and both degrees of freedom must be positive integers.

### FINVERSE (P, DFNUM, DFDEN)
### Inverse of the F-Distribution

This function computes the F test statistic for which the probability of a smaller value is P.

### HYPER (X1, X2, N1, N2)
### Lower-Tail Hypergeometric Probability Distribution

This function computes Pr (y1 ≤ X1), where y1 is a random variable drawn from a hypergeometric distribution. Using the traditional "urn" model, N1 corresponds to the number of red balls initially in the urn, and N2 corresponds to the number of black balls. Then, y1+y2 balls are randomly drawn from the urn. HYPER computes the probability of observing X1 or fewer red balls in such a sample.

All four parameters must be non-negative integers.

## NEGBIN (N+X, N, P)
## Lower-Tail Negative Binomial Probability Distribution

This function computes Pr (N + y ≤ N + X) or equivalently Pr (y ≤ X) for a random variable y which follows a negative binomial distribution. Typically, N+X is referred to as the number of trials required to get N successes. The probability of a success on a particular trial is the paramcter p. In other words, NEGBIN computes the probability of requiring N+X or fewer trials to get N successes. X is the number of failures observed before the Nth success.

N+X and N must be positive integers, and N+X must be greater than N. The parameter p may range from zero to one.

## POISSON (X, LAMBDA)
## Lower-Tail Poisson Probability Distribution

This function computes Pr (y ≤ X) for a random variable y from a Poisson distribution with rate parameter LAMBDA. In some situations, the random variable is thought of as the number of random events in some interval of time or space, and the rate parameter LAMBDA is the average number of such events expected in the interval. In other words, POISSON computes the probability of observing X or fewer events in an interval if the expected number of events is LAMBDA. You can find the upper-tail distribution by using the relationship Pr (y > X) = 1 - Pr (y ≤ X).

X must be an integer value and LAMBDA must be greater than zero.

## T1TAIL (X, DF)
## One-Tailed Probability Value for Student's T-Distribution

This function computes Pr (y ≤ X) for X ≤ 0, and Pr (y ≥ X) for X > 0 for a random variable y from a central t-distribution with DF degrees of freedom. In other words, T1TAIL computes the probability of a t value equal to or more extreme than X, taking into account the sign of X. This is often called the one-tailed significance of X.

DF must be a positive integer value.

### T2TAIL (X, DF)
### Two-Tailed Probability Value for Student's T-Distribution

This function computes Pr ( | y | ≥ | X | ) for a random variable y from a central t-distribution with DF degrees of freedom. In other words, T2TAIL computes the probability of a t value with an absolute value equal to or larger than the absolute value of X. This is often called the two-tailed significance of X.

DF must be a positive integer value.

### TINVERSE (P, DF)
### Inverse of the Student's T-Distribution

This function computes the Students's t test statistic for which the probability of a smaller value is P.

### Z1TAIL (X)
### One-Tailed Probability Value for the Standard Normal Distribution

This function computes Pr (y ≤ X) for X ≤ 0, and Pr (y > X) for X > 0 for a standard normal random variable y. In other words, Z1TAIL computes the probability of a value equal to or more extreme than X, taking into account the sign of X. This is often called the one-tailed significance of X. A statistic with a standard normal distribution is often referred to as a Z statistic, and hence the function name.

A standard normal distribution has a mean of zero and a variance of one. A normally distributed statistic can be transformed to standard normal form by subtracting the mean and then dividing by the standard deviation.

### Z2TAIL (X)
### Two-Tailed Probability Value for the Standard Normal Distribution

This function computes Pr ( | y | ≥ | X | ) for a standard normal random variable y. In other words, Z2TAIL computes the probability of a value with an absolute value equal to or larger than the absolute value of X. This is often called the two-tailed significance of X. A statistic with a standard normal distribution is often referred to as a Z statistic, and hence the function name.

A standard normal distribution has a mean of zero and a variance of one. A normally distributed statistic can be transformed to standard normal form by subtracting the mean and then dividing by the standard deviation.

## ZINVERSE (P)
### Inverse of the Standard Normal Distribution

This function computes the standard normal value z for which the probability of a smaller value is P.

### Computational Notes

Three key functions are used to generate the various probabilities—the error function, the log gamma function, and the incomplete beta function. The error function is patterned after a routine suggested by Kennedy and Gentle (1980). The method used to calculate the log gamma function is similar to that used at the University of Wisconsin computer center (Reference Manual 1410 - Probability Distribution Functions). Representing the gamma function as G(X), an asymptotic expansion is used directly when $X \geq 8$. Otherwise, the relationship $G(X + 1) = XG(X)$ is applied until the expansion can be used. The procedure for computing the incomplete beta function is patterned after the IMSL routine MDBETA, which is discussed in Kennedy and Gentle (1980). To speed up computation, a large sample approximation for the incomplete beta function is used for certain "safe" parameter values (Abramowitz and Stegun, eq. 26.5.21).

All the probability distributions are based on relatively simple functions of these three functions. Consult Kennedy and Gentle (1908) for further detail.

# REFERENCES

Abraham, B. and J. Ledolter. 1983. *Statistical Methods for Forecasting*. Wiley. New York, New York.

Abramowitz, M. and I. A. Stegun. 1977. *Handbook of Mathematical Functions*. National Bureau of Standards. Washington, D.C.

Beasley, J. D. and S. G. Springer. 1977. The percentage points of the normal distribution. Applied Statistics. 26:118-121.

Begun, J. M. and K. R. Gabriel. 1981. Closure of the Newman-Keuls multiple comparisons procedure. Journal of the American Statistical Association. 76:374.

Bickel, P. J. and K. D. Doksum. 1977. *Mathematical Statistics*. Holden-Day. San Francisco, California.

Bingham, C. and S. E. Fienberg. 1982. Textbook analysis of covariance - is it correct? Biometrics. 38:747-753.

Bishop. Y. M. M., S. E. Fienberg and P. W. Holland. 1975. *Discrete Multivariate Analysis*. MIT Press. Cambridge, Massachusetts.

BMDP-83. Dixon, W. J. (ed). 1983. *BMDP Statistical Software - 1983 Printing with Additions*. Berkeley, California.

Bowdler, H., R. S. Martin, C. Reinsch and J. H. Wilkinson. The QR and QL algorithms for symmetric matrices. Numerical Mathematics. 11:293-306.

Bowker, A. H. 1948. A test for symmetry in contingency tables. Journal of the American Statistical Association. 43:572-574.

Box, G. E. P. and G. W. Jenkins. 1976. *Time Series Analysis: Forecasting and Control*. Holden-Day. San Francisco, California.

Bradley, J. V. 1968. *Distribution-free Statistical Tests*. Prentice-Hall. Englewood Cliffs, New Jersey.

Brown, M. B., and J. K. Benedetti. 1977. Sampling behavior of tests for correlation in two-way contingency tables. Journal of the American Statistical Association. 72:309-315.

Chatterjee, S. and Price B. 1977. *Regression Analysis by Example*. Wiley. New York, New York.

Clarke, M. R. B. 1981. A Givens algorithm for moving from one linear model to another without going back to the data. Applied Statistics. 30:198-203.

Conover, W. J. 1971. *Practical Nonparametric Statistics.* Wiley. New York, New York.

Conover, W. J. and R. L. Iman. 1981. Rank transformations as a bridge between parametric and nonparametric statistics. The American Statistician. 35:124-129.

Cook, R. D. 1977. Detection of influential observations in linear regression. Technometrics. 19:15-18.

Cook, R. D. 1979. Influential observations in linear regression. Journal of the American Statistical Association. 74:169-174.

Cook, R. D. and S. Weisberg. 1982. *Residuals and Influence in Regression.* Chapman and Hall, New York.

Cooper. B. E. 1968. The use of orthogonal polynomials. Applied Statistics. 17:283-287.

Cox, D. R. 1970. *The Analysis of Binary Data*. Chapman and Hall, London.

Daniel, C. 1976. *Applications of Statistics to Industrial Experimentation.* Wiley. New York, New York.

Daniel, C. and F. Wood. 1971. *Fitting Equations to Data*. Wiley. New York, New York.

Dineen, L. C. and B. C. Blakesley. 1973. A generator for the sampling distribution of the Mann-Whitney U statistic. Applied Statistics. 22:269-273.

Draper, N. R. and H. Smith. 1966. *Applied Regression Analysis.* Wiley. New York, New York.

Durbin, J. and G. S. Watson. 1950. Testing for serial correlation in least squares regression I. Biometrika. 37:409-428.

Durbin, J. and G. S. Watson. 1951. Testing for serial correlation in least squares regression II. Biometrika. 38:159-178.

Durbin, J. and G. S. Watson. 1971. Testing for serial correlation in least squares regression III. Biometrika. 58:1-19.

Elnot, I. and K. R. Gabriel. 1975. A study of the powers of several methods of multiple comparisons. Journal of the American Statistical Association. 70:351.

Federer, W. T. 1957. Variance and covariance analyses for unbalanced classifications. Biometrics. 13:333-362.

Fienberg, S. E. 1980. *The Analysis of Cross Classified Categorical Data.* MIT Press. Cambridge, Massachusetts.

Gentleman, W. M. 1974. Basic procedures for large, sparse or weighted least squares problems. Applied Statistics. 23:448-454.

Gordon, H. A. 1981. Errors in computer packages. Least squares regression through the origin. The Statistician. 30:23-29. (See also Casella, G. 1983. Leverage and regression through the origin. The American Statistician. 37:147-152.)

Haberman, S. J. 1972. Log-linear fit for contingency tables. Applied Statistics. 21:218-225.

Haberman, S. J. 1978. *The Analysis of Qualitative Data.* Vols. I & II. Academic Press. New York, New York.

Hald, A. 1952. *Statistical Theory with Engineering Applications.* Wiley. New York, New York.

Hanke, J. E. and A. G. Reitsch. 1989. *Business Forecasting.* Allyn and Bacon. Boston, Massachusetts.

Heisey, D. M. 1985. Analyzing selection experiments with log-linear models. Ecology:66:1744-1748.

Hill, G. W. 1970. Student's t quantiles. CACM. 13:619-620.

Hollander, M. and D. A. Wolfe. 1973. *Nonparametric Statistical Methods*. Wiley. New York, New York.

Iman, R. L. and J. M. Davenport. 1976. New approximations to the exact distribution of the Kruskal-Wallis test statistic. Communications in Statistics. Ser. A. 5:1335-1348.

Iman, R. L. and J. M. Davenport. 1980. Approximations of the critical region of the Friedman statistic. Communications in Statistics. Ser. A. 9:571-595.

IMSL - International Mathematical and Statistical Libraries, Inc. 1975. *IMSL Library 1 Reference Manual*. IMSL, 7500 Bellaire Blvd., Floor 6, GNB Building, Houston, Texas.

Jolliffe, I. T. 1982. A note on the use of principal components in regression. Applied Statistics. 31:300-303.

Kennedy, W. J. and J. E. Gentle. 1980. *Statistical Computing*. Dekker. New York, New York.

Lehmann, E. L. 1963. *Nonparametrics: Statistical Methods Based on Ranks*. Holden-Day. San Francisco, California.

Ljung, G. and G. E. P. Box. 1978. On a measure of lack of fit in time series models. Biometrika. 65:297-304.

Lund, R. E. and J. R. Lund. 1983. Algorithm 190. Probabilities and upper quantiles for the Studentized range. Applied Statistics. 32:204-210.

Majumder, K. L. and G. P. Bhattacharjee. 1973. Algorithm 64. Inverse of the incomplete beta function ratio. Applied Statistics. 22:411-414.

Martin, R. S., C. Reinsch and J. H. Wilkinson. 1968. Householder's tri-diagonalization of a symmetric matrix. Numerical Mathematics. 11:181-195.

Mercier, L. J. 1987. *Handbook for Time Series Analysis*. AFIT. Dayton, Ohio.

McCullagh, P. and J. A. Nelder. 1983. *Generalized Linear Models*. Chapman and Hall. London.

Montgomery, D. C. 1991. *Introduction to Statistical Quality Control*. 2nd. ed. John Wiley and Sons. New York, New York.

Morrison, D. F. 1977. *Multivariate Statistical Methods*. 2nd. ed. MacGraw-Hill. New York, New York.

Nash, J. C. 1979. *Compact Numerical Methods For Computers: Linear Algebra and Function Minimisation*. John Wiley and Sons. New York, New York.

Nelson, L. S. 1984. The Shewhart Control Chart - Tests for Special Causes. Journal of Quality Control. 16:237-239.

Oliver, I. 1967. Analysis of factorial experiments using generalized matrix operations. Journal of the Association of Computing Machinery. 14:508-519.

Pregibon, D. 1981. Logistic regression diagnostics. Annals of Statistics. 9:705-724.

Royston, J. P. 1982. Expected normal order statistics (exact and approximate) Applied Statistics. 31:161-165.

Rubin, D. 1972. A non-iterative algorithm of least squares estimation of missing data in any analysis of variance design. Applied Statistics. 21:136-141.

Ryan, T. A. 1960. Significance tests for multiple comparison of proportions, variances, and other statistics. Psychological Bulletin. 57:318-328.

Scheffe, H. 1977. *The Analysis of Variance*. John Wiley and Sons. New York, New York.

Seber, G. A. F. 1977. *Linear Regression Analysis*. John Wiley and Sons. New York, New York.

Shapiro, S. S. and R. S. Francia. 1972. An approximate analysis of variance test for normality. Journal of the American Statistical Association. 67:215-216.

Shapiro, S. S. and M. Wilk. 1965. An analysis of variance test for normality. Biometrika. 52:591-611.

Siegel, S. 1956. *Nonparametric Statistics for the Behavioral Sciences.* McGraw-Hill. New York, New York.

Smirnov, N. V. 1939. Estimate of deviation between empirical distribution functions in two independent samples. Bulletin Moscow University. 2(2):3-16.

Snedecor, G. W. and W. G. Cochran. 1980. *Statistical Methods.* 7th ed. The Iowa State University Press. Ames, Iowa.

Velleman, P. and D. Hoaglin. 1981. *ABC's of EDA*. Duxbury Press.

Weisberg, S. 1982. *MULTREG User's Manual.* Technical Report #298, School of Statistics, University of Minnesota. St. Paul, Minnesota.

Weisberg, S. 1985. *Applied Linear Regression.* 2nd ed. John Wiley and Sons. New York, New York.

Weisberg, S. and C. Bingham. 1975. An analysis of variance test for normality suitable for machine calculation. Technometrics. 17:133.

Welsch, R. E. 1977. Stepwise multiple comparison procedures. Journal of the American Statistical Association. 72:359.

# I N D E X

# THE MENU

### Data Management

- Data entry
- Edit data
- Transformations
- Stack/unstack
- Omit/restore cases
- Sort cases
- View data

### File Management

- Retrieve
- Save
- Close
- Merge
- Summary file
- Import
- Export
- Log file
- Delete files
- View ASCII file

### Summary Statistics

- Descriptive statistics
- Frequency distribution
- Histogram
- Stem and leaf plot
- Percentiles
- Box and whisker plots
- Cross tabulation
- Scatter plot
- Breakdown

### One, Two & Multi-Sample Tests

- Paired t test
- Sign test
- Wilcoxon signed rank test
- Two-sample t test
- Rank sum test
- Median test
- One-way AOV
- Kruskal-Wallis one-way AOV
- Friedman two-way AOV

### Linear Models

- Correlations (Pearson)
- Partial correlations
- Variance-covariance
- Linear regression
- Best subset regressions
- Stepwise regression
- Discrete (Poisson) regression
- Logistic regression
- One-way AOV
- General AOV/AOCV
- Eigenvalues - principal comp.

### Association Tests

- Chi-square test
- Kolmogorov-Smirnov test
- McNemar's symmetry test
- Two by two tables
- Log-linear models
- Correlations (Pearson)
- Partial correlations
- Spearman rank correlations

### Randomness/Normality

- Runs test
- Wilk-Shapiro/rankit plot

### Quality Control

- Pareto chart
- P chart
- Np chart
- C chart
- U chart
- X bar chart
- R chart
- S chart
- I chart
- MR chart
- EWMA chart

### Time Series

- Time series plot
- Autocorrelation
- Partial autocorrelation
- Cross correlation
- Moving averages
- Exponential smoothing
- SARIMA (Box-Jenkins)

# NOTES

# NOTES

# NOTES

# NOTES

# NOTES

# NOTES

# NOTES

# NOTES